CARL ALEXANDER

Carl Alexander
Being an Island Boy, 1939-1957
Copyright © 2024 by Carl Spiegelberg

All rights reserved. No part of this book may be reproduced or transmitted in any form or by any means without written permission from the publisher and author.

Additional copies may be ordered from the publisher for educational, business, promotional or premium use.
For information, contact ALIVE Book Publishing at:
alivebookpublishing.com

Book design by Alex P. Johnson

ISBN 13
978-1-63132-227-3 Paperback
978-1-63132-229-7 Hardcover

Library of Congress Control Number: 2024904185

Library of Congress Cataloging-in-Publication Data
is available upon request.

First Edition

Published in the United States of America by ALIVE Book Publishing
an imprint of Advanced Publishing LLC
3200 A Danville Blvd., Suite 204, Alamo, California 94507
alivebookpublishing.com

PRINTED IN THE UNITED STATES OF AMERICA

10 9 8 7 6 5 4 3 2 1

CARL ALEXANDER

BEING AN ISLAND BOY
1939-1957

Carl Spiegelberg

Alive Book Publishing

Dedication

I want to dedicate *Carl Alexander* to the loving memory of my parents Charlotte Harrison Spiegelberg and Carl Henry Spiegelberg. They raised my brother, sister and me in Honolulu's Manoa Valley with care and love. They were exemplary parents who instilled in us strong family values that have kept all of us close to each other over the years. Charlotte and Spieg are gone now, but they were an essential part of my story. I miss them.

Acknowledgements

Writing is most often a solitary pursuit, but when I wrote *Carl Alexander*, I found collaborators looking over my shoulder who were of tremendous support to me.

First, my appreciation goes to my friend James O'Hara for his contributions in several areas: information about the publishing industry, copy editing, manuscript formatting and, in particular, his encouragement. Support like his is highly energizing.

The content of the book is supplemented by memories from my sister Aileen Spielberg Wilder and my brother Harrison Spiegelberg and his wife Patti. Patricia Palmer Azzone and her sister Sharon Palmer Wittington, family friends and neighbors when I was a child, contributed their memories about Manoa Valley and our lives when we were children. The chapters about *Red Hale*, especially *My Japanese Grandparents*, could not have been written without the vivid memories of family friends Seiko Ogai Oshita and her sister Atsuko Ogai Kato who lived at *Red Hale* when they were children. I have greatly benefitted from the inciteful comments and encouragement from my writing class in Rossmoor, a senior living complex in Walnut Creek, California. I also want to thank my husband Janek Bubela for his encouragement and his extensive technical help with the computer.

Contents

Foreword...11

To The Hawaiian Wall......................................17

Small Kid Time in Manoa.................................33

Fort Street and Downtown Honolulu.............65

Waikiki, Then and Now....................................77

The S.S. Lurline—A love Affair........................99

The Mainland, Another Place........................121

Coming to Terms with Punahou—and Myself.............167

Living With My Stagestruck Right Brain....................205

My Secret, Then and Now..............................265

Red Hale..349

The Chippendale Chair...................................353

A Miracle Suburb on Yonder Beach.............371

The General and Camp McKinley................387

Susan and Hoste at Washington Place........401

Charlotte and Spieg in Waikiki and Manoa...............427

My Japanese Grandparents............................459

Epilogue...477

The Southern Cross, a One-Act Play..............479

Foreword

C*arl Alexander.* Carl Alexander were my given names. Carl was from my father whose German parents had anglicized his name to Carl. My middle name was from my maternal great uncle Alexander Davis who had served gallantly in the U.S. Army for many years.

Therefore, my parents had reached into both sides of my family to give me names. The following auto-biography is primarily about me, so my given names seemed to be an appropriate title for this book.

"Always write about what you know." My several writing teachers over the years taught me that primary lesson, that first tenet of good writing. So, along with trying to show and not just tell and using the active voice whenever possible, I have followed their advice and, consequently, my words have flowed easily when I reach into my own memories.

The gathered Hawaiian stories in this book occurred in a relatively untroubled and unspoiled time before statehood and mass tourism changed Hawaii's landscape. These snap shots of my formative years took place before the jet airplane intruded on my quiet childhood, before extreme traffic congestion and freeways crisscrossed Honolulu, before the Hawaiian sovereignty movement changed the Islands' culture, and before Honolulu became a high-rise city. World War Two had come and gone when I was a little kid, and Hawaii would not become the fiftieth state of the union until 1959 after I had gone away to college on the mainland. The subtitle of the book includes the years 1939 to 1957. 1939 is the year I was born, and 1957 is the year I left Hawaii to go away to college. I have gone back to Hawaii for many visits, but I never returned to live, so I have used 1957 as a convenient end point for my story. Some of my chapters do exceed that year, but 1957 is the finality of my living in Hawaii.

One day about 35 years ago, perhaps it was sometime in the early eighties, my childhood adventures in Honolulu's Manoa Valley prompted me to record what I remembered. "To The Hawaiian Wall," the first piece in this collection of memoirs, was the result of that prompting.

And then I couldn't stop myself. I was caught by a writing bug that wouldn't leave me. My memories came fast and persistently, until, after some years, I had unwittingly recorded a montage of the Hawaiian part of my life – my childhood in the 1940s, including the war years, and my teen years in the 1950s. I hadn't set out to do that, but now I see I have summoned up a collection of memories to leave to my descendants and perhaps anyone else interested in these particular Hawaiian yesterdays. I decided to answer questions and reveal secrets that my descendants might one day ask about me and my time living in Honolulu. Here are some of those answers.

Unfortunately, the urge to record my childhood came at a time when I had already lost the sources for prompting and confirming my memories. My parents and grandparents were all gone, and there was no one left for me to ask questions of. But there was one exception to that: I was lucky to be friends with the oldest living daughter of my "Japanese grandparents." In her '90s, Seiko Oshita was blessed with an acute memory of the lives and occurrences in my writings about Honolulu of another era and Red Hale (*ha-lay*, Hawaiian for *house*). Red Hale was the name of my maternal grandmother's house on the seawall near Diamond

Head and serves as an example of what happened in the transition from an extensive collection of large beach houses to the high-rise neighborhood that Waikiki became. I never lived at Red Hale, but my childhood visits and Seiko's lively memories provide outlines for my Red Hale chapters.

Seiko was particularly helpful with my chapter called "My Japanese Grandparents" which was about her parents who served as nanny, housekeeper and cook at Red Hale. Seiko, who grew up there at a time before I was born, was invaluable in my writing. My six chapters about Red Hale turned out to be a self-contained collection so I have placed them separately in the second half of the book. For them, I relied on family lore, my memory, Seiko's memory, and family letters, travel journals and diaries. The rest of the pieces in this book are about various nostalgic aspects of my mid-twentieth century beginnings: my adventures in our neighborhood rain forest, my education, my early travels, my sexual orientation, my Manoa Valley neighborhood and Honolulu, the city I grew up in.

Because I was an island boy, these chapters tell tales that all begin in Hawaii. Some of them then move to the mainland where I spent most of my later life. But, for the mostpart, these chapters tell island tales of a certain era. But there is also some pertinent history scattered throughout the book. I have arranged it in three parts: the first nine chapters tell tales of my childhood life in the 1940s and '50s; the second part, *Red Hale*, contains six chapters about the family house in Waikiki that cast a spell on me when I was a child, and the third part is a one-act play, "The Southern Cross," based on characters and incidents from my *Red Hale* chapters. As each chapter was written separately, there may be some repetitions throughout the book.

Although this book is made up of a collection of separate memoirs, one should see the sum total of them as an autobiography. After reading them, you will have a fairly complete picture of who I am, Carl Alexander, and the life I led in Hawaii in my childhood, teenage years and my later adult life on the mainland.

The photographs that illustrate the book are personal or family photos that mirror the times I have written about. I hope that they and my memories reflect the quieter and more innocent time and place in which I grew up, a Hawaii of another era. These are true stories. I have written about what I know. I hope my writing teachers would think well of me.

Our house at the dead-end of Keahi St. just before the trail led to the Hawaiian wall

To The Hawaiian Wall
(1944 – 1950)

At times when my friends and I had tired of riding bikes on our dead-end street, building forts in the back yard, or playing hide-and-seek and tag, our attentions turned to adventures farther afield – what we kids called the "*kahuna* (priest or sorcerer) cave", Manoa Falls – and the Hawaiian wall. The cave required a trek up the side of the steep mountain, the falls were a couple of miles away, but the wall lay only a few hundred yards through often soggy *hono hono* grass toward the back of Manoa Valley. It extended through a forest of Guava, Mango and *Kukui* trees, and, for all intents and purposes, served as the *mauka* (toward the mountains) boundary of my early childhood.

These were the first few years after World War Two when I was about six through nine years old, and developers had not yet altered the natural landscape of our neighborhood. My parents had recently stored away the gas masks and blackout curtains that had been fixtures of our wartime lives, and Hawaii had not yet been aroused by enormous passenger jets that would thoroughly alter its landscape. Manoa was still a quiet *cull-de-sac*, essentially a suburb of greater Honolulu that afforded the children who grew up there the safety to explore their immediate world on their own. There were no electronic toys or televisions to keep us indoors in those days so we were thrust outside into nature for our childhood adventures.

Most of upper Manoa was still a luxuriant rain forest at the head of a broad valley, a territory large enough that, when I was very young, I wasn't even conscious of living on an island. This wet world of 160 inches of annual rainfall is the home of surging clouds and mist that impart mystery to the many waterfalls that nestle in the crevices at the back of the valley. All of that water is collected when the trade winds dump their payload on Manoa's mountains. The gentle patter of an approaching shower can suddenly turn into a thunderous roar that, then, just as quickly, passes leaving a gentle trickle from leaves and eaves. In this aftermath, the relieved calls of doves and mynah birds usually accompany the appearance of a rainbow.

We lived in the last house on our block-long dead-end street, and we looked out on a jungle where the tops of Kukui trees punctuated the dark forest with sun-splashed patches of lighter green. This view was circumscribed by almost perpendicular stone cliffs that rose about a thousand feet above us. There, about a third of the way up the mountain, was the *kahuna cave*. It was probably just a large cavity in the rock created by erosion, but it was big enough for us to have a picnic in, and our imaginations saw a home for *kahuna* magic.

We would get permission to cut through a neighbor's back yard, and then the route up the cliff took us through trees that clung to the steep incline. Hand over hand, we would pull ourselves up by grabbing branches and climbing over fallen boulders. Suddenly, we emerged in the sunlight on the face of the mountain. We could see most of the eight square miles of Manoa Valley and a good part of Honolulu from up there. Kahunas or not, we always wondered what use the early Hawaiians had made for *our* cave.

As we ate our peanut butter and jelly sandwiches, we could look down to distant Waikiki where a solid fringe of coconut trees was only broken by the tiny pink cupola on top of the Royal Hawaiian Hotel. Another part of this vertical orientation was an early childhood confusion of *up* and *north*. For a time, we were convinced that Santa Claus lived in a house with an exotic chimney that was *up* on the ridge above us. We had learned that chimneys had something to do with Santa, and, from that vantage point, it was no wonder he could look down on us to see if we were naughty or nice.

Despite our childhood fantasies, we had no way of knowing in those quiet post-war years that our playground would imminently be changed. But, in the meantime, we amused ourselves with treks to Manoa Falls, another outing that required sandwiches and shoes. On our way was the old Chinese store on East Manoa Road where we bought cracked seed and shave [sic] ice. The trail to the falls had us scratching through Lantana, climbing over tree roots, ducking under low-hanging branches and easing through a bamboo forest. Part of the adventure was seeing a mongoose dart across our path and attacking each other with pieces of what we called "the shampoo plant." I think it was a variety of Ginger that had a soapy flower. Once everyone's hair was sudsy, we rinsed off in the pool at the base of the falls. The soap was like that from the Aloe plant and was good for treating the scratches we had collected on the trail.

Heading home, we collected wild orchids, Job's Tears, Koa seeds and Kukui nuts which we strung together as necklaces. We tried to sell these harvests (no lemonade stands for us) to our parents and neighbors. We would also forage for Mountain Apples, Guavas and Mangos that our mothers would turn into jelly, sherbet or chutney. Some of the overripe fruit would ooze under our feet and might be used for throwing at each other or a grumpy neighbor's screen door.

A section of Manoa Stream hadn't yet been paved over with concrete in the early '50s. We made our way past *kapu* (no trespassing) signs on empty lots and through the Japanese flower gardens to that area of the stream where we could swim. We caught little shrimp we called crayfish with bread on the end of a string, but we always released them as they were too small to eat. Multi-colored Rainbow Fish with long tails went home with us to circle in our aquarium. One time, a collection of Pollywogs grew into frogs and took over our garage. Mom was not pleased.

*****

But always, from my point of view, the most fascinating enterprise into our rainforest was a trip to what we called *the Hawaiian wall*.

With neighbor playmates and my younger brother, we could step off the pavement at the end of Keahi Street and follow a narrow path which led into the woods. We would ignore the *kapu* sign that indicated *no entry* and make our way up the trail which was immediately next to our house as we were the last house on the block. Our toes squished into the mud on the constantly wet trail, and the sharp blades of the *hono hono* grass and Lantana left scratches on our legs. We were terrified of setting our bare feet down on a Buffo toad, mongoose or centipede, but our fascination with the wall challenged the standard canon of childhood literature which had taught us what can happen to children in the woods. After all, we weren't too far from home and we hoped there was safety in numbers.

We called it *the Hawaiian wall* because our fantasies had decided that *Menehunes* (a Hawaiian legendary race of little people) were responsible for building it, and to go beyond it was to court lurking danger. Parental warnings, but mostly our own fertile imaginations fueled by ill-defined impressions of Hawaii's past, conjured the ghosts of *kahunas* protecting their *kapus* (taboo or prohibition). It was the possibility of a curse for accidentally disturbing a reserve of sacred bones or artifacts that frightened us the most. With attacks of *chicken skin* (Pidgin English for goose bumps) we dared each other to touch the wall, but the ultimate act of bravery was to climb over its loose stones to search for relics that we were sure lay hidden on the other side.

Our hunts were always facilitated by flashes of sunlight that managed to penetrate the dense canopy of trees. An earthy redolence rose from the forest floor as we warily lifted stones that might be protecting centipedes or scorpions – or treasure.

This adventure was long before children would be exposed to the archeological exploits of Indiana Jones, but we had been on field trips to The Bishop Museum to see the giant overhanging whale and many Hawaiian artifacts. The one of us to find a *poi* pounder or other proof of human presence would become a neighborhood hero. I had no concept of what *ancient Hawaiian* really meant then. These people might as well have been prehistoric cave dwellers in my then limited understanding of historical time.

As *Hawaiiana* wasn't yet a usual part of school curriculum at that time, a cultural awareness of the Hawaiians for a *haole* (Caucasian) boy in those post war years was solely influenced by the wax figures of Hawaiians at the museum, Robert Louis Stevenson's grass shack at Waioli Tea Room, fanciful stories of Hawaii's little people, the *Menehunes,* in illustrated children's books, and the wartime plastic ukuleles and cellophane hula skirts stored in the hall closet. *Kau kau* (food), *moi moi* (sleep), *opu* (stomach) and *pau* (finished) were just other words we were learning; they might just as well have been part of our accumulating English for all we knew. And the "little grass shacks" and "lovely hula hands" of 1940s popular Hawaiian music imparted romantic but dishonest ideas of things Hawaiian. What did all these fragments of Hawaiian lore have to do with each other, and what had ancient Hawaiians been doing in our neighborhood anyway?

But then, there was the very palpable wall: about three feet high, it was built of loose mossy stones and ran east and west across our part of the valley. We knew it had been there for a long time as ferns grew from it and many of its stones had fallen and were overgrown by brush. In places, there seemed to be a pattern of enclosure around some of the trees. Had they surrounded something that was no longer there? It didn't occur to us to wonder whose land we were on, but it was clear that the wall had been left and forgotten by somebody. Walls are usually used to set off ownership boundaries, so perhaps our wall had served in that way as well. It fascinated me that the wall was evidence of human presence concealed in an otherwise natural world. My curiosity was piqued, but it would be many years, and an abandonment of the *Menehune* theory, before I would look for an explanation.

*****

Our family came to live near the wall because of my father's career at the Pineapple Research Institute near the University of Hawaii in lower Manoa and the appeal of a pre-war real estate offer for scarce fee-simple lots in a tract called Manoa Uplands. Mom and Dad bought the last two of those lots and built and moved into our house the summer before the attack on Pearl Harbor. In those days, it was the end of the road. An occasional farmer from Waianae would come to cut fresh grass for his livestock, a neighbor pastured a couple of horses there, and sometimes young couples would come and put out the street light with a stone in order to *park* on the dead-end road. Because there was no through traffic, we could use the street to play until after dark. It was a safe place in a safe time and we were allowed to roam "as far as the wall" and have as much adventure as our imaginations could conjure up.

*****

The War was over, and the century had recently passed its half way point. We had no way of knowing that our naiveté and quiet playground would soon be invaded by a battalion of bulldozers. The wall wouldn't survive those post-war years that had started off so peacefully. Maybe the *kahunas* had a message for us after all, as change was coming to our valley. Housing was scarce after the war, and the Bishop Estate leased our forest to a company called Island Homes which created the first tract housing development in Hawaii.

The sounds of machines and the smell of diesel and freshly turned earth dominated our lives as the mysteries of the forbidden world beyond the wall were invaded and destroyed. We watched with fascination and sadness as workmen cleared the land for roads and housing sites. One day the bulldozers arrived on our street, plowed up the *hono*

hono grass and Lantana, knocked down the Guava and Mango trees and pushed through the wall, scattering its stones. The haunts of *Menehunes* became ordinary backyards and those Hawaiian artifacts that we had never found were buried under pavement and houses forever.

We could no longer play in the safety of our dead-end street which now connected to a new subdivision. All the new homes generated traffic that rushed through our accustomed playground. But ironically, the changes to our neighborhood seemed insignificant compared to what happened to the rest of Honolulu in the 1960s and '70s. Manoa seemed to stay relatively the same – cool, quiet and low-rise. Our house still looked out at Manoa Falls and the near-vertical cliffs, but the sidewalk no longer came to an end. I would walk up the street in the direction of the wall, but the bicycles and cars in driveways disoriented me. I had difficulty remembering exactly where the wall had stood, or, indeed, if I had imagined the whole thing. Yet, if I let my eyes go out of focus, looked over the new rooftops and ignored the traffic, the mountains looked the same. The cave was still there, and the chimney of *Santa's house* – more overgrown now – could still be seen on the ridge. There must have been a wall.

*****

Those events happened over seventy years ago. Memory fades with the passing of time, but, occasionally I flash back to our childhood rain forest adventures. Years after that heyday, when I came home to help sell my parents' house, I had the time to look for some answers to my questions about the wall. I contacted an old family friend, Beatrice Krauss, who had lived all her life – most of the twentieth century – in

Manoa. I met with her twice in her home shortly before she passed away. She told me that in the old days the valley was divided down its middle between the *ali'i* (ruling class) and commoners. Our neighborhood – and the wall – were on the *ali'i* side where the air was fresher and cooler when the afternoon sun baked the Woodlawn side of the valley. In the late eighteenth century, Queen Ka'ahumanu, the favorite wife of Kamehameha l, became Queen Regent *(kuhina nui)* on his death. In order to escape the summer heat of Waikiki, she built a beloved summer cottage – her "wooden house of green shutters" – in the cool upper reaches of the *ali'i* side of Manoa.

Today, there are only guesses as to where her house actually stood, but speculation suggests that our wall could have been part of her large estate which, in typical Hawaiian fashion, would have been enclosed by stone walls. C.S. Stewart, in his *Visit to the South Seas* (1829), describes the home "on the height of a gently swelling knoll, commanding, in front, an open and extensive view." Our wall sat on a raised side flank overlooking the "vast wide valley" just as Stewart described it. Another theory is that Ka'ahumanu's home was a few blocks down the valley close to the intersection of Manoa Road and Oahu Avenue near the present day Waioli Tea Room. At one time that land belonged to Kamehameha the Third and, most probably, this royal title had led back to Ka'ahumanu. In *Manoa, the Story of a Valley* compiled by Manoa residents, we read, "a little village grew up in the area" as it became the seat of government when she was staying there. "A village" would suggest a good deal of activity and people to support, necessitating a large tract of land. Our wall was about six blocks away and was very possibly part of her royal enclosure and the lands that were later leased by The Bishop Estate to Island Homes.

In 1832, when Ka'ahumanu was dying, she asked to be taken to her summer home in Manoa. The large Queen was pulled up the valley in a cart flanked by ceremonial feathered *kahilis*. Beside her was a copy of the newly translated Hawaiian version of the King James Bible which she had commissioned just before she died. Could our wall have been a witness to that scene? Was it part of the enclosure of her estate, a confinement for animals, or part of a taro terrace in her kitchen garden?

All of these possibilities remind me of what I have seen under the overgrowth in Halawa Valley on the east end of Molokai. The *heiaus* (pre-Christian place of worship), fish ponds and taro terraces on that island have, so far, been spared, but Manoa's ancient infrastructure, of course, have not. I wondered what further stone structures had existed before Honolulu's other subdivisions were built. It didn't seem logical that our wall had existed alone. What else had been lost? Or were Manoa's stone structures in place because of its important proximity to the royal seat at Waikiki?

The "Ka'ahumanu theory" would have dated the wall's origin to the early nineteenth century. But a different starting point – a much earlier one – became another possibility. The wall could have been part of a *heiau* of the "stone people, "as Bea called them, who lived there without *kuleana* (ownership) boundaries long before Ka'ahumanu. My imagination pictured something from pre-history. Indeed, there turned out to be a pre-historic connection to the stones that filled the valley and gave these people their name – and another possibility for the wall's existence.

When my parents were landscaping their property, I would sometimes help my father prepare the soil by collecting the stones that lay or were buried everywhere. Just as the Hawaiians had done before us, he used our stones in mortarless walls to enclose and terrace our property. Our wall in the forest looked very much like my father's garden walls, which was not surprising as they were both products of the last volcanic eruption on the island. That had deluged the valley with lava from Mt. Tantalus, pushing Manoa Stream to the east, and acting like a dam, holding back alluvial soils turning Manoa Valley into a very fertile garden. The eruption had also covered the landscape with stones. Like New England farmers of old and the stone people, my father had cleared his rocky soil by building walls.

The era of "the stone people," Bea told me, was long before the critical mass of native population led to the organization of chiefdoms. The land divisions of the time, *ahupua'a*, were pie-shaped wedges that ran from the reefs to the mountain tops and included the arable land in between. Our neighborhood would have been part of the Waikiki *ahupua'a* that extended to the top of the Ko'olau Mountains at the head of Manoa Valley. The lands of Manoa were vast, rich and handy to the royal enclave at Waikiki, and there is evidence of extensive human use. Taro terraces, *heiaus* and enclosure walls would have been the infrastructure of that society. Our wall could have been a part of any of these, but in 1819 the early religious system was abolished and the *heiaus* destroyed. It's not probable that our wall was part of a *heiau* that escaped this destruction. Most Taro cultivation was focused primarily on the central and southern parts of the valley so that is not a probability either. But the wall could very well have been an enclosure for animals or food plants. Or it could have been part of a surrounding statement of ownership around Kaahumanu's estate.

*****

Eventually, feeling that my search for the wall's story had gone as far as it could, I left the investigation and saw my Hawaiian wall inquiry as a *cold case*. But sometimes, new evidence can turn a cold case hot again. And a chance encounter did just that. A new theory presented itself in the backyard of a neighbor. Not long ago a casual conversation with my sister in Oregon led me to an acquaintance of hers named Mark Vossbrink whose family home was near us in Manoa Valley at 3314 Halelani Drive. Not far from our Hawaiian wall, his home sits on a sunny knoll with an expansive outlook down the valley to Waikiki just as C.S. Stewart in his *Visit to the South Seas* (1832) describes the site of Ka'ahumanu's Manoa home.

I arranged a time to visit Mark's brother Tony and his mother at their home so I could see for myself. When I stepped into their backyard, I was struck by the similarities to the historical descriptions. That backyard is only a few blocks from where our wall had been, and an ancient *hau* tree (a member of the hibiscus family) dominates the garden just as C. S. Stewart had described. Tony showed me a news article from 1932 which described a group of ladies from the Daughters of Hawaii organization researching and seeking out this site in order to make suitable ceremonies in Ka'ahumanu's memory on the hundredth anniversary of her death. This happened over twenty years before the land was developed by Island Homes. The ladies reported the thicket of *hau* trees that, now grizzled and overgrown, is still there. And C.S. Stewart had also described *Ohia* and Eugenia bushes that also remain there.

Most convincing of all, however, are remnant slabs of an old coral foundation which had supported a structure of some sort. One dimension of the structure is about sixty feet which would suggest a large house and was probably suitable for a queen. There is also a rock that possibly served as a garden seat for Ka'ahumanu. My cold case had been reopened in a neighbor's backyard, and I could now see that our wall was possibly part of the outlying infrastructure for this royal retreat.

When all was said and done, however, I realized I didn't need to have a definitive answer to the mystery of our wall. My satisfaction had been in the process of the search, and, as a consequence, I am no longer the naïve *haole* boy who thought of the Hawaiians in terms of grass shacks, cellophane hula skirts and *"lovely hula hands."* I had not set out to write another chapter in the now too familiar story of change in Hawaii, nor had I intended to tell a tale of the prevailing vogue for Hawaiian archeology. But it seems as if, in my attempt to recall a part of my childhood in Manoa Valley, that, perhaps, I have done both. In those days, in the middle to late 1940s, the wall was only a part of my childhood adventures and its disappearance did not have the metaphorical value it has taken on since. However, our childhood exploits did occur shortly before the jet age, Hawaii's period of greatest change since European contact. At the time, during my childhood, the destruction of the wall was a harbinger of greater change to come that we did not yet have the perspective to understand.

Today, in an age of rank commercialism and over-development, Hawaii seems to be struggling to preserve and connect to its unique and disrespected past. Our wall was just one of many lost remnants of Hawaiian culture, but my memories of it serve as a personal connection to old Hawaii and some of its cultural sentiments – the importance of *mana* (supernatural or divine power), and *a'ina*, the land. Our wall had a powerful *mana* that remained with me through the years. Even in the wall's absence, its spirit has the power to cast a benevolent spell, and I want to think that it also casts a protective spirit over the land it stood on – that the *a'ina* of Manoa and *mana* of the wall are still a part of me and each other.

Manoa Valley where we had so much fun

Small Kid Time in Manoa
(1939 – 1953)

1939 – 1945
Very Small-Kid-Time

The day ahead always seemed full of tempting promise on mornings when, still in bed and after pulling up the Venetian blinds, I could look out of my bedroom window and see Manoa Valley's tallest peaks without their usual shroud of clouds. We lived at the end of a dead-end street where the valley's rainforest was our next-door neighbor, and the early 1950s housing development hadn't yet blocked my bedroom view of the back of the valley. The usual clouds hanging over Manoa's peaks (thought by early Hawaiians to be the home of the gods) didn't always bring rain. And on infrequent days when the crisp jagged silhouette of Manoa's mountaintops stood out against a clear blue sky, I felt a quickening in the pit of my stomach which urged me out of bed.

Those sparkling mornings didn't happen all the time – only when the nearly constant trade winds diminished and didn't blow the windward clouds to our side of Oahu. The forest on the mountains would shine with various hues of green, and anything seemed possible – especially on Saturdays. Dad was at home, and weekend breakfasts were in order. Sundays always meant wearing shoes and the interruption of church and Sunday school. But the promise of Saturdays was special. Before the end of 1953 when television first came to Hawaii, time moved more slowly for kids, and the auspiciousness of the glistening mountains promised me that a lot could happen in a single day. Our neighborhood was nestled against the mountains on the western side of Manoa Valley about three blocks mauka of Waioli Tea Room. Keahi Street's short block ended where the rainforest began as there were no streets or houses beyond our own.

*****

It has been said that a child becomes an autonomous being when he or she is about four years old. I was born at the end of 1939 so, for me, that would have been during the Second World War in late 1943. I do know that my recollections from that age are more reliable than earlier ones and have provided glimpses of my very *small-kid-time* (pidgin English for *childhood*) world. I think it was at that age that I realized my individuality and wondered, as most kids do, if I had been adopted. As it turned out, I hadn't. And it really didn't concern me much to know if we were rich or poor. Parental conversations about money led me to think we were somewhat the latter (as a scientist, Dad had an academic salary), but that information didn't alter my life. It was also about then that I looked beyond our walls and sought membership in a tribe of kids who lived in our neighborhood.

It seems that most children share beliefs and a kid-time mythology in addition to those of their parents. There was a disheveled bag lady, probably homeless, (long before there was a general homeless problem in our cities), who sometimes roamed our neighborhood. We kids believed she was a witch and lived in the forest, and that gossip turned her into our own version of Boo Radley from *To Kill a Mockingbird*. At times, our tribe kept its secrets by speaking pig Latin (*ig pay, atin lay*) and pidgin English (*howzit?* and *da kine*). When one of us stepped out of line, we would point and chant *ahana koko lele* (*shame on you*). Pretty please, patty cake and goody, goody gumdrops were also part of our lexicon, and we entertained each other with sophisticated riddles like *what's black and white and read all over?*, and warnings like *finders keepers, losers weepers and* accusations as to who among us had cooties. Other rhythmic phrases like *liar, liar, pants on fire; smarty pants, smarty pants;* and *it's not fair; it's my turn* and *I'm going home* filled out conversations.

We passed notes in school, whispered secrets, had our feelings hurt and called each other names: *crybaby, sissy, liar,* and the admonition *sticks and stones will break my bones, but words will never hurt me.* We would punch each other on the shoulder and mutter *pass on, no pass back.* We snitched on each other at times, and, like many kids, we couldn't wait to be grown-up. Each year we would exchange valentines with everyone in our class at school. For the most part, we remained in our kid-time bubble which was filled with beliefs that guided our lives. *Never step on a crack, or you'll break your mother's back.* We tried to adhere to that wisdom just as we would religiously check under our beds to make sure there was no bogeyman. Linked pinkie fingers sealed a bet or a promise, and if you crossed your eyes too much, they would stay that way. You could go blind if you touched yourself down there, frogs would give you warts, and wishbones could bring good or bad luck.

When I was young, and sometimes even today, my family called me *Carlo*, a nickname that probably originated when my younger brother tried to say my name. Mom was a housewife, a *career* that occupied many mothers then and put her in charge of our safety. Our sister Aileen wasn't born until 1946 so, during the war, my younger brother and I shared our middle bedroom. Grandma, Mom's mother, had the third bedroom down the hall. Bedtime was probably about eight o'clock in those early days, and we would often go to sleep after a story listening to the wind battering the rain on the roof and through the trees.

What could have been a bogey man in our dark bedroom was, in the light of day, only a pile of clothes stacked on our rocking chair or hung on the clothes tree. I was afraid of the dark when I was very little, and heights still make me weak in the knees. And there was the fear of snakes although we didn't have to actually worry about them in Hawaii. But we did have geckos which we simply called lizards. In the morning, window screens and walls might host those overnight visitors. They seemed harmless to me, and we had heard that they helped keep the cockroaches in check so we always gently rescued them and put them outside.

My stuffed panda would observe me from the bed as I exchanged my pajamas for shorts and a striped t-shirt. Papaya from our backyard and weekend waffles or pancakes were also part of the promise of Saturdays. In the winter, when temperatures sometimes plunged to sixty or below (a *freezing* 53 degrees was reported one year), we would huddle around a small space heater that got us through the chilly breakfast hour. Another endearing winter memory is that Dad would sit on cold toilet seats to warm them up for us.

*****

My *small-kid-time* happened in the Territory of Hawaii, so *T.H.* was part of our return address until 1959 when Hawaii became a state. Mom and Dad couldn't vote for the president until then, but we did have local elections. Every two years, on *vote-for-day*, we would go to a temporary booth in a Manoa park. We didn't have zip codes until 1963, and area codes were officially started in 1947, but I don't remember them then. That was probably because we didn't make many expensive long-distance calls. Our phone number had only five digits – 98876. Mom's calls from Manoa Valley to Wahiawa, where Dad sometimes worked on his pineapple field studies, was considered long distance despite it being only 24 miles away.

"Don't let the screen door slam!" would inevitably ring out as I headed to the garage and driveway after breakfast.

Ultimately, all three of us spent our childhoods with that refrain in our ears.

"I won't. I promise." I would answer back. But that promise was quickly forgotten until the next time.

This was always followed with *be careful!* even though Mom and Dad didn't have to worry as our one-block *cul-de-sac* was pretty much traffic-free then. Another admonition – *it will spoil your appetite* – was a periodic warning. Even at school, our tribe was constantly barefoot, a circumstance that moved with us through our small- kid-time and accomplished the leathery bottoms of our feet (*Kalua feet* we called them.) and inevitable stubbed toes. Mom would fix that problem with an ever-present bottle of mercurochrome; taking splinters out of us was another necessary remedy.

With Dad finishing his coffee in the dining room and Mom at the kitchen sink, I was usually greeted with the aftermath of a night in our rain forest. The rising steam from the asphalt smelled of dampness which would gradually evaporate as the sun rose higher. The hopeful cries of doves and mynah birds announced the drying out, and a smashed Buffo on the road would sometimes be a casualty of its nocturnal wanderings.

Each morning I would help Dad measure the overnight rain in his rain gauge next to the driveway. He tracked the rainfall for the University of Hawaii, and, by the end of any year, we would have had over 100 inches. The tops of Manoa's mountains would have over 200 inches, and Waikiki would have only twenty. All that rain, at times, curtains of rain, made our garden grow, and there were constant chores to help Dad keep our plot of the rainforest manicured – mowing the lawn with a heavy manual mower, edging with a hand clipper, trimming the Crotons, Hibiscus and Heliconia — and lots of weeding. Dad's ultimate nemesis was the crabgrass that invaded our lawn. Mom's chores, including all the jobs to keep our home running smoothly, included shopping at Piggly Wiggly on King Street. My jobs were to help dig out the crabgrass and carry and put away the groceries.

The Hawaiian word *manoa*, the name of our valley, means *vast* or *wide*, and, indeed, it is the largest of the valleys that help partition Honolulu into some of its distinct neighborhoods. It took many millions of years of volcanism and rain to create Manoa, and, in the eighteen-hundreds, it was home to extensive Hawaiian residence and taro cultivation. The nineteenth century also saw Hawaii's first commercial plantings of sugar cane, pineapple and coffee in Manoa Valley. The perimeter of the valley's approximately eight square miles circumscribed my early childhood and dictated how and where I played. Our picture window looked out on a lot of open space, a vast view of the rain forest that included waterfalls and rainbows. In the winter, Manoa Falls would swell to several times its usual size and sometimes bring flooding to Manoa Stream.

Our view of the valley floor was dominated by Japanese vegetable and flower gardens, especially Manoa lettuce and gladiolas. Some of those farmers were said to be squatters who settled in Manoa when they had fulfilled their contracts on the sugar plantations. They would take their vegetables to markets downtown and flowers to Moiliili where there were a number of Japanese flower shops. On the other side of the valley was another suburb called Woodlawn, named after an early dairy. The Chinese Cemetery there would occasionally interrupt our play with reverberating strings of firecrackers and a brass band which attended the dead. Those funerals always meant long processions of cars from the mortuary to the graveyard and the customary food (fruit and *manapua* or pork buns) left on the graves. On our side of the valley the air was cooler because the heat of the afternoon sun was blocked by the precipitous western ridge of the valley that rose above us. The early Hawaiian *alii* (ruling class) historically summered in our neighborhood because it was sheltered from the heat.

*****

With the screen door once again slammed and my promise not to do it again, I would help bring in deliveries sitting inside our open garage. There were bottles of milk and eggs from the University of Hawaii Dairy in lower Manoa. A gallon jar of fresh guava juice which lasted us a week came every Saturday. A Manoa Bakery delivery truck brought sweet rolls and coffee cake, and, later in the day, even a Dairymen's ice cream truck with its classic bell found us in our remote neighborhood and brought us running.

Our short *cull de sac* was a safe setting for most of our outdoor play. Keahi Street was part of a subdivision called Manoa Uplands and was as far back in the valley as roads would take you in those days. As we lived on the edge of nature, I was always engaged by the pressing rain forest. A fascinating weed that we called *sleeping grass* folded up or *went to sleep* when you touched it. We had a Schefflera tree in our front garden. The main amusement of that tree was its two-foot-long branches that had a slight hook at their ends. We could swing them around our index fingers, and centrifugal force kept them spinning. The dried seed pods of African Tulip trees were shaped like boats, and we would sail them in the gutter after a rain. Macadamia nuts from our backyard met their demise on our driveway when we pounded the very hard shells to get out the meat that Mom would roast for us. Wild guavas and mangos and the honeysuckle climbing around the garage provided sweet between-meal treats at any time.

Riding my tricycle up and down our sidewalk gave me my first sense of geographical freedom. That range would be extended by a number of blocks when I learned to ride a bike, and much later, even farther, when I could borrow the family car. Kid-time freedom also included climbing in the trees in our yard – Mango, Lychee and Macadamia. I especially liked climbing in the twisting branches of the *Christmas berry tree* in our side yard. We called it that because its bright red berries bloomed at the end of the year. Our family decorated with those berries and their dark green leaves during the holidays the way people use holly on the mainland.

The Japanese attacked us shortly before Christmas in 1941, but blacking out our windows because visible light was forbidden during the War didn't prevent us from having a lighted Christmas tree that year. It may have been a potted Norfolk Island Pine because war jitters had probably interrupted the shipment of Douglas Firs from Oregon. In years when we did have mainland trees, we loved lying among the presents, looking up at the lights and smelling the fir branches.

Today, years seem to go by quickly, so Christmases come all too soon. But in those kid-time days it seemed to take forever for Christmas to finally roll around. When it did, it was time for going to see the Christmas windows downtown at Liberty House, visiting Santa at Sears and hunting through Christmas catalogs. We carefully picked out just the right tree, and it was we kids who were trusted with carefully draping the icicles on the branches and placing a star on the top. Sometimes we were guilty of snooping in closets to find unwrapped presents. Our stockings were always pinned to the bottom of our beds because we had no fireplace. I guessed that Santa came in the front door. Then we took turns opening our presents under the tree. We believed in Santa Claus then, but we also believed in the Easter Bunny, the sandman and the tooth fairy.

The War

In retrospect, there was a world war taking place until I was six years old, but that extended drama didn't ever mar my anticipation of play and adventure. Pearl Harbor was several valleys and ridges to our west so we didn't experience the actual attack in Manoa, and I don't remember being frightened. I was free to enjoy that time of stuffed animals, chocolate milk, digging a hole to China, cartwheels and somersaults, piggy banks, daily doses of cod liver oil, Animal and Graham Crackers and sitting at the *kid's table* when we had guests.

I would be two years old on December 8th, the day after the bombing, and the family was probably getting ready to go to St. Andrews Cathedral on that Sunday morning. The radio announced, *this is not a drill! Everyone take cover.* I was only two, but I guess my parents must have stayed home from church that day.

To secure public safety, martial law was declared from the end of 1941 to Oct. 1944. This led to local internment camps for some Japanese people and a large stamp that said *Hawaii* on all our paper money. That allowed the government to only devalue the Hawaii currency in case of further invasion. The *war effort* involved scrap drives so we dutifully saved old tires, tin cans, paper and even the foil linings of cigarette and gum packages. Each house was supposed to have an air-raid shelter, and I think ours must have been in the large basement area under the house. In 1943, there was a wartime outbreak of Dengue Fever that required inspections and regular spraying of DDT. Men in trucks would come around looking for standing water that might breed mosquitos. Another sign of the War in Manoa was an extensive neighborhood of Quonset huts that provided military housing near the University.

I was not yet in school during the War so every day held new enterprises that engaged me. One of those was helping with Dad's victory garden where, as a botanist, he grew everything you could think of, including rhubarb and peanuts. There were lines at grocery stores and rationing coupons for things like butter and gasoline, but you couldn't get those from a victory garden. Another job for me was mixing the yellow coloring tablet into the white margarine so we could have a butter substitute. Our lives were hidden behind blackout paper which covered all the windows. A neighbor, Mr. Palmer, was our area warden whose job it was to see if anyone had any light leaking when air raid sirens sounded after dark. He and the city made sure that the street light outside our house was turned off for the duration. A curfew at dusk turned the city dark and allowed only very necessary night driving; special headlight coverings had a slit that focused the light onto the ground. The government distributed gas masks that were kept ready. Kids couldn't attend school without them and an ID card which recorded their blood type. We discovered we could use those fearsome looking masks in our play as they made us look like aliens.

Wartime nerves generated lots of persistent rumors. Some said that a Japanese parachutist had landed at the back of the valley, and, as we were the last house before the forest, we were nervously on the lookout. A few neighbors had heard that the Japanese had poisoned our water supply, so some collected rain water for drinking. People were wary of possible sympathizers, and one Japanese family on our street lost its Japanese-speaking grandfather to a local internment camp. He was suspected of using a short-wave radio to communicate with the homeland. Because of these scares, some people evacuated to the mainland, including our good friends the Keplers and the Tattersons who never returned.

Another very engaging presence of the War in Manoa was a small Army camp on the next block. It was probably established right after the bombing as no one knew what would happen next. There was a strong fear of further invasion. The camp was situated on a gentle rise that had a clear view down the valley to the ocean and to the back of the valley in the opposite direction. I think I remember a tank being there, but it may have been an anti-aircraft gun pointed at the sky and toward the ocean beyond Waikiki where barbed wire lined the beach. A slightly older neighbor girl remembers selling Kool-Aid for five cents to the very friendly soldiers and also teaching them how to do the hula.

    I was still young enough then that playing outdoors kept me close to home. My imagination would guide me in building towns and roads in the dirt and driving my toy cars and trucks on them. When I was about four years old, my father's brother came to visit on his way to serve in the South Pacific. I had never met an uncle before, and this one was full of songs and stories. Uncle Herb brought us toy World War Two airplanes that I flew over my pretend towns. When playing outdoors, I always had to be wary of centipedes. About three inches long with a blue line down their backs, these sinister looking creatures lived under rocks. I was taught to slowly lift them, but I wasn't always careful enough. Another childhood danger was also regularly being stung by yellow jackets which built nests hanging under the leaves of *ti* plants.

    On hot days, Dad would sometimes set up a lawn sprinkler on our front lawn. My earliest memory of playing with a neighbor took place on that lawn. Tricia (Patricia Palmer), who lived a few houses down the street, and I were about the same age, perhaps four, and were old enough to know about *playing house*. She, of course, was the mother and made mud pies to be served at our *tea parties*. I dutifully played the father. My brother had recently been born and was lying peacefully in his crib when we got the bright idea that he could complete *our family*.

Somehow, we were able to get him out of his crib to what we had set up to be *our house* on the lawn. My horrified mother quickly came out of the house when she discovered the kidnapping. As she rushed Harrison back to his crib, she probably heard me indignantly announce, "We're playing house, and we need him! He's our baby!" I've sublimated the consequences of that event, but I do know that that is my first memory of interacting with my younger brother. He had been born prematurely and was in an oxygen tent at the hospital for a time. No wonder Mom panicked when she saw what we had done.

Although we were spanked now and then, I don't think we were chronic *problem kids*. I'm sure we *did* get into fights, threw temper tantrums that tried Mom and Dad's patience once in a while. I remember having the taste of soap in my mouth just once. Today, I wonder what I must have said in polite company. Sometimes, trouble could be brewing, and we would hear, "It's awfully quiet in there. What are you kids up to?"

I began to hear strange names like Hitler and Tojo sprinkled into Mom and Dad's conversations. They had lived through the Great Depression so there was also table talk about the starving children in China, and we tried not to leave food on our plates – except maybe lima beans and Brussels sprouts. Sometimes those could be secreted to the kitchen sink in the bottom of a glass of milk. We always had breakfasts and dinners together in the dining room and learned not to talk with our mouths full and to keep our elbows off the table. Running with scissors was a *no-no*, and we kept metal objects away from electric sockets. We said *please* and *thank you* and tried to look people in the eye. I did have the bad habit of chewing my nails, so I was threatened with chili powder on my fingertips. And there was the classic *if Johnny jumped off a bridge, would you do that too?* Another recurring warning was, *"If you keep this up, you're going to drive me to Kaneohe* (where the crazy house was, *Hale Pupule.)"* And sometimes: *"Don't you dare, mister. I've had quite enough of that."* I don't remember what *this* or *that* were, but Harrison and I (and later Aileen) got through small-kid-time with no more stumbles than most kids.

1945 – 1952
Bigger-Kid-Time

The war was over, prosperity was on the horizon, and Grandma went to live with Aunt Peggy on the mainland. We had an available bedroom so a young Japanese woman named Sadako Shimabukuro (we called her *Dako*) came to get her room and board with us for about five years and to help in the kitchen. Dako worked for the state court system. She never governed us, and she became our friend. Harrison and I even stayed with her and her family in Laupahoehoe on the Big Island. Dako remained our family friend until she died in 2015 when she was ninety years old.

No matter who was cooking, Mom or Dako, food in our small-kid-time was limited in Hawaii. We did always have fresh pineapple in the frig which Dad brought home from his Wahiawa experiments. And I'm sure we must have eaten well in our victory garden days, but after the War, we relied on food that could be shipped from the mainland. Most of that came in cans. I only knew peas as small mushy green balls and canned spinach as slimy strings. I didn't know what a fresh zucchini looked like until I was into my teens. I just thought it was gummy green pieces mixed with stewed tomatoes as it came out of the can. Lunch often meant opening a can of Campbell's soup. Our favorites were Chicken-noodle and Chicken Gumbo which contained an exotic vegetable called okra. Even some meat came in cans in the form of Spam, Vienna Sausages and canned hams.

Some of our favorite meals were Chinese food brought home from the Golden Duck restaurant in Makiki and Hawaiian food from the Chun Hoon Market in Nuuanu. Actually, all three of us ate the very nutritious Hawaiian staple *poi* from the time we were infants as almost all kids do in Hawaii. Another favorite was any meat cooked in soy sauce, garlic and ginger, a ubiquitous island flavor. Mrs. Nishioka, our house cleaner, sometimes came to cook when Mom and Dad entertained. Her specialties were a Japanese dish called hekka served with rice, and shrimp curry with all the condiments. Today, Hawaii has access to lots of fresh vegetables that are grown in the islands, and the cans we used to rely on gradually moved out of our lives.

*****

In the fall of 1946, I started first grade at Teacher's College – we called it *T.C.* – across from the University of Hawaii. Today it is called The Lab School and is where the University trains teachers. As I did that, I moved into *bigger-kid-time,* and play on Keahi Street began to change as well. With smart-ass irreverence, we would sometimes call our valley, our greater playground, *Manure Valley.* And there were now other playmates besides Tricia, my *playing-house* friend. Our upper middle-class neighborhood of single-family homes – no one had heard of co-ops or condos then – was made up of an ethnic goulash. There were a number of *haole* (Caucasian) families, of course, but there was also a melting pot of others: Rowena Wang was Korean, Nancy Gail Kisheda and Lester Ikeda were Japanese, George *Boy* Kaholiwai was Hawaiian, Timmy Toner and Sammy Olivera were Portuguese, Mr. and Mrs. Levine were Jewish (Mr. Levine wore his hair very long, and we called him *Jesus*), the Cintrons were Cuban, our next-door neighbors, the Changs, were Chinese, Diana McIntyre was Spanish and Trisha Palmer was Norwegian - and I was German, Danish, English and Irish – pure *haole*.

Trisha, Diana McIntyre and I were about the same age and were in the same grade although we didn't attend school together until senior high at Punahou School. Trisha and Diana lived next door to each other and were close friends, and I lived a few houses up the street. I could often hear them giggling over secrets that I wasn't a part of. I remember that Diana wore a beautiful fresh flower in her hair almost every day of her life. Diana's father was a sea captain – *Captain Mac* we called him – and he commanded ships, the Waialeale and the Hualalai, that sailed to the outer islands. Captain Mac was bigger than life, and we would regularly see him walking on our street in his pajamas smoking a large cigar.

Every summer, our neighbor, Mrs. Fujimoto, imported four other playmates, her niece and three nephews from the Big Island, to join our tribe. One year at her house I was trying to cut up a pineapple with a machete, and I have a major scar on my left hand to this day. I don't ever remember considering the races of any of these friends. They were all just kids we played with. During the war, one could hear the enemy being called *Japs* (mostly by servicemen), but we never did so as we had very close Japanese friends who were like family to us. Not realizing its implications of correctness then, we *did* sometimes chant, "Ching Chong Chinaman, sitting on a fence, trying to make a dollar out of fifteen cents." I encountered a much more complex racial perspective when we first went to the mainland. Interestingly, except in the military, there were no African-Americans in our neighborhood, or the islands, that I knew of. If there had been, I'm sure they would have been invited into our games as all the others were.

As a pioneer baby boomer, my sister Aileen joined us on June 8, 1946, so there then would be three of us letting the screen door slam, and my brother and I would have somebody new to tease. Aileen was a towheaded tomboy, and she eventually joined all of our street games. She became great at barefoot football and riding bikes. As the youngest of us, she was always tagging along, wanting to be included in everything. We never owned a dog, but, at one point, we acquired a cat from the Humane Society, and Aileen named him Cadillac. At that time, those fancy cars had exaggerated tail fins, and our cat always sat with his haunches sticking up like the fins of a classic '50s Cadillac. In the early fifties, we had two parakeets, one yellow and one blue, that our parents, good old-style Republicans that they were, named Ike and Mamie. When she was little, Aileen had an ambition to be a garbage man, and she would ride on the fender of our car wearing a sailor hat as she had seen the garbage crew do on their trucks. In this same tomboy vein, she hated the patent leather *Mary Jane shoes* and frilly dresses she had to wear to Sunday School.

On the island of Oahu, there were only a few destinations that could excite a trip anywhere, but I don't remember ever having *island fever* back then. That would first happen with the prospect of going off to college when I was in high school. We did take our first train ride, Oahu Railway's last, in 1947 when we went from downtown to Haleiwa and back. We could drive around the island in our 1939 Studebaker in a day, but, for me, a more interesting outing was a trek through a jungle over the *Pali* to the windward side of the island. There was a meandering road that took us up Nuuanu Valley through a forest of hanging vines and deposited us at the very windy viewpoint at the top. The Upside Down Falls there were created by the severe winds against the cliffs that blew the water upward. Then a very narrow road twisted us down the other side past several hairpin curves. We always leaned into the mountain because we thought it would prevent us from going over the edge.

As a slight digression, I will move us out of Manoa Valley for a year and take us to Riverside, California where Dad had a sabbatical leave in 1948-'49. (More on this later) I was in fourth grade, Harrison was in first, and Aileen hadn't started school yet. We discovered a new place called *the mainland,* experienced snow for the first time, fought off bouts of homesickness and were forced to wear sweaters, coats and shoes. Once school was out, we went on an extensive road trip as far east as Chicago before coming back to Manoa Valley and fifth grade for me at Teacher's College.

*****

Parents didn't arrange play dates or sleepovers in those days. Getting together for games on our *cul-de-sac,* where much of our outdoor playing took place, was less formal. To find a playmate, we would simply go to their house and yell up at a window: *Can Trisha come out to play?!* Sometimes getting together meant having a picnic. We would all go home to have our mothers pack a lunch – a sandwich along with a peanut butter jar full of milk. Each time, we would try to think of a new place to go, but we always ended up sitting in the same spot on the curb in front of the Kisheda's Panax hedge. We celebrated each other's birthdays with presents and games such as pin-the-tail-on-the-donkey; suffered through measles, chicken pox and broken bones together and shared stories about losing our tonsils or adenoids.

After the war, some of us were old enough for play to take us away from our immediate neighborhood. We could walk or ride bikes about a mile to what everyone called *the village*. The old Chinese store on East Manoa Road was the first stop. There we could buy *see moi* and cracked seed (Chinese preserved fruits) for five cents a bag, *manapua* (pork buns) for a dime, *shave* ice and the miracle of something new to Honolulu called bubble gum. Lowrey Avenue would take us across Manoa Stream on a rickety wooden bridge. The village, which we treated as our neighborhood *downtown*, was the site of old Manoa Elementary School where I later attended sixth grade. There were also Manoa Market (today it's a Starbucks), a barber shop with two Japanese barber ladies where I received my first, perhaps tearless, haircut. There was Manoa Pharmacy run by a Japanese man named Warren (we just called it *Warren's*), Manoa Bakery (for five cent donuts) and another drugstore (part of Manoa-Woodlawn Super Market) that had a soda fountain and lunch counter. I liked their hamburgers, cherry Cokes and a drink called a Green River made of lime syrup. Our allowances

(25 cents a week at first, and later, a dollar) were mostly spent in these places. Ten-cent comic books were my favorite purchases. I wish I had valued those comics more as they would be worth a lot of money today.

Before the invention of skateboards, Legos and even Hula Hoops, we played outdoor games on driveways and sidewalks. We never paid much attention to what time of the year it was as seasons all ran together in Hawaii for kids, but we could always count on some rain in Manoa. We did notice when it was summer because we were out of school, and we knew that Christmas, even without snow, came in the winter. There was always time for London Bridge is Falling Down, jump rope, leap frog and hop scotch which required a piece of chalk for drawing the squares on the sidewalk and a token for throwing; a set of six-pointed metal pieces and a rubber ball were needed for playing jacks. Sometimes we would bicker about cheating and whose turn it was. And there were declarations of *kapu*. That was Hawaiian for *forbidden,* but we used it as a verb to mean *that is mine* as in *I kapu that ball,* the way mainland kids would say *I dibs*. Some of us had swings in our backyard, and spinning tops, yo-yos, water pistols and shooting marbles got a lot of consideration too. The clear ones were called purees, and there were cat's eyes, and *bombuchas* (Pidgin slang) which were the big ones we used to knock our rivals out of a circle.

But the sidewalk game that got the most attention used the caps from the tops of milk bottles. We would dry the caps in the sun until they were stiff and then used them as tokens to flip over other kids' caps from a pile. You got to keep the ones you flipped. Was it like gambling since you would bet so many caps each round as the pile grew? And was it cheating to tape two caps together as your token? That game isn't seen anymore, even in schoolyards. Milk comes in cartons now, and video games, social media and texting seem to have taken the place of most of our outdoor games that we loved so much.

Rainy days – and there were lots of them – moved us indoors, and *w*e had a large repertoire for that as well: in addition to keeping up with a pen pals, we had Tinker Toys, Lincoln Logs, Pick -Up -Sticks, Silly Putty, a Slinky and an elaborate Lionel train set that Harrison got for Christmas one year. We could also be found sprawled on the floor – we spent a lot of time sprawled on the floor – with jigsaw puzzles and coloring books (trying to stay within the lines), Monopoly, Checkers, Chinese Checkers and card games like Old Maid, Go Fish and "fifty-two pick up." We traded playing cards which we collected and categorized in shoe boxes. There were sections for people, scenery and animals and everything else. One section was for horses, and a prize card depicted the famous race horse Man of War. Because of the popularity of trading cards, stores began selling brand new cards in wrapped packets. But I thought that was cheating.

One year, we set up a neighborhood library. We taped lending cards in our books, loaned them to the younger kids and tried to collect fines if they weren't returned on time. We also started a hand-printed neighborhood newspaper and charged ten cents for subscriptions. We never had complaints even when we tired of that project and moved on to something else.

In the early '50s, Harrison had a paper route near the *village* and I subbed for him sometimes. About that same time, he and I twice left Manoa and attended an Episcopal summer camp at Mokuleia on the North Shore. Our dorm was a war-surplus Quonset hut, and we spent our time doing woodwork, ceramics, painting, archery, baseball, swimming and hiking. I was very impressed with the closing ceremony on the night our parents came to pick us up. At dusk, a metal cross covered in burlap and soaked in gasoline was attached to the reef and set on fire. The flames rising out of the surf provided a theatrical finale for our two weeks away from home.

Almost traffic-free, Keahi Street was the setting of many of our neighborhood games. Our telephone and electric lines were underground, and there weren't many parked cars then so we had lots of room to run, skate and ride. None of us was what is today called *streetwise*, but our street was our playground. After school and on weekends, before or after homework, we would try to gather a quorum of playmates and choose a game from our repertoire. Some of our games were as simple as tag, Mother, May I, jump rope and flying kites made of newspaper and Panax branches. Other sidewalk pastimes required equipment we had received for birthdays or Christmases: a red wagon, a scooter, a pogo stick and a pair of stilts. One could regularly hear the crack of croquet mallets, the whoosh of badminton birds and the clang of horseshoes on our front lawn.

As it was easy to organize, the universal children's game hide and seek was our favorite. We would choose who would be *it* by standing in a circle and chanting *Jan-ken-po, I can show* which was a Japanese version of *paper-scissors-rock*. At the end of the game, if everyone hadn't been found, someone would shout *olly olly oxen free*, and the last players would come out of hiding.

Some of our outdoor games required teams: Run, Sheep, Run, Kick-the-Can, Dodgeball and Capture the Flag. Other games were less formal when we made up the rules. Cowboys and Indians (not politically incorrect then), probably inspired by cowboy movies, needed cowboy hats, homemade bows and arrows and cap guns. Most often we would simply point our fingers and say, "Pow! You're dead." The game of *war* used ill-advised slingshots with berries or pebbles. We would shout, "Bombs Away!," something we had heard a lot during the War.

Dad had bought an Army surplus pup-tent that served us when we camped out overnight in the front yard and read comic books with a flashlight after dark. But sometimes, *roughing it* defeated us, and we would end up in our own beds. *Knights of the Roundtable*, probably inspired by another movie, required capes and wooden swords. We gave each other dorky names like Sir Lester of the Lake and Sir Gaines of the Gulf.

Barefoot touch football was played on Lester Ikeda's front lawn and on the street. Again, Mom's antibiotic *Mercurochrome* became a fixture in our lives because of stubbed toes from drop kicks and scraped knees from falls. We learned to ride the bikes that we had received for Christmas, and the street became our highway. We would attach playing cards to our wheel spokes to produce a clicking sound that we imagined sounded like a motor. I remember attaching my transistor radio to my bike's handle bars to replicate a car's radio. We put roller skates on our shoes with skate keys we were always losing. Roller Derby at the Civic Auditorium was the inspiration for the derby we staged in Lester's garage. There were metal poles that we would skate around and swing on. We gave each other names like Blonde Bomber, Cherry Rockette and Blossom Rodriquez that plagiarized the names of the tough Roller Derby stars.

They always seemed so tough, and we thought water-based tattoos made us look tough too.

Waioli Tea Room was a commercial cafe for lunch and dinner in a beautiful garden setting about three blocks from our house. It was connected to a Salvation Army home for orphaned and *wayward* girls. Some of them worked in the café in order to meet the general public and learn *the arts of gracious living*. We called them *titas*, a Hawaiian word meaning *sister*. On another level, *tita* referred to the fact that they were a bit rough around the edges, and were sexually experienced, we thought. They wore large earrings, cuffed Levis and aloha shirts with the sleeves rolled up and too much make-up. We got a kick out of watching them with their boyfriends at our bus stop which was near their dormitory. The *titas* fascinated us, but we watched them from a safe distance. One time at Manoa Stream, a gang of them took over our skinny-dipping site. The pool wasn't big enough for all of us, and, intimidated, we scrambled home.

Before television became a Saturday morning babysitter in the mid-50s, the Pawaa Theater on King Street hosted The Mighty Mouse Club. The theater always smelled of popcorn and butter, and for nine cents – I always wondered why not ten cents? – you got a Buck Rogers serial, previews, a full-length cowboy movie (usually Lash Larue, Johnny Mack Brown or Roy Rogers), games and prizes on stage and a Mighty Mouse cartoon. The Porky Pig Club was held at the Kaimuki Theater, and I think the Bugs Bunny Club was at the Kapahulu. Mom would drop Harrison and me off with a dollar, and we were good for the whole morning, including Raisinetts, Milk Duds and popcorn. I also liked something called Lick-M-Ade. It was flavored powder that came in little envelopes. You would tear open the envelope, pour the colored powder into your hand and lick it off your palm. It was a great way to get very sticky before the movie was over.

The Pawaa on Saturdays was a great gathering place for kids. Our playmate Diana was a bit older and worldlier than the rest of us. We would sit a few rows behind her and her boyfriend Sammy in order to watch them *making out*. We were very impressed with Diana's seasoned sophistication that, at one point, involved an *I'll-show-you- mine, if-you-show-me-yours* conversation. Would that have been like playing doctor? I don't think I ever actually did that, but I'm pretty sure the discussion involved Diana – or was it Tricia?

1952 – 1957
Adolescent Kid Time

During the years of new construction, our street games were played on a different playground: the foundations and studded walls of new houses. Our expeditions to the Hawaiian wall, the cave, Manoa Stream and Manoa Falls were also replaced by other enterprises that would draw new parental warnings for our safety. After the workmen had gone home at the end of the day, we played on the footings of new homes, chased each other across floor beams and, accompanied by the smell of diesel oil, tar and freshly turned earth, we would climb on the parked bulldozers and imagine them to be wartime tanks.

As the houses neared completion, we wondered who our new neighbors would be, and we played our game of hide-and-seek in the bedroom closets and kitchen cupboards of the new homes before the carpenters finally locked them up. Our picture windows that had looked out on the lush valley now showed us a field of tract homes instead of the Japanese gladiola gardens we used to look down on. More important for me, I could no longer see Manoa's cloudless mountain tops from my bedroom in the morning. There was now a house right next door to us on the *mauka* (mountain) side.

In 1954, we discovered a place called Rainbow Rollerland on Keeaumoku Street. You could roll around a huge oval to the accompaniment of music on skates that laced up and didn't require an elusive skate key. At first, the goal was to merely remain upright, but, as time went on, we also mastered the art of skating backward. It all felt very grown-up and allowed us to mix with kids from other parts of the city.

Once TV had come to Honolulu in late 1952, the Saturday morning cartoon clubs became a phenomenon of the past. At first, we were drawn to the televisions we could see in store windows or in the appliance department at Sears. Then we found out that one of our neighbors was the head engineer at KGMB, the first TV channel in the islands. The Lindemans had a television set, of course, and on Friday nights we would often gather for *Ozzie and Harriett, Dragnet,* and *I Love Lucy*. In 1954, Harrison bought us an eighteen-inch Crossley set with his paper route money, and we eased from radio to TV.

But earlier, *Charley McCarthy* and *Amos-n-Andy* on the radio had forced us to use our imaginations, so those shows actually seemed more vivid than the very old movies, cooking shows and test patterns that KGMB first broadcast in black and white. We had already experienced TV on the mainland in 1948/'49 (*Howdy Doody, The Lone Ranger* and *Milton Berle*) which happened to be the first year of regularly scheduled network shows. But in Honolulu we were *glued* to anything that moved or appeared on our own screen. We were also very proud of the metal novelty on our roof. That aerial announced to the whole neighborhood, *we have a TV set!* Once-in-a-while, the winds of upper Manoa would require climbing up to adjust the reception. Eventually, everyone had one of those contraptions on their roof, so we just became one of the neighborhood crowd.

There was opportunity for *kid-time* pranks that today we're not very proud of. I remember that some kind of fireworks bomb went down a sewer blowing off the manhole cover and shattering some windows. That happened on a New Year's Eve when other firecrackers and cherry bombs were being blown up under people's windows. Always, the next day, streets and yards were littered with red paper from the exploded crackers. And it was hilarious at the time when we would order Chinese food or a taxi to a neighbor's house and then peek out a window to witness the confrontation at their front door. Much less sinister was calling someone to ask if their refrigerator was running and then suggesting that they *run after it.*

An older teenager named Billy Linus lived a couple of blocks away from us. He owned two horses and would occasionally bring them to the end of our street to graze. Billy was handsome and the girls were interested in him. He was fun, and he taught us to ride his horses. He also took us for jaunts in his Cadillac convertible. But Billy also had the reputation as a *bad boy* because he sometimes got himself and some of us in trouble. One year, that trouble was connected to trick or treating when he dug holes in a lawn, put blue dye in a fish pond and threw rotten guavas at a front door. The police were called, but I don't remember my parents being involved. Billy probably smoked cigarettes, but he didn't pass on any bad habits to us, and harder drugs wouldn't be seen for another decade or so. Apparently, he continued to live on the edge, and we later heard he went to prison for a time.

*****

As small-kid-time eased into adolescence, we graduated from bare feet to wearing flip flops and eventually to shoes when school or jobs required them. Maybe it was because of the family budget, but, for some reason, I was sent from the private U.H. Lab School to the public Manoa Elementary School for sixth grade. Besides shoes, my teen years brought about a driver's license and several jobs: as a janitor for summer art classes at the Honolulu Academy of Art, as a McInerny's clothing salesman at the then-new Ala Moana Center and as a tray boy at the Dole Pineapple Cannery. The driver's license gave me more freedom of movement when I could borrow the family car.

My world expanded when I developed new friendships with Lloyd, Michael and Timmy who lived on nearby Huelani Drive. Our next-door neighbor Gaines Medley was also a close pal. Sadly, we watched his house burn down one Saturday morning in 1955, but we were glad they rebuilt and continued to be our very good neighbors. A connection with Gaines' father put Harrison, Gaines and me on the pit crew for the stock car races at the old Honolulu Stadium. Helping with those jalopies was a great rush for three young boys, and we got the idea for our own demolition derby on Keahi Street. Our bikes took a beating when we tried to recreate that mayhem.

Perhaps it was because we were now teenagers and had a store of new hormones, someone had the idea to throw a party that would involve music, dancing – and the opposite sex. The only place we could find to do it was in Lester's garage which wasn't very romantic, but we decorated with crepe paper, brought in an old 78 RPM record player and dredged up some neighbor girls to join us. They may have been Diana, Tricia and Gloria Canlis whose father owned a popular Waikiki restaurant. Aileen also may have been part of the mix as were Lester's sisters Marcia and Joann. Enterprises like that led us to consider the way we looked. Our longer hair needed grease so we could comb it into what we called a chicken or duck ass (CA or DA for short). Hair from both sides met at the back of the head to form a look that we must have picked up from older more tough guys. I think we may have played spin-*the-bottle* at that event, but mainly the party was for dancing. My favorite song at the time was Tony Bennett's *Rags to Riches*, but we also had on hand *Oh, Mein Papa* (Eddie Fisher), *That's Amore* (Dean Martin), *Secret Love* (Doris Day), and S*h-Boom, Sh-Boom* by the Crewcuts – all clearly from an era before Rock and Roll.

In 1957, the last year of my Manoa childhood, I graduated from Punahou School and went off to The University of Oregon. *Kid-time* on Keahi Street had been a happy time for me, and now it was over. But our valley still calls to me even after all these years.

2021

I live in California now, but I occasionally visit Keahi Street because my brother Harrison and his wife Patti live next door to the house we grew up in. Harrison couldn't drag himself away, and in 1980, he built his own house on the second lot Mom and Dad purchased in 1940. I try to imagine the small-kid playground of our old *cul-de-sac*, but it's no longer the traffic-free playground we enjoyed during our kid-time bubble. It seems a lot smaller today and so much more crowded as parked cars now crowd the curbs. Could we have really played touch football, roller skated and ridden our bikes there? So much happened on that street then that I wonder if we could ever have been bored, a common childhood condition. Did I ever have to ask Mom, *what can I do today*?

A new generation of kids can no longer experience the adventures in the rain forest that we did. The Hawaiian Wall has, of course, disappeared under a subdivision, and the cave entrance on the mountain is overgrown with Kukui and Albezia trees now. The part of Manoa Stream where we had skinny-dipped is a hardscape concrete spillway, and some say that isolated Manoa Falls can be a dangerous destination.

All but one of our old neighbors are gone now – moved or passed away – so my brother no longer knows everyone on the street. Our friend Diana died of a heart attack in 1999 when she was sixty years old. Tricia lives in Portland, Oregon, as does my sister Aileen. Tricia and I are now eighty-four years old (2023) and are still very close friends. Except for all the new houses, our old neighborhood hasn't changed the way the rest of Honolulu has. The hum of the city with its high-rise density and freeways still does not penetrate our valley. Manoa has been spared the forests of high rises that crowd the rest of what has become the most isolated major city on Earth.

But Manoa Valley was a safe place and, except for the war years, we lived there in a safe time. We didn't realize how good we had it then. We were allowed to roam as far as the wall, the stream, the falls and the cave and have as much adventure as our imaginations would allow. We were lucky to have grown up in a multi-ethnic melting pot that seemed to exist without racial prejudice. Today, kids growing up on Keahi Street experience a totally different kid-time than we did in the 1940s and '50s. A preoccupation with social media and more stringent admonitions for safety keep kids indoors so the interaction of outdoor play doesn't happen much anymore.

When Mom and Dad bought their two adjacent lots in upper Manoa in 1941, the area was considered isolated and soggy, and they paid ten cents a square foot for them; today, those square feet are each assessed at over $300. Their fortuitous decision to buy those lots was rewarded with a rare place to live and raise a family. My brother and sister and I spent happy small-and-big-kid-times living where we did. It didn't seem special or unusual at the time, but, from the vantage point of 2024, I think we lived there in a magical window of time and place. As Honolulu has fanned out across the southern side of the island, Manoa has become very central to everything, and its wet world is prized for its lush coolness. It is close to Waikiki, Ala Moana and downtown, and it has the comfortable suburban atmosphere that it always had. And occasionally, there are still those sparkling days when clouds don't shroud the tops of the mountains. When I am home in Manoa, l can still feel the tug of excitement that those rare days had always set in the pit of my stomach.

While heading to San Francisco recently, I was sitting on the left side of the plane. At a distance, I strained to see the neighborhood our tribe had inhabited. But there it was, looking so small that I wondered how all that childhood could ever have taken place there.

Our neighborhood tribe: I'm at the bottom right.

Our tribe has a Halloween party - I'm in the clown outfit.

Fort Street when I was a kid

Fort Street and Downtown Honolulu
(1947 – 1955)

Even as a child learning to speak my first language, English, the word tripped easily off my tongue. *Ho-no-lu-lu.* It was easy to say, but I certainly thought it was an odd sounding collection of vowels. Very early on, I was taught to connect that funny sounding word to the city I lived in. No one ever affectionately called it "the city" as they do in San Francisco. It was just Honolulu. Other exotic cities on my small-kid-time radar, Hong Kong and Bangkok, for instance, also had peculiar sounding rhythmic vowel-filled names, and I wondered if that was an indication of an exceptional city.

Honolulu was just a medium-sized city then (about 300,000 or so in the 1940s when I was a kid and well-over a million today), but those four rhythmic syllables didn't seem like a proper name for a city of any kind, even if it was secluded in the middle of an ocean. New York, yes. Chicago, yes. They sounded like real cities. But Hono-lulu? Or Hana-lula, as some tourists call it. It sounded like baby talk or something from Dr. Seuss to me. In high school English class, I learned that Edgar Allen Poe had used lots of vowel repetition and rhythm, or *assonance,* so I came to accept the name of my city as part of that same tripping language I was learning in addition to English.

My Hawaiian dictionary tells me that the descriptive word *Honolulu* means *sheltered harbor* – *hono* (harbor) and *lulu* (sheltered). The dictionary also includes *calm water* as a variation. If one surveys the scene where the tiny village of Honolulu began welcoming sailing ships in the 18th century, it is clear that the harbor is protected in several ways: the Koolau Mountains guard Honolulu from major trade winds from the north. In addition, an encompassing coral reef that stills incoming surf also keeps the ocean at bay from the harbor just as it does from Waikiki and all of the southern side of the island. And, if one looks to the south, less than a mile away one can see another low slice of land called Sand Island. In addition to some light industry, a public park and, fittingly, a Coast Guard station, Sand Island guards the harbor from the incoming Pacific. Honolulu, indeed, had its origins at a sheltered harbor on an island called Oahu – *the gathering place.*

I knew Manoa Valley where I grew up was a part of Honolulu, but regarding the greater city, it was the designation *downtown* that meant Honolulu to me. I was always excited to hear "we're going downtown" as that meant a trip out of the valley to a more bustling and interesting part of the city. And, in those days, *downtown* primarily meant our main shopping district on Fort Street. Ala Moana Shopping Center hadn't even been thought of yet. Fort Street was the major hub of activity – all the major stores were there, The Liberty House, Kress, Kramers, McInerny and Andrade. None of those establishments were chain stores from the mainland, except, of course, for Kress. But they were all part of our shopping mall of the day, the five most important blocks of Fort Street.

The street was named for an old Russian fort built near the waterfront of coral blocks cut from the reef. In 1815 Kamehameha the First had granted some Russian whalers and fur-traders permission to build a storehouse near the harbor. But, instead, they began building a fort and then raised the Russian flag over it. It was the largest structure in the islands at the time. King Kamehameha reacted, of course, and had the Russians removed. Those Russians, challenged by stronger Hawaiian forces, moved on to Kauai and built another fort where ruins can still be seen today.

But the Russian presence had proved one thing to the Hawaiians – a fort was needed to keep our unwanted strangers. The Hawaiians finished building the fort and mounted guns for that purpose. At mid-century, the 1850s, the fort was also used as a jail to keep unruly drunken whalers off the street. In 1843 the English arrived and managed to rule Hawaii for about a year. They then decided there was no commercial or strategic value for them possessing the islands. And in 1849 the French attacked the fort because of the persecution of Catholics and the repression of French trade. After about a year, when their demands were met, they, too, withdrew.

In 1857, after some quieter years, it became clear that the fort was no longer necessary for defense, and it was demolished. I knew the English had ruled Hawaii for a time; one just has to notice the Union Jack on the Hawaiian flag to know that, and the fact that the islands were named for the Englishman the Earl of Sandwich at one time. But my research also told me of the invasions of the Russians and the French, and that was new information to me. And, speaking of invasions, today no fort is going to turn back the invasion of millions of world tourists who arrive every year.

Originally, a simple trail from the fort heading toward the mountains became the real estate that resulted as Fort Street. The trail was paved in 1881, and it became a two-way street when automobiles arrived near the turn of the twentieth century. Because of its proximity to the harbor, property on the street increased in value, and all the important businesses moved there.

    I discovered the street when I was taken there by my parents when I was a child. I loved the bustle of the fashionable shoppers, the honking traffic, the bells of the streetcars and the neon signs and display windows that showed off what was inside the stores. Waikiki Beach was a growing tourist center but was not yet the focus of the city's economy. I suppose the main streets of Honolulu today are Kalakaua Avenue in Waikiki and King and Beretania Streets that cut across the city. But in the old days, downtown Honolulu and Fort Street were where the city shopped and conducted most of its business.

*****

    Very little looked as I remembered it. I searched for hints of a seventy-year-old childhood landscape I held in my mind, but there was nearly nothing. The five blocks of Fort Street that had been the focus of downtown Honolulu for me when I was a child and teenager didn't look anything like what they had been, and now they even seemed inhospitable. I felt out of place and wanted to move on, but I had made a purposeful expedition in June of 2022 to let the camera in my mind search for remnants of a more-lofty time gone by. I was waiting for the frisson, the shudder of excitement, I had always felt as a child when going downtown to this grown-up landscape. Since my dad had not worked in that part of town, downtown was not every-day familiar territory for me when I was little. Our occasional trips to that greater world always registered heavily on me – church at St. Andrews Cathedral, Dr. Marshall at the Medical Group, clothes shopping with Mom, and trips to the main post office and library. I always wore shoes when we went downtown, confirmation that downtown was an important destination.

When I was in high school I had a membership at a fitness center (Rex Ravell's Heath Club) near Fort Street, and, as a teenage *flaneur* (French for a dallier who strolls about idly taking in the sights), I always took advantage of being in town to wander along Fort Street and in the surrounding neighborhood checking out everything for what was new. The early bones of Fort Street were not new, but there were always changes in the store windows, new books and magazines in the bookstores, and new and different well-dressed grownups doing their shopping.

My reminiscent visit to Fort Street last summer happened on a Saturday, a day that seventy years earlier would have hosted well-dressed ladies and their families shopping in Honolulu's premier emporium – its Main Steet, its main drag, its Broadway, its Rialto. But there were no well-dressed ladies; there were no well-dressed people at all. And no one was shopping. Most of them barefoot, they were all just hanging out – on a bench, on the ground, some sleeping, some just staring. Brown paper bags containing bottles and the remains of fast food decorated the scene as did a derelict shopping cart or two and some half-hearted graffiti that had not been painted over. Fort Street seemed to have become these people's living room, but where, I wondered, were their bedrooms?

Maybe, if I had gone there on a weekday I might have seen some better-dressed business people who had spilled over from Bishop Street, but, on this day, Fort Street was nearly desolate, hosting a current urban reality. It was clear that this mostly-idle community was there because its members had no place else to be, and some of them were most likely homeless, or *unhoused* as they say today. There was a place on a bench where I could have joined one of them – I really wanted a personal story – but a pungent odor kept me at bay. Another reason for that scene may have been because of the Covid pandemic, but I saw no masks. Fort Street had become a refugee hang-out, a rec-room for downtown's underclass and unhoused.

I looked away from this disappointing scene on the street, let my eyes go out of focus and hoped to see, at least in my mind's eye, the businesses that had brought people there at one time – the banks, the restaurants, the theaters and, most of all, the world-class stores. Almost all of the hardscape, the buildings themselves, were still there, but what had been inside of them had decamped for other homes or gone out of business. The Fort Street banks, of an era before my time, had long ago moved to Bishop Street, a few restaurants were now on side streets, and the old Russian fort was, of course, a part of distant history.

Fort Street was never a major thoroughfare; it was only two lanes wide, but, in its time, it was the most important street in the city. Old photographs show that it even had streetcars long ago. The street imported all the best-known goods and labels from the mainland, Europe and Asia.

My earliest memory of Fort Street was going to Kress, a store that we used to call a five-and-dime. I remember going on the bus with my grandmother and sometimes with my mother in the car for what, among other purchases were things they called *notions*. Those turned out to be accessories for their sewing: thread, buttons, snaps, zippers and pins and needles. We also bought notebooks and pencils and pens and other school supplies there every August. All of this was fairly inexpensive then, although I suspect some of it cost more than five or ten cents. No matter what Grandma was paying, I was always fascinated with the magical pneumatic tubes that whooshed cylinders with sales slips and her money (no credit cards then) to an unseen mysterious place. Soon, just as magically, the container would whisk back with change and a receipt. It seemed like something out of science fiction to me.

But the best part of going to Kress was sitting with Grandma at its serpentine lunch counter and soda fountain. The counter zig-zagged in and out so you were always facing other diners across from you. It was great for people watching. The kitchen grill made the whole store smell of cooked hamburgers which I was always lovingly treated to along with a piece of apple pie and a root beer float. We would sit on turning stools along with other well-dressed shoppers and office workers all of whom wore hats in those days. I didn't wear a hat, but Grandma did – this was the 1940s, after all – and I loved mixing with all the other grown-ups who also wore hats. Some of the ladies wore gloves, but almost all of them wore hats. All the hats made this downtown place very special compared to our suburban home in Manoa Valley. The mother of my childhood friend Tricia was a milliner at The Liberty House, and I suppose she created some of the hats I saw on Fort Street.

Even Woolworth's, a later five-and-dime store, brand new when I was a teenager, had disappeared from the corner of Fort and King streets. That store had always smelled of roasting nuts and hamburgers. But their lunch counter also offered something new to me and to Honolulu, something called a submarine sandwich. Perhaps it was called that because of its elongated shape. Those submarines were filled with layers of sandwich meat, mayonnaise and cold slaw, and, along with a cherry Coke, I loved them.

And then there was Ciro's restaurant on Hotel St., around the corner from Fort. I never ate at Ciro's as it was a grownup kind of place. But, I was fascinated. In my wanderings, I would peek inside now and then. It was dark and mysterious and smelled of smoke and alcohol. There were well-dressed adults (more hats) sipping cocktails and eating lunch in red leather dining booths. Now there is only a McDonalds on Fort Street, the closest thing to a restaurant that still exists there.

The downtown shopping area also had two music stores where, after a submarine sandwich, I could sit in a soundproof listening booth to sample records. Those stores were two of my regular stops where I would listen to all the latest popular music and Broadway show tunes. The Honolulu Book Shop was also a great place for browsing, – I have always been a reader – and the nearby block-long Alexander Young Hotel, a holdover from the days before Waikiki had all the first-rate hotels, had the best bakery in the city just off its lobby – a great stop for a donut or a bear claw.

Looking in the other direction, toward the corner where King Street meets Fort, I could see where another important landmark of my childhood had been. I was horrified to see that The Liberty House, at one time Honolulu's premier quality department store was now a Walmart. A Walmart? How had Fort Street come to that? And now (2023) it has been announced that even Walmart is pulling out, leaving Fort Street and its mall even more bereft.

Originally a German-run establishment, Hackfeld and Co. became The Liberty House just after the first World War for geo-political reasons. As a young adult, I remember The Liberty House being in San Francisco too, and then Macy's bought the whole chain, and closed the store for good in 1998. My brother and sister and I went to The Liberty House with Mom every year for back-to-school clothes. Excitedly, we got to ride the elevator to the upper fourth floor at a time when elevators were few-and-far-between in Honolulu. In addition to my fascination with the elevators, I was drawn to the machine that allowed you to see the bones in your feet when buying shoes. The Liberty House was full of wonders.

In December, we always made a trip to town to see Fort Street's Christmas lights which were festooned above the traffic. And we also went to see The Liberty House's store windows with holiday displays some of which were mechanical and actually moved. As a little kid I wondered how Santa could be at two stores – Sears and Liberty House. We always visited him twice. Now filled with plastic from China, I felt insulted by the Walmart that had replaced the festivities of my favorite store. I hate to think it could happen on Fort Street, but Walmart has also become a setting for mass shootings in some parts of the country.

Fort Street Mall's current footprint revealed none of the other names I remembered. McInerny's, another high-end emporium was also gone from the street. I felt very sophisticated one summer when, home from college in Oregon, I worked in their Ala Moana Center store selling clothing and high-end accessories. I had an employee discount and wanted to look like the well-to-do customers. And where was Andrade that also had sold luxury clothing, and the Indian-owned Watamull's, and Kramer's men's store and the ritzy women's store The Ritz? As Honolulu has morphed into a high-rise city, the older and lower buildings of that shopping area have become an island of a time gone by.

Sadly, downtown Honolulu is not alone. The current scene on Fort Street is a familiar one across the country. By the late 1940s, traffic congestion and a lack of parking foretold change for Fort Street, and as the new concept of enclosed shopping centers came along in the 1950s, older businesses flocked to them, and original city centers emptied out. All those enterprises were left with no customers – and no life that I wanted to be a part of. In Honolulu, it was the Kahala Mall in 1954, and then Ala Moana Center in 1959 that decimated downtown. And now we hear from around the country that even much newer shopping centers are retreating too. If the shopping centers hadn't decimated the stores back then, Amazon and the internet have done so now.

In 1968, Honolulu's city fathers decided to do something about its downtown exodus. They removed the cars, planted some trees, put in some benches and declared Fort Street to be a mall. But, in my mind, this is a misnomer; the fix has not taken. Fort Street Mall, that sad new landscape, has not disguised the absence of a lofty heyday gone by.

Another part of that heyday for me was the Honolulu Magazine Store, a favorite haunt when I was a teenager. That shop had offered news and magazines from around the world that fed a growing curiosity about my expanding universe which included my growing awareness of sex. And now it, too, is gone.

The Princess Theater, one of Honolulu's movie palaces when I was a kid, was on Fort Street. Just past its ornate plant-filled lobby, and greeted by reverberations from a gigantic pipe organ, there was a raked stadium-style auditorium that seated 1600 people. The Princess hasn't even left a footprint as a new building replaced it in 1969. I loved going downtown on the bus to see first-run movies in that huge ornate palace.

And after the movie, as the teenaged *flaneur* I had become, I'd wander Fort Street and the surrounding neighborhood, soaking in all that was new: the latest magazines and books, the submarine sandwiches, the ever-changing store windows, the well-dressed shoppers in hats, the latest Broadway show albums, a donut at the Young Hotel Bakery and a peek inside a smoke-filled grownup restaurant.

I could always count on finding those amusements on or near Fort Street in a Honolulu of a time gone by. I miss them.

Waikiki Beach Then and Now

Waikiki, Then and Now
(1946 – 1957)

Well, I think they may have finally done it – turned Waikiki into Miami Beach – with a little bit of Times Square and the Las Vegas strip thrown in for good measure. Could "they" be the tax–greedy Honolulu City Council which has consistently signed off on projects for hungry developers? Miami Beach had a hundred-year head start at pouring resort-intended concrete, but now Waikiki has caught up, and, as some have long feared, surpassed it. For a long time, there had been frequent warnings in editorials and letters to the Honolulu Star-Bulletin and Advertiser: "If we're not careful, we're going to turn Waikiki into Miami Beach." "Too much concrete, a loss of coconut trees and open space, the beach hidden by towers and not much Hawaiian about it anymore."

It isn't even easy to find Hawaiian music in Waikiki today. At one time, Waikiki exported its Hawaiian music from under the banyan tree at the Moana Hotel. *Hawaii Calls*, hosted by Webley Edwards, was a significant avenue of musical communication between Hawaii and the mainland from 1935 to 1975. They would even put the microphone at the water's edge so the lapping waves could be heard around the world. Today, the sunset cocktail hour at the Halekulani is the last place I know for old style Hawaiian music in Waikiki. The diverse musical tastes of millions of paying tourists dictates that traditional Hawaiian music is seldom heard at the beach any more. Many visitors are only interested in where *Magnum P.I.* or *NCIS: Hawaii* is filmed, where to get a Mai Tai and where to buy name-brand luxury goods. Kalakaua Avenue is now one of the top high-priced shopping areas in the world, so Waikiki has become a version of Rodeo Drive as well.

I hope I'm not being too hard on, arguably, Honolulu's main tourist attraction. Some may consider this memoir a mean-spirited screed, but it isn't intended to be so. It just disappoints me to see that, as in Times Square and on Hollywood Boulevard, you can now pay to have your picture taken on Kalakaua Avenue with costumed super heroes or cartoon characters like the Smurfs. And there are noisy street hawkers selling cheap jewelry and souvenirs, unsightly racks of tourist brochures on almost every corner and lumbering tour buses that spew exhaust everywhere. Honolulu has had a downtown *red light district* since World War Two, but some streetwalkers have now migrated from Hotel Street to Waikiki to seek business from conventioneers and tourists.

The S.W.A.T. (Special Weapons and Tactics) Gun Club offers *real guns and factory ammo* at a shooting gallery on Kuhio Avenue. Why would anyone go to Waikiki to shoot M-16 automatic rifles? When I recently saw pitchmen handing out flyers for that, I thought of it as a *final nail* in Waikiki's coffin. But then I realized that *final nails* and *strqws* have been accumulating steadily for some time. In 1962, for instance, the 25 story Foster Tower bisected the iconic view of Diamond Head. And in 1971 the 32 floors of the Sheraton Waikiki Hotel brought an out-of-proportion, bulky eye-sore to the skyline and obliterated the beach and seawall that was there. Could an earlier *nail* have been driven in 1959 when the first passenger jet plane set down in Honolulu?

A personal *tragedy* was the loss of the beautiful and iconic

Waikiki Theater in 2005. *The Waikiki* was one of America's most unusual movie theaters. Built in 1936, its stylish art deco façade was gently stepped back from the street with a tropical garden and a fountain lit by colored lights. This soft open space took up a good deal of real estate which became more and more valuable for other uses. The theater's owners replaced this softness which used to be part of the human scale of Waikiki.

The theater's very dramatic interior included a lighted rainbow arching over the stage and two artificial coconut trees flanking the movie screen. The audience was surrounded by a rain forest of plaster and papier-mâché plants and projected clouds that drifted overhead on the ceiling. A team of classy usherettes wore red sashes and feather leis and knew how to make the audience feel welcome. I loved going to the movies there, especially on Friday nights at 10:15 when the theater organ would play, and festive *first vue* showings premiered the following week's film. The charm of The Waikiki has also hosted a number of searchlighted world-premiers over the years. Now, all this unique glamor has been replaced by yet another generic and bulky shopping center that, like most Waikiki developments, is built to the edge of the sidewalk.

All of that accumulated concrete has replaced a Hawaiian sense of place in Waikiki by eliminating open space, lawns and thousands of coconut trees. Originally the International Market Place had a lovely large lawn as its focus. OK, in someone's favor, *they* **did** preserve the iconic banyan tree in the new center, but a "village-like" lightness has been replaced by a warren of concrete high-end shops and restaurants including a prominent Tesla showroom, of all things. An attempt at open space on Lewers Street has provided a small lawn, but, unfortunately, that has been accomplished with artificial turf. The old wooden fence that once protected the extensive gardens of the Royal Hawaiian Hotel has been replaced by two generations of bunker-like shopping centers. The reduced garden is still there, but one can only see it by negotiating a collection of expensive shops. I wonder if the Moana Hotel in 1901 or the Ala Wai Canal in 1922 to create more buildable land could have been other *final straws*, or at least warning signs of what was to come.

*****

But, at one time, I loved Waikiki. It wasn't yet the world-famous resort area it was to become. It was an accessible playground where one could have a meal and a drink, see a movie and enjoy some great people watching. For me, the mid-to-late '50s was a, dare I say, *golden age* in Waikiki. Part of my fascination was due to the fact that it was still a place for heightened glamour and, sometimes even movie stars. But, even as a kid or teenager, I could go there too. Tops and the Jolly Roger were great casual places after a movie or a party. The Gourmet and the Merry Monarch were fancier places, but the Canlis Charcoal Broiler was the fanciest and most beautiful of all – iconic '50s architecture, orchids everywhere and elegant Japanese servers in kimonos. All these places are gone now, replaced by hotel rooms, apartments or high-end shops.

Up to the 1970s, traffic was still manageable in Waikiki even if we had to compete with scores of pink tourist jeeps provided by Henry Kaiser. It was even easy to park in Waikiki back then. I could always count on free parking along the Ala Wai Canal, in the Zoo parking lot or at Fort

DeRussy. My brother could even park right on Kalakaua Avenue across from Kuhio Beach when he went there to surf. Today, a careful parking strategy is necessary if one opts to go there at all. Sadly, there's not much to go for anymore, not even a movie. At one time, there were five movie theaters in Waikiki, but now there are none. The land became too valuable, and now only provides those luxury stores that are mostly patronized by foreigners. The food in Waikiki is expensive, and hordes of lockstep tourists jam the sidewalks like in Las Vegas. Joni Mitchell was presciently correct when she wrote a song called *Big Yellow Taxi* in 1970. She wasn't writing about Waikiki, but she was right on when she pointed out that *they paved paradise and put up a parking lot*. Today, it's too late to save the fabric of the low-rise Waikiki I used to love. The multi-layered variety of the neighborhood is gone. Almost everything looks the same with stores all selling the same souvenirs from China and the Philippines.

*****

My mother was born in Waikiki in 1910 and she grew up at the end of Kalakaua Avenue near Diamond Head. When I was a child I would hear her complain that the neighborhood "just isn't what it used to be," and she would hesitate about going there. Apparently, she had *last straws* too that turned her away from the gentle nostalgia of the *Waikiki* that she knew in the teens through the 1930s. At the time, I couldn't understand that. I saw Waikiki as exciting, a place where all of Honolulu's most interesting action was. But at some juncture there was a tipping point for me too, and now a highest profit-per-square-foot mentality has erased the human scale that used to be. I guess I've turned into the curmudgeon that my mother had become. Just as she did, I dearly miss the Waikiki that I remember from my childhood and teen-age years.

*****

When I was a child in the 1940s, our family (two parents and three kids,) would occasionally get in the family pre-war Studebaker after dinner and, often in pajamas, we would go on sightseeing outings before bedtime. We loved going to Dairymen's Ice Cream Parlor at the corner of Beretania and Keeaumoku Streets for dessert. It was a drive-in, but we wouldn't sit in the car. We would always go inside for vanilla, chocolate or strawberry (the only flavors then) ice cream cones or milk shakes. Now Dairymen's is gone, replaced by a medical office building in 2010.

Another before-bedtime-jaunt was to Fisherman's Wharf at Kewalo Basin to see the unloading of whopping tuna from the sampans and fishing boats. The slippery fish were unloaded onto pallets which were then moved into the very fishy smelling cannery. It was a bustling scene which transformed the huge creatures into cans of tuna that ended up in our sandwiches. I don't know if he was inspired by our visits there, but years later, my brother Harrison worked at that cannery. His jobs were to stack cases of canned tuna in the warehouse and to rip the heads off the fish so the innards would come out to be used for cat food or fertilizer. But now the Hawaiian Tuna Packers cannery is no longer there either.

Sometimes we would go downtown to look at Honolulu's underlayer on Hotel and River Streets. Dad would have us roll up the windows and lock the car doors. I didn't know what the threat was, but there were plenty of sailors and colorful ladies wandering the streets looking for something. One bar on Hotel Street was called Club Hubba-Hubba, a rhythmic name that has stuck in my head as a touchstone for nighttime grown-up pleasures. This downtown scene was left over from World War Two, but, even now, it has a life because of all the military still stationed on Oahu.

But the excursions I loved best were our outings to Waikiki. To me, that is where the most interesting action was, and we didn't have to lock our doors. (Today, one might think twice about that.) I even loved the pulse of the word – *Wai-Ki-Ki* – which seemed to accompany the throb of the neighborhood's heightened activity. It meant *spouting water* which referred to the fresh water springs in the long-ago duck and taro ponds.

Starting at McCully Street, we would slowly ride along Kalakaua Avenue, Honolulu's *great white way*, toward Diamond Head looking at the tourists, military guys and lighted signs. We didn't have neon or signs that moved in Manoa Valley so this was an exotic novelty.

Waikiki was obviously a place for fun, and all the engaging neon made it seem like the center of a festive playground. There was elegant and expensive Lau Yee Chai with its iconic moon gate and Chinese garden. P.Y. Chong's was across the street. Stewart's Pharmacy with its popular fountain and dining counter was on the corner of Lewers Street. Other restaurants were the Green Lantern, the Blue Ocean Inn, the original Canlis Charcoal Broiler and the South Seas. I was especially impressed by a red neon sign – the restaurant may have been The Barbecue Inn – that had a moving pig and touted barbeque dinners. The quasi-Tudor Waikiki Tavern with its carousel bar had its own rakish orbit of action as did the Waikiki Bowling Alley next door.

Along with all the shops, restaurants and hotels, there were two movie theaters, the Waikiki and the Kuhio, with lots of neon to set off their marquees. The exotic architecture of the Hart Wood designed building that housed Gump's was a favorite of mine and, thankfully, has survived as a Louis Vuitton store. Hawaiian ladies sold leis on the sidewalk next to the fence that surrounded the Royal Hawaiian Hotel, and, amongst all the tourists and fun, there were cottages and small houses that made Waikiki a residential community. Just a few of those cottages remain as tourist shops today. Not every block sported an ABC Store then; there was a drug store, a service station, a clothes cleaner, a shoe repair shop and a Piggly Wiggly, places that supported a neighborhood where ordinary people lived.

Albeit a showy one, Waikiki was just another neighborhood of Honolulu. There was no sense of the single-minded place of entertainment it was to become. The International Market Place, built in 1957, didn't even exist yet. We didn't think in terms of a world-famous resort; we just enjoyed evening outings to look at the sights and tourists that my scientist father jokingly called *touri fungundi*. Sometimes, we would stop at Kau Kau Corner for a treat, and now I don't remember how a coin-operated condom machine in the men's room was explained to me. Kalakaua Avenue was not a one-way street in those days so we would often turn around at Kapahulu Avenue and drive home to Manoa Valley by reversing our tour.

*****

Pearl Harbor was bombed the day before my second birthday so I was a child during World War Two and the immediate post-war years, and I was a teenager in the 1950s. My early memories fall into those two decades, years when I had to be taken to Waikiki and those when I could go on my own. I see now that I was getting to know that neighborhood at the same time I was getting to know myself. It influenced how I saw the world and how I fit into it. In the '40s there was nothing taller than the five-story Moana Hotel, or maybe the top of the vertical Waikiki Theater sign. There was nothing alarming about it at the time, but, starting in the mid-1950s, gradual development gently began to raise the skyline over the tops of the coconut trees.

Those family after-dinner jaunts to Waikiki generated some of my earliest impressions of Honolulu outside Manoa Valley. I also have memories of where we took swimming lessons at the old YWCA beach club next to Fort DeRussy. A thirty-story apartment building named the Waikiki Shores has replaced it. There is even a 38-story Trump Tower a block away. But in the 1940s, a wonderful mature *hau* tree sheltered a picnic area next to the beach there. We would have our swim lesson and then eat our lunch of tuna sandwiches and deviled eggs. Mom would always let us climb in the maze of the *hau* tree before we went home to Manoa.

When we were a little older, we would practice what we had learned in those swim lessons. This happened sometimes at Gray's Beach next to the Halekulani Hotel and on the offshore rafts at Fort DeRussy. The place we liked best, however, was the Waikiki Natatorium on the beach across from Kapiolani Park. Opened in October, 1927, it was a one hundred by forty-meter (twice the length of an Olympic size pool) plunge that some people called *the tank*. The water was from the ocean and came and went through open sluice gates. Duke Kahanamoku competed in an opening day (October 24th, his birthday) swim meet there, and Tarzan Johnny Weissmuller swam there too.

I didn't know what *natatorium* meant then, or that it was a memorial to the fallen of World War One, but we loved going there to ride down the huge slide that careened us into the salty pool. The top of the slide may have been about 250 feet above the water, but it seemed even taller to us then. We would line up to climb the stairs that took us to the top where we could turn a faucet that sent water down to make the slide more slippery. There were also five levels of platforms from which you could jump or dive. This was much scarier than the slide because we didn't have as much control. We would dare each other to jump from the very top. I remember sticking to the slide, but once we were in the dark water, there were also fears about sea life, including eels, which could lurk there. Sadly, the Natatorium was closed in 1979 after thirty years of neglect, and it has been boarded up since then.

Other trips to Waikiki before I was ten years old were for picnics in Kapiolani Park, outings to the Honolulu Zoo and trips to the old aquarium. Sometimes we would go to the Kodak Hula Show which was presented for tourists in a park near the Natatorium. Occasionally, we had birthday parties at one of Waikiki's movie theaters before going home for cake, ice cream and pin-the-tail-on-the-donkey. The luxury of the Royal Hawaiian Hotel was a particular interest after a neighbor told me about the splendor of the women's restroom. Of course, I have never seen it, but I decided then that the Royal must be the peak of elegance and I would someday stay there. That has not happened yet, but it did give me a lifetime interest in iconic hotels.

*****

Until the mid-1950s when tall concrete began to block our view, we could look toward the ocean from our street in upper Manoa Valley, and we could faintly make out a little pink cupola that peeked above the fringe of coconut trees at the beach. That was the decoration on top of the Royal Hawaiian Hotel, and it was the only evidence of a structure we could see from upper Manoa. In 1955, however, a twelve-story apartment building called the Rosalei Apartments was constructed on Kai'olu Street near the Ala Wai Canal. It was Waikiki's first high-rise building, and it made a startling statement. The construction of the Rosalei began a cacophony of pile drivers, squealing saws and drumming hammers that, for decades, has accompanied life in Waikiki. Eventually, construction cranes became known as a new *state bird*.

The Rosalei is still there, but it has been dwarfed by much taller buildings in a concrete jungle. But, at the time, I thought it exciting to have such a *tall* building in our city. It was probably another warning sign of things to come, but it was still a long way from being a tipping point for me. In the meantime, I was always fascinated by the height and design of the new buildings, especially in my college years on the mainland when I would come home in the summer to see what had popped up in the previous year.

*****

Hawaii's economy met a significant milestone in 1950 when tourism exceeded defense spending for the first time.

The growing visitor scene in Waikiki presented some teenagers (shared stories tell us we weren't alone) with opportunities for mischief and, sometimes, mayhem. It was only a phase, and our parents would have been horrified, but we (my brother and some of our friends) realized oats could be sown in Waikiki. We knew it was a neighborhood for fun, and we were determined to have some of our own. Eventual driver's licenses provided access for teenage pranks, and we all went along with it as no one wanted to be called *chicken* or a *ding-a-ling*.

Ridiculing the tourists and military (very politically incorrect now) was part of the *fun*. With peeling sunburns, pink and white skin and Hilo Hattie outfits, they were easy targets of disrespect. We called the sailors *swabbies* (I guess because they *swabbed* decks) and *shark bait* (because of their white skin), and at times we tried to get them to buy beer for us. Appalling as it seems to me today, we would sometimes *moon* and throw water balloons at the passing parade from the back seat of our car. One might excuse this behavior as *boys-will-be-boys*, but at least we weren't *TP-ing* innocent people's houses. I don't remember whose idea any of that was (we had no ringleader), and we certainly weren't a gang in the sense of tattoos or greased hair. We were just a group of friends, mostly my younger brother's group from junior and senior high school which I latched onto at times.

In the long run, we succeeded in getting kicked out of the Reef, the Edgewater, the Princess Kaiulani and the Hawaiian Village Hotels. We accomplished that by *playing tourist*, pretending to be hotel guests and sneaking in to use their lounge chairs and fresh water pools. These exploits were similar to our dressing up and blending into departure crowds on ships at the harbor. With much less security in those days, we could crash farewell parties on board.

With an eye out for security guards, we would try to look like hotel guests by carrying a camera and wearing sun glasses and *aloha wear* as most of the tourists did. Of course, we didn't have a room key, but we would synchronize our stories as to what room we were in and vaguely say our parents were nearby. This usually gave us some time to stretch out in the sun and use the pool. It was a more innocent time in Waikiki, and sometimes we would get away with it. But often we wouldn't. I think it was primarily the challenge that entertained us.

The Hawaiian Village Hotel, built by Henry Kaiser in 1957 with pieces of wartime surplus, was a favorite as there were a number of small pools that dotted gardens around tourist cottages. Originally, the hotel had an actual *village* atmosphere as there were no high rises there yet, and the war-surplus cottages had been decorated with coconut fronds on their roofs. When we eyed a suspicious guard, we could move on to another pool and then to the next. When all else failed, we would move on to the Kaiser Lagoon where we could swim freely. Another favorite was The Reef Hotel that had a fascinating bar underground next to the swimming pool. Called Davy Jones Locker, the bar looked through a large window into the deep end of the pool. We would go underwater and wave at the patrons who were sipping cocktails in the bar. There were even incidents of pulling down shorts for them. At one point, I think a lounge chair with one of us sitting in it may have gone into the pool as well.

In the late '50s, when we thought we looked old enough (mustaches were tried), we fabricated false IDs so we could get into the Shell Bar at the Hawaiian Village to hear the exotic sounds of Arthur Lyman and Alfred Apaka, and at Duke's in the International Market Place to hear Don Ho. We tried to look like grown-ups, but we always hunkered down a bit to be less conspicuous. Not in Waikiki, Honolulu's only burlesque theater, the downtown Beretania Follies, was another challenge for our fake IDs. We liked sitting near the front for an obvious reason but also so we could harass the strippers with catcalls. Some of them may have been Tempest Storm, Blaze Starr or Sally Rand.

One of our compatriots in crime was our next door neighbor whose father was the Exalted Ruler of the Elks Club. The old four-story Castle mansion near Diamond Head was their club house then. We would go there in the evening, and, while the Elks were sharing secret handshakes and having their *exalted* meetings, we would play hide-and-seek and tag in the nooks and crannies of that Victorian labyrinth. There was a billiard parlor in the basement and we would slide down the banister of the huge central staircase. We could play there until 1959 when after many years (it was built in 1890) of termites and salt air, a demolition led to a new club house on the site. The Castles were neighbors of my mother when she was a child, and she would play some of those same games there with her playmates, the Castle children.

*****

"We're going to the beach! We're going to the beach!" I joyfully chanted as I jumped up and down on my parents' bed. That's only a flicker of a memory from my early childhood, but it still reminds me of the excitement I always felt at the prospect of going to Waikiki. Sometimes it was a trip to Grandma's house on the seawall near Diamond Head, sometimes it was for one of our swimming lessons, and sometimes it was for a picnic to play in the water and sand. Inflated inner tubes, water wings, pails and small shovels were inevitable props at those early picnics. Mom was always our lifeguard, and she dispensed careful admonitions to not go in the water if we had eaten anything. I learned early that *cramps* were to be avoided at all cost.

Later, when we were teenagers the purpose of the beach was to socialize, people-watch and get a tan. At times, if we weren't careful, these efforts produced sunburns and a week of peeling skin. No one talked of skin cancer or the need to cover up with sun-block then. As a matter of fact, the most popular lotion was simply coconut oil that had been infused with a bit of iodine. We believed that that mixture, which had no sun-blocking attributes, provided the richest tans. We would lie on Japanese grass mats that could be bought in any drug store. The water was mostly for cooling off before applying another layer of oil and tan. We thought sun glasses provided a touch of glamor and mystery.

I always thought the most interesting part of the beach was in front of the Royal Hawaiian Hotel, the Uluniu Swim Club and the old Outrigger Canoe Club. The beach was relatively wide there, and a sense of glamor was added due to Waikiki's most elegant hotel. The wartime barbed wire that had protected the beach from invasion had been removed by then. The catamarans and outrigger canoes pulled up there and so did the professional Hawaiian beach boys who would finesse the tourists with ukulele music, surfing lessons and even romance.

Once in a while the gang would go to the beach in the evening. We would bring snacks and beer (perhaps acquired from our *friends the swabbies*), and, barefoot, we would join others with the same idea and park ourselves on the sand next to a low pink wall outside the Royal's Monarch Room. We weren't willing to pay the cover charge or two-drink minimum, but we were close enough to hear the music. I remember hearing the Cazimero Brothers and the Kingston Trio there. It was like being at a party, and sometimes we went skinny dipping before going home.

The Halekulani Hotel was another source of free music, usually Hawaiian, that we could hear from the seawall. We paid for concerts at the Waikiki Shell in Kapiolani Park, but we always sat in the cheap section on the grass with a drink cooler, beach chairs, blankets and the smell of *weed*. The futuristic geodesic dome at the Hawaiian Village was another venue for concerts, but now the then-iconic Kaiser Dome has been replaced by a 25-story tower.

As time went on, Waikiki came to mean more than raising hell to us. Our life of *teen-age crime* took a back seat as we grew older and learned that trouble making wasn't the only way to have fun in Waikiki. I even worked there during three different summers when I was home from college. My first job was as a bus boy at the Makahiki Room, the main dining room at the Hawaiian Village. Another bus boy job was at the new Outrigger Canoe Club near Diamond Head.

But the job I liked the best was at the Reef Hotel in the summer of 1959. Our home in Manoa had been designed by Roy Kelley's architecture firm, and this family connection put me at the front desk of his hotel for the summer. We handled registrations and check-outs, keys, mail and messages. The Kelleys owned the hotel and lived upstairs in a penthouse. Every morning Roy and Estelle would come down to inspect the lobby and front desk and wish us a nice day. I worked with their daughter Pat who was my immediate boss. Pat was a lot of fun and she organized the rest of us for adventures including going out on the tug boat with leis over our arms to greet hotel guests arriving on the Lurline or Matsonia. Pat's brother-in-law Chuck Rolles opened Chuck's Steak House nearby at another Kelley hotel, the Edgewater, where he essentially invented the long-time ubiquitous concept of the self-service salad bar.

Some of the Reef's guests were young college-aged women who were part of what we called *the co-ed scene*. A summer program in the '50s and '60s brought college girls to many hotels in Waikiki under the pretext of taking classes at the University of Hawaii. Some of these courses were inconsequential efforts like Hula dancing or Basket Weaving. But, the bottom line was to have a relaxing and, sometimes, romantic summer in Hawaii. Dances were held – often at the Ala Wai Clubhouse – at which the girls could meet local guys. Those dance events were very popular as the co-eds were on the make just as the guys were.

*****

In all our years of having fun in Waikiki – the hell-raising and the more-gentle variety – we didn't really notice the creeping accumulation of concrete that was gradually changing the neighborhood. There must have been a first tipping point, however; perhaps it was the dramatic implosion of the mere 20-year-old Waikiki Biltmore in 1974 that made us take notice. That event made way for the Hyatt Regency Hotel adding 1,230 rooms and replacing 10 stories with two 40-story skyscrapers right across the street from the beach.

In the 1980s and '90s developers "discovered" an approximate 36 square-block-area at the Diamond Head end of central Waikiki that had been nicknamed *the jungle*. A lack of serious maintenance because it was ripe for development had allowed hundreds of cottages and small homes to deteriorate and their gardens to become densely overgrown. Low rents had made the jungle popular especially with a bohemian party-crowd. Sex, drugs and flower children predominated until it was all razed and replaced with numerous thirty-or-more story apartment buildings and hotels.

Even the cottages at the low-rise family-run Halekulani Hotel – today the most tasteful redevelopment in Waikiki – was replaced in 1984 with two 25-story towers. One by one, the low buildings along the beach were replaced – a rampant *Miami-Beachification* – first by the 25-story Royal Hawaiian Hotel Tower, then the 30-story Outrigger Hotel (replacing the original Outrigger Canoe Club). The village quality of the Hawaiian Village Hotel where, at one time, we had tried to outfox hotel security guards, has been replaced by six high-rise towers. And the Japanese owners of the old eight-story Surfrider Hotel on the beach want to replace it with 25 stories next to the Moana Hotel. A massive skyline is one thing in a place like New York City, but cutting off an iconic beach is another matter.

*****

Waikiki tipping points have come and gone, and more may be on the horizon for other people who don't share memories with me of Waikiki in the 1940s and '50s or with my mother in the 1920s and '30s. The physical location is the same as we remember – a relatively dry climate, a sandy beach, warm water, gentle surf and *mauka* trade winds. Diamond Head is still there, somewhat obscured from certain view-points now, and, thanks to King Kalakaua, Kapiolani Park still provides the lungs of Waikiki as 160 acres of open space. Tourists still come for all of those reasons, but they now experience them through the prism of a concrete city, not the gentle community that I remember. Those tourists are part of the ten million visitors who bring nearly two billion dollars a year to Hawaii. These figures could not exist unless a lot of concrete had been poured since the 1950s. Waikiki's 284 hotels now provide 57,148 rooms that accommodate those crowds. It seems as if the charm that made Waikiki attractive in the first place had to be destroyed for the sake of making it very profitable.

The innocence of our long-ago family jaunts to Waikiki to see the neon lights could not happen in the same way now. And, of course, my childhood view from Manoa of the Royal Hawaiian's pink topknot has long disappeared behind a wall of hotel rooms. Even Waikiki's 12-story first "skyscraper" from the '50s, the Rosalei Apartments, has disappeared behind that wall. I wonder if teenagers still sew their oats in Waikiki as we did. And where do families go to the beach there? And where do they park? The only thing I would go there for today is to hear Hawaiian music at the Halekulani Hotel at sunset. Oh – and to stay at the Royal Hawaiian Hotel for a night or two if I could afford it.

Currently (2023), there is discussion in Hawaii that Waikiki has finally reached a saturation point and cannot handle more visitors. Some new development is happening at Ko Olina on the Waianae Coast of Oahu, and, of course, the neighbor islands continue to build for tourists. The economy relies on it. But *my Waikiki* is a place of the past, and, unfortunately, it has become the Miami Beach of the Pacific. As long as they last, my memories will have to serve me.

The S.S. Lurline

The S.S. Lurline
A Love Affair
(1948 – 1957)

S.S. Lurline (lure – lean)

The thing I love most about passenger liners is the way they look from the outside, at least the way they used to look – sleek, symmetrical, not top-heavy, with a scale and proportion always pleasing to the eye. With cleaving prows and stepped back decks, those earlier ships were a vision of the future from a previous age. But before April 22, 1948, when I was eight years old and had never been away from my home in Hawaii, I wasn't aware of ships like that or the unexpected world they were a part of.

That April day was an especially busy one at Honolulu Harbor as thousands of people stood in line from 9A.M. to 10 P.M. to tour the Matson Line's refurbished S.S. Lurline which had returned to Honolulu after serving as a troop ship during World War Two. As I was to find out, the Lurline was one of those cleaving, symmetrical ships.

My fascination, essentially a love affair with beautiful passenger liners (unlike today's monstrous ungainly cruise ships) and the travel and adventure they offered began that day when I went with my parents to see the Lurline's postwar transformation. Actually, they would notice those changes as they had known the ship before the War. But for me, this would be an original and consciousness altering experience.

The arrival of the new Lurline was one more indication that life was returning to normal after the War, and the crowd hummed with anticipation. The historical significance of this event wasn't clear to me then, but I was aware that something important was happening. Finally, the crush on the gangway gave way and we stepped onto the renovated ship. The first thing I noticed was the smell of air-conditioned newness – fresh paint and new furnishings combined with a scent of flowers that were on display everywhere. Air-conditioning had not been part of my life before this, and an all-air-conditioned ship was a post-war revelation to everyone.

And then marvels unfolded. I think it was the Lurline's *dollhouse* quality that fascinated me the most. How else could an eight-year-old kid have seen it? There, under one roof, were a restaurant, shops, a library, a night club, a children's play room, a gymnasium, writing, smoking and card rooms and living rooms that transformed into bedrooms. There was even a swimming pool. There was something neat and comforting about this self-contained floating microcosm of an astonishing world I hadn't yet experienced, and, best of all, this enormous doll-house was going to go to places I longed to see.

Actually, few people in Hawaii had encountered what we were seeing, as the ship was decorated in a new mid-century style that came to be associated with the 1950s. Even as an eight-year-old, I think I felt the shock-of-the-new. Our house in Manoa Valley, built in 1941, was decorated with Victorian furniture and oriental carpets inherited from my grandmother's home – a look that did not prepare me for the mid-century style of the remodeled Lurline.

I learned later that the tour we took was part of a

celebration that had begun the day before when the Lurline was the star of what must have been Hawaii's most elaborate *steamer day* ever. Governor Stainback had declared April 21, 1948 *Lurline Day*. Early that morning Navy bombers and Army B47 Thunderbirds had swooped over the ship as she rounded Diamond Head, and biplanes flew overhead with banners that proclaimed "Aloha, Lurline." Over eighty surface craft – tugs and yachts from the harbor and outrigger canoes from Waikiki – greeted her with whistles and horns and escorted her to Honolulu Harbor. An enormous orange crepe-paper lei, the largest ever made, was dropped around her bow as she arrived at Pier 11 which had been elaborately decorated with flowers and palm branches by the ladies of The Outdoor Circle organization. Hawaiian priests had conveyed blessings of the Hawaiian gods to the accompaniment of hula dancers and The Royal Hawaiian Band.

A few days earlier, The Honolulu Star Bulletin had proclaimed the Lurline to be a ship *as fine as the finest on any sea! You'll see her on the morning of April 21 rounding Diamond Head . . . gleaming white against the blue water of Hawaii . . . a creation of luxury and beauty . . . proudly sailing home.* The paper declared this day to be a full-scale salute to tourism, Hawaii's third industry (behind the military and agriculture – predominantly sugar and pineapple), which, by 1950 would annually bring 50,000 visitors and $35,000,000 to the islands. These numbers seem naïve today, but passenger jets would not be part of the tourism picture for another ten years.

After that first encounter with the Lurline, my personal radar began to work overtime picking up blips that hadn't registered before. There were exotic advertisements for the Matson Lines in National Geographic and Life magazines, which always showed ecstatic beautiful people being luxuriously pampered. And in those days, the newspapers regularly published glamorous photos of arriving Hollywood stars and other celebrities, and I found dockside farewell scenes of my parents covered in leis in family photo albums.

I was particularly taken with the colorful Matson brochures with deck plans that laid out the geography of the ships and supported the intricate dollhouse quality that fascinated me so much. One day, I came across a large plan of the Lurline – each of the six decks was 27 inches long and four inches wide. Here was a project. I had never spent a lot of time with model airplanes, but I decided to build the Lurline using these layouts as templates. Backing the paper plans with cardboard, I constructed the ship using pieces of balsa wood to separate the levels for proper deck spacing. Railings were created with thread, ladders with toothpicks, and the swimming pool with tin foil. Today, it sits on the top of a bookcase, not quite finished and covered with dust, but it is still able to kindle some of the excitement I always felt at the sight of the ship or the sound of her name.

The name *Lurline* has always had the power to jump off a page at me the way words will do when they have a personal psychic attachment. When I hear it, there is a euphonious peal that invokes exotic romance. *Matsonia, Monterey, Malolo* (flying fish) – yes, there is a auditory tug in those names as well, but for me, *Lurline* had the most resonance. The most popular explanation for this name is that the ship was named after Captain William Matson's daughter. But Matson records show that Lurline Matson wasn't born (1890) until three years after the first Lurline was christened. Perhaps she had been named for the ship.

Furthermore, the word *Lurline* could be a variation of *Lorelei,* the mythological siren of the Rhine who lured sailors to their deaths. Captain Matson was an opera lover and the libretto of a popular mid-nineteenth-century grand opera called *Lurline* was found among his papers when he died. It is the story of a water nymph who used her sultry voice and long blond hair to lure her elusive lover to his death so they could be united in spirit. A mural depicting this theme dominated the main dining room of the ship I knew; it showed a sailor lashed to the mast of his ship with wax in his ears to protect himself against the guile of Lorelei, or Lurline.

Another story that connects Captain Matson to this name focuses on sugar king Claus Spreckles who frequently hosted the young Matson on his yacht *Lurline*. Perhaps the captain borrowed that name for a ship, and a daughter. Or maybe Spreckles had heard the same opera. Nevertheless, both men seem to have been taken by this nymph with a seductive voice and golden hair.

Hawaii has seen at least five Matson ships christened Lurline, including a modern freighter launched in 1973. In 1887 William Matson's original Lurline, a two-masted brigantine brought miscellaneous supplies to the Islands in exchange for sugar. Disabled by a storm in 1915, she was set adrift, and, for years, occasional mysterious sightings fascinated the public. Even before that disaster, in 1908, the three-week crossing from San Francisco to Honolulu on that first Lurline was improved upon when the first steam powered Lurline, carrying fifty-one passengers, made the trip in a week.

In 1927 Matson made the decision to build three $8,000,000 ships (Mariposa, Monterey and the third Lurline) that would also serve Los Angeles and take passengers to Australia, New Zealand and various south Pacific islands. This Lurline, in her post-war guise, was *my Lurline*. She was built in Quincy, Massachusetts and launched in July, 1932 with a maiden voyage in January of 1933. On December 7th, 1941, she was on her way to San Francisco when war broke out. The day after she arrived she was turned over to the government and her gleaming white exterior was covered in gray and camouflage; luxurious furnishings were stored and beds became bunks as she was turned into a seagoing barracks for 4000 service men including soldiers of the famed 442nd Regimental Combat Team. She survived the war with one close call, a narrow escape from a torpedo near Samoa. After a $20,000,000 conversion at Alameda Shipyard, she sailed for Honolulu – and into my life – on April 16, 1948.

*****

There were nine years between my 1948 tour of the ship and the fulfillment of a nagging daydream. I did eventually sail to San Francisco on the Lurline, but first I had to complete my childhood and maneuver through adolescence, a time when the spell of the Lurline never left me. I now wonder just how normal it was for an eight-year-old to be mesmerized by a ship. Shouldn't I have been playing marbles or collecting bottle caps and baseball cards? But some of my most indelible memories from those years include the romance of the ships – dockside arrivals, lei sellers touting their wares, local boys diving for coins – and the most exciting part of boat days, the sailings. Sometimes I went with my parents to see people off to the mainland, but there were also teen adventures when friends and I would roam the boat to see how many farewell parties we could crash. We always called the Lurline the *boat*, perhaps because of the expressions *boat day* or *steamer day*, the local name for a day of arrival and departure.

It seems unbelievable today, but in the mid-fifties, before the need for heavy security, we could go aboard without question and wander around as if we were meant to be there. Counting on the crush of excitement to preserve our anonymity, we would try to slip into crowded staterooms to join the whirl of lei-covered passengers and guests. The sounds of clinking glasses and Hawaiian music and the pungent smell of plumeria and pikake always accompanied these scenes. To this day, I associate those sensations with the revelry of boat day. But then the warning gong would inevitably sound and *all ashore who's going ashore* would ring out. That announcement is no longer heard on ships as tight security keeps visitors away. But in those days we'd obey the order and make our way down to join the continuing celebration on the pier.

The Royal Hawaiian Band would tune up for its send-off and hula dancers would start their show. Streamers began to be unfurled, and a near solid web of multi-colored serpentine was woven between the ship and the dock. Passengers and well-wishers would search for each other on decks and dock, goodbyes were shouted and leis were thrown. At four o'clock the deep trumpet of the Lurline's horn was the cue for the band to launch into *Aloha, Oe*, and the party neared its climax. Almost imperceptibly at first, tension on the streamers would increase and we could see that the ship was moving. Then there was no doubt when ribbons of colored paper would snap and shimmer into the ever-widening sliver of water between the ship and the dock. The shouting and waving would reach a crescendo as *Aloha, Oe* was completed along with the continuing blasts of the ship's horn.

And then, suddenly, as the ship would pass out of shouting distance, a pall of anticlimax would descend; the music would finish, and the musicians and dancers would begin to pack up their instruments. Kicking their way through discarded flowers and piles of colored paper streamers, people would move away from the dock's rail

Saturdays were always boat day for one of the Matson ships, so sometimes, when I was close enough to Honolulu Harbor, I would listen for the trumpeting of the ship's horn at four o'clock – and know that streamers were tearing and one of the white ships was backing away from the pier. At other times I would manage to be at Waikiki so I could watch as the ship disappeared around Diamond Head and pointed herself north-east toward California.

*****

My fantasy of traveling on the Lurline was nearly fulfilled just a year after her homecoming tour. In 1948 Dad was awarded a year-long sabbatical leave to study citrus fruit in California. That was my first trip away from Hawaii, and in 1949, at the end of a summer road trip, our family and our car were booked to return to Honolulu from San Francisco on the Lurline. But that's when the imposing shadow of longshoreman boss Harry Bridges and the consequences of a protracted stevedore strike entered my consciousness. Of course, I knew what shipping strikes were because in Hawaii they could mean no Christmas trees or a shortage of toilet paper. A potted Norfolk Island pine was no substitute for the trees that came from the northwest, and the hoarding of toilet paper became a bothersome necessity.

I can remember my father gnashing his teeth every time

Harry Bridges' name was heard, for now we were stranded on the mainland with the car we had purchased to drive around the country that summer, and school was going to start in a week. Some quick maneuvering found us space on the S.S. President Wilson, which could essentially drop us off by tender in Honolulu without docking and facing the authority of Mr. Bridges. The Wilson could then proceed with the rest of her passengers to Asia.

But the President Wilson would not be sailing for a couple of weeks. The family budget was overdrawn after a long summer trip and we found ourselves experiencing scenes from *The Grapes of Wrath* in a rundown auto court in east Oakland. After our two weeks with part of Oakland's underclass, we boarded the ship and headed home. After five festive days to Honolulu, other more fortunate passengers were going on to exotic places called Yokohama and Hong Kong. But we were ignominiously put on a tug boat and tendered into Honolulu Harbor. Our Studebaker would be sent to us after the strike. I was a few weeks late starting fifth grade, but it had been a memorable five-day adventure. I couldn't help remembering, however, that it was not on the Lurline.

When I finally did fulfill that dream, it was as part of an annual fall migration of students to colleges and prep schools on the mainland. Ever since the California gold rush, students had been traveling by ship to and from Hawaii. In the mid-nineteenth-century it was closer and less hazardous for Californians to come to Hawaii for an education than to go overland or around the horn to east coast schools. By the late '50s, lots of the student traffic was on those *college sailings* that we called *the college boat*.

Once I had seized on the idea that I could sail on the

Lurline to the mainland for my freshman year of college, my parents heard a lot about it.

"It would be just as cheap as a coach seat on an airplane," I pointed out. "I'd be in an inside stateroom with roommates. That would be cheap. About $150." I had done some research.

"Who do you know that will be doing that?"

"I've heard of a lot of kids from my class who are signed up."

"We'll see" That response was inconclusive, but at least they were thinking about it. And I knew they knew about the tradition of college boat sailings.

Two days later, I heard their decision. "We think it would be a broadening experience for you, and Aunt Peggy and Uncle John could come from Salinas and meet you. We don't want you in San Francisco by yourself. And then you could stay with Uncle Dick in San Leandro. And they could put you on a train to Eugene."

As it turned out, I left the islands as a permanent resident for good that fall. But at the time, no such finality was in my thoughts and I spent the summer in a whirl of teen-age socializing and a hellish job at the Dole Pineapple Cannery which couldn't dull my sharp anticipation of that September sailing.

That happened in 1957, a relatively innocent time that seems more distant now than the sixty years ago that it really was. Going away to college on the Lurline meant much more to me than the fulfillment of a childhood dream. I was only seventeen and I was leaving home to go across an ocean. The anticipation of my first adult adventure mixed with fear and excitement about leaving my family produced a heavy overload. Those feelings were accomplished by a summer-long round of farewell parties and trips to the airport as, one by one, members of my social group went off to the mainland to school. By the time of my sailing in early September, those farewells had become frequent enough that our crowd had dwindled to a precious few.

By the 1950s, the Lurline had become a classless ship so most of her was mine to explore. She carried about 750 passengers – tiny by today's standards, but she seemed enormous to me – and I was just as dazzled by her self-contained universe and mid-century look as I had been nine years earlier. Only this time I was the one peering over a stack of leis around my neck and the shipboard party of friends and family was mine, not one I was sneaking into with my friends. As part of a dramatic perspective adjustment, I was looking down at the pier as the ship pulled away, not the other way around. Then, framed by sightings of flying fish at the beginning of the trip and sea gulls as we neared the coast, the next five days passed quicker than I would have liked.

In compliance with local tradition, I threw most of my leis into the water as we passed Diamond Head to ensure I would return to Hawaii. I pictured them washing up against the sea wall at my grandmother's house where I had spent lots of time as a child. But they may not have all washed ashore after all, as I never returned to the islands to live permanently. In explaining this custom, I started some new friendships with a group of kids my age who were returning to the mainland after spending the summer in the islands.

I don't remember anything of my older roommates in our claustrophobic inside cabin; I do remember sleeping in an upper bunk and naively confusing the intense air-conditioning with colder air as we approached the mainland. As it turned out, that cabin and upper bunk served only for rest stops between escapades exploring the geography of the ship and getting lost in the labyrinth of the *dollhouse*. Tucked into an upper deck, I discovered two very special lanai suites which had their own outside decks. Most of the monster cruise ships today devote many decks to these lanai cabins, but in those days, they were unique and represented a touch of rare luxury.

There was no casino, disco, giant theater for Broadway shows, bowling alley, bumper cars or rock-climbing walls on the Lurline. And we had to do without the spas, pizza parlors and computer centers that are all amenities on cruise ships today. It must have been because we were at sea that we kids were able to drink the champagne. Today, cruise lines use any opportunity to sell alcohol, but that was pretty tame on the Lurline. We happily filled our days with what now seem like shipboard activities of another era: horse races, bingo, skeet shooting and shuffleboard. We learned to dance a corny tourist version of *Lovely Hula Hands*, were served tea and bouillon in deck chairs – and ate.

For years, I saved the stylish dining room menus along with the passenger list and daily ship newspapers. Now these are sought-after collectors' items, but one day they were missing from my college trunk where I thought I had put them. I wish I had realized their value as I've replaced a couple of the menus at a high cost. There were choices on those menus that were vaguely French and what I thought to be *haute cuisine*: frog legs, oysters, snails, caviar, hearts of palm salad, vichyssoise, Baked Alaska and Cherries Jubilee. That sort of fancy fare is old fashioned today but was fairly standard in better restaurants in the fifties. But not at my house, so I felt a rush of new- found worldliness when I sampled all of it. I can't say the same of the champagne that laid me low at the captain's party. In an *au courant* butch-waxed flat top and white sport coat and buck shoes, and trying to juggle a cigarette and a champagne glass as I had seen them do it the movies, I felt passably sophisticated but must have looked pretty silly. My pictures show a skinny kid who was trying to play grownup – and to this day I have never liked champagne.

The Lurline's tiny pool was the center of our daytime social life as we tried to polish off our tans before getting to San Francisco. When the air got colder as we neared the coast, we changed to sweatshirts, and then, before we were ready for it, the San Franciscans started picking up their favorite Top 40 station on a portable radio.

"We must be pretty close now. I just picked up KGO playing *Jailhouse Rock* and *My Special Angel*." We all gathered around the radio.

The ship's mood was festive but wistful on the last night. Our bags were packed and the band's Hawaiian music had been replaced with *San Francisco, Open Your Golden Gate* and *California, Here I Come*.

We seemed to be moving in slow motion as we sailed under the Golden Gate Bridge at dawn. Of course, the ship had slowed down and the bay was calm, but perhaps also because I wasn't ready for the trip to end. Wisps of fog lay over Alcatraz and the empty streets that climbed the city's hills; lights were still on in most of the buildings, but they gradually flickered out as we neared Pier 35. The morning light revealed San Francisco to be a delicate white city. My Brownie snapshots show a gentler silhouette of San Francisco than what one sees today. But this was definitely the big city to me as I had grown up in a place where the skyline had not yet started to change. Except for Aloha Tower which had been the last thing I saw as we left Honolulu Harbor. Its ten stories, long the tallest building in the islands, had seemed to scrape the sky.

And then abruptly we were at the dock and the slow motion came to a grinding halt. I was jolted into a speeded-up reality, for there, suddenly were my Aunt Peggy and Uncle John who collected my luggage and took me to the Top of the Mark on Nob Hill. I could look down and see the Lurline docked at the pier and I felt grateful for the crossing I had experienced – but I was also feeling sad. At 4 o'clock she would be sailing back to Honolulu without me. Two years later I repeated this trip on her sister ship the Matsonia, but it was not the same; it was not the first time and it was not the Lurline.

*****

The following summer I worked as a desk clerk at The Reef Hotel in Waikiki. The most exciting part of that job was being part of the hotel greeting party for Matson passengers. We would go out on the harbor tug early in the morning and board the arriving Lurline or Matsonia as she came around Diamond Head. Supplied with vanda orchid leis, our job was to welcome and pre-register guests of the Roy Kelly Hotels. Then, and this was the best part, we would arrive at Aloha Tower amidst the fanfare of boat day. The docking was always at nine A.M. and, just seven hours later, the ship would sail at 4 o'clock and head back to California. This was the fastest turn-around time for any passenger ship in the country then.

I have lived in the San Francisco area for many years, and

until the Lurline was taken out of service in 1970, I could never pass the Matson ticket office at Union Square without looking at the newest promotional brochures. And on boat day, as in Honolulu, the ship's horn could be heard at 4 o'clock; sometimes I was in the right place to see one of the white ships sail out under the Golden Gate Bridge.

*****

Breakfast in San Francisco and dine in Honolulu, proclaimed the airline ads in the late 1940s and early '50s. That meant a grueling twelve-hour flight in those days, but it was a clear challenge to the five-day crossing that Matson offered. Time was becoming valuable and Pan American and United Airlines had now cornered that market. But, for a brief time, Matson tried to compete. In the late '40s the line purchased two Douglas DC-4s and named them Sky Matsonia and Sky Lurline. These planes took passengers one way so they could sail back the other. It was the custom of the planes to make a low pass in mid-ocean in order to salute the ships. But Pan Am persuaded the government to use anti-trust legislation to get Matson out of the airline business. And so, the company began its gradual retrenchment from the enterprise of luxury tourism to that of carrying freight.

In 1927 Matson had decisively moved into Hawaii tourism when it opened the iconic Royal Hawaiian Hotel. Other Matson hotels followed – the Surfrider in 1952 and the Princess Kaiulani in 1953. But the expense of pleasing passengers on the ships and also visitors in the hotels eventually became too great. Ships have always been Hawaii's lifeline, but the Lurline and her sisters were extravagances that Matson could no longer afford. First, the Matson airliners disappeared as did the boat trains from New York and Chicago which connected passengers to ship departures in San Francisco. Then the Waikiki hotels were sold to Sheraton in 1959. That same year, on July 29th, Quantas announced jet service from Sydney to London via Honolulu. It would now take less than five hours to get to San Francisco. *Breakfast in Honolulu and lunch in San Francisco*, the ads might have said then. *Hawaii welcomes the jet age* heralded the newspapers, but Matson would not participate in that greeting. In 1969, Matson was still the largest U.S. shipping line, but after ten years of jet-age competition, the Lurline had reached the end of her usefulness. 593 peacetime crossings and 600,000 passengers were indicative of a glorious career, but in 1970 Matson sold the Lurline to the Greek line Chandris Ltd. for three and a half million dollars.

*****

And then one day, years later, I was jolted from the calm of my morning ritual of coffee and The San Francisco Chronicle. *Floating Hotel Hopes Go Down with the Ship*. It was Tuesday October 24, 2000; a minor news story and the word *Lurline* on page 21 leaped off the page at me and I felt a wave of disbelief and shock. The Lurline had gone down off Cape Town, South Africa on its way from Tampa, Florida to the scrap yards of India, and no explanation was given for the sinking. But, perhaps, as some have suggested, she was sunk to collect on insurance because a crash in steel prices while she was on the way to India made the insurance more valuable than the scrap metal. The *hopes* in this headline referred to a much-ballyhooed 1999 plan to rescue and restore the Lurline to its pre-war art-deco glory and open her as a hotel at Fisherman's Wharf in San Francisco. It was planned to be a historic time capsule of 1933 with *porters in uniform, masses or red roses in crystal bowls and silver place settings.* This would not be the mid-century modern Lurline that I remembered, but I felt it would be an appropriate last act to return her to her home port.

I was wrenched back to the reality of the newspaper. *The dream is over,* the developer announced. *It's gone. This is not the Titanic, and we are not going to raise her from the bottom of the sea.* It would have cost four million dollars to berth her in San Francisco. *What it came down to was that someone had to write a check for a lot of money. No one did.*

I went through a period of mourning for the Lurline. *Sunk off the African coast, scrap yards?* The incongruity astonished me. I fought with images of her lying on the ocean floor off the Cape of Good Hope. Lines from a Thomas Hardy poem, *The Convergence of the Twain* ran through my head – *moon-eyed fishes query 'why all this vain gloriousness down here?* Hardy's poem is about the Titanic, but I imagined fifties Polynesian furnishings providing homes for sea creatures half way around the world from where they belonged. Perhaps she was in good company, I rationalized. Many other great vessels have met such fates. And maybe, after all, the indignity of a scrapyard was too great a burden for her to bear.

The Matson ships, but particularly the Lurline, have been and still are an important part of the iconography and mythology of pre-jet travel to the islands. That time has taken on a distinction, for we now look back from an era when a glut of cruise ships goes virtually everywhere on Earth. These behemoths don't look like real ships to me, but ungainly floating bunkers. Aesthetic scale and symmetry are absent; the proportions are all wrong; they are top-heavy tubs designed to pack in as many paying customers as possible. Everyone can take an aimless cruise to nowhere. Some people even live on these ships which often seem like retirement communities at sea. The ships no longer provide exotic privileged transportation, but popular diversion that sometimes can carry disease.

*****

It has been said that we are the product of our first twenty-five years, and some would narrow that to our first ten. The experiences and icons we chance upon in those years can shape us and give value to our lives. When I was eight years old the Lurline touched me with an emotional charge that wouldn't let go. In my childhood years, she was a symbol that was stamped on my developing psyche to the extent that some of my dreams took place on her, and I wished the impossible, that I could transform my surroundings into her image.

When I was a teenager the Lurline became a tangible metaphor for, and connection to, the larger and more sophisticated world I was exposed to in the movies and on television. The culture and urbanity of New York City, for example, were potent temptations for an isolated island boy and I associated the glossy sophistication of the Lurline with the life that I would, one day, surely live in New York City.

As a young man living in San Francisco, any sighting of the Lurline on the bay served as a touchstone that could instantly transport me to Hawaii and my childhood. Today, the Lurline is gone and it doesn't hold the prominent place in my consciousness that it once did. But I can't help appreciating my parents' wisdom in taking me to see the Lurline when I was eight years old, just an age when my view of the world was ready to expand and embody an experience that I would take with me throughout my life.

Afterward

There is a complicated history surrounding the final years of the Lurline. Try to bear with me. The story is confusing as the company changed the names of its ships for various reasons. If we count Matson's original brigantine and the more recent freighter and container ship, there were six Lurlines – I think. In 1963, the ship built in 1932, the one I toured in 1948 and later sailed on in 1957, suffered massive engine failure that was too costly to repair. She was then sold to the Greek owned Chandris Lines which refitted her as an emigrant ship and renamed her Elinis. She carried passengers from Piraeus to Sydney and Amsterdam. She was laid up in dry-dock at Piraeus from 1980 to 1987 and then sold to a Liberian company which had her scrapped when she was fifty-five years old. That was *my Lurline*.

The last passenger liner named Lurline (1963 – 1970) was actually the second rechristening of a ship that started as the S.S. Monterey in 1932. She was one of three ships (Monterey, Matsonia and the third Lurline) that Matson built in that year. The government took her for the war, but when business was booming in 1956, Matson repurchased her, named her the Matsonia and put her in service with her sister ship, the Lurline. When that Lurline was disabled and sold in 1963, Matson rechristened the Matsonia with the flagship name Lurline to satisfy public nostalgia. In 1970, this Lurline was also sold to Chandris Lines and renamed Britanis. Kept in service until 1996, she was retired and dry-docked in Florida. If I read this history correctly, it was this ship, not the actual ship I had sailed on, that sank on her way to be scrapped in India.

In 1973, Matson again used the legendary name Lurline for one of its ships. This time it was a freighter which still serves as part of Hawaii's lifeline to the mainland. And now Google tells me that in 2020 Matson christened an even newer Lurline, a container ship that is Matson's fastest and largest ship. But, after unraveling this history, I realized that none of it greatly mattered, as it was the mythical image of the Lurline that was important to me, not the actual body she inhabited. The Lurline of my memory will always be there – sleek and symmetrical, with cleaving prow and stepped back decks and still promising privilege and luxury.

Exploring the Lurline – September 1957

On Sailing Day – September 1957

The Airport Photograph

The Miracle of Snow

The Mainland, Another Place
(1948 – 1958)

The Airport Photograph

The three of us, my younger brother and sister and I, were wearing what we thought of as our Sunday School clothes, and certainly we would not have been barefoot on what was, clearly, an important day. Aileen was three years-old, Harrison was seven, and I was nine. Harrison and I were in matching aloha shirts and atypical long pants, and all of us had on plumeria leis along with some made of candy that were usually meant for children. For island kids, these usually aroused more interest than flowers that could be picked in any garden. The challenge was to not consume the leis before they could serve their symbolic purpose on travel day. We were familiar with the aloha ritual of leis, but this was the first time we had all been wearing them at the same time.

With wide-eyed expectation, we were posed in front of one of the bamboo-sheathed columns that characterized the *old* Honolulu Airport. There was an innocence in our faces that didn't anticipate the life changing adventure we were about to have. Something just outside the camera's view had caught my brother's and my attention. Perhaps we were being encouraged to smile by our ever-attentive mother. In a clean white pinafore, our towheaded sister Aileen didn't seem to notice the distraction and grinned happily for the camera.

I had found the photograph in one of my dad's meticulous

files marked *Mainland – 1948/49*. Dad was a scientist – a plant pathologist who specialized in pineapples – and it was his habit to collect data on almost everything. The airport picture was a small part of a much larger time capsule that would send me off to write this memoir. But I was initially drawn to this photo as it captured a festive and ceremonial beginning of a, clearly, significant event. It was early in September of 1948, and the three of us were about to leave the islands for the first time. Significantly, I was clutching a coat in my left hand, a clear sign that the destination was probably a place called "the mainland."

Another Place

I wonder if the Human Genome Project has identified an innate stamp for curiosity or wanderlust. If so, I am sure I was hard-wired with a restlessness that focused my imagination on more distant horizons than the ones I was born with. Or perhaps it was my Sagittarian stamp that imbued me with the spirit of a nomad. At any rate, if there hadn't been an identified place called *the mainland* for me to wonder about, I would have had to invent it.

But there was a *mainland*, and, not long after learning I lived on an island, this *other place* was in my consciousness. At various times, I heard it as *the coast,* or *California,* or *San Francisco,* but the context of the references led me to suspect these were generally the same place. By the time I knew I lived in the middle of the Pacific Ocean on one of the Earth's most isolated pieces of land, *the mainland* was a familiar designation if not a totally clear notion. *Islands* were an early geographical concept for me so I assumed the mainland was another, perhaps more important, island. If it was a *main* land, was it superior in any way, and were we inferior for living on our smaller island? Questions like these transformed the mainland, which I came to suspect was a much larger place than what I already knew, into an early touchstone for a wider world to investigate.

They're going to the coast . . . when I was in California . . . next time we're in San Francisco . . . But most often I heard it as *the mainland* so *the mainland* is what this place came to be for me too. It seemed that one went *up* to the mainland (*we goin' up da mainland* I would sometimes hear in pidgin English), so I thought of it as north of us and wondered if it had anything to do with Santa Claus. Grown-ups referred to it a lot and eventually taught me of its vital relationship to Hawaii. Maps revealed that it was not an island, it was not nearby, and, indeed, it was a much larger place than the small island I lived on. It was not long before I set my sights on going there. Was it in my genes or just the challenge of geographical distance? Certainly, the isolation of my home filled the outside world with compelling intrigue.

As I got older, a gradual understanding of geography allowed me to expand the frame through which I saw the world until it also encompassed the mainland. At first, I only knew the well-worn rattan furniture on our indoor lanai; then my consciousness broadened to include our front yard that was enclosed by a mock orange hedge and plumeria trees. But soon, the extent of my outlook took a quantum leap as if a powerful camera had zoomed out. Our house looked out on a panorama – the amphitheater of the back of Manoa Valley. There, massive, nearly vertical mountains towered over a rainforest, and waterfalls poured out of shadowed notches on the cliffs. What else was in those shadows, and what, I wondered, was on the other side of those mountains?

The pointing of a finger sometimes accompanied the direction of the mainland and corresponded to the source of the trade winds that often rushed down our valley. Frequent rain storms producing imagination-inducing rainbows also came from there, and I was convinced that there was something unexpected beyond what I could see. Usually, these mountains were shrouded in clouds, but on some days in the wintertime when the trades stopped blowing, their tops were completely clear, and my mind would ignite with a sense of heightened accessibility to what I was certain lay beyond.

To the left of our house, outside the mock orange hedge, lay Keahi Street and, at a distance, the ocean laced with the tops of coconut trees. But when I turned *mauka*, toward the mountains, there was a much closer and looming presence. We lived at the end of a dead-end street, and a protective *kapu* (forbidden) sign guarded a trail that meandered through tall grass into the forest. My tenuous sense of direction didn't allow me to know that the trail faced northeast, and 2500 miles away, over unbroken ocean, was that place called *the mainland*.

Quickly, my known world grew to include the rest of our broad valley; then there was Diamond Head where my grandmother had lived on the seawall, and Waikiki, a gathering place for visitors from the mainland. I got to know downtown Honolulu and, significantly, its harbor and airport – and then the whole island. Like Jeepers our neighbor's dog, I was always ready to leap into the car and go somewhere. At first, my need for adventure could be satisfied by a short excursion beyond Diamond Head to Hanauma Bay and the Blowhole, or a slightly more enterprising ride to the windward side of the island on the hairpin turns of the old Pali Road.

A lengthier outing was rarer and would essentially take us around the Koolau Mountains. Occasionally, accompanied by *I wanted the window seat; boys, stop poking each other*, and the inevitable *are we there yet?*, we would make our way around the island in our black pre-war Studebaker sedan that was outfitted with running boards and a stick shift on the floor. Such a family road trip took a whole day on narrow two-lane roads and stretched to the edges of what I knew – Rabbit Island, Chinaman's Hat, Sacred Falls, the Crouching Lion, and Kahuku where an abandoned sugar mill served in my imagination as an *ancient* ruin.

We would often stop for lunch with our friends the Sheltons at their beach house on Kawela Bay and then continue past the high surf on the north shore to Waimea Falls. A country general store in Haliewa where we could get *shave ice* was our farthest destination. Then we would turn inland, back toward Honolulu, through the pineapple and sugar cane fields. From there, we could see the sun setting behind another mountain range, the Waianaes.

One year, soon after World War Two, we rode the old Oahu Railway on its final run to Haleiwa and back. This was my first train ride, but it marked the end of railroads in Hawaii, and I wouldn't get on another train for many years, that time, on my way to college on the mainland.

For a time, these undertakings provided sufficient satisfaction for a curious kid who loved to move, but, always, no matter what the adventure, we would inevitably end up too quickly where we had started. As I grew older, this circumscribed itinerary began to feel restrictive. I was eager for something more. It wouldn't be long before *the mainland* was the answer to that call.

Island fever, a burning desire *to get off the rock*, didn't strike until I was a teenager and faced the prospect of going away to college. Earlier, it was just healthy hard wiring that drove my interest in the outside world. Some families did escape to the mainland for safekeeping during the war, but we were islanders on my mother's side so, for us, there was no thought of leaving. I had to be satisfied with the pictures that came to us in National Geographic and Life magazines – exotic images of wide open spaces, large cities, deserts – and snow.

When the war was over and I was in school, geography was my favorite subject. I loved filling in blank maps with colored pencils, providing the names of countries and capitals. Sometimes I could be seen curled up with a world atlas, and I started a stamp collection that taught me poetic sounding names like Hong Kong, Bali, Goa, Fiji, Togo, Singapore and Bora Bora. I could see the airplanes that flew over Honolulu and ships that sailed past Diamond Head. Family photos showed festive dockside sendoffs. In one picture Mom was smiling at the camera having just covered Dad with leis. He was leaving to finish his PhD. Residency in Madison, Wisconsin.

There were stories from neighbor kids who had visited family on the mainland, and I wondered when we would do the same. Although Mom had been born in the Islands, Dad's family all lived on the mainland so there were also photos of places like St. Louis, Missouri; Kennewick, Washington; Edmonton, Alberta; Portland, Oregon and San Leandro, California. These images held the promise that perhaps, someday, my parents would take me with them on another trip. And, indeed, it was not long before they did.

The Map on the Terminal Floor

In 1927, twenty years after it had been built, Honolulu's airport attained the status of Honolulu International. Between 1939 and 1943, the nearby Keehi Lagoon was dredged for runway material and provided a landing place for Pan American's pontooned Flying Clippers. The Clipper era was a colorful time that existed just before I was born. By 1948 and my first trip to the mainland, Hawaii was known as *The Crossroads of the Pacific,* and the Honolulu Airport was just shy of being the third busiest in the United States in terms of aircraft operations. To a wide-eyed nine-year-old, it seemed like a very busy place in terms of people too. My attention quickened whenever we went to the harbor or airport. Early on, I made a vow to go someplace on one of those ships or planes.

The airport was small then, almost quaint compared to today's huge complex, but to a child in the 1940s, it seemed enormous. The main terminal housed a large space decorated with tropical plants, *lauhala* wall matting and bamboo-covered structural columns. The focal point on the tile floor was a large map of the world that showed Hawaii prominently in the center of five continents. In this rendering, Hawaii, indeed, did seem like the *crossroads of the world,* and I felt that the airport fully deserved its *international* status.

With all those destinations, the possibilities for adventure seemed endless. That floor was always crowded with spirited well-dressed people covered with flowers. Today, the scent of plumeria or *pikake* can transport me back to that terminal which always seemed to be hosting an elegant grown-up party. Those festivities were infused with a hubbub of Hawaiian music, animated conversation, passengers being paged, flights announced, and, above all, a feeling of expectation and excitement.

Even as a child, I could see that the airport was a special place for privileged people. In the 1940s, before jets revolutionized the industry, air travel was still rare and special. An airplane trip was not the casual event it is today. Through their advertising, the airlines created a romantic aura around the adventure and glamour of flying that tempted people to get on board one of those planes. Certainly, I was not immune to those efforts.

In 1948, my dad was given a sabbatical leave from his position at The Pineapple Research Institute, and we went to live in Riverside, California for a year. He would study at the old Citrus Experiment Station that, in the future, would become a campus of the University of California. But another important reason for the trip was to enlarge the world for three kids who had never known anything but an island. In order to be enrolled at the start of the school year in September, Mom and Grandma took my brother and sister and me to Southern California; Dad would join us in January.

*****

Neighbors had given us candy leis in celebration of our trip, and we proudly wore them when playing or riding our bikes. They served as a boast to our friends that we were about to go away. Finally, we were driving out of Manoa Valley toward the airport, and I turned back to catch sight of the retreating mountains I had been eager to go beyond. My excitement kept me from realizing it would be over a year before I saw those mountains again.

At the Pan American counter, we provided our ages and

birthplaces and weighed our luggage and ourselves on a large scale. Pan Am Operations needed this information to calculate the correct weight and balance of the plane for safety. Before heading to the upstairs lounge to wait for our flight, Harrison, Aileen and I, in our plumeria and candy leis, were posed for that departure photograph I would find many years later.

Ringing chimes and an authoritative voice announced, *Pan American World Airways' flight number seven is now ready for boarding at gate number three.* We stepped across the tile map on the floor, and I traced the straight line our plane would take to Los Angeles. Moving out of the terminal, I felt a wind from the warming propellers that was blending the smells of airline fuel and the flowers in our leis. All the passengers were dressed for the occasion – in suits, high heels, hats and gloves – and many carried Pan Am flight bags and coats that would be needed for arrival in another climate.

Guitars and ukuleles brought a troupe of hula dancers to life, and they began their traditional aloha sendoff. With our tickets checked, we passed through a gate in a simple chain-link fence that separated us from the plane. There was no cavernous jet-way or complicated security to negotiate. Since Dad would not be joining us until January, he and family friends had crowded to the chain-linked barrier to wave to us as we walked to the plane. As if part of a ceremonial ritual, we climbed the stairs to the plane's door and turned back toward the crowd. Newspapers often showed important people waving in this pose. Those pictures had come to symbolize the glamour of air travel for me, and I didn't want to let go of the moment, so my mind recast it in slow motion. But then, too quickly, the camera sped up, as I stepped inside the plane. Magically, I had been transformed into a member of an exclusive club of privileged travelers.

Night Flight

By today's measure, our DC-4 was tiny, but it seemed immense to me. As were all commercial planes at that time, ours was a retrofitted troop and supply carrier from World War Two. One aisle down the center divided two seats on either side of a cabin that held about fifty passengers. There was a closeness in the cabin as air-conditioning had not yet come to airplanes, but after take-off, this would be relieved by recirculated air from the outside.

Stewardesses were busy getting passengers seated and storing coats and leis. In 1948, these young women were no longer required to have nursing credentials, load bags or clean the cabins. They did, however, have to be single, not wear glasses, and meet certain height and weight requirements. These were the early days of the *coffee, tea or me* mythology when all flight attendants were female, and young and pretty too.

While Mom was busy settling Aileen for the night, Harrison and I were busily investigating anything mechanical we could lay our hands on. There were built-in ashtrays, swiveling nozzles to let in outside air, switches for reading lights and, before we could be stopped, a button to call the stewardess. We rummaged through the seat pockets for scrapbook treasures: post cards, stationary, maps and airline brochures. I collected everything, including an airsickness bag that I had to have explained to me.

With three excited kids to shepherd to Riverside, Mom had her hands full so Grandma tried to keep Harrison and me from annoying each other or other passengers. At first, I was too preoccupied to notice Mom's nervousness, but that would become clear after take-off – and for the rest of the flight. This was long before movies would be shown in the air, but we were entertained with sets of pin-on Junior Pan-Am Wings, coloring books, playing cards and plenty of two-pack packages of Chiclets. These were neat benefits that came with flying, but the purpose of the gum and mysterious bags soon became clear. The plane was unpressurized and would have to fly no higher than 12,000 feet, well within a zone of regular air pockets.

The plane's door was locked shut, and we rumbled across the tarmac to the end of the runway next to the ocean. Then slowly, we swung around to face the mountains. The roaring propellers increased their pitch, and a rush of anxiety shook me as I momentarily lost faith in what I had been told about the laws of aerodynamics. Then we were successfully in the air, and I could look down on the pale green terminal building which wished us *Aloha* in oversized lettering on the control tower. Suddenly we were over Honolulu Harbor, and then we were passing the mountains of Manoa Valley and then leaving Diamond Head behind us.

This was a single class airline, and the long flight times in this pre-jet era allowed what today would be considered first class service. Trays did not come down from the seat in front, but, set out with linen and an orchid, were placed in slots in front of each of us. There were hot towels, shrimp cocktails, steaks and a complimentary package of cigarettes. In segmented compartments on the tray, dinner was served with utensils, dishes and salt and pepper shakers that reminded me of toys. After dinner, the setting sun was behind us; we were just above the clouds which gradually reflected pink, then red and then black as we flew east to California.

Mom's main focus was watching over Aileen, but, as the night wore on, I realized she had other things on her mind as well. It was her first trip since the war, and it might even have been, as it was mine, her first flight ever. Unfortunately, she is no longer here to ask that question of. The only family records of previous trips I had seen were *steamer day* photos of ship departures. Airplane travel was new to most people then and could make anyone nervous, especially my mother.

It was six years before the John Wayne film *The High and the Mighty* would teach us the concept of *the point of no return* on a twelve-hour flight over open water. Indeed, there was nothing between Honolulu and Los Angeles so this may have been the longest uninterrupted over-water flight on Earth. Despite prevailing tail winds, this range was a challenge to the DC-4s. With a cruising speed of 204 MPH and a distance of 2140 miles, we might have been flying on fumes at the end of our flight just as John Wayne would do in the film. I lay awake as Mom nervously responded to each change of sound in the engines, and, with every shudder of the plane, she gripped the arm of her seat. It was a long night.

After a breakfast served on more dollhouse dishes, we arrived in early morning fog at the Los Angeles Airport in Inglewood. I could see that mom was relieved to be on the ground, but a fear of the unknown and the reality of being so far from home engulfed me, and I was instantly homesick. I missed my father, and, so far, my dream of the mainland was more frightening than I had imagined it would be.

The sun burned away the fog and some of my misgivings as we drove east to Riverside. There was family history attached to this town as my maternal grandfather had come there seeking therapy for tuberculosis in 1890. He had sailed around the Horn from Northern Ireland when he was nineteen and lived in Riverside for ten years before moving to Hawaii for an even warmer climate. One evening he met my grandmother at a party given by Queen Liliuokalani at her home, Washington Place - and he decided to stay.

Culture Shock

With half the population in 1948 than it has today, America was beginning to gain a foothold in what would become a roaring post-war economy. The country was heading into its most prosperous decade. There weren't many two–car families yet, but there was no need for two incomes either. In the next ten years, America would be the richest and, so we were told, the happiest country in the history of the world.

Baby boomers had made their first appearance, and life expectancy was 62.9 years. An annual average income was $2936, and a typical new home cost $7700. Bread was fourteen cents a loaf, gasoline was sixteen cents a gallon, postage was three cents, and an adult movie ticket cost sixty cents. This was before the advent of ballpoint pens, TV dinners, shopping malls and supermarkets, but Hotpoint had introduced something they called *push button cooking*, Birdseye had begun marketing frozen peas, and a Japanese company called Honda had just started selling motorcycles to Americans.

Riverside was still a healthful utopia with a gentle climate, clean air and endless orange trees. Colorful orange crate labels promoted Southern California as a romantic cornucopia of wholesome beauty. Freeways and smog were still in the future, and voracious developers had not yet thought to chew up the orange groves and replace them with concrete and asphalt.

Founded in 1870 on land that was once a Spanish Rancho, by 1948 Riverside was a town of 45,000 people. It looked nothing like Honolulu, and, in the beginning, I suffered from culture shock and a continuing bout of homesickness. Riverside was flat, land-locked and on the edge of a large desert. Less delicate looking date palms had replaced our familiar coconut trees; there was no encircling ocean or looming mountains, and the air had a strange smell. This was before the blanket of smog covered Southern California, but the dry desert air mixed with the seasonal smudge pots to protect the orange groves from frost was a far cry from the trade winds of Manoa Valley. I missed the predominant green of Hawaii which contrasted with a desert beige surrounding Riverside. And the light was different – the high brightness of Hawaii contrasted with a subtler palette. The angle of the sun produced subdued pastels, but, in time, I came to appreciate the purple shadows cast on Mt. Rubidoux in the evenings.

Seasons change subtly in Hawaii (as a small kid, I was never sure what season we were in) so I was not accustomed to bare branches or streets filling with colored leaves in the fall. Nor had I imagined anything that would put me inside bulky layers of clothing or cause me to give up my barefoot life and become a tenderfoot. In Honolulu, a seasonal chill would mean any temperature below sixty. Winter always forced us to huddle around a tiny electric space heater near the breakfast table, so the fireplaces and steam heat in Riverside were exotic novelties.

We lived next door to our friends the Keplers who had fled Hawaii for safety soon after the bombing of Pearl Harbor. They arranged for us to live next to them on 8th Street (now University Avenue). Probably built in the 1920s, our rented house was an ordinary single-story structure in a neighborhood that had seen better days, but we leased it for $125 a month in order to be near our friends. With windows and construction meant to solidly keep out the cold, this was clearly a mainland house of an era before my time. The late 1940s were well-before the now seeming innocent wave of juvenile delinquency that swept America in the 1950s. But we became accustomed to the unfamiliar habit of locking our doors at night.

I knew that mango, papayas and guava came from trees, but now I saw that walnuts, apricots and oranges did as well. Our Riverside back yard produced what the Honolulu Piggly-Wiggly had provided at home. Behind these trees was another mainland peculiarity, a service alley that led to our garage. The house was on the main street in town and was equidistant from the Citrus Experiment Station where Dad would work, and downtown, where the elaborate Spanish-gothic Mission Inn was testament to the healthful destination that Riverside still was.

Acculturation

Aileen was not yet in school, but Harrison was in first grade and I was in fourth at Longfellow Elementary School. Housed in an ornate two-story Victorian building, the school was equipped with unfamiliar cloakrooms and crackling radiators. Our desks had lids that opened up to store books and inkwells for dipping pens or pigtails. Always careful to avoid the sixth-grade bullies, we would walk to and from school each day in the cumbersome shoes we were learning to wear; part of this routine was the temptation of Mooney's mom-and-pop candy store that reminded me of the Chinese store at home on East Manoa Road; but in Riverside, there was no *crack* seed, *see mui*, *shave* ice or *manapua* (pork buns). Instead, we spent our pennies on jawbreakers, Tootsie Rolls, wax lips, Sugar Daddies, Necco Wafers, candy cigarettes and a new sensation called bubble gum.

As in Hawaii, other students represented a mixture of races, but now there were new ones: Hispanics and African Americans rather than Asians and Polynesians. These races were distinct minorities at that time, but in Hawaii, we had grown up in a comfortable melting pot – at school and everywhere. In Riverside, the other students and I sometimes had difficulty understanding each other. The Pidgin English and Hawaiian words I had grown up with were useless. *Howzit* became *howdy*, *soda watah* became *soda pop*, *shave ice* became *snow cone*, and shoyu became *bug juice*. Hawaiian references to the landscape and direction (*mauka*, toward the mountains, and *makai*, toward the ocean) were replaced with words like *mesa*, *arroyo* and *seco*. *Pau* (finished), *puka* (hole) and *pilau* (dirty) were gradually eliminated from my vocabulary as they drew blank stares or misunderstandings.

The attack on Pearl Harbor had happened only seven years earlier when I was two, but that event, and Hawaii itself, were clearly not part of my classmates' awareness. I think my brother and I were seen as exotic, sometimes barefoot, visitors from across the sea – foreigners from an outpost that might as well have been in deepest Africa. Hawaii's status as a territory rather than a state was an unfamiliar concept to most of our classmates. My teacher encouraged me to give a presentation about my *homeland*, and I had to convince my audience that we didn't wear grass clothes or live in grass houses.

In those days, Hawaii kids grew up with a more exotic palate than mainlanders did. After all, *poi* was likely to be our first solid food. This was followed as a natural course by *lomi lomi* salmon, *lau laus* and *kalua* pig. It would be years before mainland menus were as cosmopolitan as they are today. We had come from a place where Asia influenced our food and tastes. Now we had to do without *gai-see-min* and shrimp Canton from the Golden Duck in Makiki, Mom's curry with rice, coconut and chutney; and *hekka*, *sukiyak*i, *saimin* and, in those days, even sushi. We had none of the fresh pineapples, guavas, mangos or papayas that had always been in our kitchen at home. On the other hand, in Hawaii, it had always been a challenge to find affordable fresh mainland produce that had to be shipped to us.

Mom wasn't happy with the never-ending challenge of keeping us fed, but with Grandma's help, we made do with tuna and peanut butter and jelly sandwiches for school lunch and various meat loaf and casserole recipes for dinner. There were no real convenience foods then except, of course, the frozen peas that Birdseye was offering and various Campbell's soups. The rest of Mom's days, I assumed, were taken up with chores like putting laundry through the wringer and hanging it out in the dry desert air. In the winter, makeshift clotheslines were arranged indoors when soot from the smudge pots would blacken everything. And, of course, there was gossip with Charlotte Kepler next door, riding herd on three kids and seeing us through lost teeth, measles and chicken pox which we mistakenly came to associate with the mainland.

In 1948, one million American homes had television sets. One of those was a 15-inch Crosley at a neighbor's house around the corner on Mesa St. where a provocative rooftop aerial announced this to the whole neighborhood. Television would not come to Hawaii until the mid-fifties so this riveting miracle – as grainy and snowy as it was – had us glued to that set every Friday night. After an initial fascination with the test pattern wore off, the main attraction was a puppet named *Howdy Doody*. But we were also entertained by *Kukla, Fran and Ollie, Bozo the Clown, The Milton Berle Show, The Lone Ranger* and *The Cisco Kid*.

Because Hawaiians could not vote in national elections, being on the mainland for the 1948 presidential race was of great interest to my mother and grandmother and would introduce me to the world of partisan politics. Mom and Grandma, along with many other islanders, were staunch Republicans at that time and preoccupied by the Communist scare that was gripping the nation. I overheard a great deal of animated talk in our house, and next door at the Kepler's, about the imminent Republican victory of Thomas Dewey. But in November, Harry Truman's upset sent tremors through our two households. Apparently, this was very bad news for the anti-Communist movement and gave encouragement to the Joseph McCarthy era that followed. Today, I am decidedly objective in my politics, but that 1948 election was a seminal lesson in how our government works.

An upside of not being home for Christmas was having a real mainland tree instead of the potted Norfolk Island Pine we sometimes had to settle for. In Hawaii, Santa often arrived on a surfboard so I was hoping for some of the exoticism of snow and jingle bells that mainland Christmas cards always showed. But we were living in Southern California so there would be no white Christmas; we did, however, have some fascinating mornings of frost that crunched under our feet. We borrowed ornaments from the Keplers and enjoyed the familiar custom of choosing toys from the Sears-Roebuck Catalog. I think that was the year of my chemistry set.

As telegrams and long-distance phone calls were mainly reserved for emergencies in those days, communication with Dad across 2500 miles of water was a challenge, especially at Christmas time. One solution was a newsy monologue he wrote, recorded and sent to us on a 78-RPM vinyl disc. Recently, I listened to that recording after seventy years. I didn't recognize Dad's voice at first as he sounded so young. He told us about seeing Santa and his reindeer downtown at Liberty House and how quiet the neighborhood was since we had left. He mentioned the various invitations he had had for Christmas dinner and entreated us to *be good and mind Mommy* so Santa would visit us on 8th Street. And he signed off singing *Jingle Bells* and invited us to join in.

But there were also occasional expensive long-distance calls. These would be prearranged through letters, and at the appointed time we would huddle around the phone with our scripted notes. These were overseas calls so it made sense to shout our conversation until, too quickly, the operator announced that our three minutes were up. We also managed to shrink the miles on some Saturdays by listening to Webley Edwards' *Hawaii Calls*, broadcast from the Moana Hotel in Waikiki.

On one January afternoon in 1949, Mom stood out on our back porch and felt something in the air. The sky was clouding over, and the temperature had been dropping all day. Mom was an island girl so there was no reason she should have had such a premonition – but she did, and her forecast came true – snow! The unlikely storm we experienced in the next two days is still remembered in Southern California as if it were a hundred-year flood. Riverside is near the Mojave Desert and it never snowed there except in the mountains. But in 1948, it did.

Slipping on the back stairs, we ran out in our bare feet and touched the flakes to our tongues. In one night, the world took on an altered appearance. The walnut, apricot and orange trees were given a fine coating of white, and we set about gathering up enough snow to build a snowman. The ground was covered with only an inch or two, not enough for school to close, but we treasured it and argued with the Kepler kids over whose snow belonged in whose yard. In a few days, our snowman had disappeared as had the white groundcover, but the memory of this first encounter with snow has remained.

Across the street was a large orange grove that gave us bright colored fruit and the smell of blossoms in the spring; in the winter, we had the smell of soot and dirty coating on the window sills and furniture from the smudge pots that kept the oranges from freezing. These navel oranges were first planted in 1871, and the climate soon encouraged a major industry. In 1949, the endless orange groves set against the palm trees and snow-capped mountains were still essential parts of the iconography of Southern California.

Harrison and I and our neighborhood friends considered *our orange grove* across 8th Street to be a private forest playground. There, we dug an underground fort, and, with slingshots, decoding rings with secret whistles and caps in our toy guns, we played war, cops and robbers, cowboys and Indians and chased the jack rabbits which made their home there. Squirrels, blue jays and the rabbits had replaced the familiar wildlife of Manoa Valley, the mongooses, centipedes, Buffo toads and mynah birds. Kids played outdoors a lot more then as we had no electronic toys or daytime TV to distract us. But we had to adjust to being indoors in the winter, something we had never thought much about in Hawaii. So, on days when we couldn't go out, we had our Erector and chemistry sets, a wood burning kit and a board game called Candy Land – and *The Hardy Boys, Boy's Life Magazine* and lots of comic books.

Over thirty years ago, I made a trip to see what had happened to our Riverside neighborhood. The grand Victorian Longfellow School had been replaced by a nondescript institutional building; our 8th Street house was abandoned and derelict, and, sadly, in place of our orange grove across the street, there were ugly chain motels and restaurants. The Fox Riverside Theater had been saved, and the Mission Inn still attracted tourists, but nothing else seemed the same. Innocently, at mid-century, it hadn't occurred to most of us that paradise might one day be lost under pavement, and all of California would be threatened – and now Hawaii too.

California Dreaming

By the end of 1948, I had become a provisional *mainland haole*. The shoes I was forced to wear had tenderized the soles of my feet, and I had adjusted to long pants and cumbersome layers of clothing. Harrison and I had made new friends with whom we shared the wonders of television and snow and our make-believe exploits amongst the orange trees. It was a relatively safe time, so, on Saturday afternoons we could walk downtown on our own to explore the Mission Inn and go to the movies at the elaborate Fox Riverside Theater. *The Wizard of Oz* had just been rereleased, and we roared at Abbot and Costello and fantasized during the cowboy and gangster movies and Buck Rogers serials that inspired the scenarios we sometimes acted out in our orange grove adventures.

No longer homesick, I had temporarily become accustomed to my new neighborhood and town. Along with reciting poems by Henry Wadsworth Longfellow and the multiplication tables, Longfellow school was teaching me that Riverside was only a small part of the mainland; I was studying U.S. geography and learning that there was much more to experience than the world I had recently adjusted to. I sent for free brochures of national parks, and, for Christmas, I received a View-Master slide set. This low-tech device came with stereoscopic discs that, when held up to the light, revealed three dimensional images of the natural wonders of Southern California and much more of the mainland too.

We were all waiting for Dad's arrival from Honolulu to venture out on some family road trips. But on January first, we went to Pasadena with the Keplers to see The Tournament of Roses. Hawaii is known for its flowers, but I had never seen anything as spectacular or theatrical as that parade. Dad arrived later in January having missed the big snowstorm and the Rose Parade, but, now that he was with us, we could join the exuberant culture of the open road that was gathering momentum all around us. By 1949, Southern California had become the focal point of America's growing love of the automobile. Freeways had not yet been built, but drive-in movies, restaurants and miniature golf courses dotted the landscape, and people thought nothing of driving long distances to get somewhere.

Those miles of roadways were beginning to host attention-getting monuments to commercialism and, sometimes, bad taste. An array of ersatz tackiness was designed to convince travelers in moving cars to stop at commercial attractions and tourist traps, and I was susceptible to all of it. The giant pineapple that looked down on the Dole Cannery in Honolulu had transfixed me as a kid. But in California, that kind of kitsch was everywhere. There were diners shaped like chili bowls, pigs and coffee pots. You could buy baked goods in windmills, and what was not yet called fast food out of giant ice cream cones and Indian tepees. In Hollywood, there was even a restaurant in a very large brown derby hat. And everywhere, there were outlets that looked like oversized oranges that served freshly-squeezed juice for a dime. This whimsical roadside architecture extended to ordinary buildings and homes. What I would later learn to be English Tudor, French Norman, Colonial revival, art deco, art nouveau, and Spanish Mission were styles that decorated every neighborhood and looked to me like the settings of movies or illustrations out of story books.

Before we left Hawaii, Dad had ordered a 1949 Studebaker Champion. We felt lucky to get our car as there was still a steel shortage because of the war. This was the postwar era when automobile design was beginning to take a streamlined leap into the future. Cars were increasing in size and sophistication, a trend that would culminate in the automotive excesses of the late 1950s. Our long and low, beige and tan Champion came with a wrap-around rear window and looked nothing like the stunted all black sedan with running boards that had been our car at home. Although power steering, overdrive and automatic transmissions did not exist yet, this sleek machine symbolized a new age to me, and I loved its smell and chrome details that reminded me of the Buck Rogers movies I had been seeing downtown. Los Angeles seemed to be a city of the future too. Its flat landscape encouraged trips of sprawling distances that put a lot of miles on our odometer in the next few months. There would be weekend drives to beaches, mountains and deserts that could not be compared to the circumscribed jaunts around our small island at home.

This was seven years before Disneyland would make its debut and eventually spawn many other elaborate theme parks. But Knott's Berry Farm, then just a fried chicken and berry pie restaurant with an artificial ghost town for kids, was a popular family destination – as was Farmer's Market, another concept that seemed to have arrived from the future. This was a few years before Ala Moana Center was built on dredged coral near Waikiki, so the complex on Fairfax Avenue, actually a very large food court and fresh produce market, was the first shopping center I had ever seen.

The late 1940s were a part of the golden age of movies, and many of its icons were not far away. I loved movies, and now we were living close to where they were made. Pictures from my movie star scrapbook at home came to life when we went to see Sunset Boulevard, Hollywood and Vine, the Hollywood sign and Grauman's Chinese and Egyptian theaters.

California kids learned about their Spanish heritage in fourth grade, so I earned extra credit for visiting the missions at San Juan Capistrano and Santa Barbara. We discovered that the beaches in those places were not like the ones we knew in Hawaii. Surfing was not yet the rage it would be in the 1950s, and the water was cold. But Mom entertained herself in Laguna Beach searching for Fiesta Ware and Catalina Island Pottery, and I was absorbed by the animal shows at the San Diego Zoo, the brand-new 200-inch telescope at Mount Palomar and my first trip to a foreign country when we went to Tijuana. More roadside phantasmagoria turned up as we ventured east to the desert and mountains – pyramids, pueblos and covered wagons dispensed gasoline, and giant coffee cups, donuts, sombreros and Arabian palaces sold food, drinks and souvenirs.

The Orange Show in San Bernardino annually celebrated the citrus industry with gigantic displays made of fruit and reminded me of the floats in the Rose Parade. There were date milkshakes in Indio, and tourists in imitation western wear and wealthy land-owning Indians driving Cadillacs in the still small and exclusive Palm Springs. And, coming to life from Friday night television, the Cisco Kid and his sidekick Pancho led a parade down Palm Canyon Drive on horseback. The Palms to Pines Highway took us up to Idyllwild and to more of the exotica of winter. This time, in the mountains, there was lots of snow to go around. We discovered the distinct mainland pleasures of making snow angels, throwing snowballs, and sledding down hills that reminded me of *ti* leaf sliding on the muddy slopes of Manoa Valley. All of this snow was in the context of fun, and it wasn't until years later I learned what the discomfort of a real mainland winter could be.

The Mainland Untamed – *The Yellow Brick Road*

It was always our intention that our biggest exploit, a

major road trip, would happen when school was out in June. This would be both educational for us kids and nostalgic for Mom and Dad, and we would visit far-flung family most of whom I had never met before. Living in Hawaii, we were as *far-flung* as any in the family, and I grew up never knowing any of my cousins. I guess Mom and Dad thought it was time to rectify that. We had never gone on vacations, two weeks or otherwise, when I was younger. Families tended to save up time because going to the mainland in those days was a big event. So, our trip around the country in 1949 was thanks to saved vacation time and the fact that we were already on the mainland for Dad's sabbatical leave.

In the summer of 1949, long distance auto travel was gradually becoming an American habit, and tourists were taking to the open road. Hawaii was too small to have an *open road*, and you couldn't drive around the mainland in a day as we had driven around Oahu. A trip to the mainland was a much bigger commitment before jet travel, and islanders would sometimes make a grand tour that might last several months. So, on the day after Longfellow School released us for the summer, our futuristic Studebaker rolled slowly out of the alley behind our Riverside house, and we began a summer-long progress around the country.

Along with routed Triple A maps and guides and a book of restaurants recommended by Duncan Hines, the car had been loaded with enough provisions to supply two adults and three kids for nearly three months. Gasoline was cheap in 1949 so we would drive up the west coast to Canada, cross the Canadian Rockies, and then go down through the Midwest as far east as Chicago and return to San Francisco to sail home with our new car in September. This would be the most important adventure of my life up to then, and it could only have happened in the wide-open and, in places, still untamed spaces of the mainland.

On every day of our trip, I was struck viscerally by an unbound spaciousness, expanses of land that stretched in every direction under a seemingly endless vault of sky. I had learned about the world in a place where mountains always restricted a distant view, and the sky hung over an ocean, not unlimited landscape. The Triple-A maps allowed me to trace our progress. In addition to the routes that were marked out for us, the maps showed a lot of enticing emptiness too. Those marked routes indicated where we were going, but each mile of getting there was part of a journey into the unknown.

The Federal Interstate Highway System (today's interstate freeways) had been planned in 1944, but by 1949 had not yet been built. Compared to today, there were about a million fewer miles of road then and a fraction of the cars that now exist. Our trip happened just before auto travel exploded with the advent of the interstate freeways. Some people were still traveling by rail, and, although we saw some drivers pulling sleek Airstream trailers, this was well before the appearance of recreational vehicles.

We certainly weren't pioneers. I suppose Lewis and Clark could be credited with the first trans-continental sightseeing trip. In 1804, they started out on a two-year trek from St. Louis to the Pacific Ocean and back. A hundred years later, in 1903, the first cross-country auto trip was accomplished in 64 days. Today, one can rush from coast to coast in 4 or 5 days but experience little more than exit signs and indications for gas, food and lodging. The initial trans-continental road, the Abraham Lincoln Memorial Highway from San Francisco to New York, was completed in 1915. In

1925, the world's first motel charged $1.25 to stay overnight in San Luis Obispo, and in 1926, Henry Ford significantly lowered the price of his Model A. During the Depression Dad and two of his brothers crossed the country on partly-paved roads in a Model T with a couple of pup tents. Americans were gradually freeing themselves from the constraints of the railroads and taking to independent travel. At the same time, we were traveling in 1949, Jack Kerouac was moving around the country writing his iconic *On the Road*. Highways and back roads were beginning to snake everywhere, and there were enough support businesses for an extensive family road trip to be possible.

Our tour coincided with that reality in a time when the infrastructure of tourist facilities had not yet taken on the slickness of a golden age. Corporate monoliths like Holiday Inn had not yet homogenized the country and chain stores and networks of outlets for food and lodging hadn't done so either. Each town we came to was unique, and the places we stayed or ate in had a distinct identity. This filled me with a daily anticipation of discovery that cannot be experienced today except on some back roads that are now seldom traveled.

Today's back roads were the main roads we traveled on in 1949, and those two-lane highways presented daily challenges – narrow shoulders, inconsistent guard rails and the visceral thrill of negotiating sharp turns or roller coaster hills. There were panicky episodes of pressing the pedal to the floor to pass slower traffic, and, because the pieces of highway were not yet part of a seamless system, dealing with puzzling detours that sometimes sent us off on dirt tracks and once into a cornfield. Just as she had reacted to our airplane flight from Honolulu, Mom was a panicky driver from the front seat or the back.

Sitting in the back seat with Harrison and Aileen, and perched on a piece of luggage so I could see the unraveling road ahead, I was surrounded with maps, tour books, the national park brochures I had sent for, my Kodak Brownie camera and my View Master slides. We would usually drive three or four hundred miles a day, a distance that, at first, this Hawaiian kid had trouble grasping. I would trace the blue and red highways on the map and wonder what Oakville, or Maverick, or Cedarvale, or Gladstone or Dateland or Pleasant View would look like after we had gone around the next bend or risen over the next high point that prevented us from seeing the far horizon. The map would also show me the dotted scenic routes – the rivers and lakes and elevations, and the borders of the parks, and I would try to imagine the coming landscape. We were driving into the unknown, following a yellow brick road that, surely, led to an Emerald City or, at least someplace that was new and totally different from what we had seen the day before.

Cars weren't equipped with overdrive then, so we didn't think of rushing from place to place as freeways demand today. The two-lane highways followed the natural contours of the land rather than cutting through them. Much of this landscape was overspread with classic family farms that I had only seen in picture books; they came with silos and windmills and wonderful red barns that displayed advertisements for Nehi Soda or chewing tobacco. These farms bore no resemblance to the dairy farm in lower Manoa Valley that I had visited on field trips. Roads went through all the towns instead of bypassing them, and there were no suburbs or ugly commercial strips to get through. Often it was the matter of a speed limit or a single stoplight that forced us to really see Main Street and experience the fabric of even the smallest wide places in the road. Ten years later, we would undertake a similar trip, but by then, the traffic sped to the horizon and bypassed the hills, valleys and small towns that gave texture and character to the land. But in 1949, I could still be excited by the fantasy of what we would encounter in *Oakville* when we cleared the next rise.

By the middle of the afternoon, I would turn to the Duncan Hines and AAA guides to help decide where we would eat and spend the night. The listings provided stars that indicated quality and price, but I was attracted to the names that stirred me, like *Pirate's Cove Café, Dixie Grill,* or *The Red Barn Steak House.* Many of the places had the words *café, grill* or *diner* attached to them. I was especially taken with the chromed railroad cars that sported shiny lighted jukeboxes and smelled of cooking grease. *Nutrition* and *cuisine* were not common concepts then. Except for some hamburger places in the Midwest called White Castle, there were no fast food outlets as we know them today. McDonalds had not been thought of yet, and pizza was not part of the American diet. Duncan Hines seemed to prefer good plain American food, so we dutifully ate in places that announced *good eats, home cooked* and *the best food in town.*

When we weren't staying with friends or relatives, the AAA Guide led us to lodgings that cost no more than eight dollars a night and had evocative names like *Twin Pines, Trail's End, Lakeview,* or *Eagle's Nest.* They were sometimes called *cottages, cabins or tourist courts,* but *motel,* a new word in everyone's vocabulary, was most common. There were few *inns, lodges* or *resorts*; bed-and-breakfasts had not yet appeared, and Holiday Inn wouldn't exist for three more years. I loved the electric signs that announced these places, often with flashing neon arrows or masses of lightbulbs that turned on and off to suggest movement. Most often, the motels were arranged as an open-ended court around a lawn with trees and sometimes a pool. None of these places took advance reservations or was attached to a chain.

There were no driving distances in Hawaii that called for an overnight stay, so this world of roadside food and shelter was all new to me. Before this trip, I had never stayed in any commercial lodging, and I loved the surprise of opening the door and choosing beds in a new home each night. There were no television sets, and few had phones, but, as the Bates Motel was not yet a part of our cultural heritage, they were all clean and safe and had miniature bars of soap and paper bathmats with the outlines of feet to show where you were to stand.

Dad's *Mainland – 1948/'49* file provided a very complete time capsule of that summer. In addition to brochures, menus, place mats and AAA maps, there were his meticulous notes, including mileage, prices and *scientific* commentary. His comments reminded me that our trip had begun with a furtive effort to elude the law. There had been a misunderstanding over the terms of the lease on our Riverside house, and the landlord had a son in the California Highway Patrol. A lawyer had advised us to sneak out of town to avoid a wrangle that might delay our trip. The night before our *escape*, we had hidden our loaded Studebaker in a neighbor's garage and, like outlaws in a gangster film, we had stolen away before dawn. With an eye on the rear-view mirror and an effort to keep within the speed limit and use back roads to avoid the Highway Patrol, we gingerly made our way north through California hoping our license plates wouldn't give us away. We eventually found asylum at the Oregon border.

The rest of California was not quite as dramatic as our departure from Riverside, but the images in my View Master slides and mail-order brochures came to life at Death Valley, and then at Sequoia and Yosemite National Parks, Big Sur, Monterey, the coastal redwoods and a city I would live in or near for the rest of my life. I fell in love with the still small city of San Francisco for all the reasons that many people refer to it as *America's Favorite City*. Here was a new world of skyscrapers, suspension bridges, cable-cars and auto ferries that Hawaii had never seen. Mom was on a quest for Dungeness crab, and Dad was looking for the summer fruit of his boyhood in the Midwest and in Washington state. This had always been rare and expensive in Hawaii, especially during the depression and the war.

Crossing the border into Oregon had more significance than saying goodbye to the California Highway Patrol. Hawaii does not share political borders so I got in the habit of looking beyond the signage for the instant gratification of cultural or visual differences that might match the state boundaries. It wasn't until we got to Crater Lake that we finally felt we were in a new state. And then we drove through Eugene where ten years later, I would begin four years at the University of Oregon. We stayed with one of Dad's brothers in Beaverton outside Portland. Uncle Herb and Aunt Vera put Harrison and me in a pup tent in their deep and wooded back yard. How was I to know there were really no bears out there?

Vashon Island is a very rural suburb of Seattle and can be reached by regular ferry service. Mom's sister, Aunt Peggy, and her husband, Uncle John, had been living there for a few years, and our visit turned out to be more than a family reunion. The island was a setting for long walks and blackberry picking, but behind the scenes, there was a drama taking place. We had been summoned to spirit Aunt Peggy away from an alcoholic husband; this involved a diversion and escape under the cover of darkness on a night train to Santa Barbara – a touch of *film noir* at its best.

Harrison and I mercilessly satirized a very British stopover in Victoria, B.C. High tea at the Empress Hotel was the climax of this with lots of *Cheerio, pip, pips* and toasts *to the Queen*. We were suddenly eating in very nice restaurants which now I attribute to favorable exchange rate. Mom and Dad had honeymooned at Lake Louise, and I had lived my early childhood with a painting of the lake that they had paid ten dollars for in 1938. So, for nostalgia's sake, we headed into the Canadian Rockies and the Columbia Icefields. The glaciers were not melting then, and they became an exotic highlight of the trip. They couldn't have been more antithetical to what I knew in Hawaii. And there were animals, lots of them – bears, antelope, elk, moose, Bighorn Sheep and lots of little creatures called chipmunks.

One evening, we innocently ended up in Missoula, Montana because it was time to stop driving, or perhaps because Dad was drawn to university towns. The preoccupation of settling into a new motel prevented us from noticing what was next door. Frantic fire engines at two A.M. were the first indication – and then we were evacuated and put at a safe distance from what turned out to be a coal storage dock surrounded by gasoline tanks. Morning revealed nothing but ashes of the coal dock and the news that other fires had happened all over town. Missoula has always been attached to that fire for me, and a new vocabulary word – *arson*.

The information for Yellowstone Park had moved to the top of my collection of brochures, and I had been previewing what I would see there with my View Master slides. Like Hawaii National Park near the Kilauea volcano on the Big Island, the hot earth at Yellowstone seemed to be alive with geysers, steam vents and bubbling sulfur pots. As in the Canadian Rockies, we saw animals everywhere – buffalo, bears, elk, chipmunks – and families of prairie dogs which watched us roll by from their villages near the highway. Most of these animals are now in decline, and the prairie dogs are endangered. But we saw this park and other national parks at a time when human population didn't overwhelm them as it does today.

Having crossed the Continental Divide we descended out of the Rockies. The Triple-A map didn't promise us any interesting geography for a thousand miles. There would be most of Wyoming, the northeast corner of Colorado, the long way across Kansas and the width of Missouri before we reached St. Louis, Dad's birthplace. I overheard Mom and Dad ominously discussing the humidity of the Midwest in the summertime and the fact that Kansas was a dry state. *Humidity* and *dry* did not compute for me until we experienced a dew point that far surpassed the worst Kona weather at home and stopped to purchase a couple of bottles of bourbon before we crossed the Kansas state line. We did not miss having air-conditioning as it didn't exist in cars then, but we found some relief with departures before sunrise and damp towels over open windows. Apparently, bourbon and soda over ice in the evenings helped a lot too.

The highway across Kansas ran for five hundred miles through endless cornfields, and I looked for anything to break the monotony. At home, we always had the mountains as orienting landmarks, but the Great Plains had nothing but water tanks with the town's names on them and out-of-proportion grain elevators. Most of the communities had at least one of those oversized structures that towered over the towns they looked down on. From a distance, they loomed with the promise of an *Emerald City*. But this mirage always melted away as we arrived at the reality of Main Street.

There is something in me that wants the world to conform to the imagery from the movies, and I had been looking for MGM's Kansas from *The Wizard of Oz*. All of the cornfield monotony had me hoping for a tornado, and I vainly searched for funnel clouds. One day, we did have a healthy hail storm that forced us off the road, but I held out the hope for a twister, maybe just a small harmless one.

In 1949, my parents and many others believed that a car radio, much less the cell phones of today, was a dangerous distraction to driving so we had to find other diversions to fill the monotony of the *boring states*. There were no Nintendos, computer games or I-Pods to keep our eyes glued to our laps, so when Harrison and I weren't busy poking each other or teasing Aileen, we were forced to connect to the world we were passing through. Sometimes we would ride the wind with the palms of our hands out an open window or count far-ranging license plates, or look for a new variety of road-kill and the then easy to recognize models of postwar cars. We loved the sequential Burma-Shave signs that were strung along the highways: *His face was loved by just his mother. He Burma shaved and now- Oh Brother!* Larger billboards were another oddity as they had been outlawed in Hawaii.

Often, there were invitations to stop for free ice and water, cheap souvenirs, home cooked food and caged exotic wildlife. I was particularly susceptible to the roadside attractions and tourist traps that passed themselves off as *zoos* or *wonders of the world*. *See the Buffalo! See the Jaguar! See the two-headed calf* or *Experience the Force Field of Mystery!* After paying to see our first sad and mangy buffalo, it became more difficult to convince Mom and Dad to stop. But there was a snake farm that I'll never forget. Maybe Dad thought it would be educational as we had no poisonous reptiles of any kind in Hawaii. The snakes were displayed on colored velvet cushions with jewel-like lighting that highlighted the brilliance of their skin. None of these places sold T-shirts in those days, but they did sell souvenirs, and I started buying bits of quartz, mica and what I was led to believe was a bit of petrified dinosaur bone. That piece held center place in a significant rock collection that I took home to Honolulu.

Childhood literature had taught me that trolls, ogres and Gypsies were often involved in treachery and sometimes stealing babies. I was pretty sure that ogres and trolls were fictional, but I hadn't made my mind up about Gypsies yet. At any rate, we didn't have them in Hawaii as far as I knew. I was about to find out they existed in the real world.

Gypsies, I was to learn, traveled in caravans just as they did in story books. But, in 1949 America, their chosen modes of transportation were large fin-tailed Cadillacs and Airstream trailers. One night, on the way to St. Louis, we stopped in Independence, Missouri, the home of our new president, Harry Truman. In the late afternoon, we checked into a perfectly ordinary looking motel, and, while we were away at dinner, so did the advance party of a tribe of Gypsy tinkers. Initially, a few of them had settled into a couple of rooms but then had moved in many more of their tribe and set up a camp and metal workshop in the woods behind the motel.

By ten p.m., all of these ingredients – Cadillacs and caravans, steaming caldrons in the woods, a large tribe of Gypsies, exotic music and lots of alcohol – had created a situation that drew several police squadrons and all of the guests from their rooms. The motel management served coffee and donuts while we watched the colorful confrontation. The peace had been disturbed, and Gypsies would never again remain on the pages of storybooks for me.

Historically, St. Louis is where the west begins, and we had traveled a couple of thousand miles to get to that beginning. Dad was born there in 1898, and he searched, somewhat in vain, to find remnants of the old German neighborhoods he remembered. Here and there he found recognizable street names and a few turn-of-the-century landmarks, but, for the most part, he had to be satisfied with a newer St. Louis. I remember the famous zoo and its animal shows and a creaky wooden baseball park where we ate peanuts and hotdogs and watched the Yankee Clipper Joe DiMaggio challenge the St. Louis Browns.

It was in St. Louis, a city that borders the south that I first became aware of racial segregation and the Jim Crow laws that were still very much a part of reality then. At least publicly, Hawaii was known for its racial equality, and I had had friends and classmates of many backgrounds. But none of them were African American, and there was no culture of *coloreds only* in the islands as I was shocked to learn about here. I went back to Hawaii with a new appreciation of our remarkable melting pot.

Home air-conditioning had not yet become the summer panacea it is today. We endured clammy Midwest evenings with pitchers of iced tea and lemonade along with lots of sauerkraut, German potato salad, corn on the cob, watermelon and other favorites from Dad's childhood. At Uncle Paul's house we sat in front of an electric fan inside a screened porch that protected us from flying creatures, but I was dazzled by the phenomenon of lightning bugs. I learned the mainland sport of capturing them in a bottle before setting them free.

In the late 1940s, Honolulu was still a low-rise city if you didn't count the anomaly of ten- story Aloha Tower. I had seen lots of skyscrapers in the movies, and although New York would have to wait for another trip, I was primed to experience a city of them. Chicago would be our farthest destination, and it fulfilled that expectation. The Museum of Science and Industry was an interactive fantasyland for kids and adults with buttons to push and cranks to turn that gave us automated glimpses inside the human body and the world of the future. It would take Walt Disney six more years to create a theme park that would rival that.

But the climactic attraction in Chicago was *The Greatest Show on Earth* – the combined Ringling Brothers and Barnum and Bailey Circus under the big top on Soldiers' Field. Very small circuses had made their way to Honolulu, but this was show-business on a grand scale, and it provided me with an obsession that electrified my psyche for years. As I did with anything that captured my imagination, I later tried to recreate what I could of it in our backyard at home. I didn't know it then, but this may have been an attempt to hold on to a phenomenon – a circus that smelled of sawdust under a massive tent, *the big top* – that would soon be a part of the past.

The way west took us through South Dakota and Nebraska, two more *endless* states, but this time we had the diversion of The Black Hills, Devil's Tower, Mt. Rushmore, a petrified forest and an underground cavern called Wonderland Cave. We were seeing another new variety of roadkill and the lure of more kitschy businesses that were shaped like what they sold. There were monumental statues of dinosaurs and Paul Bunyan, free ice water at Wall Drug Store on the plains of South Dakota and photo opportunities of the world-famous *jack-a-lope*.

We arrived in San Francisco to news that the longshoremen were on strike and so we wouldn't be able to sail home on Matson's S.S. Lurline. The next ship we could get on was the S.S. President Wilson. Our well-traveled Studebaker would be shipped to us after the strike. Money was tight after the summer-long trip so we waited a couple of weeks in a place that could have been right out of *The Grapes of Wrath*. The Oakland Auto Court seemed to be the end of the line for some people's California dreams. But this was a temporary way station for us, and a highlight of each day was hitching a ride on the truck that came to deliver ice. Dad's notes recorded that we had traveled 13,465 miles before we finally boarded the ship that took us home.

Home Again

One morning in late September, we rounded Diamond Head on the S.S. President Wilson. There was an anti-climactic quality to this homecoming as there would be no festive greeting by The Royal Hawaiian Band at dockside. We were tendered ashore with other Honolulu passengers to avoid the striking stevedores. Our Studebaker would be delivered to us when the strike was over.

As the Wilson moved closer to meet the tender, Honolulu looked small to me – there were no mainland big-city landmarks I had become used to. Comfortably nestled in a jungle of coconut trees, the pink Royal Hawaiian Hotel and the white Moana Hotel quaintly dominated the skyline at Waikiki. Nobody knew that only two decades later, they would be lost in another jungle - of high rises. Over their shoulders and beyond Waikiki were the green mountains of Manoa Valley still covered with clouds. They looked the same as I had left them a year before, but something had changed in me, and I saw them in a new light. I was now an eleven-year-old fifth grader and considered myself very worldly and well-traveled. I had three countries and seventeen states to my credit, and I wondered if I would be content to be back on the farm – was Hawaii still big enough for me? I had a nagging feeling that my curiosity and wanderlust had merely been whetted.

*****

As the century eased into its second half, the Honolulu airport continued to set my daydreams on edge. In the sophisticated Sky Room, you could order a famous flaming sword dinner and watch the traffic of planes on the runway below. The well-dressed grownup farewell parties were still set to Hawaiian music, flowers and expectation. And the map of the world on the airport floor with Hawaii at its center still held the promise of endless adventures.

But there was something new at the airport too. Pan American and Northwest had started flying double-decker sleepers, the Boeing Stratocruisers. Accessed by a spiral staircase, a cocktail lounge and bar was housed in a prominent bulge that protruded below the cockpit. Nicknamed *the pregnant guppy*, these were the 747s of their day and flew 55 passengers in unmatched first-class luxury. Advertisements touted the gratification of *champagne flights*, and whenever I saw the Stratocruisers being fueled, I jokingly imagined that champagne was being pumped into that underbelly. The era of the Stratocruiser came and went before I could fly on one, but they held my imagination for the time they existed – until the Lockheed Constellation replaced them in the late 1950s.

Common island propaganda told me I was lucky I lived in Hawaii, and now that I had been away for a year, I knew there was some truth to that. But the mainland had awakened a contradiction in me as well. Radio, movies and now television were filling me with another message too. The mainland was beginning to seem like the real world; at least it was a lot bigger with many more possibilities. Anticipating statehood, Hawaii optimistically called its annual fair *The 49th State Fair*, but, so far, distance and the limitation of propeller aviation had contradicted that attempt to ally ourselves with the other forty-eight states. As the time approached for me to consider a college on the mainland, friends and I began to think in terms of *getting off the rock*. We talked of *going to America, going stateside*, going to the BIG island, and to *haoleland*.

At the same time my generation was longing for the *real world*, we chauvinistically defended our own. We harbored a condescension toward the visitors and military personnel who came from there – the coast-*haoles* who roamed Waikiki with their white or pink skin, sun burns, tacky island outfits and cameras. They were an imported breed that stained us with its misunderstandings. This cultural divide pulled us in two directions, but the force of gravity produced by the mainland could not be denied.

The Mainland – Tamed

In the fall of 1957, I returned to the mainland on the S.S. Lurline, this time to go to the University of Oregon. And then, ten years after our time in Riverside, Dad was given another sabbatical leave in Corvallis, Oregon which was near Eugene and my university. That summer we took another lengthy road trip, this time in a 1959 almost day-glow aqua Plymouth Fury. I think the excessive extravagance of automobile design had reached its zenith. As big as our '49 Studebaker had been, this car was even larger – *a boat* some people called it – long and wide, with unnecessarily exaggerated fins, and encrusted with chrome, it featured a push-button transmission and overdrive.

Those ten years had also made a big difference in American culture and life on the open road. The romance of the road had become much less adventurous, and it felt as if we had become common tourists rather than the bold travelers we had been in 1949. The predictability of a franchised America now robbed us of anticipating what might be around the next bend of the road. We were eating and sleeping in homogenized places with corporate names in the outskirts of towns rather than in them. The restaurant food was often the same everywhere, and there was no longer the surprise of opening the door to a new home each night. The land was more tamed and paved over as highway engineers had flattened its contours. Two lanes had given way to four or more, and our car's overdrive sped us from place to place bypassing many of the towns. The freeways had supplanted the old main roads, and many of the towns' businesses were stranded and ignored.

Our way west had taken us across three time zones and

eight states on *the mother road*, Route 66. Through literature, music and television, this was the most famous road in America then, and its waitresses, truckers and motel clerks still supplied a welcome hint of that earlier time before America became so generic.

Pins on the Map of the World

December 27th, 2007 – I am finishing this memoir as my ship is approaching the island of Bora Bora, another part of the world that I had just begun to see when I first flew to Los Angeles in 1948. There are still some unfamiliar places on the map, but, for the most part, the continents that surrounded Hawaii on the floor of the old Honolulu Airport are no longer *terra incognita*. The entire planet has become what *the mainland* was for me then – a concept, not just a place, the challenge to be anywhere that I am not. I am still the hard-wired seeker I started off to be, and, as a Sagittarian archer, I will keep placing new pins on the enormous world map that covers one wall of my study. And I will continue to thank my parents for turning me at age ten into a citizen of the world – by taking me to the mainland where an island boy had to begin that process. I was at the right age for my mind to latch hungrily onto everything new. And almost everything I experienced in those travels *was* new and unlike the place where I grew up.

Sometime in the last sixty or seventy years, Hawaii stopped being the exotic childhood home where I started out. In those days, Hawaii was relatively isolated from the mainland and considerably insulated by distance. Certainly, there had been earlier cultural infusions from the Chinese, Japanese, Portuguese and Filipinos – but those had happened before I was born and were a part of the exotic mix I grew up with. Before jet planes, television, the internet and a tide of mainland commerce and culture, Hawaii had settled into an almost Darwinian cultural quarantine. Like those animals imprisoned on their island in The Galapagos, we had maintained our unique identity back then.

In contrast to the mainland, Hawaii is still a softer place, and I am always astounded by its isolation when I see its mountains or city lights after five hours of uninterrupted ocean. But the pace and culture of the whole country has become homogenized, and Hawaii's Eden has not escaped that process. No one thinks we live in houses or clothes made of grass anymore. In 1958, jet planes allowed the masses of the world to join us, and the heft of mainland culture has taken its toll: first, transcribed television and then satellite direct transmission, drive-in movies, enormous shopping centers, pizza parlors, a forest of high-rise buildings and the *Mauka* Arterial freeway. The onrush of acculturation has continued with the internet, email instead of five-day letters, and even Walmart. Today, a ten-year old traveler would not experience the stimulation or otherness as I did when going to the mainland for the first time. Today, he would step off a jet plane into a larger version of his own world.

But, at one time ... a serpentine of images floods over me: two-lane highways meandering over an unaltered landscape, wild animals at the roadside, thriving main streets of small towns, Indian teepees and covered wagons selling hot dogs and milk shakes, Burma-Shave jingles strung along the highway, a drunken gypsy caravan, a conflagration that almost destroyed a town, healthy glaciers covering mountain tops, desert sunsets, a backyard snowman, orange groves filling the landscape, a three-ring circus under the big top –

a world before freeways and smog and a homogenized America. Many of these memories will never be experienced again – by ten-year-old boys, or anyone.

The parade of imagery has run its course, and my mind puts nearly seventy years in rapid rewind. In an instant I am fixed on my childhood mountains in Manoa Valley that, at one time, had focused me on the world beyond. The mountains are still there, and they look the same, but the world on the other side of them has changed irreparably for me. I'm glad my discovery of the mainland - that *other place* that filled my childhood imagination – happened when it did, when there was still a vast difference between it and where I was from. The frisson I felt from that otherness is what set my wanderlust on fire, what sent me searching for the wider world.

Punahou's Class of 1957

Coming to Terms with Punahou —and Myself
(1953 – 1957)

The events portrayed in this memoir are told from my personal point of view and may not reflect what others may have experienced at the same time. While admittedly a literary cliché, this is basically a tale of teenage angst in negotiating the sometimes-daunting social labyrinth of high school. I have tried to be honest with myself and my material in hopes of touching a chord or, at least, jarring loose some interesting memories of a time gone by. It is now clear to me that by going to school at Punahou School in the nineteen-fifties I experienced a very rarified and narrow slice of life.

June, 1957 — —The Great White Father and I

The Great White Father looked down at me and shook my right hand, and I reached for the diploma with my left as I had been instructed to do, and I realized that my time at Punahou School was nearly over. Lurking at the edge of an excited euphoria were touches of relief that I was too preoccupied to examine closely. It would be many years before I fully understood them.

Nearly seventy years later I tried to make out the tiny faces in our graduation photograph. I would need a magnifying glass to see the details. I count 269 of us, boys in the center and girls on the sides, posture perfect and attentively focused on Miss Murray as she led us in singing our graduation songs. For many years, I could remember the names of those songs, and their Hawaiian lyrics would easily run through my head, but now they are gone. I do remember that we finished with Punahou's alma mater *Oahu'a* as tears and *chicken skin* (goosebumps) filled the gym. We all look so young and beautiful, the guys in our white dinner jackets and red carnation boutonnieres and the girls in full white skirts and red carnation leis. The gymnasium stage was flanked by ceremonial *kahilis* and a large **57**, the class numerals, was framed by a rendering of Punahou's main gates. I suppose this was done with crepe paper and chicken wire – or could they have been real flowers?

An hour earlier, we had lined up with our assigned walking partners – some pleased and others chagrined by whom they were placed with. Then *Pomp and Circumstance* sounded and we marched – a bit fortified in some cases – into the gym and took places that had been designated by our singing voices. Chaplain Rewick read an invocation, two classmates gave inspirational speeches, and our principal, Mr. Curtis (*Uncle Walter*), presented the class to Dr. Fox, *The Great White Father*. That name wasn't official, of course, but he was tall and handsome and had a full head of wavy white hair. A Hollywood director couldn't have cast a more likely candidate as the president of a distinguished prep school.

Desperate not to trip, and with an out-of-body sensation, I had made my way across the wide stage. Irrationally, I wondered if my classmates knew who I was. After four years of quietly searching for a place in the social fabric of my class, I felt anonymous. *Who is that kid?* I imagined some of them asking. And then there was 1957's gift to Punahou (some remember it was a fountain of some sort), and then, confident we knew everything we would ever need to know, we marched out singing a student-written song. And then we were *pau* (finished).

But there was also a graduation party in Waikiki on the roof of a World War Two bunker at Fort DeRussy. Champagne punch and, surely, flasks of other things, whetted our thirsts to dance music by a group called the Hollywood Flames and entertainment by a folk singer named Josh White. Then a sunrise at Sandy Beach and, just to make sure we could all still function, breakfast at Dole Hall on campus. And then we were really *pau*.

The Anxious Prospect of a Reunion

"Fifty years later" it said. A printed blue and gold flyer had been pushed to the back corner of my desk, and periodically attracted my attention. It seemed too daunting to deal with at the time so I conjured up pressing priorities and there it sat. It was 2007 and Punahou's class of 1957 was going to have its 50th reunion in June – fifty years to the day since we had walked across that gym stage. This would involve an elaborate week of activities and parties culminating in the annual alumna*e luau* honoring our class under a very large tent. That persistent document was a request for a personal biography that would be included in a *fifty-years-later* memory book. I continued to hesitate, alternately trying to avoid dealing with it and then, once I got started, becoming obsessed.

Eventually, guilt and periodic email reminders were too much for me to ignore. It was slow going at first, but then, as memories began to emerge, I found myself enjoying the process. I dutifully wrote about how my family had come to Hawaii and where life had taken me since graduation. But, even before the bio was finished, I had a nagging feeling that something was being left out. There was more to my relationship with Punahou than I was telling. Curiosity had drawn me to a few other reunions in the past, usually with my classmate Tricia for moral support, but there was always a lot of anxiety involved, too. And I certainly had mixed feelings about our looming half-centennial in June.

My bio for the reunion book met the deadline, but a voice in my head pestered me that there was still more to say. I needed to exorcise something that had been tucked away for a long time. I needed to make a journey – both physically and emotionally– to treat a wound that had never healed.

So, in February of 2007, three months ahead of our reunion, I returned to Honolulu to attend the annual Punahou Carnival which, in two days, would raise over a million dollars for scholarships. It had been fifty years since my last Carnival, and retirement from teaching high school in California had given me a window of time to attend. Besides, there was an opportunity to work with a few of my classmates in one of the carnival booths, and I wanted this contact before mixing with many more of them at our reunion in June. I had resolved to attend the February and June events, mostly to do away with some of the ghosts from the four years I spent at Punahou in the mid-fifties.

The Culture of Punahou – Then

I see now that when I started high school in 1953, I was not fully prepared for the rarified world I was entering. Public schools and the tiny classes at Hawaii Episcopal Academy

(Hawaii Preparatory Academy today) on the Big Island had not prepared me for the well-heeled system of values at Punahou or the size of its student body. As a shy kid who was nearly a year younger – my birthday was in December – than many of my classmates, it was difficult to find a place in what I then perceived as the school's tradition-bound ethos of privilege and entitlement. We were being educated to be leaders of the community, and a self-conscious vanity hung in the air; in subtle ways, we taught each other to be smug about being Punahou students. This school is a very different institution today, but then it still seemed to be an isolated ivory tower that gave admissions priority to missionary families, the children of the mostly Caucasian-owned corporations that drove the island economy, children of military officers, alumnae (my mother) and faculty and Hawaiians with scholastic or athletic prowess.

Many of the students had been together at Punahou since kindergarten, or had come with each other from private and public feeder schools such as Hanahauoli and Lincoln. Some were related to well-connected establishment families and the *wasp* world of boardrooms, polo fields and private clubs. In essence, it was my first encounter with Hawaii's class system, and I felt ill-equipped to find my place in it. I had not heard it expressed before this, but, yes, Punahou seemed to be a school for rich *haoles* (Caucasians). *Haoles* had never been a majority of the island population, so Punahou, in my day, did not reflect a realistic racial balance. I was a *haole*, and my father was a professional, a research scientist, but we were a middle-class family, and my parents struggled to send my brother and sister and me to Punahou. I can think of no other term but *culture shock* to describe my experience when I began my freshman year.

I entered high school, *the senior academy*, at a time when Dr. Fox was in the process of transforming Punahou into the egalitarian first-class institution that it is today. When he arrived in 1944, it was predominantly a Caucasian school that only offered about 300 scholarships; otherwise, it was a place for those who could afford to pay for it. He was still adjusting inherited racial quotas dating from the 1890s. By the mid-1950s, Punahou admissions were decidedly based on merit – and sometimes, athletic ability – not racial quotas. But the student body still did not realistically reflect the true mix of races in the islands.

A lot of careful retrospection and self-knowledge has now taught me that I overreacted to what Punahou seemed to be. I lacked the proper perspective to see the big picture, and I felt like an interloper on a club that I didn't feel I belonged to. I imagined that most of the students were living much more exciting and glamorous lives in places like Kahala and Nuuanu. I was from upper Manoa Valley and felt isolated from the *real life* that was surely going on elsewhere.

I learned quickly that it would be necessary to have good athletic ability or an outgoing personality to find a niche. Unfortunately, I had neither. I was an awestruck, tongue-tied, skinny kid. I had disturbing fantasies (fueled by the back pages of comic books) of sand being kicked in my face at the beach. I worried too much about what others thought of me. I wish I had seen that most of them weren't even noticing me at all. They were probably struggling with their own challenges of self-acceptance and fitting in. Mrs. Erwin was the school psychologist, but you didn't go to her for self-image problems. She administered the kinds of preference tests that suggested career choices. Mine revealed that I'd make a great undertaker! That news troubled me, but, then, many of today's vocations didn't even exist then.

In spite of being trapped inside a contentious psyche, I was excited by the rich experience of going to school at Punahou. I was smart enough – not one of the top *brains*, I had a B plus average – and I was very observant. I noticed the cliques and eventually learned who everyone was. I never wanted to miss anything, so, though obliged to look on from the sidelines, I studied the campus life that was going on around me. I loved the variety of classes and the beautiful college-like campus and was fascinated by the traditions and activities; I went to the football games and attended some of the dances. After a time, I found a niche to quietly become part of – today I would probably be called a *drama geek*. Tongue-tied in my real life, I was comfortable speaking the words of others on stage.

I, too, became prideful, and yes, a bit narcissistic, to be going to what is arguably one of the best schools in the islands and one of the most respected prep schools in America. But I wanted to be part of the student social scene as well. True success, it seemed to me, came only if you were part of the conspicuous in-crowd. I wanted to be as cool as the beautiful people I saw around me.

I remember that there were other black sheep in our class, but I was so quiet that it didn't seem that I made much of an impression on the school's radar. It was probably this that kept me from being a noticeable outcast. Today, there are some who tell me they thought of me as the brainy type, but I only saw myself as shy and frightened. It's certain that there were others who were experiencing what I did, but it wasn't something you shared, and we struggled in silence.

It has taken years to realize it, but I didn't have the empathy then to know that everyone else was living in the disquiet of their own misgivings – about who they were and how they fit into the culture of high school and Punahou. After all, we were teenagers. Experts tell us that children learn their physical world much sooner than they do their social world. Teens are ruled by ego rather than compassion as they have not yet developed the empathetic front part of the brain as adults later do.

There was no high-tech cyber bullying as there sometimes is today, but subtle psychological intimidation was a regular thing. I don't remember a single heart-pounding day that I didn't feel some self-consciousness or distress, and the worst part of it was I thought then that I was the only one.

I can remember exactly where I was – and the whole incident happened in seconds. But fifty years later, these few moments are as indelible as if they happened yesterday. I was coming down the steps next to the boy's Physical Education building, Armstrong Hall. Three confident and self-involved girls from a younger class, strangers to me, were approaching, and, as we passed each other, one turned to her friends and said, in reference to me, "I don't like that boy!," and then they disappeared laughing. Stung with embarrassment, I took this to be proof of my inadequacy, and buried myself deeper inside the shell I had been building. I must admit that, because of the fear of rejection, I never greeted anyone first; I always waited to see if others would recognize me. I now see that that was a fine way to insure my isolation. Maybe that girl could see the fact that I came off as unfriendly.

Those *mean girls* didn't know who I really was – someone who wanted to be anything but the quiet, serious person I seemed to be. They probably saw me as anti-social and aloof, *stuck up* as many Punahou students were accused of being. I didn't have the self-confidence to let this incident roll off my back; it got lodged in a crevice of my mind and at regular intervals presented itself. As a teacher in a public high school for thirty-seven years, I relived the universal teenage angst in the lives of my students. I always saw them through a prism of my own unease at Punahou.

Punahou on my Mind

At first, Punahou to me was just the stone wall my family drove past every time we came in or out of Manoa Valley. The wall was covered with vines and flowers that, miraculously, only bloomed at night. I wondered what was on the other side of that wall of Night-blooming Cereus.

Rising up behind the wall was an old stone building crowned with an eye-catching blue and yellow dome, and a few blocks away was another colorful dome, this one red and yellow. The colors of the Punahou dome were buff-n-blue, I was told. *Blue* was clear to me, but what was *buff*? At any rate, that other dome, the red and yellow one, was on the Roosevelt High School campus. I didn't understand the rivalry between Punahou and Roosevelt then, but I *had* discovered a distinguishing feature of high schools – those bright colored domes with school colors.

I learned that my mother had graduated from Punahou in 1929, and in 1936, her wedding bouquet had contained flowers from the wall. How was this possible? Those flowers only bloomed at night. I supposed that they might have been forced to bloom in a closet and then rushed to St. Andrews Cathedral for the afternoon ceremony. Years later, when I learned how hallowed the Night-blooming Cereus were to Punahou, I wondered if special permission had been granted.

Before Punahou, school happened in other places for me: grades 1,2,3 and 5 at the Teacher's College at the University of Hawaii (today it is the University Laboratory School); 4th grade at Longfellow School in Riverside, California; 6th grade at Manoa School up in the valley, and 7th and 8th grades at Hawaii Episcopal Academy in Kamuela on the Big Island. But Punahou held the most prominent place in my consciousness. As a child, I was taken to community and student theater productions at Dillingham Hall and summer swimming lessons at the Punahou pool. And I wondered about the large colorful class numerals painted on Rocky Hill above the campus. One day, I helped break my brother's collar bone when we were playing at something called *the Punahou swing (*when two people would swing a third person between them). I learned that this originated in the nineteenth century when new students were flung into the lily pond on campus.

But the most exciting event happened every February. Punahou Carnival script was a regular stocking stuffer in our house, and we had from Christmas to the beginning of February to look forward to using it. In five-cent increments on sheets worth a dollar, these tickets provided entrée to such amusements as pony rides and cotton candy in my early years, and a Ferris wheel and bumper cars later on – and shave ice, and meat sticks, and saimin and sushi, and Punahou Carnival hamburgers and malasadas and *skill games* where you could win prizes for knocking over milk bottles or dunking a popular senior student, and a stage show with dancing girls, and . . . in some years lots of rain and a field of mud. But the main appeal of the carnival was that it provided a safe weekend of freedom away from parents and a tantalizing brush with the adult world.

Eventually, I heard other kids in my neighborhood reporting about going to school at Punahou. The advantages of being educated there weren't clear to me then, but stories indicated that there was something extraordinary behind that wall of night-time flowers. But I sensed controversy too. Why did some people refer to it as P-U nahou as if there was something smelly about it? And were Punahou students really *stuck-up*? And why, as was rumored, did they run the risk of getting beat up near some of the other high schools?

And then it was announced that my brother and sister and I would go to high school at Punahou. We would be legacies through our mother, and scholarships would help pay our tuition. It was probably best that my unsettling questions weren't immediately answered, as the prospect would have been even more intimidating. But all of this would eventually become clear as I came to understand Punahou's distinguished but controversial reputation.

A School with a History

Punahou's self-conscious sense of tradition and history can be traced back to the royal patronage and blessing that nurtured its founding. The campus lily pond, while not at Punahou's educational center, is certainly the explanation for the school's location. It was the fresh water from this natural spring that made *Ka Punahou (new spring)* one of the choicest tracts of land in Honolulu. King Kamehameha the First had given this prime property to his loyal chief Kameeimoku in gratitude for his support in the conquest of Oahu. Two generations later, Chiefess Liliha and her husband Boki controlled these lands, until, in 1829, he disappeared during an unsuccessful search for sandalwood in the

South Pacific. To protect his interest while he was gone, he trusted the land to the Congregational Missionary Reverend Hiram Bingham, and then – and here the story begins to sound like a soap opera to me – Queen Regent Kaahumanu, who had become a strong supporter of the missionaries, convinced Bingham to put her in charge so the acquisitive Liliha couldn't demand the return of *Ka Punahou*. It was Ka'ahumanu who suggested this property go to the missionaries as the site for a school.

In 1831, the Hiram Binghams came to live at *Ka Punahou* in a thatched adobe cottage and, respecting her roots in New England and Hawaiian custom, Mrs. Bingham had walls built around the property and is thought to have planted the first of the Night-blooming Cereus. But originally it was the water from the spring that made this place special. Today, the lily pond and the chapel that sits beside it is the most beautiful part of the campus and has become a sacred focus of tradition and esteem.

At first, it was to be a school for the children of the *alii* (ruling class) to elevate Hawaii to a state of Christian civilization, but a lack of funds delayed this, until, eventually, The Royal School was established downtown for them. Not wanting to mix with the Hawaiians, the conservative New Englanders continued to send their children to eastern mainland schools. But these difficult separations came to an end when a thousand dollars of missionary funds was set aside in 1840, and the decision was made in 1841, to found a boarding school for the children of Hawaii, which initially meant the missionaries' own offspring. 1841 is the year Punahou uses to date its founding. On July 11, 1842 fifteen mission children sat down at the first school west of the Rocky Mountains, Punahou School and Oahu College, to be empowered as respectable citizens and leaders of the community. The school went through a number of name changes in its early history – Ka Punahou (1849), Punahou School and Oahu College (1853), Oahu College (1857) and finally Punahou School in 1934. Over a hundred years later after its founding, in the mid-1950s, I experienced that same sense of entitlement when I came to Punahou.

In the mid-1950s Hawaii and Punahou were much more exotic and isolated places than they are today, and the cultural changes in the next infamous decade were not yet imagined. In many ways, Honolulu was still a small town in an insular territory, and even then it wasn't unheard of for some mainlanders to think that we lived in grass shacks. This physical isolation focused our attention on local issues that became magnified as if under a microscope. In Hawaii, the pigeon English question *Where you wen grad?* referred to high school, and the answer could convey high or low status and almost everything else anyone needed to know about you.

When I came to Punahou in 1953, It had been nearly ten years since the Army Corps of Engineers had returned the campus to Punahou after World War Two, and Dr. Fox was still in the process of widening the diversity of the student population. Political correctness was not yet a concept, nor was women's liberation, the sexual revolution, the civil rights movement or the internet, and Punahou students could blithely be as narcissistically self-involved as they wanted to be. From our midcentury and post-war vantage point, we imagined that our generation represented a grand culmination of history.

But we did respect the status quo and obeyed the adults in our lives. The free speech movement and the Vietnam

War riots were nearly a decade away, and most of us had never heard of marijuana. Our parents were mostly Republicans in the old sense and comfortably fit into the established power structure of the islands. Most of our mothers stayed at home to oversee our welfare. School was secure and predictable; cigarettes, being late, cutting class, or being too close to our partners on the dance floor were pretty much the most serious of our crimes. Guns and school shootings were still a generation away. In those relatively quiet Eisenhower years, an average income was $4,500; a new house went for under $12,000; gasoline was twenty-two cents a gallon; a year at Harvard cost $800, and annual tuition at Punahou was $275. Today it is nearly $25,000 each year for kindergarten through twelfth grade.

In that chaste era, it was pretty normal to go steady without "getting to third base," and our parents almost never divorced. We listened to The Kingston Trio, Johnny Mathis and Pat Boone sing songs like *Tom Dooley*, *Chances Are* and *Love Letters in the Sand*. Even the threat of something called "rock and roll" was exemplified by the stainlessness of *Don't Be Cruel*, *Blue Suede Shoes* and *The Rock and Roll Waltz*.

*****

My four years at Punahou were framed by incidents of triumph and tragedy – two events that were stamped indelibly on my consciousness. The first, in the fall of 1953, was a victory celebration that was unlike anything Punahou had ever seen. In the first few months of my freshman year, Punahou gradually marched to its first football championship in 29 years. As each game ended in victory, there was a mounting excitement that culminated in a dramatic "squeaker" when we beat St. Louis High School by two points. This came to be known as *the game*, and it started a winning streak that continued for many years.

Later that night, after the game, the celebration on the campus was so extravagant that one might think a war had ended. A pandemonium of cheers and songs greeted the team bus and the crowd sang:

"*Cheer, boys, cheer, Oahu has the ball. Rah, rah, rah, the Saints will take a fall, and when we hit that line, there'll be no line at all. There'll be a hot time in the old town tonight!*"

The lei-covered players sang their rendition of *Sons of Oahu* as they climbed off the bus to join the crowd. And then, Al Harrington, the team captain and hero of the game (several touchdowns were his doing), was carried on his teammates' shoulders under a small fortune of fireworks that lit up the entire campus. This was soon after I had begun school at Punahou, and I wondered how high school could get any more exciting than that.

Then, four years later, during the spring break of our senior year, tragedy struck. We woke up to stunning headlines that sent shock waves through our secure world. The Honolulu Advertiser's top headline for April 25, 1957 read *Trio Killed in Car Crash Here!* A terrible auto accident at Punalu'u had killed three popular girls in our class. Alcohol was probably involved, and I wondered if popularity had a price to pay. We gathered to mourn in Dillingham Hall and Dr. Fox told us it was ". . . by far the most tragic thing that had happened in my years at Punahou." The Class of '57's "deceased list" had been given a hefty head start even before we had graduated.

More Punahou Culture

Not long ago a friend flippantly referred to Punahou as *... that finishing school or whatever it was you went to.* I laughed and tried to set him straight, but then I realized that Punahou had, indeed, been a de facto finishing school. Along with our scholastic endeavors, we learned how to dress and speak and behave. It was the "finishing school" aspect of Punahou that most bedazzled but also challenged me.

The students' primary motivation for adopting this accepted behavior must have been to fit in socially, but we were also learning to gain a smooth entrée into the world of the establishment. Punahou's strict dress code controlled what we wore, and proper teachers like Miss Dunstan and Mr. Brenneman taught the art of precise speech. After all, one of the reasons our parents sent us to this school was to protect us from the corruption of the Pidgin English that defined much of the greater community.

We also learned an accepted courtliness that went with the conventions of attending social events. Punahou had major dances. some formal, some not, almost every month, and certain rules of etiquette that accompanied these events were dictated. It was like being in the adult world, especially at the dances held off-campus at places like the Oahu Country Club and the new Princess Kaiulani Hotel. There was the Aloha Dance at the beginning of the year, the Christmas dance, the Valentine's dance when the girls could ask the boys, the Holoku Ball, the ROTC Ball, and the Junior and Senior Proms.

It all seems so antiquated, almost medieval today, but the boys usually paid for an ornate dance card, and it was the girl's job to exchange dances by negotiating with their girlfriends and record them in the dance program. Everyone's dance card was full for the evening. One was always with your date for the first and last dances and the one just before intermission when there was a special entertainer. These were usually slow dances designed to ignite hormones in a fairly safe way. And later, it was often the guy's intention to see if he could get his date to Diamond Head or some other isolated spot to watch *the submarine races*, as we called *getting to third base* in those days.

It was the boy's responsibility to provide a lei and transportation, and the girl's duty was to look pretty with a tan, a new hair-do and a new outfit. It was a fate worse than death not to be asked. So, doing my part, I asked a girl to the Aloha Dance in my freshman year. I suffered the disgrace of having my mother drive us, and then stumbled awkwardly through the rest of the approved formalities like not dancing too close to your dance partner.

The Culture of Punahou – Today

Do students still learn how to waltz, foxtrot and tango at dance classes like the ones they held at the Cotillion at the Royal Hawaiian Hotel in the 1950s? Most of these social procedures we learned sixty years ago are relics of the past – at Punahou and everywhere. Today, there are no dance cards, and, quite democratically, friends can come together in groups so there is even no longer the need for a date. The Junior Prom is now known as the Junior Function and, as in our day, there are informal canteens on many Friday nights where you can just show up. But, surely, despite the passage of time, I believed that Punahou students continue to be instilled with the civilities of dress and proper behavior. In

February of 2007 I decided to see for myself.

I sat on the bench under the Tamarind tree– and I waited. The school bell would ring soon, but I was also waiting for memories. At first, I tried to envision what was no longer there – the specter of old Bingham Hall. Gradually, the Victorian details of its ornate front staircase appeared in my mind, and then the broad outdoor upper lanai (I took three years of Spanish and one of Algebra there.) where my locker had been for four years. But the surrounding geography had changed and the building's footprint eluded me. A broad lawn had replaced the road that used to enter the campus from Punahou Street. I was further disoriented by the absence of McNeil Hall, new in my time, but now replaced by the Mamiya Science Center. There was Old School Hall, where I had freshman English and Latin, just where it should be, and Dillingham Hall (Speech and Drama) had not changed. There was the buff and blue dome just where I remember it to be on Pauahi Hall. And there was Alexander Hall, a place that will play an important part of this story, where it always was.

It was a school day in February of 2007, and I had come to the campus with my camera to capture some of Punahou's current culture many years after I had experienced it. The Tamarind tree, planted by the class of 1941 to commemorate Punahou's centennial, is in the center of the main quad of the senior academy and seemed like a good vantage point to view the action. I wanted to relive and, hopefully, dispel some of the distress that had gripped me when I first came here as a wide-eyed thirteen-year-old. Punahou's values must have changed in all those years, but I was not prepared for just how much it had done so.

The bell rang, and students converged from all directions

– from the administration building Pauahi Hall (where I had had Bible Study and Speed Reading), the Mamiya Science Center (Physics and Chemistry in the old McNeil Hall), Alexander Hall (Pacific History, Geometry, U.S. History and senior English), the old Cooke Library (Typing and study hall), and several buildings that hadn't been there in the 1950s, including a new Bingham Hall. I knew that the dress code under which we had lived had evolved, especially in the '60s and '70s, but I wasn't prepared for the casual nonchalant parade that greeted me.

Was this the tradition-bound private school I remembered? Backpacks, flipflops, jeans and t-shirts and shorts? Again, the look of things was disorienting. These kids looked like members of an ordinary student body of any contemporary high school, not the fashion-conscious assemblage of beautiful people I remembered. The egalitarian desire to dress down and look like everyone else had even reached Punahou. But, of course, here the taste for grunge was somewhat sanitized. Everyone was neat and well-behaved – there were no bare midriffs or pants worn below the buttocks – but the chic swirl of fashion, so dazzling and challenging to me sixty years earlier, was gone. This Punahou just might be easier to attend than the one I had known.

When I first came to school here, I experienced Punahou through the filters of an excessive naiveté and an over-active imagination. It was not just a school but a fashionable world with a sense of place that was both fascinating and daunting. But now, as students headed for their next classes, their backpacks, shorts and flip-flops fixed my attention, and I struggled to conjure up that long-ago fashion parade in my memory.

Gradually, the pixels of that other Punahou began to

converge. The look of our wardrobe in those days was a natural result of a strict dress code. From the perspective of a skinny teenager trying to fill out his clothes, everyone seemed beautiful, and the mandatory attire only accentuated that. Backpacks and cell phones attached to ears didn't destroy the profile of our outfits then, and we all wore laced shoes – except for Lei Day when bare feet were allowed. Boys had to wear collars, and girls' dresses adhered to a proscribed length. Red carpets and runways were not yet a part of popular culture, but it seemed to me that many were competing to be the queen of the hop.

For boys, it was buck shoes, polished khaki pants, sometimes with a nonfunctional buckle at the back, and shirts with unnecessary buttons on the collars. The attire of one of our teachers from the Ivy League had impressed us with this new look, and we dutifully followed suit. Our collared aloha shirts were most often worn out of our pants, but got tucked in when we wanted to show off our very skinny suede belts. On Wednesdays, we had to wear our heavily starched ROTC uniforms. I always felt I was walking around inside an oversized layer of cardboard. Of course, there could be no *dungarees* or choked or draped pants that were common at the public schools. And there could never be a greasy *chicken ass* or hair touching our collar that would have threatened a touch of sexuality. If our mothers didn't make our clothes, we got them at McInerny, Andrade or Liberty House. I desperately tried to look like the coolest guys and would regularly inform my mother what I needed to wear.

Naturally, the girls left the most indelible impression. It was the mid-fifties, and starched crinoline underskirts were a fad, a sexy and fashionable look that took up a lot of space and attention. It seemed that more was better, and sometimes five or six crinolines inflated skirts so much that girls had to give way to each other in the hallways. The buoyancy created by all those layers of netting and air inspired a confident way of moving. Perhaps *sashaying* is the word I want. The girls all looked like Dior models. Ponytails were in vogue and many of the trendsetters wore luxuriant leis. Swaying hair and flowers, in conjunction with the swirl of those skirts, conjured up bevies of hoop-skirted southern belles.

In addition to the official dress code, there was another, unofficial one, often unspoken. There were no poodles or puffballs on skirts; this was much too common for Punahou. For some, it mattered where you got your hair done and bought your clothes; the basement salon at the Royal Hawaiian Hotel was acceptable for hair, and Winifred Dick in Waikiki and Carol and Mary downtown were respectable for clothes, and, of course, Outrigger Canoe Club logos on anything couldn't hurt. And every girl seemed to be carrying square wicker *picnic basket*-style purses that served long before backpacks became portable lockers. Carrying schoolbooks and loose-leaf folders with tabs for each class was a studied part of the look. Girls cradled these with both arms in front as ballast to counteract the sway of their skirts, and boys propped theirs on their hips at the side.

Of course, not everyone was beautiful. It just seemed that way to me. But Punahou, like any high school, had its special stars – golden girls that mesmerized me. Extra special glamour was achieved by being a cheerleader, song leader or one of the dignified ROTC sponsors. One of the girls in my class seemed to cast a spell over everyone: her style and looks cut a swath across graduating class lines. I never said a word to her in my four years of high school, but she startled me with her star quality every time I saw her.

Athletic ability and a good build conferred that status on some of the guys. Good looks and social breeding anointed the girls. They came from families that could afford the right labels and memberships in the right clubs. The culmination of this idolatry was a spring ritual when the student body conferred high status on some of these girls by choosing them to be cheer and song leaders for the following year. The cheerleaders were peppy and fun, but the song leaders seemed to have the glamour of Hollywood stars.

Lots of people could be in the annual Variety Show, but only a few had the allure to become school royalty. We voted for student body officers, too, but the theatrical quality of the song leaders was special. Moving well was imperative, and being one of Josephine Flanders' dance students was a definite advantage. But it was admittedly a popularity contest, and from ninth grade on it was fairly easy to identify who the chosen would be.

In those days, the phenomenon of the song leaders and cheer leaders was integrated into the culture of athletics. Honolulu was a small town in many ways, and high school football was a very big deal. These were the early days of television in the islands, and the professional games on the mainland were too distant to hold center stage. School spirit was a matter of pride: we wore buff and blue and held exuberant pep rallies in the gym on game days. The song and cheer leaders presided at these and were a major part of the pageantry of the games at the old wooden Honolulu Stadium, or *termite palace* as it came to be called.

In addition to my visit to the campus, I decided to visit Stadium Park that sits in a square block where the old stadium used to be. I bought some shave ice and boiled peanuts to adjust my perspective and encourage nostalgia. Looking across the park, I wondered how the old 25,000-capacity stadium could ever have fit in that space. It had to have been huge to contain the energy and excitement of those games. And didn't they hold polo matches and stock car races there too?

In my imagination, I heard the clamor of two school bands, Punahou's and our opponent's across the field. And then there were the Friday night lights and the thunder and shock waves of stomping feet rattling the creaky wooden floor boards – and a sea of buff and blue pennants and pom-poms, and banners that screamed R*ip the Roughriders, Grind the Govs* and *Trash the Tigers*. I heard fragments of cheers: "*strawberry shortcake, huckleberry pie, V-I-C-T-O-R-Y! Are we in it? Well, I guess! Punahou, Punabou, yes, yes yes!*" And then there are the songs: "*Just give 'em the hash and give 'em the gravy. Just like they do in the USA Navy! Come along, boys; treat 'em like toys! We're fighting for dear Punahou!*" And "*fight on for Buff 'n Blue,*" and "*On Oahu,*" and "*Punahou Forever.*" And there were the song leaders in their saddle shoes, blue dresses and yellow leis still performing for the crowd as if time had stopped.

But there were memories of a darker side to the stadium milieu as well. Despite a customary gesture of good will at half time when the cheerleaders and song girls traded sides and led the opponents in cheers and songs, you could still hear booing and "rap da haoles" that was born of a pervasive resentment. There was an idea that Punahou's exclusivity and money could buy football teams by offering scholarships to talented athletes. Sometimes there were fights under the bleachers, and guys from other schools would try to *scoop* or goose the Punahou girls in the crowd.

Punahou was not totally innocent of such incorrect rivalry. Every year there was a hysterical satire at one of our rallies. We were so fond of ourselves that we made fun of the cheerleaders from the public schools. It featured such girls as *Fascination Macadangdang* from Farrington, *Gracine Ginbasha* and *Sachiko Veracruz* from McKinley, *Carnation Fernandez* from Kaimuki and *Pualani Makapuuyokohamawaikikniakapueomatsu* (Hawaiian names are famous for lots of syllables.) from Kamehameha School. I wonder how they viewed us at their rallies. Today, this kind of satire is common with island comedians, but in this age of political correctness this kind of satire would never happen again at Punahou.

The ethos of athletics at Punahou is very different now. In 1970 the Interscholastic League of Honolulu was split, with the public schools going one way and the private schools another. The unfair recruiting advantage enjoyed by the private schools, particularly Punahou, was nullified, and now there are no more sports scholarships. Dr. Fox's effort to build a star-studded program is no more. Now, Punahou's major rivals are other private schools like Iolani and Kamehameha, not Roosevelt or McKinley, and the *termite palace* was torn down in 1976.

All the high school games are now played at the much larger Aloha Stadium. There are no song girls today, and those great fight songs are only remembered by alumnae support groups and junior school pep rallies. Cheerleaders appear at some of the games, but their major focus is getting PE credit, as cheerleading is now a sport in the Interscholastic League. And the glamour of the ROTC sponsors is also a thing of the past. Girls are now a part of ROTC, which is no longer required, and in 2006 Punahou's battalion commander was a female.

*****

The bell has rung, and the quad is empty now. The backpacks, cellphones, shorts and flip-flops have returned to class and I find myself sitting alone under the Tamarind tree. The campus is quiet and I wander over to the new Cooke Library and then to the front of Alexander Hall. And, again, I find myself drifting to another time.

It is Monday morning before the first bell. Laughter and the slamming of locker doors punctuate a babble of self-confidence. Girls are showing off new outfits, tans and fresh carnation leis. Guys are trying to impress each other with insults and reports of weekend conquests. I hear "Makapuu" and "Makaha" (the *in* surfing beaches) and "at the game Friday night" mixed with "at The Outrigger" (the best private beach club) and "Kau-Kau Corner" and "Kelly's." These are all the places to have been on the weekend, and everyone seems to have a story to tell. This is the front lanai of Alexander Hall, and an unspoken rule says that this is the gathering to be at.

From a safe distance and without an invitation, I would eavesdrop on this party of beautiful people as it progressed through the day. Variously, it was held on the steps of old Bingham Hall or at specified tables in Dole Cafeteria where lunch was bought – no brown bags for the beautiful people – and at the snack bar after school, or under the Monkey pod tree at canteens on Friday nights. But always, the front lanai of Alexander Hall. They were always together in twos and threes and larger groups.

"Can I have a ride?"

"I'll meet you at the dance pavilion after school."

"I'll see you at the Outrigger."

And even "Why are you talking to her? She's so unpopular."

There were no wars to protest, and our parents' politics were of little concern. I imagined intense conversations about surf conditions and cars and schemes for painting class numerals on Rocky Hill or exploding cherry bombs in study hall; which girls' bodies had started to blossom and which freshman girls were ripe for the picking; and wagers on who would have to walk with whom at graduation; and college plans and the treachery of stealing boyfriends.

These were the kids who knew how to be cool, the ones who didn't need to talk about it; they just were. My eavesdropping taught me what conferred coolness, but not how to attain it. I knew I could never become part Hawaiian or be one of Mrs. Flanders' star dancers, two circumstances that seemed to be revered by the Punahou's glitterati.

I imagined that my isolation could be cured by hanging out with the crowd that parked its cars and socialized a block from campus on Poki Street and had access to the surfing beaches, Kau-Kau Corner and Kelly's Drive-In – the crowd with the way to cash in on the value of Senior Privileges and go off campus for lunch. But I would need a car and perhaps a membership at the Outrigger. I would also need a more outgoing personality and a body that filled out my clothes better. To this end, and for a time, I attended Rex Ravelle's body building studio downtown on Bishop Street after school. That was long before ordinary people worked out in gyms, and I found myself in the exotic world of competitive body builders who oiled their bodies and wore wigs or dyed their hair. This was not what I had in mind and I soon realized that my muscles were not the bulking kind anyway.

I tried to be as inconspicuous as possible at my after-school job, but it was hard to be invisible in the school bookstore in the basement of Pauahi Hall. I imagined that working there was proof to everyone that I really couldn't afford to be at Punahou. And it was *so scholarshipish* to bring your own lunch. But once a week, my parents allowed me to leave my brown bag at home and join the ranks of the cool in the cafeteria. I always saved this privilege for the days Mrs. Early served her sautéed mahi-mahi and rice smothered in brown gravy that came with caramel cuts for dessert.

The Land of the Cool

And then everything changed for me. For the last quarter of my senior year, I had access to the "land of the cool" which I had only observed until then.

I met Sally through a friend at church a few days before that deadly auto accident at Punalu'u. Perhaps I had the cachet of being an *older man* – she was a sophomore and I was a senior. My picture in the Oahuan had me looking about twelve years old, but I **was** older and, I guess the wisdom of age was catnip to a fifteen-year-old girl. At any rate, this *going steady* episode in my high school career caught me completely by surprise. I had never had any reason to think of myself as a lady's man.

Nevertheless, I was allowed into the social circle of the *brainy/popular* group of the class of 1959. Suddenly, I had access to what I had longed for. Sally was cute and fun, and she was part of a ready-to-order, dare I say *clique?* - and she had a car! *Pooze* was a bright pink 1932 Model A Ford with a rumble seat, and it, and we, made quite a stir wherever we went. I became part of that car crowd on Poki Street and I had regular access to the popular beaches and Kau-Kau Corner and all the other cool places that everyone talked about on the Alexander Hall lanai. Sally didn't come with a membership to the Outrigger Club, but I became too busy to notice. Now, again, at the end of my Punahou career, I experienced a bout of culture shock as I went from being a *wannabe* to part of a popular crowd. True, it was someone else's crowd, and, even today, I wonder why I allowed myself to be so comfortable with this younger group when my own class continued to unnerve me. But my parents were delighted to see me blossom into a real teenager. Of course, we didn't have perspective on it yet, but we were the first generation of a thoroughly teen culture in the history of the world. That might have begun just after the war, but it wasn't in full flower until the 1950s.

After a one-month *engagement,* by May 18th, we were going steady, something many teens did for the social security if offered. By the stroke of a declaration to Sally, I had garnered all the coolness that I had ever wanted. I could relate to all the songs I was now dancing to – something we called *the bop.* There were *Party Doll, Young Love, At the Hop, Love is Strange, and April Love.* Sally and I even had *our song* – *Little Darlin'* by a group called The Diamonds.

I should have been finishing my senior theme and studying for finals, but there were beach picnics, boat rides on the Ala Wai Canal, movies at the Waikiki and Kuhio Theaters, hamburgers and shakes at Kau Kau Corner, Tops and The Jolly Roger; a rock and roll show at the 49th State Fair, and a breakfast of pancakes and poi after an all-niter to watch the Night-blooming Cereus appear on the Punahou wall with a sunrise at Makapuu beach. And parties – lots of parties.

Sally and I gave a very successful *blalah* (local hoodlums) party: everyone came wearing sideburns, chicken asses, drape pants, tight skirts and too much make-up – not very PC of us, but, of course, no one had heard of that in those days.

We celebrated our going steady and our one-month anniversary with gifts and a date to the Holoku Ball on campus. I gave her a Tommy Sands album, and she gave me a pair of Makaha shorts and a Kona hat. Sally made us matching Ivy League outfits for the dance – an Ivy League holoku with buttons on the collar to match my shirt. Before dinner at her house, her father served us each one weak Old Fashioned, and later we piled into Pooze and motored to the dance.

One day during finals weeks, because of the safety that Sally offered and this new group of *best friends,* I found myself sitting in a group autographing yearbooks – on the front lanai of Alexander Hall – that hallowed spot that I used to think was reserved only for the best. There I was among them as if I belonged, and indeed, I finally did belong because I had a group to be part of. Sally and I happily continued our rounds of going steady throughout the rest of the summer, and then I left for college in Oregon at the start of September. Our lives went in different directions, but we are still in contact with each other today.

2007: *Coming to Terms . . .*

She drives a BMW and carries a Starbucks' cup, several credit cards and her father's membership to the Oahu Country Club – and she dates Shallow Ken and Private School Scooter. The tone of this *Punahou Barbie* that I recently received in a satirical email certainly doesn't dispel the stuck up *P-U-nahou* of sixty years ago. Other reports reveal that Punahou students are still seen as "classier," and prestige is conferred on their families who are sometimes accused of not supporting public education when they send their kids there. Had nothing changed?

But, on closer inspection, and a nod to a Russian satellite in the late '50s and the social revolution of the '60s, it is clear that Punahou has gone through a cultural revolution. In the fall of 1957, just as our class had departed, Punahou was thrust into the future. Sputnik sent shock waves through every educational institution in the country. Punahou, too, would have to catch up with the Russians.

On my visit to check out the school's current ethos, I obtained a copy of Punahou's current course listing. Four years at Punahou wouldn't be nearly enough time to take all the classes that teased me from the list. The curriculum reflected a multi-culturalism that we didn't know in the '50s. Students in my day were required to take one semester of Pacific History and there was the Hawaiian Lore Club, but now courses include Hawaiian Culture and four levels of the Hawaiian language. One can also take five levels each of Japanese and Mandarin. Many Advanced Placement courses are listed, and a tempting schedule could include Advanced Photography, Digital Art, Video Art, Asian Calligraphy, Ideas in Western Literature, The Elizabethan Age, Astronomy, Anthropology, Oceanography, Robotic Engineering, Genetics, Global Issues, The History of the Sixties and Independent Study in Theater. This was all in high school.

Today, new students are given buddies, and all ninth graders go to a summer bonding camp before entering the senior academy. This places a great importance on valuing the community and acknowledging and celebrating differences. Furthermore, a community service component is integrated into the curriculum and is a prominent graduation requirement. I know that this would have made a vast difference in the isolation and culture shock that confronted me in my time. A citizenship grade is controlled by a system which allows students to work off demerits. And the dress code – today it's a quasi-uniform – doesn't encourage competition. When Punahou's dress became too lax in the 1970s, consultants adjusted it. Now, students can wear approved vendor-supplied garments that have taken the sexuality – some say individuality – out of the wardrobes. Longer, less clingy t-shirts, knee-length shorts, and Punahou logo wear keep wardrobes pretty neutral and discourage extreme peer pressure. There is no longer the message that an important achievement is to be the prettiest.

As part of my visit to the Punahou Carnival in 2007, I was able to snag one of a very few remaining seats to the annual Variety Show, a production I had appeared in several times. This year it had a James Bond theme, *Special Agent 2 – Mission: Demerits are Forever*. Even from the balcony I could tell that one of the characters wasn't played by a teenager. There was something about the stance and the timbre of the voice. It's hard to imagine Dr. Fox, *the Great White Father* appearing in a variety show in my day, but there was Jim Scott, Punahou's current president, performing along with the rest of the cast. This gesture struck me as symptomatic of a radical change in Punahou's ethos. A significant democratization seems to be part of creating a student body that reflects the makeup of the community at large. Today, Punahou is ranked on par with such eastern prep schools as Exeter and Groton. It is interesting that New Englanders founded those schools *as well as Punahou*. But, Punahou is larger (kindergarten through twelfth grade) and accommodates a wider range of abilities and ethnic backgrounds.

The *coming to terms* referred to in the title of this chapter didn't start in earnest until my retirement from teaching in 2001. Not that the cult of Punahou was ever out of my mind for very long, and not that Punahou would ever allow that. But the feeling of *ohana* (family) that Punahou tenaciously tries to foster in its graduates had eluded me – when I was a student and since then. True, I looked forward to reading the periodic Punahou Bulletin to see what the people of my day were up to. But that was mostly out of curiosity, and I couldn't imagine my name ever appearing there. By the time I left teaching, however, the empathetic front part of my brain had been developed, and I was no longer ruled by a teenage ego. I was emotionally ready and had the time to make a project of leaving peer pressure hell behind me. It was about time my name appeared in the Bulletin as an effort to dispel the anonymity I had felt for so long. All I needed to do, I discovered, was to contact our class correspondent, and my name and a personal update promptly appeared there.

*****

One day, my brother and I were leaving Long's Drug Store at the Manoa Marketplace. I looked up just in time to see a statuesque figure in dark glasses enter the other automatic door. I took one more step and suddenly I was transported once again to the front lanai of Alexander Hall. Telling my brother to wait in the car, I gathered all the self-possession that sixty years had conferred on me and I went back into the store.

She had taken off her dark glasses and I was sure who she was. Still radiant, she was the star who had cast a spell over me in high school – and she was shopping in *my* Long's. It had never occurred to me that, away from the Punahou campus, she and I would ever inhabit the same space. I introduced myself. I'm not sure she remembered exactly who I was, but I told her we were classmates in another time. And then more words tumbled out, and I heard myself telling her that she had dazzled me years earlier.

And then we were having a real conversation, and we talked about the coming reunion in June and living in Manoa Valley, and she pointed out her son who was in the next aisle. I felt as if I should be asking for her autograph, but, no, we were actually talking with each other, and I pictured us on the Alexander Hall lanai in 1957. It seemed like the easiest thing in the world. Why wasn't it then? Of course, we were both different people; no longer the misfit of my imagination, I had lived an eventful life and had nothing to apologize for.

I said I hoped to see her at the reunion, and I took her hand with a touch that I hoped conveyed the lightness I was feeling. As I walked away, I felt that a burden had lifted. And then, before I went to tell my brother what had happened, I turned back for one more look. She was still as stylish and beautiful as I remembered. It is now 2023, and, at another recent reunion I have learned that that golden girl has passed away. I was shocked and saddened.

*****

June 1, 2007. Tomorrow I will fly to Honolulu for the fiftieth reunion and I still need a suitable ending for this memoir.

Looking for inspiration, I searched through a pile of dusty artifacts that littered my desk. I had bought a magnifying glass so I could see the faces in my group graduation picture. There I was – five rows up and three to the left of center – among all those expectant faces, seemingly attentive and alert, no different from the other 268 of us. Why did I think I was an impossible misfit when I was seventeen?

I had also tracked down the recording of our graduation songs. Having finally found a machine that would play it, I discovered the sound quality was not what I remembered. But, there we were – the exuberant anthem *I Believe*, a lilting *Pua Carnation*, and the up-tempo *Hole Waimea* that was so much fun to sing. I tried to transcribe it and come up with: *Ku aka hika pahu/ ku aka awe awe/ hana lei keiki kala o hilo kini* . . . At least that's how the words sounded, but I left off deciding it was useless to drive my computer's spell check crazy. For years that refrain was tucked in my brain and I couldn't get rid of it. Eventually, time took it away – until I put the needle back on the recording. And I relived the *chicken skin* I felt on graduation night as I heard the last song, a triumphant *Oahu'a,* the school alma mater.

On the same upper shelf where I found the recording, there is my copy of the 1957 Oahuan. My picture makes me look like an innocent twelve-year-old. I am startled to find about a dozen activities next to my name. Was I really that busy and involved? Could I have had more of a high school life than I remembered?

I uncovered the biography request for the fifty-years-later memory book that I had wrestled with a few months earlier. Tucked into the form was a startling list that I hadn't noticed at first. These were the classmates who are no longer with us, and I expected to see the names of the three girls who were killed in our senior year. But I was shocked by all the others. Fifty years had taken its toll, and the length of that list made me feel like a survivor. I found the pictures I took while sitting under the Tamarind tree in February. These kids, two generations younger than I, with their backpacks and flip-flops could be my grandchildren. Perhaps this is all I needed to let Punahou off the hook and stop massaging the ache that my subconscious had grown tired of.

Yesterday, I was looking through a small book called The Four Agreements by Don Miguel Ruiz. *Be impeccable with your word; don't take anything personally; don't make assumptions; always do your best.* I wish we had all been in possession of that new age wisdom when we were in high school. Back then, I spent four years flouting every one of those rules. I hadn't yet learned that most of us were not part of that rarified in-crowd. Now, finally comfortable in my own skin and even though I'm still a relatively skinny guy, I have come to know that I was, and have always been, as cool as I will ever need to be.

With this self-assessment and the confidence of a new smile, I attended the Carnival in February, 2007 and the fiftieth reunion in June. An orthodontist had adjusted a gap in my front teeth and I was suddenly smiling more than I had ever done before. I had a great time working in the carnival hamburger booth with a few of my classmates. And in June, armed with copies of this memoir, I went to the reunion and luau. I passed around my writing and suddenly I found myself on the map. I was no longer the anonymous kid I had imagined myself to be fifty years earlier at graduation. I was now a writer who had been willing to express what many others had been feeling as well. I had broken the ice about a subject that had festered in many psyches other than mine.

There was a collective relief that we could now talk about something we had all been feeling for many years. I made some new friends at that reunion, friends who I could have been close to many years before if I had allowed it.

It is now 2023 and a recent list tells me that nearly two-thirds of our original class is gone. I seem to be a survivor. A small number of us had returned to live in Hawaii, but many of us are scattered around the country probably near the universities Punahou had sent us to. I was one of those as I live in California now. Each time I receive the Punahou Bulletin, I scour its pages for news of the school, but also to read the class notes that catch me up on the lives of my classmates. Each time I do that, I realize that, despite what I felt at one time, I am now very happy to be part of the Punahou *ohana*, the Punahou family.

Punahou's Revered Lily Pond

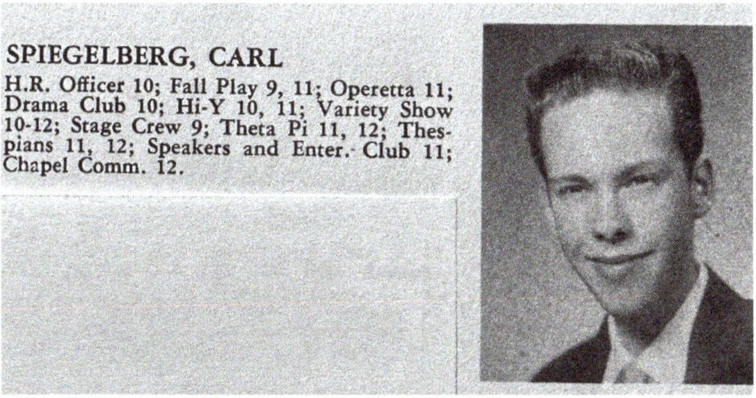

SPIEGELBERG, CARL
H.R. Officer 10; Fall Play 9, 11; Operetta 11; Drama Club 10; Hi-Y 10, 11; Variety Show 10-12; Stage Crew 9; Theta Pi 11, 12; Thespians 11, 12; Speakers and Enter. Club 11; Chapel Comm. 12.

Looking Twelve Years Old in my Punahou Yearbook

Living With My Stagestruck Right Brain
(1946 – 2023)

I have to admit that I had decidedly conflicted feelings when I retired from a successful 37-year teaching career in 2001. My high school English and Drama classes, along with the hundreds of play productions I directed, had filled those years with a lot of joy. On the day I received my gold watch, however, I was elated that getting up wouldn't happen at six A.M. anymore, my evenings would not be shackled with student papers entertaining my red pen, and sometimes contentious school politics would no longer be a time-consuming distraction. I was relieved and thankful for all of that.

But I was leaving something behind as well. For the last twenty-one years (2022) there has been an open place in my heart. I have missed playing *let's pretend* with *my family* of drama students and the great fun we had putting on all those shows together.

But neither greasepaint, footlights nor playhouses were foretold for me when I was born in Honolulu at the end of 1939. You see, mine was not a theatrical family. I wasn't born in a backstage trunk at the Princess Theater as Judy Garland once sang about. Nor was there a refrain of *There's No Business Like Show Business* sounding in the wings at my birth. My early backstory, first at Queen's Hospital and then a childhood in upper Manoa Valley, did not suggest that I would one day *tread the boards* or direct others who did that.

And, besides, I was a shy kid from the very start. So, where, I wonder, did my right brain imagination and theatrical leanings come from?

This was especially puzzling because I see now that those leanings might have entirely succumbed to my innate bashfulness before they even had had a chance to bloom. My tension-induced perspiration and heart thumps were symptoms of a timidity that often engulfed me. I didn't even have imaginary friends or a dog. That initial fear of the world may have cut short what eventually became my lifelong engagement with theater, an endeavor that requires a lot of interplay with other people. But, I didn't let it do so. I was an introvert, but I did pursue a long theatrical career in spite of that.

I'm not usually perceived as someone who would shine on a stage. My quiet nature has been with me from the very beginning. But, contradictorily, I've been tugged at by theaters and anything theatrical since I was very young. My social reticence may have been engendered because my dad was an introvert as well, I had no cousins to learn socializing with (my extended family all lived on the mainland), and I was a skinny kid with a very baby face. I was always afraid my classmates didn't take me seriously.

I was caught between a desire to hide away and a quiet urge to show myself on a stage. Self-conscious around other people, especially strangers, I was surprisingly bold in front of an audience. It just depended on which side of the *footlights* I found myself. I guess you could say I suffered from a kind of offstage stage fright, which I have learned I share with many other actors, Lawrence Olivier and Meryl Streep to name two. I am in very good company, it seems. What draws all of us to a spotlight in spite of feeling that fear? I don't think it's the mostly elusive fame and fortune. Despite our sweaty palms, some of us use that added adrenalin to intensify our performances.

I often found myself tongue tied as a kid, afraid I'd say the wrong thing, so I felt more comfortable with the security of a script. Some of my social *stage fright* has gradually retreated as I have grown older, probably because I use my acting skills to trick myself into confidence and because I've learned that the world is not my enemy. But, sometimes, at the prospect of socializing with other people, I've had to make a mental list of topics to talk about and practice things to say as if learning lines for a play. Just so, rehearsed words of a playwright are sometimes more accessible to me than my own.

I'm uncomfortable reporting that in high school, I never greeted other people first. Ever afraid of rejection, I guarded myself by not giving them a chance to offend me. As a young adult, I always hated the social dance of negotiating cocktail parties, which I sometimes went to on the off-chance possibility of meeting someone interesting. Making small talk and then trying to gracefully move on to someone else unnerved me. I usually tried to latch on to someone as a life preserver, but often I was set adrift when they, too, moved on. Even when I didn't have to use it, a restroom with a locked door was a handy escape. I could be alone to mentally recharge, check my hair and then enter the fray again.

In mapping the human brain in the 1960s, scientists determined that each of its two hemispheres appeared to have separate specialties. It seems that, for most people, one side of the brain is more dominant than the other. The left hemisphere is often host to facts, logic, linear thinking and mathematics. The right side is stronger in feelings, imagination, intuition, and the arts. My school grades have consistently shown that I am a poor math student. On the other hand, my interest in the humanities and arts, especially theater, keep the right side of my brain humming. I suppose the synapses dancing together in my right brain have also helped to energize my otherwise quiet personality. I wonder if those scientists have discovered a part of the brain that generates shyness.

My immediate family doesn't share my right brain energy or theatrical interests. Dad was an analytical left-brained scientist focused on his plant pathology experiments with pineapples and his home garden. Mom was a practical stay-at-home housewife, too busy raising three kids to follow cultural pursuits. But I wonder if there had been an artistic calling she may have ignored in order to take care of my brother and sister and me. My more athletic younger siblings displayed no theatrical bent, nor did anyone else in my extended family that I know of. Early on, my right brain indicated to me that I would not be a scientist as Dad had been, but show business was in my pulse from the start. Why was I, alone in my family, endowed with those inclinations? Half my DNA came from my mother and half from my father. If I go back far enough on my family tree, perhaps there were right-brain leanings that eventually got passed down to me.

The DNA I was born with naturally emphasized the right side of my brain, but that was only a start. I would also need external cues to set those genetics in motion. Unfortunately, the arts and pop culture didn't have a strong presence in our home when I was a kid. Maybe because it was war time, I wasn't taken to concerts, theater or even movies, and television didn't come to Hawaii until I was a teenager in the early 1950s. We didn't have a record player either, so there wasn't any background music, show tunes or otherwise, accompanying my early childhood.

But I wasn't completely deprived. Here and there, culture did sneak in around the edges. I can't remember how old I was when I was signed up for piano lessons, though eventually it became clear that my talents lay elsewhere.

"You'll be happy you took these lessons when you grow up. Playing the piano will make you popular. You can do it at parties," Mom urged.

"I don't want to be popular."

"Of course, you do. You'll understand when you're older."

So, off to piano lessons I went. Creating music is certainly a right-brain art form, but playing the piano also depends on a sensitivity to mathematical motifs and nimble dexterity, not my strong suits. Our Victorian upright piano, inherited from Grandma, sat untuned and, except for an occasional sloppy but enthusiastic rendering of *Chopsticks*, unused on our indoor lanai.

National Geographic, *Life Magazine* and, later, *Boy's Life* came to us regularly. *Life* was my favorite, and I looked forward to it appearing in our mailbox every week. All those photographs gave me an early view of the world before I was exposed to newsreels in movie theaters or on TV news shows. In addition to world events, *Life* also covered movies, theater and celebrities, all of which drew my close attention. Another, more exciting world, it seemed, lay out there beyond the confines of my childhood in Manoa Valley.

The Honolulu Star-Bulletin showed up every evening on our driveway, with its comics like *Dennis the Menace,* an attraction called *Believe It or Not* and tantalizing movie ads. And, because it was deemed "educational and a good investment" by Dad, The *Encyclopedia Britannica*, the Google of its time, had a prominent place on our bookcase. Now, the Internet has made those books practically useless.

Another cultural diversion engaged us because of the presence of a 1940s Zenith console radio in our living room. I remember the excitement of turning its tantalizing dial to find music, comedy, and especially acted-out stories. At the time, I wondered how all that content came to us without wires. We would sit around the radio with our imaginations fully tuned picturing the action only suggested by the tone of the actors' voices and sound effects. Some of my favorites were *Jack Benny, Edgar Bergen and Charlie McCarthy, The Lone Ranger,* and *Dick Tracy.*

"I want to listen to *Charley McCarthy,*" I would usually suggest.

"I want *The Lone Ranger,*" my brother would chime in.

Mom and Dad went for *Jack Benny*, but I was really happy with any of it, even the commercials: Kool-Aid, Jell-o, Ivory Soap and Coca-Cola. Because I was comfortably at home with my family, those radio plays erased my self-consciousness and any doubts I harbored about my worthiness. If plays could accomplish that, I definitely wanted more of them. They were my first brush with theater of any kind, and I was hooked. Those shows made me want to tell stories too.

In order to help tell my meandering show business tale, several aging scrapbooks, photo albums and journals have come off a shelf in my office. Filled with yellowing snapshots, slick professional composite photos, crumbling newspaper articles, a sizable collection of theater programs and personal performance reviews, they have played their part in jarring my memory of stops on my right-brain journey.

That path was further encouraged when Mom regularly took me downtown to the main Honolulu library, where I could choose books in the children's room that, early on, were read to me, and later I read myself. Of course, *Mother Goose*, Beatrix Potter and classics like *Cinderella* and *Hansel and Gretel* came first. But the Internet has reminded me of other children's books from the 1940s that we brought home from the library: *Babar the Elephant, The Wind in the Willows, Lazy Liza Lizard, Mr. Popper's Penguins, Curious George,* and Dr. Seuss's early books *Horton Hatches an Egg* and *The Five Hundred Hats of Bartholomew Cubbins.* I must admit that *Little Black Sambo* is now embarrassing and not politically correct, but I guess it was acceptable in those days. I wonder if that story is read to kids today. Those children's books always had wonderful illustrations, which helped alert my imagination, just as sound effects had in the radio plays.

One year, for my birthday, I was given a book called *Black Beauty* about a well-bred horse before the age of automobiles. I was captivated by the book, especially because it was *my* book, I didn't have to return it to the library, and holding it and turning its pages produced a muscle memory that would fuel a lifelong habit. I fell in love with words, which wonderfully spun characters and other worlds off the page to me. Soon to follow would be *Treasure Island, Robinson Crusoe* and most of the Hardy Boys mysteries.

To make reading more fun, some of my grade school teachers acted out book reports with props and costumes as if they were short plays. Another aspect of pop-culture snuck into our home when I spent my allowance on comic books. At first they were Disney and *Tarzan*, then *Archie and*

Jughead and later, *Tales Calculated to Drive You Mad*. Then I collected all the *Classics Illustrated* comics based on famous novels and plays. Mom thought that was a great idea, and she supported me spending my dimes that way.

My right brain was further tickled by class activities in grade school. Because my parents saved them for me, I have the end-of-year reports from all of my elementary school teachers. Here is what Mrs. McCleery had to say about me in June, 1948 after third grade:

Carl has a wide range of interests and shows a creative quality of mind. He made some delightful clay models, wrote a play, worked on puppets, wrote a poem and asked the teacher to help him write music for it. He is very creative in writing, painting and modeling. He enjoys sharing stories during our library period. He enjoyed having the role of The Sandman in our dramatization of Hansel and Gretel and worked hard to give a good performance. He is attentive and absorbed during the story hour.

It seems that Mrs. McCleery saw me as a third grade Renaissance kid: clay modeler, playwright, actor, puppeteer, poet, composer and painter. I now notice that most of those activities were solitary endeavors that I could pursue on my own, without interacting with other kids. Mrs. McCleery didn't mention my shyness, but I guess I did conquer that enough to play the Sandman in the *Hansel and Gretel* play.

I had no idea I was so accomplished back then. Were other kids getting those same rave reviews? What did my parents think of this kid they had produced? Of course, that glorified information in Mrs. McCleery's report was intended for them, but I wonder what it would have done for my self-confidence if I had known about it at that time too. Perhaps her enthusiastic reviews would have softened my self-doubts about not being a talented athlete like other boys seemed to be. But apparently I had compensating talents that had showed up by the time I was in third grade.

No matter if they are right-brained or left-brained or both, most kids are natural born actors. You can't avoid hearing "let's pretend" when watching kids at play. "Let's pretend I'm the mommy and you're the daddy."

"Let's pretend you are the doctor, and I'm the patient. You pretend to give me a shot, and I'll pretend to cry."

"Let's pretend I'm a cop, and you're a robber. Stick 'em up! Bang, you're dead!" we would shout at each other pointing our fingers.

We were our own audience, and there was no applause, but a lot of our games involved role-playing that imitated the lives of adults. We played school, doctor, war, and house. In between games of hide-and-seek, riding bikes and tending to my rock and stamp collections, I acted out all of those story lines at one time or another with my multi-racial neighborhood playmates. We took cues from radio shows, magazines, comic books and cowboy movies.

When we were small kids, we were living through World War Two which inspired our war games, and all we had to do to play *house* was look around us and imitate the scenarios we lived with. Playing school meant one of us would be the teacher, and playing doctor was inspired by our school check-ups at the Honolulu Medical Group. My *let's pretend* suggestions almost always leaned toward the theatrical.

"Let's pretend you're an actor, and I'm the director. Let's put on a show." It was as if I was a neighborhood Mickey Rooney and Judy Garland rolled into one.

My future as a stage director was clearly suggested early on, as everything our family did was fodder for my re-creation. I always wanted to bring the real world home with me:

Dad's office (we shuffled papers, answered our toy telephones and pretended to take notes);

Restaurants (we served Graham Crackers and Kool-Aid to each other in paper cups and on paper plates);

The public library (we took books from home and taped lending cards in them);

The Honolulu Star Bulletin (we hand printed a weekly paper for a time that we delivered to neighbors).

And the rituals at St. Andrew's Cathedral: I restaged a wedding in our living room, with dining room chairs as pews, a small table as the altar and garden flowers to decorate. As a theatrical touch, I think I even put down a white sheet in the aisle for the bride to walk on. Perhaps my brother and a neighbor friend were the bride and groom, and I was the minister. Mom, Dad and Grandma, who was living with us then, were the guests, or *audience* as I thought of them.

Although I didn't see it that way at the time, that wedding was probably my earliest outing as a director. I staged it to re-create the ceremonial quality of the real wedding that had engaged me so much. I think I instinctively knew that the St. Andrews Cathedral setting, with all its stained glass and Gothic arches, was like an elaborate theater with a section for the *audience* as well as the *performers*.

Despite my introversion, I always wanted to be the ringleader of our kid-time neighborhood enterprises. My shyness seemed to abate around close friends – and when my right brain took control at the prospect of a theatrical undertaking. I wonder if my interest in theater was a compensation for my childhood shyness. They seemed to cancel each other out. One engages the world and the other shies away from it. Everyone involved in theater has a role to play, either on or offstage. Shy people can hide inside those roles which were sometimes my social salvation when I was a kid. I wonder if other actors feel more comfortable talking to characters in a play than when confronting real people.

A particular *production* that I *ringled* was inspired by a nearby forested empty lot where someone had discarded some large packing crates. I saw the possibility of a miniature town with houses and stores.

"Let's pretend I'm the mayor, and all of you live in these houses. Who will sell things to the other people?"

I was constantly on the lookout for the possibility of a stage. There was an arch-like entranceway (I eventually learned to call it a *proscenium arch.)* between our dining room and indoor lanai where I strung up sheets as theater curtains. Any elevated area became a stage in my mind. Our front porch was slightly raised from the garden, and, because there was no railing, I would set up chairs on the lawn to create a theater. Two poles supporting the porch roof delineated our playing area, and, once again, I strung up old sheets on a wire between them. I was fascinated by curtains opening to reveal something different on the other side.

One of my Keahi Street playmates had a marionette theater that caught my envious attention. I certainly loved the marionettes – there was a king, a princess and a witch – but it was the backstage intricacy of the theater itself that fascinated me the most. I could pull open the curtain and look into the miniature layers of scenery, into the wings and onto the backdrops that could be moved in and out. The look and workings of that toy theater provided my first vision of how the backstage of a theater worked. I think my specific desire to direct plays was seeded with wanting to manipulate all those technical layers. I'm sure other boys were wrapping themselves around baseball cards, model trains and trucks. But not me. My right brain consistently reminded me that I wasn't generally a techie kind of guy, except when it came to the workings of back stage technology.

Sometimes our efforts were invented on the spot, but at least one of those plays was scripted. I recently found a roughly hand-printed one-page copy of *I Lost My Wife* in a file of childhood memories my parents had saved for me. Looking at the handwriting and my spelling, I couldn't have been more than seven or eight years old when I wrote it. I think it might have been the play Mrs. McCleery said I wrote in third grade. I have no idea what had inspired the story. And I wonder how I even knew what a play script was at that age. Here is an exact transcript of my play:

I Lost My Wife
Actors: Harrison and Aileen. (my brother and sister.)
Seen 1 [sic]
Joe comes out and looks for his wife.
Seen 2
Joe goes into his house.
Seen 3
Joe eates [sic] dinner and goes to sleep.
Seen 4 A wile [sic] later.
Joe gets up and eats breakfast and then goes out side [sic]. He sees his wife and kisses her.
The End

That cryptic opus, with an Aristotelian beginning, middle and end, and a classic denouement with a happy ending, was my first attempt at playwriting. There would be others. I seemed to know what conflict was and also how to resolve it. I guess I had an innate sense of how plays (stories) were structured. My brother and sister don't remember this play, but my copy of the script is evidence enough that at least I had written it, and I'm sure I would have wanted to stage it too. If I was seven or so, Harrison was five and Aileen was only one. I guess Harrison could have been talked into playing Joe as there were no lines to learn. Aileen was still a baby, so maybe my friend Tricia stood in, and I was the narrator. This was the kind of event that parents were dutifully required to attend. We may have received a standing ovation. We were learning that one of the best things about putting on shows was that we received the encouragement of applause. And we were probably also figuring out how to elicit more of that with curtain calls. There were lots of bows.

But the best *pretend theater* in our neighborhood was in my playmate Tricia's basement. It was a finished room on two levels, with the *stage* about three feet off the floor. We hung even more sheets on a wire stretched between two posts, and, with the guidance of Tricia's older sister Louise, we staged a program of vignettes based on children's nursery rhymes: *Twinkle, Twinkle, Little Star; Peter, Peter Pumpkin Eater;* and *Little Bo Peep.*

"I want to be the narrator," I piped up. "You guys can act out the parts."

"Why don't you stand on the right side of the stage, and little Bo Peep and Peter can stand on the left," Louise suggested.

We *choreographed* the movement with an eye to how the action looked. That would always be an important hallmark of my direction in the future. I had an artist's eye for the composition of the stage picture. Over the years, I learned that directing a show is like sculpting. You roughly mold the larger piece, then you whittle away and fine-tune until you are focused on the best version of the play's essence. Again, I don't know where all that came from; I guess it was instinct, part of my DNA.

We scrounged costumes and props from our bedrooms and closets, and, of course, our parents and friends loved our show. More applause. We had the satisfaction of a project well received and a sense of camaraderie, a feeling that has been a part of every show I have ever been involved with. The loneliness I sometimes felt as a shy kid could be assuaged by the family-like social structure of putting on a show. The production itself was the glue that held us together for the run of the project. As rehearsals turned into performances, our casts became tight-knit temporary tribes. Even at that age, I was learning that everyone had to do his part for the show to go on. Long before I knew that show business anthem, I was learning that *there's no business like show business*. And realizing that my shyness diminished when I felt I was a necessary part of the proceedings.

It now turns out that Tricia (Patricia) Palmer is my oldest friend. We are about the same age (early 80s now, 2023) and grew up on Keahi Street a few houses from each other. Our kid-time theatrical exploits cemented our friendship at an early age, and we still reminisce about the early triumphs we cooked up at her house or at mine.

"Remember the time we pretended to have a store in my living room, and we sold my mother's perfume bottles to each other?" Tricia recently asked me.

"Or the time we pretended to be the mailman and *sent* valentines?" I added.

"Or when we were fortune tellers with the Ouija Board?"

We also took dance classes together as teenagers in hopes

of being cast in musicals. Tricia went on to study dance and make a career of it as a teacher. We graduated from high school together and still make an attempt to regularly see each other. Today, she is in rural northern California and I am in Walnut Creek, California.

I had an ability to ferret out theaters wherever they were. I discovered two real theaters in Honolulu that I had access to when I could sneak in. Tenney Hall, complete with a real stage, curtains, stage lights and a raked audience area, was part of the St. Andrew's Cathedral complex. My Sunday school room was around the corner in the same building. The door was usually unlocked, and, after Sunday school, I could creep into the mostly dark theater and feel my way up some stairs onto the stage. The *ghost light,* which is required for safety on a dark stage helped me grope my way. One time, I found the rope for the main curtain and pulled it open. No one stopped me! I would peer into the dark and pretend an audience was out there.

The other real theater was an outdoor amphitheater called the Andrews Theater on the University of Hawaii campus near my Dad's office. The background scenery on a very large raised stage was an extensive rock garden of living tropical plants. There was an auditorium of possibly 5000 seats, and I think they held university graduations and perhaps Lei Day pageants there. When we were waiting to pick Dad up from work, I would sometimes sneak into the empty theater to face an imaginary audience from that stage. I attempted to be loud enough to fill that huge space.

But any theater, inside or outside, excited me. There were quite a few movie theaters in Honolulu in those days, and, once I got to be of movie-going age, I loved those too. There was lots of neon on the marquees and lofty vertical signs spelling out the name of the theater. They always had separate box-office structures, with glassed-in displays of current and coming films. The words *Now Playing* could easily set my heart thumping.

When our family was on road trips on the mainland in 1949 and 1958, I always wanted to drive to the center of every town, where the movie theaters were. I am disappointed that time hasn't been kind to downtown theaters, and most of them have now disappeared. My favorite movie theaters in Honolulu were the spectacular Waikiki and the Kuhio theaters near the beach as well as the neighborhood Pawaa and Varsity near Manoa Valley. The Waikiki had a reverberating theater organ which made festive events of seeing movies there. The post-war innovation of air-conditioning, along with the smell of popcorn and Raisinets, set off all the theaters as arresting places where good guys and bad guys and anyone else could appear on a big screen. Sadly, alll of those theaters are gone now.

Our parents took Harrison, Aileen and me to all the animated Disney features, like *Snow White, Song of the South, Cinderella,* and *Peter Pan.* And I have a clear memory of another Technicolor film from those early years, called *Lassie, Come Home* (1943). I was thoroughly taken with anything that moved on a movie screen or on TV after it came to Hawaii in 1954. But I was especially fond of big Technicolor films like *Samson and Delilah* (1949), *King Solomon's Mines* (1950), *Quo Vadis* (1951) and *The Greatest Show on Earth* (1952). Some of those were called *roadshow releases* because they were special event films, often epics with casts of thousands. The tickets were more expensive, there were reserved seats and sometimes an intermission. I was very impressed. About that same time, a dying gasp of vaudeville came to the downtown King Theater with trained dogs, song and dance acts and a movie. The heyday of vaudeville had been well before my time, so I wonder why those acts had made their way to Hawaii as late as the early '50s.

And then there were musicals like *Singing in the Rain* (1952), *Seven Brides for Seven Brothers* (1954) and the pyrotechnics and moving water of Esther Williams films. I loved the comedy of Abbott and Costello and Bob Hope, and, a bit later, anything directed by Alfred Hitchcock – *Rear Window* (1954) and *The Man Who Knew Too Much* (1956). For a time, I was enthralled by science fiction: *When Worlds Collide* and *The Day the Earth Stood Still* (both from 1951). And, as time moved on, any film directed by Billy Wilder or Federico Fellini. Throughout my kid-time movie going years, I was excited about a series of movie marvels that came to Honolulu theaters: first there was Three D, then Cinemascope, and later Vista Vision, Todd A-O and Cinerama. And back when double features were in style, I loved the idea of getting two for one.

I was susceptible to the starry-eyed photos and stories about ecstatic movie stars in magazines (*Modern Screen, Silver Screen* and *Photoplay*) which I saw in the drug store where I bought my comic books. I was young enough that I fell for the fairy tale propaganda they published. And in keeping with my desire to bring the real world home with me, one summer I created my own movie theater in a friend's darkened garage, where I set up an 8mm movie projector. Each week, I regularly listened to a radio show sponsored by Lux Soap. *The Lux Radio Theater* presented popular movies in the form of radio scripts. My heart stirred when they would announce *Direct From Hollywood* at the beginning of each program. With absolutely no thought to how talented I was, I over-optimistically hatched a plan to become a movie star. I too would appear in those movie magazines – as soon as I was discovered.

Anything with a touch of showiness engaged me as a kid. I loved people-watching at Manoa Market Place, and each year we would go to the *Aloha Week Parade* that featured floats, marching bands and princesses from each of the neighbor islands riding side-saddle on decorated horses. I have always loved parade floats, which magically move stage sets and action along the street. *The Tournament of Roses* on January 1, 1949 and again in 1958 were dramatic high points of that phenomenon for me. Hawaii had an annual *49th State Fair*, with exhibits and rides that promised more excitement. At that time, Hawaii thought it would be admitted to the Union before Alaska, but Alaska was admitted in January of '59 and Hawaii was in August. So, we became the 50th state. And then there was the Roller Derby at the old Civic Auditorium. I eventually learned that, like wrestlers, the Derby stars were putting on a show of being tough. We pretended to be them when we roller-skated on our street.

"You be the Blond Bomber, and I'll be Blossom Rodriguez," one of us would suggest.

"Toughie is my favorite. Someone has to be her."

"I'll be Toughie, and let's use our pretend tattoos to make us look really scary like they do."

There was always a Christmas play at Sunday school. I think I was a shepherd more than once. I may have said something like,

"Let us go to Bethlehem and see what the Lord has made known to us."

Or was I an elf in a grade school play? Probably both. Another yearly holiday event was the Santa Claus play presented on the overhanging roof at Sears-Roebuck on Beretania [sic] Street. I think it was to kick off the holiday shopping season and get kids to visit Santa inside the store. We usually went in our pajamas and collected as much candy as we could when it was thrown into the audience at the curtain call. Years later, a friend in high school told me she had been in those plays as part of a children's drama class. I envied her. Why hadn't Mom put me in a class like that instead of sending me off to piano lessons? Surely, I would have insisted on it if I had known about such acting classes then.

I can see now that I had a one-track mind as a kid. I never went through a time when I wanted to be a policeman or a pilot, but I did seem to know what I might do with my life early on. Mom and Dad were probably happy to see me staying out of trouble and engaging in something as wholesome and harmless as putting on shows.

When I was about six years old, I was treated to a performance of a real live play called *The Blue Bird* which was performed at Dillingham Hall at Punahou School. *The Blue Bird* is a tale of a boy and his sister seeking happiness and finally finding it in their own backyard. I could relate, especially because the two main actors were not much older than I was, and they looked like they were having a lot of fun pretending to be other people. That show was the first play in a real theater that I had ever seen. *Playhouses* and all the magic they contained had now entered my life.

Perhaps my parents had noticed my unfolding right brain and had decided to encourage it with that performance of *The Blue Bird*. Everything theatrical that I had only imagined during my *pretend theater* efforts and the radio shows came together for me in that production. Here were painted sets, costumes, props, music, lighting effects and, of course, live actors.

I quickly forgot where I was, that the Punahou School campus was just outside the walls of that theater. Through an invisible portal, which I eventually learned to call *the fourth wall,* shards of light and costumed players transformed a poor woodcutter's cabin into a hall of luxuries. I must have left Dillingham Hall wanting to be onstage with those actors. And I also wanted to go behind the scenes to see the secrets that produced all that stage wizardry. I didn't know then that in a few years I would appear on that same stage in high school plays and variety shows.

Because two high school girls in our neighborhood had lead roles, I was taken to a student production of *Arsenic and Old Lace,* also at Punahou. Again, fascinated with the technical aspects, I wondered how they got that realistic large old house onto the stage. What were those walls made of, and what would I see if I went behind them? I directed that comedy twice when I was a theater teacher years later. And that is what this memoir is slowly pointing toward – my 37-year career of teaching theater and directing plays in a public high school. This memoir is not the accumulating story of a professional actor (Hollywood never did discover me.), but of a life full of theater nevertheless.

I was not yet a teenager when I was astounded by a one-ring traveling circus that came to Honolulu from the mainland. They had brought clowns, tight- rope-walkers, and even elephants. It was performed in a tent on an open lot near the Mormon Temple on Beretania [sic] St. In Hawaii, it was problematic for a kid to run away and join the circus, but it did cross my mind. With some of my playmates, however, that circus was inevitably recreated in our backyard.

I was the ringmaster and also a clown because, as a part of trick or treating, Mom had made a clown costume for me. Perhaps I corralled some neighborhood dogs to be the menagerie, and we performed some rudimentary tumbling on the lawn. We tied towels around our necks as capes, and, after each act, we would throw our arms into the air in triumph. *Ta Dah!* Our circus acts were always heavy on grand flourishes.

When I was ten years old we went to see *The Ringling Brothers and Barnum and Bailey Circus* under a gigantic big top in Chicago. That earlier circus in Honolulu was nothing compared to the extreme pageantry and spectacle of those three rings in Chicago. Totally fascinated with circuses, I went back to Honolulu and put together another circus, even bigger and better than the earlier one. Our clowns didn't tumble out of a car as they had in Chicago, but we pretended to walk on a rope we had laid out on the grass and then marched around to a fanfare of music. Our family's first small record player accompanied us with an album of circus music provided by Mom and Dad.

In addition to the main tent of that earlier circus in Honolulu, there was also a sideshow tent with oddities that we then called *freaks*. There was a bearded lady, a fat lady, an illustrated man and a sword swallower, but the attraction that impressed me the most was a magician. I was dazzled. Objects appeared and disappeared, and he even pulled a rabbit out of a hat. I quickly put on a show for my family on our lanai. This was not the fantastic *Harry Potter*-style of wizardry from a later generation, but stage tricks with things up my sleeve and attempts at sleight of hand. My tricks with rope, coins and playing cards (*pick a card, any card*) were the beginning of my *career* as an amateur magician. I've had a fascination with the technical workings of large stage illusions that trick the audience with mirrors, trap doors and lighting.

Shortly, I received a magic set for Christmas, which expanded my act so I could present a show for kids as part of a fundraiser at Manoa Elementary School. A library book taught me how to pluck a coin from the air and how to tear up a newspaper and then restore it.

As a sophomore in high school, I collaborated with an equally magic-mad friend to put on a more sophisticated show for Punahou's annual variety show. I was the magician's assistant that time, but the directors thought it best to have a slinky girl in that role, and I was given a speaking part instead. That was even better for me as those memorized lines set me off on an amateur acting career, which has continued in fits and starts ever since. I discovered that hiding inside a character, pretending to be someone else, gave me temporary safe passage from my persistent shyness. Because of my very young looks, I was always cast as a child or teenager or was thoroughly made up to look very old. My part in that Variety Show was an old professor, and I was heavily disguised with grease paint, lines on my face and a false beard. *Grease paint* had now entered my life, but I don't think the audience was fooled. Photographs show that I still looked like a kid.

It was about that time I discovered a small store in downtown Honolulu on Alakea Street called Pop's Novelty Shop. Pop was a very friendly older Japanese man. You didn't actually go into Pop's store, but you interacted with him at a counter right from the sidewalk. Pop sold practical jokes like whoopie cushions, lapel flowers that shot out water when you squeezed a bulb and buzzers to shock someone when shaking hands. These were novelties you could also order from ads in the back of comic books; I wasn't interested in any of that.

But, to my elation, Pop also sold magic tricks, and, for a few years, I haunted his shop to see what new illusions he had brought in. I spent my allowance on tricks like rings that linked and miraculously unlinked; a wand that turned into a bouquet of flowers; scarves that changed color and small balls you held between your fingers and made one fold into another to make it seem to disappear. I didn't have a live rabbit to pull out of a hat, but, ever interested in the scenic aspects of shows, I felt my act needed a little more theatricality. I cut out a two-foot-high rabbit from plywood with a coping saw and painted it as a piece of standup scenery.

In my second year of high school Mom and Dad suggested I take an elective drama class. I think I was the youngest looking guy in the class, but I was trusted with a couple of monologues for older characters. At first, I played Tom Wingfield from *The Glass Menagerie*.

I have tricks in my pocket, I have things up my sleeve. But I am the opposite of a stage magician.

Another monologue was a speech by Petruchio from Shakespeare's *The Taming of the Shrew*.

Thus, have I politically begun my reign, and 'tis my hope to end successfully.

I directed that play with my students years later. I still love the sound of those words and can recite at least the beginning of each of those speeches. My love of Shakespeare and Tennessee Williams started in that class. Because of my continuing high school angst, Mom and Dad also encouraged me to take a Speech class. As with most people, I was afraid of public speaking because what I said were *my* words, not those of a playwright. In the same way, I was hesitant to raise my hand in any of my classes, afraid all eyes would be on me. Would I say the right thing?

My drama teacher Mr. Andrews made me realize that theater is a collaborative art form – various talents cooperating to create a theatrical work of art. We were taught about the Greek origins of western theater, including *Thalia* and *Melpomene*, the Greek gods of comedy and tragedy, and Aristotle's theater unities in his definition of tragedy. In my second year of Drama, we were assigned to put together a director's prompt book for one act of a play of our choice. I chose the comedy *You Can't Take It With You*. We had to design a set and include all the movements the characters made. For that, we learned about *upstage, downstage* and *stage right* and *left,* and the strongest position on the stage, *down center.* Years later, I directed that play twice with my high school students, and I still have that director's book.

A now brittle copy of *Ka Punahou,* our high school newspaper, reminds me that I wrote and performed in a radio play with friends. *A Pocket Full of Posies* was about a young woman trying to break into the theater in N.Y. Wouldn't you know? And when I was in tenth grade I was cast as a doddering old doctor (lots of old age makeup) in the comedy *The Man Who Came to Dinner.* I have to report that I came down with mumps just before the performances and was replaced – a disappointing setback. I learned the hard way what an understudy was. But that play is a great vehicle for high school actors (lots of over-the-top characters for men and women) and I have directed it several times during my career at Ygnacio Valley High School. Every time I directed a student as Dr. Bradley, I molded him in the image of what my high school performance might have been.

Punahou School is a college prep school, and the counseling department had us take the Kuder Preference Test to see how we should be guided toward college or a career. The results of that test shocked me. There was nothing about the arts. What had I marked on the test to make it decide I would make a good undertaker? Had my right brain betrayed me? I was very insulted. I don't remember what my counselor thought, however, she never urged me to study mortuary arts. She did encourage me to get involved in Punahou's two drama clubs: *Theta Pi* was our Punahou club, but we also had a chapter of *The National Thespian Society* for which I was the president in my senior year.

Another favorite right brain class was English, which I was happy to take for four required years. Literature was an important part of the class, and I especially loved reading plays out loud. In ninth grade we read both Shakespeare's *Julius Caesar* and Richard Brinsley Sheridan's *The School for Scandal*. These assigned plays set me off on a project to read most of the plays in the Punahou Library, and, when I finished that, I went on to read many of the plays in the main Honolulu Library. Here were stories being told almost entirely in dialogue form. I was fascinated with the playwright's challenge to manipulate the action so it followed the unities of time, place and action: one plot, a limited time frame and only one or a few locations.

I completed my play-reading project by the time I graduated from high school. Mom and Dad had tried to get me outside to play more during my book (play) worm period, but I liked being alone and reading and making a list of all those plays. I didn't know anyone else obsessively doing that, so was it weird I liked to read plays instead of playing outside with the other kids?

The Punahou library subscribed to the *New York Times,* and I got into the habit of reading the Sunday Arts and Leisure section, a pathway to the world of New York theater. Punahou also subscribed to a monthly magazine called *Theater Arts* that had reviews of current New York productions and also the script of a current Broadway play in each issue. Maybe I should have had a subscription to *Sports Illustrated,* but, instead, I decided to start my own subscription to *Theater Arts.* I was also being exposed to a lot of New York culture on *The Ed Sullivan Show* on Sunday nights. (Topo Gigio, jugglers, Senor Wences, Elvis, The Supremes) I loved all of it, but was especially taken with the excerpts from Broadway shows. My fantasies had me wandering the streets of the theater district when I could finally get to New York. That did happen with my family in the summer after my freshman year of college.

The Honolulu Community Theatre (H.C.T. is now called the Diamond Head Theater) was, and is, the most ambitious theater company in the Islands. Near the back end of Diamond Head, H.C.T. performed in the old Fort Ruger Army base movie house that was repurposed for live theater in 1952. Mom introduced me to HCT by treating me to two productions there when I was in ninth and tenth grades. The musical *Paint Your Wagon* (an earlier show by those who created *My Fair Lady*) opened up the world of Broadway musicals to me. I started a collection of original cast albums that continued to grow until today I have hundreds of them.

The following year, we went to a production of Oliver Goldsmith's *She Stoops to Conquer.* Years later, I directed my students in a production of that play, using it as a thesis project for my Master's Degree in Theater Arts. My project showed how even a comedy of manners from the eighteenth century could be approachable for modern-day high school students.

As a true drama geek, I had been happy to work behind the scenes for any Punahou production I didn't have a part in. I helped build and paint scenery and worked on prop crews. With that high school experience under my belt, I felt comfortable volunteering at H.C.T. for the prop crew for a production of *The King and I*. Here were all those layers of curtains, ropes and backdrops that had first fascinated me in my friend's marionette theater.

There was a combined backstage scent of scene paint, sizing that stretched the canvas on the flats, stage glue, grease paint, sawdust and accumulated *must* from all the previous productions – a resinous woody smell with accents of acrid electricity and sweet theatrical make-up. I now understand that ground has been broken for a brand new theater next door to the old one. That new building will have to start a history of its own evocative backstage smell. It is now 2023 and that theater has now been opened.

One evening, just after we had preset the props for Act 1 of *The King and I*, I had some time on my hands before the overture. The theater had a small outbuilding nearby, and I could see something was going on there. I wandered over and stood in an open doorway.

"Are you here to audition?" A very pretty woman with a French accent greeted me at the door.

"Audition? No, thank you. I'm just killing time before *The King and I* starts."

At that point, I noticed an older man who seemed to be in charge of the proceedings. He held a clipboard and was listening to two people reading from scripts. I guessed he was the director. He looked me over and then said, "I think we may have a part for you in our next production. Let us hear you read."

"Read? Next production?"

"It's a comedy called *The Remarkable Mr. Pennypacker*. Marcelle, give this young man a script and show him where to start. Let's do the scene where Horace spills the beans about his father."

"But . . . " I protested with butterflies batting around inside of me.

The nice man added, "What luck for us. We need to cast a teenage boy, and we'd like to hear you read from the script."

I let them know I had to work the current show in the theater, so Marcelle quickly handed me a script and showed me where to start. The boy they needed to cast, Horace the Third, is sixteen years old and very young and innocent. Apparently, I looked perfect for the part.

I was reading a scene with another actor who was playing Grandpa, the father of the title character. I realized later that the scene we were reading was a turning point in the plot.

"*My father is vice-president of Pennypacker and Co.*" I read rather hesitantly as this was a cold reading from a play I knew nothing about. "*There are two branches. One here and one in Philadelphia. He has blue eyes and brown hair and he always wears knickers.*"

"*Are you crazy?*" read Grandpa.

Grandpa must have been an experienced actor as he lowered his script and looked me in the eye. That moment of connection helped me gather my nerve, and I plowed ahead.

"*No, sir He's vice-president, sir.*"

"*Is he? Well, I'm president.*"

"*Then you must know my father*," I innocently read. When we were in production, that line always got a huge laugh. The audience already knew that my father was Grandpa's son.

The play is a charming comedy set in 1890 Wilmington, Delaware. The original production was still running on Broadway, but since Hawaii's distance from New York was then prohibitive for touring shows, H.C. T. was given production rights for many recent and current Broadway plays and musicals. Burgess Meredith was then starring in the show on Broadway. *Pennypacker* is about a free-thinking man who, as it turns out, has two families, one in Wilmington and one in Philadelphia. I was soon to add a new word to my growing vocabulary: *bigamy*.

When I finished reading, both the director and the French-sounding lady named Marcelle had smiles on their faces. I must have been who they were looking for as I was cast, given a script, a rehearsal schedule and a phone to call my parents with the news. And I still had time to get to Act 1 of *The King and I*.

Mom never became a *stage mother* in the classic sense, but she and Dad were excited for me, and I had the experience of working with adult actors in a very polished, near-professional production. We garnered rave reviews from the local critics and were sold out for most of our run. We were a hit!

"Side splitting performances," The Honolulu Star-Bulletin said.

"Superbly staged, perfectly cast," announced The Honolulu Advertiser.

The Advertiser further said, "I also was impressed by the performance of Carl Spiegelberg as Horace the Third, the one who upsets the applecart by wandering across the state line."

That positive notice was my first personal acting review. My right brain and ego were given a major vote of confidence, and the review helped pull away more layers of my insecurities. I think my *Pennypacker* experience was an important turning point in my struggle with shyness. I had been *discovered*, I thought, just by killing time in that audition doorway.

As I always did when I was connected to a show, I learned some new vocabulary. Here are some that give a sense of the play, which was set in a time of social change. In addition to *bigamy*, there were: *knickerbockers, scandalized, new woman, emancipation, liberal thinker, banns of marriage, Darwin League, bordello, bodice, George Bernard Shaw, natural selection, atheist, civil disobedience, illegitimate, bastard, Karl Marx, nudism, socialism and selective breeding*. These were not words or ideas I was learning at Punahou. I felt very worldly.

The *Pennypacker* company became a close-knit if temporary family, especially since there were about eight children in the cast. We garnered publicity in the local papers because of that. Marcelle became sort of a den-mother to us, and she coached me with my dialogue. Marcelle Corday, originally from Belgium, had been a featured player in a number of Hollywood films from the silent era through the 1930s. (*The Great Ziegfeld, Blonde Venus, Dead End*).

She took me under her wing, and I figured out that adult theater was a safe place for me in this leap from high school shows. I was too excited to let my shyness take control when I was assimilated into our accepting and generous cast. *The Remarkable Mr. Pennypacker* was grown-up real theater, not the let's pretend theater of my kid-time in Manoa Valley. Marcelle and the director, Dr. Campton Bell, taught me a lot about projection and enunciation:

"Use the big muscle in your stomach, your diaphragm. Let it help you push out the sound."

"Play to your lights and cheat toward the audience so they can see your face."

"Don't let other actors upstage you when the attention should be on you."

"Don't telegraph your thoughts before it's natural to speak them."

"Don't ever mug or overact."

With their influence, I don't think I ever became a ham actor.

I learned what the *green room* was and about well-known theater superstitions such as saying *break a leg* instead of *good luck* to the other actors, and never to say the name of the Scottish play (*Macbeth*) inside a theater. Theater has always been a superstitious business, and the origins of these two beliefs are now lost in history.

I was taught about all kinds of cues: entrance, line, lighting and, sound cues. I experienced the mental focus and deep breaths an actor takes in the private moments while standing in the darkened wings just before an entrance – and the invisible energy coming the other way from the audience out there in the dark. I found myself mixing socially with adults at cast parties. Except perhaps for the other kids in our cast, I suppose most of that *Pennypacker* company is probably gone now. Those actors had been important to my growing stage and personal confidence nearly seventy years ago.

When *Pennypacker* closed, I wanted to find a way to hold

on to what had been a major experience for me. I built a detailed model of the set, using cardboard, foil, thread, string and glue, even tiny lights I found in a hobby store. I was happy to see a picture of myself with my creation in the *Honolulu Star-Bulletin*.

H.C.T. became a habit with me. Once I got my driver's license, I spent a lot of time there on prop crews, and I ran a *follow spotlight* for the musical *Kiss Me Kate*. My friend Tricia and I worked together building and painting sets. I saw all the HCT productions in that era: *A Streetcar Named Desire, The Rainmaker, Kismet, The Pajama Game* and many others. All of those productions interested me for a number of reasons, not the least of which were the scene designs. I was particularly drawn to how the shows looked and how the sets were changed. I suppose I could have become a set designer. But, in a way, I did just that, as I always conceived and designed the sets for every show when directing my plays at the high school I taught at.

I think the evidence was too great for Mom and Dad to ignore: I was a right-brained stagestruck kid, so they agreed with me and the Punahou counseling department that I should be allowed to major in Theater Arts which, we found, was part of the Speech Department at the University of Oregon. This was well before all-consuming student debt demanded that students ignore the liberal arts in order to be economically stable. I was never urged to major in something to fall back on. The U. of O. was on the West Coast, it had an estimable theatre department, I had relatives in Oregon, and, best of all for my parents, U of O didn't charge out-of-state tuition for students from Alaska or Hawaii. So, I started college in Eugene, Oregon in the fall of 1957.

Being on my own, away from family, forced me to further crawl out of my shell. I was still a quiet guy, but I found myself making friends in my freshman dorm, in the Kappa Sigma fraternity and at the University Theater. Some of my childhood social reticence was still with me, but all the audiences I had been in front of had given me practice easing that nervousness. After all, actors have always tricked themselves into *performing for their parents* who had been their first and most accepting audience. "Look, Ma. See what I can do."

The University theater and its adjacent classroom building were in a beautiful grove of mature evergreen trees on the north side of campus. That playhouse became a home for me for four years. I could easily walk there from all the places I lived during my college years. Many of my new theater friends were anticipating going into professional theater in New York or into *the business, a*s they say, in Hollywood. So, I too, toyed with the possibility of a professional career, as I was influenced by all the aspiration swirling around me. Some of my friends were spending seasons doing summer stock in New England and summers at the Oregon Shakespeare Festival in Ashland, Oregon.

My friendships with many of those talented actors are in my rearview mirror now. I lost one dear friend way too early to Multiple Sclerosis and another to a stroke. Other friends have faded into professional old age in Hollywood and New York. Just this week (Feb. 2, 2022) my university acting friend Howard Hesseman, a well-known TV actor, has passed away.

In my four years at U of O I had large and small parts in many plays, both serious and comic, from Shakespeare to children's theater. My directing aspirations also had a workout in my junior year when I helmed two one-act plays as a sidelight of the main theater season: *The Bald Soprano* by Eugene Ionesco and *The Maids* by Jean Genet. The glowing acceptance of these productions, my active involvement in the University Theater production committee and performing in many plays granted me a major theater contribution award in my senior year, and another layer of self-confidence.

During my freshman year in Eugene, Dad was offered a sabbatical leave to study at the Agricultural Department at Oregon State University in Corvallis, about an hour from Eugene. It was great having my family nearby, but the most exciting part of his leave for me was that we would be taking a summer-long road trip following the academic year. The climax of that trip would be New York City, a place I had been fantasizing about from the middle of the Pacific Ocean for at least ten years. I researched the shows that would be playing and ordered tickets by mail. I would be paying up to $8.60, matinees and evening, for the best seats in the house. That was in 1958. The shows on my agenda included: *West Side Story, Bells are Ringing, Look Homeward, Angel, The Dark at the Top of the Stairs* and *Sunrise at Campobello*.

There were a lot of other stops on our trip across the country, but New York was always on my mind. After Chicago, we traveled east, and every mile on the Pennsylvania Turnpike was a mile closer to the Manhattan skyline. As we got close, I was on a razor-sharp lookout for the Empire State Building. And then, there it was looming beyond the New Jersey mud flats and the Hudson River.

With the Lincoln Tunnel behind us, we drove into the city that never sleeps. Rodgers and Hart's *Manhattan* ("We'll Turn Manhattan Into an Isle of Joy") became an ear-worm for me as we ticked off lots of tourist attractions. We commuted into Manhattan from Queens where we were staying with

Mom's cousin, and joined buzzing crowds, all straining our necks skyward. Steam came out of man-holes, the smell of roasting chestnuts filled the air, racks of clothing moved through the streets, doormen competed for honking yellow taxis and gusts of wind rushed up our legs from rumbling underground trains. We put dimes and quarters into slots at Horn and Hardart Automats, ate hot dogs on the street and chicken livers and Reuben sandwiches at the Carnegie Deli. All of Manhattan seemed to sport an ornamental motif of silhouetted fire escapes, wooden rooftop water tanks and banners, flags, awnings and canopies that covered sidewalks to the street.

The city felt like a festival suffused with electricity, but, of course, Times Square and Broadway were the major attractions for me. A brilliant fabric of neon lit up smoke rings blown out of the Camel Cigarette billboard, a real block-long waterfall touted Pepsi-Cola, and gigantic movie ads covered whole sides of buildings. I made a point of finding a lot of the nearly fifty Broadway theaters, regretted all the shows I would not have time to see and took pictures of the theater posters in Schubert Alley. All the layers of New York, below ground and high above, were wonderfully exhausting, and when we moved on to Boston and then Washington D.C., those cities seemed almost anti-climactic.

I would return to New York many times, once was to live for six months in 1962 when I worked at Barnes and Noble's original store on Fifth Avenue, and another time was to take a summer course in Film Study at NYU's Tisch School of the Arts. I never felt I wanted to live there permanently, especially after a New York winter, but I always relished my visits and would spend a good part of my time in Broadway or Off-Broadway theaters.

I made a foray into television in Los Angeles in the early sixties by having professional composite photos taken for possible agents and warily learning to avoid the infamous *casting couch*. It didn't send my life in a new direction, but a show called *My Three Sons* was casting young looking guys, and an agent sent me to be considered.

But I gradually came to see that the uncertain career of an actor in NY or LA was not the life for me. I would be constantly auditioning, a necessity that always brought out my insecurities. *Variety*, the show business journal, told me that, at any one time, possibly 90% of actors are unemployed. I didn't want to join the nether world of *don't call us, we'll call you*, and I gradually faced the reality that I needed more stability in my life. Besides, Mom and Dad had supported me long enough, and I needed a steady income to move myself into adulthood. Then, the possibility of teaching and directing what I loved presented itself as an alternative. Some would pejoratively say that if you can't do something, you end up teaching it. But there is more to that story, and it turned out that I could do both. I accompanied my teaching with regular stints on stage as an amateur actor.

After that first trip to NY, I finished three more years at the University of Oregon majoring in Theater Arts and minoring in English. Those two areas of focus eventually led to a California General Secondary Teaching Credential. I think my parents were relieved that I saw high school teaching as a viable future. I would have a predictable income, health care coverage and, eventually, a good retirement. None of that is possible for most aspiring actors who must constantly rely on being in the right place at the right time.

My university acting classes, first at the University of Oregon, then San Francisco State and finally at U.C. Berkeley as a grad student taught me what I would eventually pass on to my students. The lessons I had learned from pretend theater as a kid and then high school and community theater in Honolulu had set me up for formal lessons in those classes.

All of us theater geeks bonded as a close-knit family of artists who had a mission to fulfill. We would change the world, we thought. That was the era of the Beat Generation, and our bohemian pretensions took on some of that mystique – dark tights for the girls and dark glasses for the guys. The theater's green room became a second home when we weren't in rehearsal or meeting in dimly-lit coffee houses. We had all come from childhoods in which we had spent a lot of time playing make believe – pretending.

A new generation of American actors had taken to Constantin Stanislavsky's naturalistic style of acting in the 1950s, and so we did too. We built our characters by always questioning our acting choices: was it believable for the character do this, or that? What were the character's circumstances moments before an entrance? I put all of this into practice when I appeared in quite a few University productions. In some of the shows I had major roles, and in some I had walk-on parts. I was learning the lesson that *there are no small parts, only small actors.*

*****

As the professor and mythologist Joseph Campbell has wisely told us, *"We must be willing to let go of the life we planned so as to have the life that is waiting for us."* That philosophy encapsulates the aspirational transition I was going through as I finished college and began to look for a meaningful career. Teaching had never been an ambition up to then, as we theater majors had always agreed that was beneath us. It would belie our hard-wired professional ambitions. But I gradually realized if I became a teacher, I would still be able to immerse myself in my love of the stage by passing on my theatrical knowledge and directing plays. I might never see my name in lights, but that paradigm shift would provide a stable career and a consistent income.

That all came to be for me when, after student teaching drama at Berkeley High School, I earned my teaching credential at U.C. Berkeley in 1964 and chanced on a job teaching English and Drama at nearby Ygnacio Valley High School in Walnut Creek. The school had opened two years before I was hired and was then the most admired high school in our school district. Even in my coat and tie, which all the men wore at the time, I still looked as young as many of my students. My grown-up briefcase did give me some adult credibility, but, at the opening assembly when the faculty was introduced to the student body in our gymnasium, the home of the Warriors, I was met with cat calls and admiring whistles from many of the girls in the audience. What was I getting myself into? One day, a message came for one of my students. The messenger thought I was one of them until the class straightened him out. Our school attendance boundaries at that time encompassed thoroughly middle and upper middle-class neighborhoods. For the most part, students were well-behaved, and I never had to compete with drugs or cell phones in those days.

But some of my off-stage stage fright reared its head as I faced my classes in the first weeks of school. I needed to get used to my new audience – a classroom full of teenagers. I used my, by then, well-learned acting prowess to subvert the intimidation I felt. I was playing the role of an authority figure. I used my acting voice, speaking from my diaphragm, and filled the room with my command. It was a great help that I had a distinct role to play, and there were built-in expectations of me as I settled into that new role of *high school teacher*. Teaching both English and Drama gave variety to my day, and I loved teaching both. This was the secure life that Joseph Campbell had suggested was waiting for me, and I took to it enthusiastically.

Our school's cavernous multi-purpose room was not an ideal theater as it was also the school cafeteria, but it did have a large stage with curtains and some theater lights. I chose three plays to produce – fall, winter and spring – and all of them were well received. *Charley's Aunt*, a classic farce, caught everyone's interest and set up expectations for *Our Town* in the winter and the musical *The Boy Friend* in the spring. Those productions garnered a lot of attention to my drama program and helped fill my classes the following year. My shows were always successful because I chose plays according to my talent pool and shows the students could relate to. We never did plays written just for teenagers (*Where's Grandma?* and the like), but always adult shows that had shown professionally in New York, like *The Diary of Anne Frank, The Crucible, Look Homeward, Angel, Inherit the Wind, The Matchmaker* and *Auntie Mame*. As the director, I had to be conscious of what the audience experienced. I coached my actors to always be heard and their faces easily seen. There is nothing worse for an audience than straining to hear.

My English classes were not electives, and I was assigned various levels and ability groups over the years. In my last ten years at the high school, I taught Advanced Placement English to seniors. Those classes were a pleasure, attracting bright industrious students who wanted to be there. In the summer of 1986, I was awarded a place in a program sponsored by The National Endowment for the Humanities. That six-week seminar was an in-depth study of *Hamlet* in the English Department at Harvard. I stayed in a residence hall where, according to local lore, JFK had lived. *Hamlet* was a center piece for my Advanced Placement seniors for the rest of my career.

*****

Looking back from retirement on thirty-seven years of teaching, I can recognize the accumulated rich fabric that my theater program took on over time. In addition to teaching five classes a day, I always had a very busy play season of four or five productions each year, including a musical assisted by the choir teacher and a choreographer – *The Pajama Game, Damn Yankees, South Pacific, Where's Charley?, Little Shop of Horrors* and *Guys and Dolls* were some of them. I always loved my casts, but I was a taskmaster for excellence, and they respected me for that. I had become a one-man producer, director and technician for each of the productions. I was responsible for every aspect of these efforts from auditions, to selling tickets, to the closing night cast party. I wanted to keep that busy schedule so as many students as possible could be involved.

But eventually I felt overwhelmed, and I engaged students to help direct some of the shows. Seniors would vie with each other to be on two-person directing teams. I helped them choose plays ranging from Greek tragedy (*Oedipus Rex*) to Shakespeare (*Romeo and Juliet*) to Neil Simon (*The Odd Couple*) among many others. I would help mediate their disagreements – these were teenagers, after all – and see them through technical run-throughs and final dress rehearsals. Those student directors appreciated the immersive hands-on experience, and, because they came to take pride in and *own* their productions, their shows were always a positive reflection on my program.

Because they were taught in a special classroom that had a small built-in stage and some theater lights, my drama classes were held in Room 201 for my entire career. In my early years in that room, before they built the shopping center next door, the whirring trains on BART's original test run became a background sound track for my classes. As my drama program continued to heat up, I decided to create a more finished theater there, and, with the help of some parents, we extended the depth of the stage, built risers for a raked seating area, installed a lighting booth and built permanent wings on the stage. My students stopped calling our little theater *Room 201* and put a sign outside the entrance announcing it as *The Spiegatorium*. I also enjoyed the compliment of being called *Spieg* as a shortcut to my long last name.

"Hey, Spieg, how are you doing?"

"What are we gonna do today, Spieg? Are we gonna get a new project?" one of my sixth-period kids asked. I always scheduled my Advanced Drama class for the last period of the day, so we could ease into after-school rehearsal time if we needed to.

"When are we going to start our one-act plays?"

"Are you ready for a new set of scenes? We'll perform the one-acts just before Christmas break, so we need to warm up with some scenes first."

"Do we get to choose our partners?"

"Yes, if it's someone you haven't worked with before."

All this activity, extracurricular and classwork, kept me extremely busy. I was putting in lots of extra time including weekends and evenings. But with student and parental help there was always something to garner the attention of the school at large and keep my students happily occupied. We had two drama clubs – our local club, and also a chapter of the National Thespian Society. Every year, at the end of the season, we held a drama awards banquet at a local hotel or restaurant. It was always an elaborate, dressy affair with satirical skits about the season's plays, a catered dinner and a suspense-filled presentation of trophies as voted by the drama students at large. The students called the trophies The *Spiegie Awards* in honor of their teacher.

Each year we would go on a field trip to San Francisco to have lunch and see a play at The American Conservatory Theater. Further afield, there were periodic trips to the Oregon Shakespeare Festival and, even farther afield, to London and Stratford, England for ten days of theater and historical sightseeing during the spring break. I did that for seven years.

If that wasn't enough excitement, we had an improvisation league that competed with other high schools. I was never a very good improviser myself (I guess it was too close to my nervousness about impromptu social conversations.), but my students loved it. We had an annual one-act play festival to entertain invited English classes as a treat during the two weeks just before the Christmas holidays, and theater conferences at Diablo Valley College where we competed against other high schools with scenes, monologues and one-act plays.

In some years we would tour a few elementary schools

with a children's play, and most years we would take a theater presentation as outreach to our local feeder junior high schools. We held annual candy sales, usually See's suckers, to beef up the drama fund. And then there were cast parties on closing night of each production and occasional parties for my students at my house. And I was also teaching English. *Whew!*

My motivation for all this furious activity evolved over the years. When I first started teaching in 1964, it was all about my desire to get hold of the school stage and put plays on it, something I had longed to do since high school and my time at the Honolulu Community Theater. Early on, I had a nagging feeling that I should have a *real* career downtown, like some friends did, one in a tall building with an office and desk to go to, not just a classroom in the suburbs. I *did* have my teacher's desk and a lectern, but I seldom sat or stood there; I was almost always on my feet. Eventually, I realized that my classroom was a far more friendly workplace than a downtown office would have ever been. And now, post-pandemic, many of those offices are closed, perhaps never to reopen.

Although my drama classes were technically under the banner of the English Department, I was on my own, the head of my own one-man drama program. No one was ever breathing down my neck. I was my own boss, an advantage few people find in their careers. Of course, I taught my English classes to the specifications of the curriculum with novels like *The Lord of the Flies*, *To Kill a Mockingbird*, *Huckleberry Finn* and *Pride and Prejudice*. I doggedly graded essays, dutifully attended department meetings and even went on strike for two weeks in 1977.

I wanted my classes to be substantial, not just playgrounds

for easy credit. To that end, in the advanced class I included theater literature and history, along with stage makeup, theatrical costuming and principles of stage lighting. In all the classes, I required that students see at least two play productions a quarter including our school plays. Because I wanted the students to come away with lasting good memories, I required them to keep a drama notebook with all their notes, theater programs, scripts and the photos I took of them in one-act plays and scenes.

But, above all, I wanted the classes to be fun, a break from the more *sit-at-your-desk* academic requirements in their schedules. After all, I was having a lot of fun, and I wanted them to share it with me. What could be more fun than putting on plays and seeing my kids flower into full-fledged drama geeks as I had been?

I wasn't a pushover; I required a high performance level, but always with an inclusiveness that allowed for a wide range of innate talent. It was always exciting to see the students blossom into stage-struck kids following in my footsteps. I loved seeing their right brains tickled and being struck with the acting bug, a revelation that came to them after appearing in front of an audience and feeling its love for the first time.

I think the school's administration could see that I was putting in a lot of energy to create a good program. The quality of my productions made it clear that I knew what I was doing. And the healthy enrollments in my classes – for a few years I had *all* drama classes – were proof that the students, too, approved of what I was doing. After three probationary years, I gained tenure. It was that magical *tenure* that set me apart from most struggling actors.

Many of my students would re-up for further classes,

and I developed relationships with many of them that took on the feeling of friendships. We thought of ourselves as a family. As a teacher and a coach, I was no longer focused on just staging plays but on the welfare and growth of my family of students. Some of them found a home in the drama department and even, for others, a reason to come to school. I encouraged that by leaving my room open to them while I went off to brunch and lunch.

Teachers are always learning, – from their curriculum and also from their students – and I loved being able to teach what I wanted to learn. I was actually getting paid for fulfilling my creative urges: reading and teaching novels and directing plays. I also loved the academic calendar that allowed me to be a world traveler. And it was very rejuvenating to be able to start over each fall after a break and bring back new and better ways to approach the material and communicate with my students. I always hated to see my seniors leave each June. Some of them had been in my classes for four years, so it was like saying goodbye to friends. But I was gratified that some of them found me on Facebook and continued our connection. Each June I was happy for school to be out, but I always looked forward to starting again in early September. There were always more plays to direct and new students to befriend and learn from.

During my teaching career, I wasn't only keeping very busy as a coach, mentor and director; on a parallel path, I was also honing my acting skills in amateur productions. In 1967, I was in a production of Aristophanes' *Lysistrata* at the Interplayers Theater near Ghirardelli Square in San Francisco. According to a now yellowing program, I played a character named Polydorus, one of several sex-starved Greek soldiers. As it was a fairly earthy version of that comedy, we all wore full body makeup and not a lot else. I felt very sophisticated doing my part with all that bawdiness. In that same decade, I played the second romantic lead, Claudio, in Marin Shakespeare Festival's *Much Ado About Nothing*. We performed on an outdoor stage at the Dominican University in San Rafael. It was exciting to be playing with a number of professional actors.

In the early '70s, I auditioned for the Civic Arts Theater Company, sponsored by the city of Walnut Creek. This was well before the modern theater called the Lesher Center was built in 1990. The earlier theater had been created from an old walnut warehouse, and we affectionately called it *The Nut House*. I was cast in a stylish production of Jean Anouilh's comedy/romance *Ring Round the Moon*. I played the male lead, a double role of twin brothers. One of them was the romantic interest, and the other was his conniving twin. I wore a white carnation on my lapel to play the good brother, Hugo, and a red one as the evil twin, Frederick. I would exit as one, and a dresser in the wings would quickly slap another Velcro-backed carnation on me so I could reenter as the other brother. I loved showing off my versatility in those two roles and the sophistication and stylishness of our production.

The Contra Costa theater community began to know who I was, and I was cast in the featured role of Motel-the-tailor in Diablo Light Opera's production of *Fiddler on the Roof*. My part required me to wear a glued-on beard and sing a solo called *Miracle of Miracles*, an up-tempo song of romantic triumph. I was not a seasoned singer, and at the final dress rehearsal my nerves got in my way, and I came in too early on the downbeat. The orchestra spent the rest of the song trying to keep up with me. I'm glad it was just a rehearsal, of course, but, for the rest of the show's run, I was always nervous that I would make that mistake again. I never did, but I could only relax into my performance after I had sung that song. I married my fiancé Tzeitel in a musical version (*Sunrise, Sunset)* of an authentic Jewish wedding ceremony. Our production was so well thought of that we were called back for another six-week run the following spring. I worked with a singing coach for a time in hopes of having further musical roles. I also had studied modern dance in Hollywood and with my friend Tricia in Honolulu. But I never did become the triple-threat (actor, singer, dancer) I had at one time hoped to be. I was a single threat: I was an actor – and I was happy to be that.

In 1974, also with the Civic Arts Repertory Company, I played Edmund Tyrone the younger son of the Tyrone family and Eugene O'Neill's alter ego in his tragic drama *A Long Day's Journey into Night*. Edmund is a complex character: romantic, restless and sensitive as well as depressive and an alcoholic consumptive. I felt I was in excellent professional company, because a well-respected Actor's Equity (the professional actor's union) acting couple played the two lead roles, James and Mary Tyrone. I enjoyed the challenge of playing such a complex role in one of modern theater's most important plays.

I had the opportunity to stretch my directing chops when one of the two musical theater companies in our area – The Contra Costa Musical Theater – signed me to direct a production of the Broadway musical *Bells Are Ringing*. As with my directing school productions, I looked a lot younger than most of my cast, but I tricked myself into confidence and into my role as director. Unfortunately, neither CCMT or the Diablo Light Opera Company exist today for economic reasons (2023) – a great loss to the community.

After the turn of the century, I learned that there are roles for actors of all ages, and the competition with other male actors began to thin out. There weren't as many older actors competing for all those older roles. If I wasn't noticing what I looked like in the mirror, at least the parts I was playing then were good indications that I was getting older and looking more like the adult I was. These were mostly character parts, not romantic leads as in the past.

I was also regularly playing with Actor's Equity actors, and I got the idea that I could become a professional actor too. In 2003, I was cast in the classic comedy *You Can't Take It With You* at the Willows Theater in Concord. As the production had an Actor's Equity-contract, I was able to start collecting points toward union membership. One point, out of 25 needed points, could be earned for each week I was in an Equity contract production. I played stuffy Mr. Kirby, the father of the male love interest, and a number of my students came to cheer me on. "Go, Spieg," I heard coming from out there in the dark. I had directed some of them in that same play.

I continued to collect Equity points with every Equity show I was in. My strategy was to audition for productions with Equity contracts, collect my points and then pay the union dues for membership. So, in the summer of 2005, with that plan in mind, I spent six weeks training at The American Conservatory Theater's Summer Training Congress in San Francisco. As most of the other students were in the early stages of their theater training, almost all of them were a lot younger than I was. We took professional classes together: Breathing and Voice, Speech and Diction, Auditioning, Shakespearean Acting, Improvisation and Acting Techniques.

My acting resume was getting longer, and my Equity points were accumulating, but, as I got older, Joseph Campbell's admonition continued to speak to me. My ongoing right-brain trajectory was going to deviate once again. I retired from teaching in 2001, but I continued to appear in shows. My attention was now divided, however, as I also had picked up a pen and begun to write. My right brain itched for a new creative outlet. I had taught expository and creative writing for many years, but I had never made time to do it for myself, until a subject matter – my childhood and teen years in Hawaii – began to call for my attention. I had always been in love with words (always crossword puzzles, never sudokus) so this most solitary of art forms became my new *metier*.

Membership in Actor's Equity gradually faded from my ambitions. I realized that Equity membership would limit me to playing only in Equity productions, and a single production could take up to three months of rehearsal and performance time. And, besides, a happy marriage and domesticity intervened, and I was unwilling to take all that time away from my relationship. But I still had time to go to the theater, and I always felt good when I had tickets to something, most often, of course, in the Bay Area but also in Ashland, New York and London.

The final two productions of my teaching career were the comedy/drama *Bus Stop* by William Inge and Stephen Sondheim's *A Funny Thing Happened on the Way to the Forum*. To help me celebrate my retirement, I invited friends to these shows, but I had also been consistently inviting friends and having parties for most of my shows throughout my career. My early shyness and a shot of modesty reared their heads when my fans called out for *director!* I was reluctant to go up on stage. But I did love standing at the back of the house admiring what my students and I had created together.

In retrospect, I can see that my nearly 40 years of teaching happened in a fortuitous time: the suburbs were growing, California was rich enough that there was money for arts classes and the demographics of our school was such that our talented student body was interested in my drama program.

*****

Today, twenty years after my retirement, there are no drama classes at Ygnacio Valley High. The school never found the proper teacher to replace me, and the *Spiegatorium* sits dark and unused amid a downturn in the fortunes of the school.

About twelve years ago, amidst that steady decline, I went back as a volunteer to help shore up the waning program. I directed a production of *Alice in Wonderland* (lots of parts for a mixed gender cast). As I worked with those students, it became clear to me that without much more training, my cast, while interested in the project, did not have the theatrical discipline to consistently attend rehearsals (cheerleading practice was more important for some) or understand what was needed to put on a good show. In spite of those problems, with the help of some of my own ex-students, we came up with a colorful and polished production. I had hoped that *Alice in Wonderland* would jump-start the program with interested students to fill classes. But the decline continued. More recently, I donated money for some new stage lights for the Spiegatorium, and I gave advice to yet another new young teacher who was trying to build a drama program. Unfortunately, she did not have students with enough talent or interest, and now, amidst the Covid pandemic, the once lively drama program at Ygnacio Valley High School is a thing of the past.

My teaching career had always made me happy. There were those difficult days, of course (I had to occasionally deal with class clowns, and kids were always very restless just before a vacation.) but, for the most part, time went by easily, and I quickly forgot about having a *real job* in a downtown office. I realized that teaching was the ideal career for me. I wasn't married during my career so I could devote a lot of my energy to school and my students.

But in the now twenty years since my retirement, I have not been able to fill that still empty corner of my heart. I miss having my classroom as an outlet to share ideas and materials I come across in my daily life, and I feel the frustration of not being able to go back and do it all over again in the even-better way I imagine now.

I still occasionally dream about being in the classroom; sometimes it's a nightmare with students bouncing off walls, or not being prepared, or being naked in front of the class. But most of my school dreams are nostalgic. I greatly miss performing for my students. I have learned how to no longer be the shy guy who could never think of the right thing to say.

As many of my early classroom charges unbelievably become grandparents and even pass away, I regularly encounter ex-students who often do a double-take and hesitantly ask, "Did you used to be a teacher?" It is gratifying that they recognize and remember me, sometimes after many years. And it is fun to reminisce about their time with me in the classroom or on stage. I want to think that they all carry with them some of what they learned in the *Spiegatorium*. I am in touch with a number of them as friends and have even traveled with some and attended their class reunions.

As I prepare to place my photo albums and scrapbooks, guides to my long career as a theater artist, back on their shelf, my mind returns, once again, to memories of my nearly four decades of teaching and the hundreds of audiences I have faced onstage or in the classroom. Those albums allow me to set my mind in rewind, and a kaleidoscope of destinations on my stagestruck journey leap out at me. I return to my days in Manoa Valley as a shy but precocious small kid empresario: the staging of a living room wedding, simple shows for my parents, pretend plays at Tricia's house and writing and staging my first playwrighting effort, *I Lost My Wife*. When I was six or so, the stage magic of *The Blue Bird* burned in my brain. My time as a busy third-grade Renaissance kid was followed by the mounting of backyard circuses and my budding career as a barefoot magician.

Finally comfortable in my own skin, my backward kaleidoscope continues to move, and includes high school plays and variety shows, my time at the Honolulu Community Theater, and being a theater major at the University of Oregon, including an adventure entertaining our troops in Asia with the U.S.O. (That episode is recounted in my next chapter, My Secret, Then and Now)) And then there were my ambitions to become a professional actor, which paralleled a thirty-seven-year career as a high school teacher.

And now, thanks to Joseph Campbell's admonition, I have allowed myself to be a writer. No longer the timid Hawaiian kid I used to be, I have learned that there are a lot of ways to be shy. There has been an evolution from shy guy to actor/director to teacher and now writer. I realize my right brain has had quite a workout in all those years, and it's still there encouraging me to create. My nearly one-track mind led me to know early on what I wanted to do with my life. Despite my shy origins, I am proud to have touched the lives of thousands of people in my life, both as the hundreds of students in my classroom and as audience members watching me pretend to be somebody else in all those plays.

Carl as a Barefoot Magician

The Remarkable Mister Pennypacker

MINIATURE THEATRE — Carl Spiegelberg puts finishing touches on his miniature replica of a stage setting complete with lights for the Remarkable Mr. Pennypacker. The set will be displayed at 7 p.m. Friday during Punahou School's annual show displaying the students' art work of the past year. The art exhibit is open to members of the community as well as Punahou students and their parents.

Shakespeare's The Tempest – University of Oregon

Wonderful Town – Entertaining our troops in Asia – I am in the Center

My Hollywood Episode

From our School Newspaper

'LONG DAY'S JOURNEY INTO NIGHT'
Bearing the burden of their tortured past, the Tyrone family includes Carl A. Spiegelberg as Edmund, Robert Haswell as James, Del Curry as Jamie and Shirley Jac Wagner as Mary.

Fiddler on the Roof

Carl the Director

Carl in the Gay Ghetto, the Castro

My Secret, Then and Now
(1951 - 2023)

"*Simpson is a homo!*" The message was conspicuously scratched on my desk in the social studies classroom along with other graffiti meant to shock or titillate. It seemed to be deeply etched with a pen, so someone wanted it to stay there. I recognized some of the other vulgarities, but this one stumped me. Dr. Simpson was our school headmaster, but what was that pulsing word that someone was rumoring him to be? *Homo*? Scrawled messages like that aren't often complimentary so I assumed this one might not be either. Why, I wondered, was he being offended, and was the message, whatever it was, even true?

I read that cryptic communication in the fall of 1951 when I was in the first semester of seventh grade. Mom and Dad, with the financial help of Grandma, had sent me from Honolulu to Hawaii Episcopal Academy (today, at a new campus, the school is called Hawaii Preparatory Academy) on the Big Island of Hawaii. Founded in 1949, HEA was a preparatory boarding school for seventh through twelfth graders in the very small country town of Kamuela. I was probably sent to HEA to encourage me to grow up, gain confidence in myself and, perhaps, to make a man of me. With no thought that there might be some homesickness on the horizon, I was excited about going to live in a new place on the Big Island. I peppered Mom with questions.

"How cold is it going to be? (I knew it was at a high elevation.) What will we do for fun? How hard will school be in the seventh grade? When will I get to come home?"

I was a good kid, but, in retrospect, I now wonder if they were on to me – had they detected something that I wasn't even aware of? – and were they taking measures to ward off what they feared most? I know I was an overly sensitive (crowds and loud noises rattled me) and shy kid, but was I peculiar or fey in any way? Did I have a limp wrist? I don't remember one. But if I was any of those things, I now wonder if Mom and Dad had considered what might go on in a dormitory full of boys. And had they considered that they were sending a shy kid away for two very critical formative years? Were they avoiding dealing with what they must have known was going to be a time of lots of questions about my puberty?

HEA was located near the 130,000 acre Parker Ranch on a high plateau north of Mauna Kea, Hawaii's tallest mountain. On cloud-free days in winter, we could see its white top and seasonal snow line, which would dip well below the mountain's 14,000 foot peak. The climate at the school was, indeed, very cool due to its 2,670 foot elevation, and I had to adjust to wearing alien sweaters and coats, things I almost never wore in Honolulu. The school's campus was laid out on several acres, with the one-story dorm, library, dining room and classroom buildings surrounding a stone church and social hall. Our regular Episcopalian chapel services there never filled me with any parochial school guilt. That was fortunate in light of what I was presently to discover about myself.

In addition to earning good grades and trying to negotiate the mysterious hormonal changes starting to happen to my mind and body, the school provided lots of extracurricular activities. Those included horseback riding in the hills, swimming in natural mountain pools and at the beach at

Kawaihae, visiting the snow on Mauna Kea in the winter, going to witness eruptions at Halemaumau and seeing lots of movies in the town's only theater. Our excursions away from the campus happened in a large truck. We were all loaded into its open backside. That would probably be illegal today as we had no seat-belts.

I had two adventures in the second semester that I hoped would prove my manliness and make me more popular even with the older guys. One of these was going to live on a farm, and the other was a wild pig hunting expedition. By the second semester, my parents were probably tired of hearing me complain about the older bullies in the dorm, so I went to live with my classmate Fred's family on their nearby farm for a semester. One of our tasks was to feed their pigs before being driven to school each morning. For that, I excitedly learned to drive their wartime stick-shift Jeep a few years before I was eligible for a driver's license. Fred and I would climb in the jeep with a day's worth of food scraps from the kitchen. We shared the driving which we both loved doing and bumped along a rocky road to the pigsty. I must flash forward for a moment to report that, years later, probably in his early twenties, my friend Fred would kill himself because, as it was rumored, he couldn't handle his fear of his father and his guilt about being gay. That was something that neither of us knew about ourselves or each other when we were friends feeding the pigs.

A wild pig hunting expedition in Waipio Valley with family friends was another porcine endeavor. The trail head, about a thousand feet above the valley floor, looked out over the roof of a rainforest, a river and a black sand beach. The valley had been the home of Hawaiian kings in ancient times, but no one lived there when we visited. We rode mules into the landlocked valley on a very narrow switchback trail in order to capture and castrate (to keep the population under control) the feral boars. Draped over the back of one of our mules, one of those boars lumbered back up the trail with us for a luau.

I was not quite twelve years old in that first semester of seventh grade; at eleven, I was the youngest kid in the school. Puberty was circling, looking for a time to land, and I was ripe to find out what that new four-letter word on my desk meant. That information was soon forthcoming, but it would still be a year or two before I fully figured out that I was, indeed, one of those too – but, what, I still wondered then, was a *homo*?

Answers to that *Simpson/homo question,* along with other sexual uncertainties, were imminent as it became clear that my education wouldn't just be happening in the classrooms. HEA was not a large school; my seventh-grade class had only eight students, insuring personalized attention for each of us. All the school's girls were day students, but most of the twenty or so boys lived in an unadorned barracks-style dormitory of bunk beds which had to pass inspection each morning. Our communal washroom was often the site of athletic grab-ass and towel-snapping games. We younger guys were regularly made victims of that, perpetrated by some of the older guys, a few of whom liked to lord it over the rest of us. I remember another game called "squirrel" that involved playfully grabbing nuts. And some of the guys were experimenting with lighting their farts on fire. I wonder now if bending over in the shower to pick up a dropped bar of soap may have been another *sport* that some were playing. I always tried to suppress temptations for sidelong glances in the shower. Clearly, that urge should have been an indication that something unusual was going on with me.

I suppose living in our dorm was like life in an Army barracks. We younger guys were scattered around among the upperclassmen. Because we needed to stick together, and despite my quiet nature, I became friends with all of the other seventh and eighth grade boys. There weren't many of us. We could socialize in the small ping- pong room where there was a Coke machine, the kind where the classic bottles sat in cold water until a nickel (or was it a dime?) released it from its rack. We also ate chocolate and ice cream bars together. We could buy them at the little Chinese store next to the campus. Those therapeutic relationships helped stave off some of my homesickness. I was away from home for the first time and only went back to Honolulu at Christmas and Easter breaks. I always went home on the tiny airplanes flown by Cockett Airlines from Upolu Point with a stop on Maui. I wonder if any of my new buddies were also homesick, questioning physical changes or tentatively entertaining sexual fantasies as I was. Today, I realize they must have been, or was I, as I feared then, out there on my own?

So, the dorm became one of our classrooms too, where we taught each other facts of life that sometimes brought snickers or had to be whispered. I think there was a quiet suspicion among us that sex was something that only we knew about, that it had been discovered just as our generation showed up. Bedtime happened about 11 o'clock, after doing our homework at study hall in the library. Together alone, adolescent boys are probably going to turn to the topics of body functions and sex, often through a prism of salacious laughter. That was certainly the case with the guys in our dorm when *lights-out* encouraged a volley of libidinous chit-chat before sleep.

Being the youngest, and looking even younger, I probably had the most to learn, so I listened a lot. I heard bragging about sexual conquests, who had the biggest dick, who could pee the farthest and which older guys already sported pubic hair. On a typical night, I was learning new expressions like *dickhead, bullshit, shitfaced, sloppy seconds* and *getting to 3^{rh} base*. I also heard plans for sneaking cigarettes down by the stream behind the dorm. I have never had a smoking habit, but I remember choking through my first experimental cigarette down at that stream. I was coerced by some of the older guys who had cigarettes to spare. And they offered me something called Sen-Sen to cover up the smell of my breath. I wondered if smoking would make me look older. And then there was a lot of discussion about the food we were fed in the dining hall.

"What about all that mystery meat they feed us?"

"Not to mention that constant *shit on a shingle* (chipped beef and gravy on toast)?"

"Do you guys know what saltpeter is?"

"Is that another mystery meat?"

"I heard it's something they feed us so we don't get horny. I think they're loading us down with that big time."

"Well, I don't think it's working."

It now turns out that that saltpeter thing was just an urban myth, but it certainly held our attention at that time in our dorm.

I was a bit overwhelmed by the older guys, a few of whom had been expelled from other private schools. HEA was not necessarily a school for bad boys, but it offered a second chance for some. Sensing that there was something different about me, I never knew how to interact with other boys. But they all had a lot to say. So, after our teeth were brushed, I paid full attention to these conversations in the dark that regularly provided sexual wisdom, *some* of which I had never heard before. My curiosity was piqued as I quietly lay on my upper bunk, sometimes kicked from below by my nemesis Lloyd. I listened to a glossary of basic four-letter words I already knew, along with an earful about the *birds-and-bees* that I had never heard from Dad in a parental sex talk but had been sketchily filtered to me in fifth and sixth grades. Perhaps Dad's reticence to talk with me about sex – we never *did* have *that* conversation – was because, despite the fact I never played with dolls, he suspected I might be gay (that wouldn't have been his word), judging by my quiet nature – and he had no idea what to say to me. My generation didn't know nearly what kids, with easy access to the Internet, know today. I was learning some new facts of life, including that *homo* business that was continuing to rattle around in my brain.

Mr. Cameron, a single man, was one of the English teachers and also our dorm master. He had a private bedroom in our building, and his job was to keep an eye on us. At times, we were aware of him eavesdropping in the shadows of our lights-out discussions. I guess he may have had a prurient interest in what we had to say, so I guess we were being spied on. We usually went silent when we thought he was there. Sometime later, when I had learned more about gay people, I wondered why Mr. Cameron was single.

One day, I was called into his bedroom for a talk, as he thought I might have been traumatized by too much *adult information*. After all, these extracurricular lessons were not necessarily what my parents had sent me there for – or perhaps they had. That sex info *could* have been part of their plan for me to grow up.

I sat quietly in a chair next to his bed from where I could see a pile of school papers and a red pen on his desk.

"Carl, I hope you realize you can always come to me if there's anything that makes you uncomfortable here."

This was an opportunity to complain about the bullies, but I decided not to open up that can of worms. Besides, I knew it wasn't macho to be a snitch. I just said, "What kind of things are you talking about, Mr. Cameron?"

"Well, boys your age have a lot of things on their minds. Do you ever feel any questions or worry about things you hear around the dorm?"

I sensed where this might be heading, and I didn't want the conversation to go much further. Mostly, I wondered if anyone had told him anything about me. But no, I soon sensed that he didn't seem to know anything specific about my hidden persuasion.

"Do you boys think about doing anything to yourself – down there?"

Mr. Cameron had come close to a very sensitive topic, but I just said, "Not that I know of, Mr. Cameron."

"Well, I just want you to report any gossip or bullying to me. And I wouldn't write home about it if I were you. Your parents want everything to go well for you. You don't want to worry them."

I promised I wouldn't do that. I was anxious to get away.

Obviously, the school didn't want any reports of sex talk or bullying to get back home. I felt no trauma, however, and I was eager to hear more of it – but I didn't tell Mr. Cameron that. Much of this *adult info* seemed to be common knowledge with the older guys, and I wanted to be as worldly as they were.

Homo, I soon learned from our discussions, was a shortcut to a longer word that gave a name to something I had been secretly intuiting for some time. I had suspected there was something up with me, so I looked the word up in my dictionary. Webster taught me the difference between *Homosapien* and *homosexual*. I learned that the Greek root *homo* means *same*, and its Latin root means *human*, perhaps suggesting something natural about it. In addition, there was a fairly blunt definition: *desire for the same sex*. Was that natural? That idea awakened an itching corner of my brain, but our nightly discussions suggested only who among us might be participating and gave me titillating descriptions of the mechanics: what went where, who was the *man* and who the *woman*. Years later, I realized that if there were women involved, I had gotten the homosexuality thing all wrong.

"You know there are two holes in your dick, one for peeing and the other for – you know what." Here was another reference to the mechanics.

"I wonder if anyone doing any cornholing in this dorm?" was one accusatory question I remember.

"You need a lot of Vaseline for that."

"Maybe just spit."

To my relief, I didn't hear my name mentioned in those discussions, and I failed to imagine our leader Dr. Simpson involved in any of it either. But I noticed that I *was* interested and not horrified as I had been a few years earlier when I was told what men and women did to have a baby. I couldn't imagine myself ever doing any of *that* stuff. I was happy to permanently postpone doing any of it, so I privately assumed I would never be a father or get married. And Dr. Simpson *was* married, so I decided that information on my desk could just be troublemaking gossip. Maybe.

In addition to those provocative nuggets of sexual information, the dorm offered up my first brush with pornography or *porn*, as we came to call it. That was another word I had never heard before, and two juicy examples of pre-computer porn were circulating around our barracks. Perhaps acquired from someone's older brother or someone in the military, these were a printed story and a graphically drawn comic book. The mimeographed story was called *Behind the Green Door* and recounted detailed descriptions of a young woman's escapades in a sex club. Years later, in 1972, after pornography had become available for mass consumption, I ran into a popular film version of the story in a movie theatre. I assumed that durability made it a classic.

The other shared treasure was a small book of drawings depicting an encounter of a bedridden patient and his very willing nurse. *Goodnight, Nurse* provided my first graphic images of what men and women sometimes did in bed together. Both printings, crumpled with lots of wear, were carefully hidden in lockers and under mattresses, were eagerly consumed by all the guys and became the inspiration for some of our nightly chatter.

As fascinating as these two treasures were, they didn't address the subject that had interested me the most. I had been having feelings, fantasies and memories that I didn't understand or, until then, have a name for. The freely shared information told me that some of the others knew plenty, and our conversations began to sprinkle in other words as well – *queer, pansy, fairy* and *fruit* – that didn't seem approving. A new vocabulary was starting to accumulate for me along with a growing fear that I might be all alone with a secret I had to keep. A few years later, I heard a phrase that seemed to underscore the hush-hush spirit of my secret – *the love that dare not speak its name*. (This had been offered by Lord Alfred Douglas in reference to Oscar Wilde whose *gross indecency* trial made him infamous).

The now universal use of the word *gay* would not enter our culture for a few years. Gay people themselves began to widely use that term in the 1960s, and the general public caught on in the '70s. Whenever one comes across the word today, you can always tell which side of a cultural divide it was used. Its meaning of *happy* is almost never used anymore. Did *sissy or cry baby*, words from my earlier childhood, mean the same thing as *homo*? I had been called those names, but so had most other kids. I got the idea that to be called a *sissy* may have meant you acted like a girl. I never had any thoughts in that direction, nor had I ever had a desire to wear a dress despite my curiosity about Mom's shoulder pads and closet full of stylish dresses left over from the 1940s. They were like costumes to me, but I never put any of them on. I've always favored being the man I am, never a woman. It's nothing that I'm necessarily proud of, but, to this day, even with my theatrical leanings (see my Stagestruck memoir), I don't know what it's like to wear a dress – and no stilettos or mascara either.

One time at Manoa Marketplace Mom had made an almost under-her-breath but memorable comment about an effeminate Hawaiian man with bleached hair:

"My God, you would think that at least he would leave his hair alone. Don't let me ever catch you doing that. You stay away from people like that."

I promised I would, but what did she mean? And what did she know about me? As it turned out, I did bleach my hair once when I played a blonde Italian in a college play,

Arthur Miller's *A View from the Bridge*. But that was show business, not gay vanity.

I didn't want to be like that bleached Hawaiian man, I decided. Or the old Japanese man in our neighborhood who was whispered by some kids to do some pretty unimaginable things with other men. I didn't believe any of it when I was younger. But, now, some of that stuff was being addressed in our dorm discussions. I didn't want to sound too interested, so I let the information come to me. I began to cling to the idea that I was probably the only boy in the dorm with that kind of secret and that it would probably die with me.

Some of those secrets were about my attraction to other boys in grade school, long before I had heard there was anything wrong with that. Gender identity, Freud has asserted, is established by age two. So, was it wrong to have thought in second grade while I was learning to read with Dick and Jane that my classmate Sherman was cute? And what about the cute older son of our friends the Bests, or the two handsome teenage brothers who came to baby sit on the next block? I used to regularly hang out near that house, hoping for a glimpse of them. I think I remember some cute guys in my Cub and Boy Scout packs too.

One Saturday afternoon in summer, when I was probably eight years old, I was to go off to play with Jamie Best, our friends' oldest son, whom I secretly admired. I remember wanting to be worthy of him, not the sissy I sometimes feared I was. That inner homophobia, generated by personal shame and guilt, was something that would rear its head consistently in the future and motivated me to pretend I was someone I wasn't. I knew I was a boy who couldn't whistle, crack my knuckles or swear, things I suspected real boys did with ease. I sat on a rock wall across from our house waiting for Jamie and his mother to pick me up. I didn't want to look like a sissy, so I decided that throwing small rocks into the street would make me seem more masculine when they showed up. Throwing rocks like that wasn't really my thing, but I hoped this act (and I *was* acting) would present me as a real boy.

I wasn't attracted to most adult men then, as their clothing in the 1940s wasn't very attractive to me. There were high-waisted baggy pants, double-breasted suits and large floppy hats. Most men didn't wear jeans or other form-fitting clothes in those days. I do remember one exception to that rule: my fifth grade teacher, Mr. Larkin, was very handsome. I remember a crush on him that I now think my mother shared. But comic books *were* a source of my nether region fantasies. Why was I a fan of any comics with men in tights, and why was Tarzan my favorite character? The back covers of the comic books regularly had ads for body building schemes, and the *after* photos always earned my careful attention. Then there were pictures of nearly naked tribes in National Geographic and the men's underwear ads in the Sears-Roebuck Catalog.

When I was about six years old, Mom took me to a Walt Disney film called *Song of the South*. It starred a good-looking boy about my age named Bobby Driscoll for whom I developed a strong childhood crush. I now know he went on to lead a tragic adult life involving drugs and an early death. But I also loved two later films with him called *So Dear to My Heart* and *Treasure Island*, however I never told anyone why. I was also attracted to another child star named Dean Stockwell, who played the title role in a film called *Kim*, based on a novel by Rudyard Kipling. I wonder if those pre-pubescent crushes might have labeled me *pre-gay*. As an adolescent, I was very taken with Robert Wagner, Tab Hunter and Rock Hudson. And some of them, it turned out, actually *were* gay. It wasn't until years later, with accumulated perspective, that I realized the guys I was attracted to steadily grew older as I did. And I have always wished I looked like the men I was drawn to.

By the time I was in junior high school at HEA, I was also attracted to some girls, which was very confusing. Something had moved me beyond that stage when most boys found girls disgusting. There wasn't a *no-girls-allowed* sign on my bedroom door, and I had moved past the *I'll-show-you-mine-if-you-show-me-your's* temptations. And then I saw two films at the onset of puberty that starred Jeff Chandler and Debra Paget as father and daughter: *Broken Arrow* (1950) and *Bird of Paradise* (1951). In one, they were an Apache chief and his daughter and in the other, Hawaiian royalty. They were beautiful people, especially since they didn't wear a lot of clothes in either film. I was turned on by both of them.

Even when I was having these confusing movie crushes, I was also infatuated with some of HEA's day-student girls because they were pretty. I was afraid of most girls then, but there were occasional mixers in our social hall, and Clarrie was the girl who appealed to me the most. I didn't know what girls expected of me then, but she was blonde, pretty and she liked to laugh. We danced to 78 records under festoons of crepe paper wrapped around the rafters. I wondered if I might have a split personality or, as I thought years later, that I had been experiencing an early glitch of bisexuality. I guess I hadn't yet distinguished between aesthetic beauty and sexual attraction (handsome vs. sexy). It was people's faces and personalities that attracted me the most then. I now see that, in lieu of a health class that taught about sex, it was puberty I needed to help me untangle that knot, and, I suspect, so did most of my seventh-and-eighth-grade friends. But we had no health classes at HEA.

Then, indeed, puberty did make a direct hit. In my second semester, I turned twelve and entered a nexus of childhood and adolescence. I got taller; my voice deepened from its conspicuous squeak; hair started to grow under my arms; oily skin and pimples began to dominate my complexion, and sexual imagery that I couldn't share with anyone began to fill my head. Suddenly, it seemed, my body was under new management, and I wondered if that was happening to all my friends too.

There was obviously something different about me – I wasn't athletic, I didn't tinker with old cars and I wasn't interested in most girls – I felt powerless to overcome that. But I wanted to be like everyone else. I didn't want to feel puny and have those forbidden thoughts. My internal *homophobia* continued its hold on me, and, to borrow a metaphor from the future, I tightly locked my *closet door.* Now I know that most gay boys develop that homophobia, and some carry it with them through life. We develop a cautiousness as a way of protecting ourselves. I don't think we ever totally lose it. There's always a background feeling that something in us doesn't measure up to the expectations of the straight world.

I never did learn to whistle or swear much, but my deepening voice was a fortuitous aid in keeping that closet door shut, as was the firm handshake I was trying to cultivate. But I was a skinny kid and looked about half my age – maybe even a bit androgynous at that time. Compared to the seemingly self-confident older guys, I was afraid of who I was. I regularly checked myself in the mirror for the image

I hoped to achieve. Puberty had not yet brought a beard or mustache – I began shaving in high school – but I practiced standing up straight and, despite being a shy kid, looking people in the eye.

Perhaps the most noticeable evidence of my puberty was the condition of the laundry I was regularly sending home to Honolulu. Mom had set up a plan for me to send dirty laundry in a special mailing container every two weeks. New stiffened cream-colored stains began to appear on my sheets and underwear that, at the very first, I didn't have an explanation for. I knew I didn't want the other guys to see them, but maybe they were also hiding stains from me. At first, the stains were produced by dreams I wasn't even aware of, and, then, once I could conjure up erotic images, I learned to create the feelings on my own. I discovered I could achieve that feeling by quietly pressing myself face down on my mattress. With a little motion, I could add to the stains in my underwear without anyone knowing. The nocturnal emissions thing had snuck up on me, and I think I had the opposite of what is today called *erectile dysfunction*. And I was powerless to stop sending those stains home to my mother.

As my hypochondriacal mind was always looking for trouble, I wondered if there was something wrong with me. I never mentioned my condition to Mom, but I'm sure she noticed the stains. What she didn't know yet was that they were inspired by fantasies of other boys. She was the daughter of very conservative nineteenth-century parents, and all of them, unfortunately, passed on some of their notions about sex to me. Grandma always asserted that polite people never talked about sex. None of what I was experiencing was ever mentioned by Mom or Dad, so I had no idea if I was the only one. Those Victorian attitudes stayed with me – until eventually a stronger self-image and a discovery of marijuana in the 1960s put me more in the moment and softened that sexual guilt.

Back in Honolulu, in the year before I went to HEA, I had had a friend in sixth grade. Tommy lived on the next block and now and then he invited me to what he called his *Blackhawk Club*, which met, away from his parents, in a crawl space under his house. The club members were just the two of us as far as I knew, and the main activity was to experiment with techniques of masturbation, jerking off, something he had already discovered, but I had not. "You just have to play with it, and it'll get hard." He seemed to get a lot of satisfaction showing me what he had already learned, but when I tried to do what he was doing, it didn't work in the same way. I was only eleven in the sixth grade, and I later realized that my time hadn't come yet.

But the next year in boarding school my time *had* come. My hormones had found their reason for being, I figured out what Tommy had been trying to show me as those stains began to collect on my sheets. I was too young to look for explanations for my private fantasies then. Possibilities came to light, however, about a decade later when my parents and I were looking for reasons for what had been happening with me. But, back in sixth grade, I was just trying to keep my secret – from Tommy and everyone else. Today I wonder if Tommy needed my presence to fulfill his fantasies. Why didn't he just do it by himself? Did he have designs on me that could have been fulfilled if I had been able to share what he was doing? Would we have been *messing around*, something I have heard other boys say they did when they were kids? Might he have, indeed, been my first sex partner? Tommy ended up marrying and having children so, perhaps what he wanted from me back then was just my company and validation he wasn't doing anything wrong. I would have discovered masturbation on my own – all boys do – but I have to thank Tommy for being my first mentor in that department.

When I first heard the metaphor *coming out of the closet*, I could only picture the door of my bedroom closet, and, later, debutantes coming out in society. In hindsight, I was definitely *in the closet* during those school years in the early 1950s. Being *out* publicly was almost unknown in those days. I wasn't even *out* to myself, because I thought I was the only one who felt the way I did. And who would I confide this information to, anyway? Certainly not my parents. Surely, I thought, I was the only one who had such uncommon and unnatural feelings. I assumed I'd be alone behind *my closet door* for the rest of my life.

An isolation and loneliness set in that I would subconsciously harbor for many years. I thought that to be lonely was a shameful thing, so I tried to hide it by pretending to be what I wasn't. In some ways, I became a loner so my guarded secret wouldn't slip out. I yearned for friends, but my shyness and insecurities were often interpreted as arrogance or conceit. I wish I had learned to smile more back then. I learned that lesson after some years of therapy and the work of an expert orthodontist who fixed a self-conscious gap in my upper front teeth. And after I learned it was OK to be just who I was.

*****

In 1953, I finished my two years of junior high school at

HEA and was brought back to Honolulu to live at home and attend Punahou School for senior high school. My secret followed me there, and I began to hear other references to who I was afraid of being. Maybe I *wasn't* the only one. Guys at Punahou passed around the idea that you were a *queer* if you wore green on Thursdays; I was thankful for that warning and was always careful not to do so. And, just to be safe, I avoided lavender and other exotic colors too. For a time, I found myself checking other guys' wardrobes on Thursdays for that evidence. In my sophomore year, I succumbed to a fad for pink long-sleeved shirts worn with cuff links, a skinny suede belt and black pants. There were two cute football players in my class who wore those shirts, and I wanted to look like them. Pink certainly wasn't lavender, nor was it green on Thursdays, but I think you really needed to be a sturdier guy than I was to successfully carry off that fashion craze.

The high school grapevine also taught me that there was a special handshake involving one's index finger that would reveal who you were. But I waited in vain to feel that shake. My gay sense of others wasn't honed yet, so if there were any other gay guys at Punahou, they didn't reveal themselves. There were some guys who performed in the annual Variety Show, as I did, and a couple who were cheerleaders, but those associations didn't mean much to me then.

I never heard anyone directly call me a *queer* or a *homo*, but those epithets were freely thrown around. I dreaded that I might see my name scratched on a desk, as I had seen Dr. Simpson's name. And all of us guys, I now presume, were trying to hide inconvenient swellings in our pants no matter what the inspiration. It wasn't always easy to stand up after class without carrying my school books in front of me.

When I was a junior, a scandal erupted when one of the male French teachers was fired after being caught with a sailor in a parked car. I took careful notice: there was **another** one. I wasn't completely alone. But I didn't want to end up like him.

As an insecure kid, I wasn't consciously looking for a girlfriend, but, in my senior year I stumbled on a chaste (never any French kissing) relationship of convenience (You would always have a date on Saturday night.) with Sally who *was* looking for a boyfriend, and I seemed to fit the bill. Maybe I was cute enough or maybe she just liked the sensitive type. At least this relationship put a stop to the inconvenient and embarrassing questions as to why I didn't have a girlfriend. Much later, that same embarrassment applied to why I wasn't married.

One day, after having her hair done, Sally confided in me that her gossipy hair dresser was *that way*, as she put it. Apparently, he was effeminate and spoke with a lisp. So, *there was* still *another* one. From her description, I didn't want to be like him either. And then there was that effeminate Hawaiian man Mom had gossiped about. Just how many of us were there? I was on the lookout, but positive role models weren't coming my way.

When I was a teenager, I loved going to downtown Honolulu on the bus to browse in bookstores and record shops. Yes, there were such places then. There was also a magazine shop on Fort Street that I liked. They had all kinds of titles from the mainland that opened my eyes to a new world. A magazine called *One, the Homosexual Viewpoint* was published by the Mattachine Society, a homosexual organization founded in 1953. Suddenly, I saw that there were *a lot* more of us. And there were theories about what caused our feelings. I carefully looked through the magazine and found an address in California. I can't remember how I had them sent as I don't think my parents found out, but I ordered a number of back issues and waited anxiously for them.

Those magazines offered lots of information about another persuasion on the other side of my closet door – if I was ever to open it. I can still feel the shudder of inclusion I felt when I first opened a copy of *One*, which showed me in black and white that other homos existed – more evidence that I, indeed, was not alone. I began to look between the lines of anything I read or saw on a screen for more evidence of that new world. In that same store, I leafed through another, more academic, magazine called *Sexology*. I glanced at some of its articles in the store. From then on, and even today, there are words that leap out at me from a page: *sex* and *homosexual* – and even just the letter *X* – were some main ones. They always seem to shout at me and gently make my heart skip a beat.

But the most titillating section of that store was where they kept the nudist and body building publications. I now realize those magazines were just a legal way to publish naked pictures. The most amazing one to me was called *Physique Pictorial*. It came from Los Angeles and featured animated erotic photographs of almost naked guys. Despite the near-nudity, there was a playfulness in the photos that added an air of innocence. Were these guys all like me? None of those homoerotic photos were explicitly pornographic, but they came very close. I had to have one of those magazines, so I stole it by slipping it into my school books. It was the only way, as I was much too unsure of myself to face the clerk and pay for it. I hid a number of those magazines on an upper shelf of my bedroom closet, along with my issues of *One Magazine*. If Mom ever found them, she was silent about it. Our major showdown had to wait for a few years, when I was a junior in college.

By the time I graduated from high school and went away to the University of Oregon, I had figured out the manly way to cross my legs, how to check my fingernails, how to carry my schoolbooks at my side, how to light a match, how to hug in a manly way and, most critical of all, not ever to let my wrists go limp. I don't know if I ever threw a ball like a girl, but that, and the fact that I was a scrawny kid, had been a sensitive issue for me since grade school, when the process of choosing sides for games was always torture. I didn't even feel comfortable with the unstructured playtime of recess. I never knew what to say to the other kids. I much preferred the order of the classroom, where I knew what was expected of me.

In high school, I had a few secret attractions to guys, but those were all quiet thoughts. I silently pretended to tolerate periodic *fag* jokes from some guys, but I was too unsure of myself to call them on it. During those same high school years, I served as an acolyte at St. Andrew's Episcopal Cathedral. I wore a white robe, and my main job was to light and snuff out the candles on the altar. It didn't occur to me then, but, today, with all the church-related sex scandals (primarily in the Catholic Church), I wonder if I was ever vulnerable to being molested. As a senior at Punahou, during my *girlfriend/going-steady episode*, I was part of a social group that entertained each other at parties. It was years later that I realized that three of us in the group were gay – and maybe more. Were we unwitting *birds of a feather*?

*****

In September of 1957, on my way to college in Oregon, I sailed to San Francisco on the Matson liner Lurline, without having kissed a guy or had sexual contact with anyone of either sex. There had been some chaste kisses with Sally in our drug and alcohol-free era, but no man but my father had ever kissed me. My closet was still well shut.

I had nagged my parents to let me stay in San Francisco on my own for a few days, but that idea was out of the question. They seemed to know something about that city that they didn't want me exposed to. I just wanted to explore the big city and go to some professional theater. But my aunt and uncle from Salinas were dispatched to meet the ship, escort me on a day of sightseeing and then deliver me to another aunt and uncle in San Leandro. I stayed with them until it was time to get on a train and go north to Eugene and the University of Oregon. There, a bigger world might present new possibilities for me.

In my freshman year I was totally focused on my studies in the theater department and in pledging the Kappa Sigma Fraternity. It was the era of *big man on campus,* and I thought the fraternity would bring me a step closer to that ideal. But I was much too busy and preoccupied to notice any gay people who were probably all around me – certainly in the theater department and maybe in the fraternity too. I had walk-on parts in a couple of plays (*The Teahouse of the August Moon* and *The Way of the World),* and I made a number of theater friends as well. In the fall of my sophomore year, I was perfectly cast in a small part in *A Streetcar Named Desire.* I played a very young and tender newsboy who comes to collect for the newspaper and then is seduced by Blanche DuBois. I still looked about half my age.

I hadn't come to the realization yet that my theatrical activities didn't totally engage with my preppy life in the fraternity. But I did move into our fancy brand-new chapter house and tried to be a good frat brother. Sometimes that required me to join testosterone-fueled plans for panty raids, something I didn't entirely understand. I also heard discussions about certain *townies* who were thought to be *easy*. And there were beer busts in our rec room at which we determined who were the hottest girls. Luckily, I was learning skills in my acting classes for that, so I sometimes timidly chimed in:

"The girls at the Alpha Phi house are pretty cool," I suggested one night after having at least one beer under my belt. "And their house is just across the millrace from us."

Would we be stealing their panties or just inviting them to a social? I wasn't sure.

As part of my attempts to fit in, – I wore a butch flattop like many of the other guys, and I bought my clothes at a campus shop that sold only the most recent collegiate fashions. Clint DeShazer was, perhaps, my best friend in the fraternity, and many years later we learned that we were both gay. But our locked closet doors allowed us to keep our secrets from each other and to pass for straight in the frat house. In order to ease our way in life, the goal of passing for straight became an ongoing challenge for many of us. I never moved or talked in a feminine way, so that was a head start and a leg up for me. In spite of my quiet nature, I could pass.

Two fraternity incidents in my freshman year that both involved vodka fortuitously strengthened my, perhaps questionable, straight credentials. A house party in Portland, where some of us had gone for a football game, revealed to the other guys that I was a cocksman. After drinking too many screwdrivers, I grabbed my date and began dramatically making out with her on a staircase. It was all an act, but, thanks to the vodka, that was just what I needed to show the other guys that I was one of them.

I never, as a child or now at college, got into a physical fight with anyone, something which might have verified my masculine credentials. But further proof that I was just a regular guy happened on a Friday night in the spring. Some of us were in the habit of piling into a car with a vodka bottle to go to the drive-in movies. Two of us were secured in the trunk so we wouldn't have to pay. Designated drivers were not a thing then, but after a long double-feature, we arrived back at the curb in front of the fraternity. I stumbled and fell into the gutter where I threw up and then was found and rescued by the fraternity president. He got me to the sleeping porch where I could recover. Though it was clear I couldn't hold my liquor, I was now seen as one of the boys because I was willing to drink with them and invite a wicked hangover.

*****

After the run of *A Streetcar Named Desire*, a Northwest Drama Conference at The University of Washington in Seattle was announced. Several of us decided to carpool to the event. I didn't anticipate that such a theater gathering would thrust me into a crowd that I had been wondering about since seventh grade. On Saturday night after a performance of an in-the-round production of Shakespeare's *As You Like*

It, a bunch of us piled into a car to go to an after-party. I will always remember that production because of what happened next. That car ride would steer my life in a new direction and cautiously inched my closet door ajar.

Because we were all jammed into the car, I was sitting in the backseat on someone's lap. I hadn't even glimpsed who it was, but I began to feel movement under me. Once we reached the party, he and I made eye contact, and I later ended up spending the night in his apartment.

"I'll get you to your ride back to Eugene tomorrow," he promised. Charlie was a University of Washington theater student, a little older than I was, and had curly red hair. He was attractive and I guess he thought I was too.

With a lot of excitement, fear and fumbling, I tried to reference information from our lights-out discussions in my HEA dorm. Some of that spotty know-how came vigorously to life. But Charlie was the experienced one, so I let him take the lead. Except for my one-sided masturbation lessons from my sixth-grade friend Tommy, that was my first consensual sexual experience of any kind. Here, finally, was a positive role model and a spring awakening for me.

My first-time anxiety kept the extreme thickness of lust at bay, but I experienced the clean musky smell of kisses from another man and what razor burn feels like. My excitement was tempered by the unfamiliarity of what we were doing. I felt an out-of-body remove as I looked down at what was going on. As with my seduction by Blanche in *Streetcar*, this seduction happened because of my very young looks. I was 18 years old, seven years since *Simpson is a homo* had leapt off of my social studies desk into my consciousness.

Still trembling from this life-changing experience, I went

back to Eugene and the frat house a changed man. It was hard to keep my mind on my studies for a while, as I contemplated what had happened. My closet door had swung slightly ajar in the sense that there was now at least one other person who knew I was queer. From then on, I was on the lookout for others. Years later, I learned a term for the ability to do that: *gaydar*.

The rest of my four-year career in the theater department had me cast in quite a number of plays. In addition to that tender paperboy in *Streetcar*, there was Trinculo, a court jester in Shakespeare's *The Tempest* and Rodolfo, a young blond Italian immigrant who is accused of being gay in Arthur Miller's *A View from the Bridge*. In an acting class, I played Tom Lee, a prep school boy who is similarly accused in *Tea and Sympathy*. There seemed to be a pattern in those roles. Maybe my directors sensed something about me too.

Up to that time, I hadn't really thought much about what had made me a member of the club referenced on my HEA desk. But that one-night stand in Seattle got me thinking. When I first read about the subject, probably in *One Magazine* or *Sexology*, the idea seemed to be that it was a mental illness, and I wondered if I could one day be cured. At least I wasn't a schizophrenic, and the exciting novelty and mysterious intrigue of my new existence made me wonder if I wanted to be cured anyway. And then, in 1973, the American Psychiatric Association finally decided that homosexuality was not, indeed, a psychological disorder.

There were other theories as well. Too much female authority over a boy could be the culprit. My mother and grandmother were dominant influences on me when I was very young. As the firstborn, I was fussed over and watchfully protected. *Don't play with matches. Don't run into the street*. Could all that fussing have been the cause of a prolonged infancy? Or was I gay because my neighborhood playmates then were mostly girls. There were boys on other blocks, but on our street, it was mainly those girls and me. As the only boy, I was always assigned to be the father whenever we played *house*. Another theory was that having gay desires was a normal developmental phase, and I'd grow out of them. Would I wake up one day and be straight?

Another popular explanation was having a suffocating mother and a distant father. Indeed, I had a quiet introspective father and an outgoing mother who loved a good party. Dad was a serious introvert as I turned out to be. He was always focused on his experiments or his garden, and we never played ball or went on camping trips together. The main thing we did do together was to pull crab grass and weeds out of the lawn. But I always felt I was under his watchful eye, and I had to do it his way.

I'm sure my father loved me, but he didn't always know how to show it or how to serve as a positive male role model for me. I longed for him to say he loved me or was proud of me. I'm sure now that his not knowing how to do that negatively affected my self-esteem. But I would occasionally go shopping or out to lunch with Mom. Today, that scenario sounds pretty gay to me. I wonder if anyone ever called me a mama's boy? As most kids do, when I was a teenager I went through a period when I didn't want to be seen with her and insisted on being dropped off at least a block from wherever I was going.

Nature vs. Nurture seemed to be the overriding idea behind all of this speculation. There now is some disagreement over the existence of a specific gay gene, although same-sex attraction does appear to be influenced by a mixture of genetic and cultural causes. I have known two sets of gay male twins, which suggests the possibility that Nature is the cause. I believe it was purely Nature that made *me* who I am. Long before I even knew what a homo was, I felt unintentional attractions to other boys. I *must* have been born this way. I have blue eyes and light brown (now gray) hair, I'm six feet tall, weigh about 165 pounds – and I am a gay man. Many on the other side of the political divide would like to think it is a choice. But, with the social stigma on being gay when I was a teenager in the 1950s, why would I or anyone have chosen it? There is also a mistaken assumption by some that gay men are attracted to all other males including children whom they want to molest. That was never the case with me or any other gay man that I know.

In California, where I live today, sodomy laws made me a criminal until 1976, and I still am vulnerable to discrimination in some states. In 2003 the Supreme Court struck down same-sex sodomy laws, but housing and health care bias are still very legal in some places, especially in the south where we are punished for something we didn't choose. As I write this memoir in 2020, the Supreme Court has just made it illegal to discriminate against LGBT people in the workplace – but only in the workplace.

In gay circles, one sometimes hears, *"I didn't choose to be gay; I just got lucky."* I don't know if it was luck or not, but I do know it is in my DNA, and I wonder who I inherited it from. One of my father's brothers was a bachelor. Could it have been Uncle Fred? As far as I know, I am the only gay person in my family – my introverted isolation has always wished there was another one to keep me company – but there *are* stories (and at least one book) about two brothers on my mother's side of the family: James and Joshua Speed (My grandmother's middle name is Speed.) were close friends of Abe Lincoln. James became Lincoln's second Attorney General and Joshua was a very close (some say *intimate*) friend of Lincoln from his boyhood in Illinois. That was seven or eight generations ago, but I am a blood descendant of Joshua Speed, who was perhaps in a sexual relationship with Abraham Lincoln. Maybe, as distant as he is to me, Joshua Speed could have been the reason I was wired this way.

In my search for a better understanding of myself, I began reading – some fiction, some non. There was a lot of lurid pulp fiction that presented the idea that all homosexuals were lonely and unhappy (*Summer in Sodom, Perverted Passion, Gay on the Range*). Those kinds of books show the more seamy and tragic side of gay life, often with a suicide. I didn't read much of that. But there was Gore Vidal's *The City and the Pillar*, which does not end tragically. And James Baldwin's *Giovanni's Room* which ends ambiguously but with a sense of hope. Walt Whitman, Tennessee Williams, Truman Capote, Christopher Isherwood, Carson McCullers and Jean Genet have presented the subject in their own ways.

I haven't been able to find a current reference to it, but I found a nonfiction paperback when I was a teenager called *The Tenth Man* which concluded that every tenth man is a homosexual. After reading that, I found myself counting men in public. I'm not sure if his theories are still accepted, but in 1948 Alfred Kinsey's *Sexual Behavior in the Human Male* put men on a scale from 0 to 6. 0 was exclusively heterosexual and 6 was exclusively homosexual. Kinsey saw this behavior as perfectly natural. Just how gay was I, and how natural was that? Today, long after growing out of my early and passing attraction for girls, I feel I am a six on Kinsey's scale. Outside of necking and basic fumbling foreplay, I have never had sex with a woman. At one time, I wondered if kissing a girl might change me. It didn't. However, I never wrapped myself in a totally gay identity; I am not a *professional gay*. I don't demand that everyone I know or everything I do must be gay oriented. But I can't deny my Kinsey marker.

*****

Home in Honolulu for the summer of 1959 after my sophomore year in Eugene, a family connection put me in a job as a clerk at the front desk of the Reef Hotel in Waikiki where the lobby was always bustling with mainland and international tourists. I loved the job, which I now see sometimes put me in the presence of other gay men.

I wondered why I kept getting looks and smiles from a good looking – tall, dark and handsome – guy who came every morning to have coffee with the woman at the tour desk across the lobby. I tried to concentrate on my duties:

"Your mail, sir; room keys go here; a message while you were out."

But the man, whom I thought could have been a film star, would not leave my mind. Today, I can't remember that heartthrob's name, but, by the end of the summer, I thought I had been in love, but then was heart-broken because, for him, the security of a wife and child was too much competition for a nearly virginal and underage college boy. That was the first time I had been dumped, but I couldn't tell Mom why I was inconsolable for nearly a week. I did learn that he was a reporter for the Honolulu Star-Bulletin and the woman working at the tour desk was his wife.

That storyline had unraveled one day when I was waiting for the bus after work. Mr. *Handsome* pulled up in his convertible and asked if I needed a ride.

"Are you going my way?" he asked.

"Maybe. Which way are you going?"

"Where do you live? I can take you home."

With a very brief negotiation in which I put up little protest, I got in the car.

It was when he put his hand on my knee that I realized what he was up to. How did he know I would be open to that? Instead of taking me to my house, he took me to his bedroom. His wife was still at work, and I could hear his daughter happily playing outside in the yard.

Mr. *Rights* have come and gone in my life, but that second one has always remained with me. Here was another positive role model: queers could look like that, have a responsible career and even be married. I was flattered that this handsome stranger had chosen me. My very brief affair with that reporter had thrust me from ordinary *teenagedom* into grownup *Life* with a capital L.

Later that summer, another chance encounter erased my brief heartache. One day, after work at the Reef, I was walking up Beachwalk, the short street that led from the Hotel to the bus stop on Kalakaua Avenue. Beachwalk was mostly a street of small private hotels, but there was one old house that had seen better days. A group of about four guys in Bermuda shorts was sitting on the porch drinking beer and laughing.

As I passed, I heard some whistles and cat calls.

I looked around, but I was the only one on the sidewalk.

Were they whistling at me?

"Hey, cutie. Come have a beer with us."

Cutie? Me? I thought.

"I'm on my way to the bus," I stalled.

"Do you work around here?"

"I'm a desk clerk down the street at the Reef."

"You can catch your bus later! Come say hello to us. We won't bite."

"My parents expect me," I hesitantly protested.

My resolve to catch the 5 o'clock bus was weakening. I was intrigued, but why were there only guys in that group? None of them seemed effeminate in any way, so I didn't come to an obvious conclusion. But then there was the fact that one of them had called me *cutie*.

With my heart pounding, I made a sudden and portentous decision to join them.

I crossed the street.

But where are the women, I naively still wondered. *And how do they all know each other?*

The old bungalow, probably from the 1920s, had been turned into a bar called the Beachwalk. I was nineteen years old, too young to be drinking legally in Hawaii, so I hesitated. But, shaking inside, I did accept that beer.

I still was questioning why there were only men, but, not being as dumb as all that, I suddenly realized what I had stumbled into.

At that point another guy appeared in the doorway. He winked at me.

"So, you're a local guy?" I glanced over to see a ruggedly handsome man, probably a few years older than me, in a short-sleeved shirt and a stained apron.

He asked me my name, and then, "Do you want a

hamburger to go with that beer? Have you been here before?" That was his version of the common pickup line "Do you come here often?"

I assured him it was my first time.

"Where do you live?" I think he was interested in the fact that I wasn't a tourist. And all of them, I later realized, were taken with me because I was a new face. As I grew older in the gay world, it became clear to me that being a new face was always a valuable asset.

We exchanged names. His was Duke Braddock, a name vaguely suggestive of a football field or boxing ring to me.

"I live with my parents in Manoa Valley, and, yes, I'm a local guy."

"Oh, you live with your parents? Just how old are you, anyway?"

"Old enough to have a beer," I lied. I was expected home for dinner, so, no, I didn't want a hamburger. The other guys could see Duke's moves on me and let him take the lead.

"You, young man, are a fox."

I didn't know what that meant, but his tone made it sound complimentary.

By now I had forgotten about the time. I was fascinated too.

I now see that meeting a group of other gay men was bound to happen sometime. But crossing Beachwalk that day had thrust me onto a new life path.

Duke, I soon found out, was newly out of the Navy and was working at the Beachwalk making and serving hamburgers, as the law said they had to serve food if they sold alcohol. His interested attentions dragged me out of my closet a little further and, within a week, he became my first boyfriend or, in the parlance of that day, *my lover*. Today, that term sounds very old fashioned and literary to me, but that was the word that was used then. My high school girlfriend had not been a sexual affair, so this was all new to me. Was it like being married, I wondered?

I didn't foresee then that my affair with Duke would set off a long, checkered career of relationships. It foreshadowed six future lovers of two years or more each, in addition to a number of briefer affairs and quite a few one-night stands. The Beachwalk was the first gay bar I had stumbled into, and my gay education began to inch forward. As you will eventually see, going into the Beachwalk and meeting Duke that day was a major turning point in my life.

Hanging out with Duke necessitated weaving stories for my parents as I tried to keep my secret from them: *I had to stay late at the hotel. I took a walk down the beach. I did some shopping. I was browsing in a bookstore.*

Duke had a car, and one day he drove me home. As chance would have it, Mom and Dad were in the garage. I don't remember what I told them about him – probably that he was someone I met when working at the hotel. We got together after my duties at the hotel at his small place on Royal Hawaiian Avenue, when I could come up with a credible story for Mom and Dad.

Duke was instrumental in showing me that gay life was a cultural lifestyle as well as a sexual persuasion. That life seemed like a sophisticated bubble distinct from, but parallel to, my ordinary existence. A lofty tone and vocabulary accompanied this new life, and I was excited to be a part of it. I had to be careful to present myself differently according to whom I was with. I began to lead two lives, and my closet door was necessary to keep them separated.

At first, before I realized the size of this new-found

group, I had the false impression that all people in the bubble knew each other. Duke was very outgoing, and he seemed to know a lot of people. One of them was Barbara Hutton's gay cousin Jimmy Donohue, who lived in the $300 a night (astronomical then) penthouse of the Surfrider Hotel. There I was, an ordinary kid, mixing with the super-wealthy. I could see that being cute and having a membership in *the club* gave entrée, in lieu of money and social standing.

My shyness in school had prompted a longstanding yearning to be a member of a group, any group, and now I felt my search for belonging to something had found one. I was no longer peering in from the outside. I had become a member just by being who I was. Because the club was secret then, membership was all the more intriguing and fun. The renegade spirit of this sub-culture intrigued me. Until then, I hadn't thought there was anything particularly noteworthy about me, but now there was the club membership that endowed me with something unique. As I wasn't a brawny guy, I never considered myself good looking, so it was a startling revelation that I was attractive to some other members of the club – as was my conclusion that being gay gave one twice as many options as being just straight, if you wanted to partake in those ways.

Homo – the word continued to rattle around inside me – had been the first entry in my new secret vocabulary back in seventh grade. Now there were many others that spun around the focal word *gay*. One of that word's meanings is *bright and showy* and, as I have read, it began to be commonly used in Britain at mid-twentieth century. Could *straight* come from *straight and narrow* or the Boy Scouts' oath to be *morally straight*?

I learned that there were two other identifying gay associations: *butch* and *nelly*. I'm pretty sure I wasn't *nelly*, but I'm not sure I was *butch* either, an adjective that carried a lot of heavy expectation. At times I heard myself referred to as a *twink*, a gay word suggesting youth and cuteness. I encouraged myself by noting that at least I didn't act like Liberace, whom my parents watched on TV every week. Looking back from a more liberated era, I can see that his image was what being gay meant to earlier generations. If you didn't act like him, it was much easier to pass unnoticed. My formative gay years came too early for easy lessons on how to be gay from TV's *Will and Grace* in the 1990s. In 1982 a mainstream film called *Making Love* had finally shown characters who reminded me of myself. Until then, gay roles had always been tragic victims, villains or comic relief.

Two of my other early gay vocabulary words were *queen* and *chicken*. Because of my age and young looks, I was definitely *chicken*, and Duke, I learned, was a *chicken queen* or *chicken hawk*. The club's vocabulary, sometimes not for public use, came to me thick and fast after that: *cruising, trick, faggot, glory hole, blow job, daisy chain, jail bait, rough trade, fellatio, swishy, pinkie ring, sugar-daddy, camp, horny, sixty-nine, lesbian, sodomy, dildo, KY Lube, orgy, hung, size queen, hustler and*, not the least, *the closet*.

I came to realize there were all kinds of gay men. There were some, like me, who were ordinary looking guys, and then there were some we called "old queens" who stuffed socks in their pants to enhance their wares. I tried to avoid people like that. My early gay education was happening in Hawaii, so the Hawaiian word *mahu*, meaning *a homosexual of either sex, crept* in too. I learned that the Hawaiian culture reserved an elevated place for *mahus*, who were seen as a respected third sex. Another Hawaiian word, *Aikane*, means *intimate friend of the same sex* or *trusted partner*.

That secret language sometimes felt like communicating in code. Although I didn't do so, I learned that, for shared gay satire, some guys called each other *Mary*, and the pronouns *she* and *her* were used a lot, along with the greeting *get you, girl*. I attempted to use some of it, but, as an introvert, I had trouble integrating any flamboyance with who I really was. *Fa-a-abulous!* was sprinkled here and there, and some gay men revered and imitated bigger-than-life women like Bette Davis, Mae West and Tallulah Bankhead. Judy Garland, I learned, was a gay patron saint, and, from her, came the gay euphemism *friends of Dorothy* as a secret password.

In those days, my identification was checked every time I went into a bar. The drinking age in Hawaii was twenty then, but I was barely nineteen, and I probably looked twelve. In college, I had discovered that changing just one number on my driver's license was enough to fake my ID. With Duke's help, I discovered other gay bars in Waikiki. Honolulu was not a huge city then (a bit more than 300,000 people in 1958 and about a million today) but as a beach resort, there was a lot going on for gay people, especially in Waikiki.

There was a two-story building across from the zoo that, over the years, was home to a number of gay bars. The Clouds, where night club singers performed, was on the top floor. I remember hearing Nancy Wilson early in her career there. The Little Dipper, a smaller bar for socializing and cruising, was on the street level. The Beachwalk was at the other end of Waikiki, so the stroll between those bars on

Kalakaua Avenue always presented the further possibility of brief encounters. When I went to these places alone, I had to get up my courage by walking around the block to help allay my self-consciousness and anxiety about being in a place I still wasn't sure I belonged. But, because I was apparently a cute *chicken*, occasional encouraging glances and drinks were sent my way. *"This is from the guy sitting at the end of the bar."*

To use one of my new vocabulary words, Duke was solidly built – *hunky* we would say today – and definitely *butch* with a butch sounding name: Duke Braddock (today that name could be a gay *nom de porn*). I had found out that one of Duke's great uncles was James Braddock, a well-known professional boxer in the 1920s and '30s, so, indeed, he came by his boxing ring image honestly.

Duke was very inclusive, liked to have a good time, and had a few friends who were drag queens. They were local *girls*, and I remember one time hanging out with them while they were dressing up for a Saturday night. Slinky dresses and exaggerated wigs were strewn around the room.

"Girl, you're not going to wear that old thing, are you?"

"Come help me put my hair up, Miss Thing, and mind your own business."

"Where are we going tonight?"

"First our usual promenade along the Avenue and then a fashionable late appearance at Yappy's."

"I guess we have to pin on our notes."

Without wanting to dress or act like them, I was immediately attracted to the high attitude, theatricality and sense of humor that was part of their sub-subculture. Gay humor is often a parody of heterosexual behavior seen through gay eyes. All these guys had *drag names* which was part of the fun. Some of them were: Cherie Amour, Jasmine James, Honey Divine and Sasha DeVille.

For a few years, there, indeed, was a bar called Yappy's on Kapahulu Avenue, where the law allowed drag as long as there was also a pinned-on note saying *I am a boy* – just so there was no confusion. Today, drag queens have become a major face of the gay community, big business with *RuPaul's Drag Race* on TV and controversy in places like Florida. But, in the 1950s, they were even more forbidden and illegal than ordinary gay people. Most gay men – doctors, lawyers, teachers, politicians etc. – aren't often obvious, so, for the general public, the more-showy drag and leather sub-cultures are more visible faces of homosexual life. I was never a member of either of those groups, but I was a careful observer of the varied texture of gay life that was spinning around me.

*****

With a promise and a plan to meet again, Duke and I parted at the end of the summer. I went back to school in Eugene where I prepared for being part of a show sponsored by the U.S. State Department. The USO was sending college theater groups to entertain the troops in Europe and Asia. Being on the West Coast, we were assigned to Asia, and we toured with a musical comedy called *Wonderful Town* with music by Leonard Bernstein. Fifteen of us played all the parts and performed all the technical jobs as well. We became a traveling troupe of players thoroughly embedded with the military, including our transport, billets and access to post exchanges. With all our needed shots, we toured Japan, Korea, Okinawa, Iwo Jima, The Philippines and

Guam. After two months on the road, we returned to Oregon by way of Honolulu where I was allowed to remain at home for Christmas.

Several of us in the troupe were gay, and my friend Hugh, a few years older than I, served as a gay mentor to me as Duke had been in Waikiki. Back in Eugene, Hugh had introduced me to gay cruising spots like the Greyhound bus station and rest rooms in the basement of the University library. But I must say, places like that made me uneasy. They were too public and too risky.

Some of our adventures on the road competed with our onstage show. It was in Japan that I learned what crab lice were when a freckle started making its way across my forearm. Where had that come from? Military medics cured me with a shave and a bottle of Kwell.

One night, Hugh and I were *cruising* around the Ginza (like Times Square) in Tokyo, where we met two Japanese guys who were pretending to look in store windows. They were wearing very high wooden platform sandals and kimono outfits.

At first there were just exchanged glances. But there were two of them and two of us, and Hugh and I were up for an adventure. We communicated with broken English, very limited Japanese – and a lot of pantomime.

I had known how to count to ten in Japanese since I was a kid (*ichi, ni, san, shi* etc.) but what good was that going to be? I also knew that *ohio* meant *good morning*, but that was also of no use as it was evening.

Konichiwa means *hello*, so we started with that. And we realized that yes (*hai*) and no *(te)* might come in handy – if the proceedings got that far.

"You American guys?" they asked timidly.

"*Hai*," we replied. That one came in handy right away.

We tried to explain the show we were in and why we were strolling in the Ginza. I guess we seemed safe enough for them, and they invited us to their nearby apartment.

"You come our house. We have tea."

That seemed harmless enough, so we agreed to follow them to their very small apartment. At first, it was all very polite with cups of tea and gentle chat. Eventually, after Hugh and I had run out of things to pantomime, and they had exhausted their careful, hesitant English some of which I'm sure was lost in translation, we had to announce our eleven o'clock curfew. At that point the proceedings got much more physical, and we had to fend them off. That was followed by *arigato* (thank you) and *oyasumi nasai* (goodnight).

Another time, we were taken by taxi to what was promised as a *special private show*. After quite a few back alleys, we were led upstairs for a startling presentation performed by two naked young ladies and some rubber accoutrements I had never seen before. Years later, only Tijuana (with a mule) and Bangkok (with ping pong balls) would top that.

Hugh and I remained friends for many years, and he later ran the prop department at Columbia Studios and was a producer at Warner Brothers. He could get me on the studio lots where I loved watching movies being made.

*****

In January, I was back in Eugene for my junior year. The plan was that Duke would come to join me, but, obviously that could never happen in the fraternity house. So, I set about finding another place for us to live. Even though I had suffered through *hell week* and was formally initiated, that move and the distractions of my more artistic life in the University Theater began easing me away from my life as a frat man. For $45 a month, I found a house from a much earlier era on an alley near Max's Tavern which, ironically, was a favorite fraternity hang out. That small house was the setting for my first time living anywhere unsupervised.

It was mid-winter and a wood-burning furnace in the basement supplied the only heat. I had to do something fast, so I ordered some wood. I was a Hawaii kid and had no idea what I was doing. I ordered one cord of wood – I thought I'd better start off small – and I came home after class that day to find that the cord of wood had buried my backyard. Duke arrived in the nick of time, I learned what a cord of wood was, and, with his help, we chopped it into smaller pieces and figured out how to keep warm.

That winter, I was appearing in Arthur Miller's *A View from the Bridge,* playing Rodolfo an Italian immigrant who is falsely accused of being a homosexual. And in March I was stage managing a production of *The King and I*. Gini Chapson, a girl who had been a year behind me in high school in Honolulu, was one of the dancers. Gini and I hadn't known each other at Punahou, but we became fast friends at the U. of O. and we were close friends until a recent stroke (2021) took her from me. But back then, her life took a dip when she was expelled by the University for consistently violating a curfew. She didn't want to return to her parents in Hawaii, so she asked to move in with Duke and me. Duke got a job delivering drugs for a pharmacy, Gini hung out with her friends, and I struggled through lots of distractions to go to my classes and do my studying in the library.

I've sublimated a large part of what I was telling my parents about all this. They seemed to accept the sketchy details because I was also passing on made—up names of girls I was *dating* to give them a degree of hope and to keep them guessing. At the end of the spring term, all three of us, Duke, Gini and I, moved to Hollywood for the summer. I did this under the pretense of taking needed theater classes at UCLA and seeing about breaking into films or TV. I found an agent and was suggested for a show called *My Three Sons*, which was casting boyish looking guys. As it turned out, that show did not change my life.

Some of my old letters to my parents reveal that, instead of Duke, I had made up a name of a friend I called *Bob Strickland* (where did I get that name?), because Duke's name would have alarmed Mom and Dad. What, they would wonder, was he doing with me on the mainland? Duke and I moved into an apartment in The Highland Tower near the Hollywood Bowl, and Gini lived near the Sunset Strip. I commuted to UCLA for my theater classes, Duke managed Delores Drive-in at Wilshire and La Cienega where he earned an exorbitant $20 a day and where the car hops were all young gay guys. Gini went about her life as a cashier at Gino's Bit, a jazz coffee house on the Strip.

That new city, with all its distractions, further increased my gay vocabulary: *leather queen, deviate, sodomite, pederast, vice squad, sea food, hot, piss-elegant, light in the loafers, gay as a goose, nancy-boy, top* and *bottom, cut* and *uncut* and *bisexual*. Duke had lived in Hollywood before he had gone to Hawaii, so he had friends with whom we hung out – trips to the gay beach in Santa Monica and outings to gay bars. One of Duke's favorite hangouts was a coffee house on Hollywood Blvd. near Highland called Coffee Dan's. We could walk there so it almost became a second home.

One night we were caught jay-walking on our way to a bar popular with college-age guys called The Red Raven on Melrose Avenue. We were flirting with danger in an era of extreme harassment of homosexuals, and the cops arrested us and took us to the Hollywood precinct station.

"Look at that; we've got ourselves some *Nancy-boys*. Do you know why you are here?"

We were silent. "I guess you guys are lovers, not fighters." I didn't know what they meant by that, but they were correct; I was not a fighter. We felt lucky, when, after about an hour of being made fun of, we were let go with a warning. Now I don't remember what that warning was for: jay-walking or being gay?

Because of a misunderstanding and some meddling by one of Duke's friends, he and I pulled away from each other by the end of the summer. I felt adrift. Duke had been a gay mentor to me ever since I had first stumbled into the gay culture in Hawaii. Now alone, I went to live on Fairfax Avenue near Farmer's Market. Then, one day I met Don Britton on Hollywood Boulevard. The Boulevard was home to lots of movie theaters, stores that sold movie memorabilia, coffee shops and Fredericks of Hollywood, a famous store for sexy women's wear – and a lot of hustlers and gay cruising. I was tired of living alone, so I went to live with him in a platonic relationship on Wonderland Drive in the hills above Laurel Canyon. I guess I had stepped into the questionable role of being a *kept man,* as I wasn't paying any rent, and I had to supply yet another new address for Mom and Dad. Their heads must have been spinning.

*****

It was at this time that my *artistic* lifestyle back in Eugene finally caught up with me. When I escaped to study in the library, Duke and Gini had been having parties in our place for mostly art and theater students. Then our artistic household became locally infamous and, somehow, word of our living situation got back to the University administration. Students weren't to live unchaperoned with the opposite sex in 1960, nor were they to live with the same sex when the relationship was a sexual one. They had gotten me on two counts, I thought.

Mom and Dad were notified by the administration that I had been expelled because of my unorthodox living arrangements. Actually, my sexual relationship with Duke was not included in the accusation (living with a woman was my main crime), but I was hustled back to Honolulu, still with no evidence that Duke had been with me on the mainland or that I was gay.

That was all about to change, however. The following dramatic events finally ripped me from the closet and revealed my secret to Mom and Dad. It's interesting that none of this would have happened in a slightly later era. In ten years being gay wouldn't have been an issue with the University, and, just the next year, the U. of O. had so many students that women were allowed to live on their own where they pleased.

Back in Honolulu, I tried to toe Mom and Dad's line, but temptations got the best of me one night. I met a guy in Waikiki who was staying at the Princess Kaiulani Hotel. I called my parents in the morning to say I was OK and would catch the bus to come home.

Ominously, Dad said, "Wait for us there, and we'll come get you."

Wondering what was up, I waited on a bench under the *porte cochere*. When my parents pulled up to the hotel, I automatically reached for the handle to the back seat.

"No, sit up here in the front with us," Dad said. Now I was really alarmed. I smelled trouble.

"There's no room for all of us." I protested. Why were they putting me between them in the crowded front seat?

"We want to talk with you, Honey," Mom answered.

After I squeezed in between them, I noticed Mom was holding a letter. I could see it was addressed to me.

Mom always drove, as Dad had vision problems, and cars were starting to line up behind us. She pulled away from the hotel, and found a place to park at Ala Moana Park.

"We want you to open this letter and read it to us."

Mom handed me the unopened letter that I could clearly see was from Duke. The post mark was Los Angeles, I recognized his handwriting and, if you held it up to the light, the words *love, Duke* could be read through the envelope.

"Open the letter and read it to us," they repeated. I could see where this was heading, and, with sweat on my brow, I refused. Because of the source of the letter, I could easily guess what this was all about. But why did we have to talk about it in the car? Was it something they didn't want my brother and sister to hear at home?

And why would Duke have sent a letter to me at my parents' house anyway?

As in a Victorian novel, where the story line might be unraveled by a crucial letter, my intrigue was ripped open by a similar plot device.

"If this is about Duke, I've already told you how I met him at the Reef Hotel."

"We think there is more to the story, and we want to get

to the bottom of it," Mom said lighting up one of her Lucky Strikes. She had a bad habit that would sadly eventually kill her, but she did this now to try to relax. I could see there were tears in her eyes that I didn't know how to stop.

"There's nothing to tell," I interrupted. "Duke is living in Los Angeles and I don't talk with him anymore."

"So why is he sending letters to you? And saying *love, Duke?*"

I didn't have an answer for that and didn't know what else to say. We were at an impasse; our confrontation came to a standstill.

"You're always keeping tabs on me," I protested.

"We're doing it for your own good. We don't want you in any trouble." Mom put out her cigarette, and I could see there were more tears. Dad suggested we contact someone who could mediate for us.

"Let's find a psychiatrist," Mom suggested. We found one by looking in the Yellow Pages in a nearby phone booth.

Dad made an emergency appointment. Dr. Silverman's office was downtown on Bishop Street, and we soon found ourselves in his waiting room, all of us silent, with me staring at the floor.

When we were moved into his office, and after some discussion and questions, Mom finally came to the point. "We have had suspicions about our son, and we can't seem to communicate about it with him." The jig, indeed, was up.

With our whole story spilled out, Doctor Silverman thought about how to handle the situation. After a lengthy pause, he told Mom and Dad, "This is not an uncommon story. You have a homosexual son, and there's nothing to be done about it. It isn't anyone's fault. Carl is who he is and, unfortunately, it is you who will have to make an adjustment.

I can help you with that. I can help Carl adjust to this too, if that is what you want me to do."

To use a corrupted adjective from the future, I guess you could say that Mom and Dad had *outed* me. As painful as this was, there was some relief in this *outing*. I would no longer be living a lie. I think this was the moment I fully realized I was a separate entity from my parents. All of my dancing around the gay life had instilled in me a personal identity thoroughly different from the one they had tried to imprint on me.

I could see that they had been gathering evidence for some time, and this letter was the final straw. As it turned out, I never did read that letter, which went home with them.

Now, I wonder when their suspicions had begun; had something happened when I was a kid that started their doubts about me? Surely, they had noticed that I wasn't athletic, I loved books, movies and theater, and I had a growing collection of Broadway show recordings. When other boys were collecting baseball cards, I was memorizing show tunes. Was that the start? Or had they just written all that off as the interests of, to use some gay euphemisms, an *artistic, creative, sensitive or sophisticated* boy?

Dr. Silverman clearly understood the situation. This was not something that could be changed in me. He did agree to write a letter to the University saying, "Carl is a young man with an active curiosity. He has been investigating various lifestyles, and this was merely a phase that he has grown out of."

None of that was true, of course, but, ultimately, it did get me readmitted to the University if I agreed to live in a dormitory and quietly finish my studies. In the winter term,

I did just that with my tail between my legs.

But the night after the meeting with Dr. Silverman, my mother had an extreme reaction to all the revelations, and she went screaming from the house. I heard her moan "Nooo! It can't be." There was more, but then she became completely incoherent. Feeling totally responsible yet helpless, I followed her to the street, but I found myself tongue-tied. I had long wondered what a nervous breakdown was, but now I saw that this probably was one. She disintegrated. A dam had burst releasing what had been building in her for some time. Mom had been paying careful attention to the *red* and *lavender* scares (*commies and queers*, some said) which led to rooting out communists and homosexuals from the government. President Eisenhower had caused just that to happen. The fact that I could be blackmailed as a national security risk or arrested on a morals charge was too much for her to bear. For Mom, it was like losing a child – her son – her firstborn. She probably thought I was doomed, as she would have had no idea that gay liberation would change all that in the future. At that point, I had no idea either. I'm sure Dad quietly reacted the same way, but he buried it inside himself. But I wanted them to love me for who I really was.

I felt responsible for their distress, but I didn't yet have a solid perspective on what I could have done to avoid it. Events had tumbled down so fast I couldn't keep up with ways to prevent them. I wish I had had the strength and foresight to hug them and tell them that all would be well. But, at that point, I didn't know that it would be. I would also like to go back to the Hawaii Episcopal Academy and the seventh grader I used to be and give him the same hug and message. I look back at pictures of myself from that time, and I almost weep for my innocence of what was still to come.

You see, when I was born, I had been nicknamed *the crown prince*. I was the firstborn, I was a boy, and I was the son who would produce children and carry my father's name forward. Dad's brothers had only girls, and, as it turned out later, my one brother had only one daughter, so he would not carry on the name either. I felt very sorry and guilty for what I had put everyone through and that I would not be preserving the Spiegelberg name for future generations as I had been expected to do. At least Mom didn't tell me she *felt like a slug had slithered out of (her) womb* as a friend's mother had told him. But there would be no grandchildren from me. And I was no longer *the crown prince*.

Letters from Mom and Dad followed me back to the University. "We've found a camp that will help you get rid of your problem." That was a miracle I'm sure they were praying for. They were not religious fanatics – Dad was an ordinary Lutheran and Mom a low-church Episcopalian – but they were grasping at straws because they loved me. Eventually, I had to tell them I didn't want their letters if they were going to insist on that. I realize now it was probably gay conversion therapy they had found for me, which attempted to change people into what they are not. I'm glad I didn't go for that torture; it probably would have involved hypnotism, shock therapy or even a lobotomy. One of the methods was to show erotic gay images and then apply an electric shock. As my gay DNA is an essential part of me, I'm sure I wouldn't have changed, even if I had gone through that. Many other young gay men and women were not as lucky in avoiding that trauma.

*****

I completed the winter and spring terms in Eugene, and then was allowed to go to San Francisco for the summer, if I took some still needed classes at San Francisco State College and lived in a dormitory. I was back in the city I had been forbidden to linger in a few years earlier – and in which I would live a good part of my life in the future. Because I wasn't going to just stay in the dormitory all the time, I met a guy at a gay bar called the Hideaway in the Tenderloin and, needing a place to live after the summer session, I went to live with him on Twin Peaks. I've totally blanked out on what I told Mom and Dad about this latest maneuver and yet another new address.. I stayed with Bert until it was time to go back to finish my very last term at U. of O. in the fall. I wasn't asked for rent, so I guess I was a kept man once again. Bert worked for American Airlines as the head of the catering department at the San Francisco Airport. For the rest of the summer, I worked on the dishwashing line that cleaned everything that came off the planes. Bert asked me if I'd like to come to New York with him after my final term. He was from there and was being transferred back home.

In the meantime, I wound up my studies at the end of the fall term, and then I *did* go to New York until the end of May. I had been fantasizing about living in New York for a long time, but after spending a messy winter of snow, slush and having a seemingly unending cold, I was ready to come back to the west coast in the spring. I entertained myself with the 1961/62 Broadway theater season and worked at Barnes and Noble's original bookstore at 5th Avenue and 20th Street. I stayed with Bert (whom I never considered one of my lovers) for a time and then went to live (rent free, once again) with Oliver in his elegant brownstone on 35th Street near 5th Avenue. My final New York address was in Jackson Heights, Queens, where I went to live with my mother's cousin Nick and his wife Ruth.

During my stay in New York, I wrestled with the Selective Service over my draft status. The Vietnam conflict was starting to be heard of, so I nervously took the physical on Whitehall St. in lower Manhattan, and I was given a ZXX rating. I think that was one notch before 4-F. On their form I had checked: *worries a lot, chews nails and suffers from a nervous stomach,* so I was spared the horrors of boot camp and eventually dealing with the *don't ask, don't tell* policy. The draft board was probably being more-choosy then, as the war hadn't really heated up yet. There was a box that said *homosexual,* but I didn't check it. I'm sure they must have figured me out anyway.

*****

I took a train back to Oregon, where I went through my graduation ceremony. And then I promptly met another guy. OK, I was starting my career as a serial monogamist. Patrick and I moved to San Francisco by way of the Seattle World's Fair and initially lived in a cheap room in the Tenderloin over a colorful establishment called the Peacock Club. We had come to San Francisco at the height of the beat generation, so we indulged in a lot of jazz and poetry in North Beach. The hippies were yet to come.

One day, Marian, the lady who managed our building, called us in.

"The man who lives next door to you has a complaint.

I know these walls are flimsy, but he says, in his words, you have been *acting like girls.*" Pat and I stared at each other. Had we been giggling too much or was it something else?

"We're sorry we're making too much noise," I offered.

Pat chimed in, "He must be imagining things. As you can see, we are not girls."

At any rate, our clean-cut denials were believed, but we decided the Tenderloin was not the neighborhood for us. We found more suitable lodgings near Buena Vista Park, until Pat was drafted into the Army and sent away to Fort Ord.

Through some friends, Pat was connected to a cross section of underground life in San Francisco. We would go to after-hours jam sessions at Jimbo's Bop City in the Fillmore area, a jazz club called the Blackhawk in the Tenderloin, beatnik coffee houses in North Beach, a British pub called the Edinburgh Castle and to the Missouri Mule, the first gay bar near what would become the gay Castro district. We saw some of the first pre-porn underground movies by a gay renegade filmmaker named Kenneth Anger. After Pat had gone into the Army, I moved across the bay to Berkeley, where I worked on a secondary teaching credential at the University of California.

At that time, Berkeley was ground zero for a major shift in American culture. 1963/64 saw the beginning of the free speech movement led by Mario Savio and the early stages of the hippie movement. Pot, patchouli oil, flower power and long hair began to dominate our lives. JFK was assassinated that fall (I remember learning about it when coming out of class that day. Everyone remembers where they were.), and, amid tear gas attacks and other chaos, I finished my studies and became a high school teacher of English and Drama. I would happily teach those subjects for 37 years at

Ygnacio Valley High School in Walnut Creek, California.

When I was going to school at Cal and in my early years of teaching in Walnut Creek, I would now and then get over to San Francisco on Saturday nights, usually to a bar called the Rendezvous. It was near Union Square at the top of a long staircase, and we would say *we were climbing a stairway to heaven*. All those good-looking guys seemed to know each other, but occasionally I got to know some of them too. Like the Red Raven in Los Angeles, the bar's clientele were mainly guys in their twenties and those who appreciated them. On Sunday nights, there was a popular sing-along that we called "choir practice." This was interspersed with lots of checking each other out, the main reason for being there.

In that era, and even today, many teenagers, including some of my students, latched on to the word *gay* (*that's so gay!* they would say) to describe anything they thought was suspect or weird, but I never heard them call me that. I was honored that they did call me *Spieg*, a shortcut for Spiegelberg, a nick name that my father was called all his life. Even though I had reached an age when being single looked suspicious, I have to give credit to *my kids* and the rest of the faculty for accepting me for who I was. At one point, I even stopped dredging up dates for faculty functions and just went alone.

As I looked not much older than many of my students, it was easy for me to see that some of my students, male and female, had innocent crushes on me. It was only my sport coat and tie that told anyone I was the teacher. Most of my students wanted to be in my classes. Teaching turned out to be a very good career for me, with Advanced Placement English and Drama as highlights. I also taught several elective classes: Speech, Creative Writing and Film Study. And I directed hundreds of plays, from Sophocles to Neil Simon, with Shakespeare and lots of musicals in-between.

*****

I never lost a job or got beat up, and my parents never disowned me. I considered myself lucky during that dark age for gay people. However, I did yearn for the *it's-OK-and-we-love-you-anyway* speech, which never came. Only twice was I under any immediate threat for being gay during the 1950s and '60s period of entrapment and raids. My generation overlapped those two decades. In the former, we were all in the closet, and in the latter, we had all started drifting out. One incident was when we went to the Hollywood jail for jaywalking into the Red Raven, and the other was a raid on an early '60s party in the Haight-Ashbury neighborhood of San Francisco. I don't remember how I ended up at that party, but my teaching career and I did survive the raid. Loud music and disorderly conduct, especially same-sex dancing, drew the police. Quite a few drag queens were part of the crowd, and, as the police pounded on the door, lots of false eyelashes, high heels and over-the-top dresses were abandoned on back fences, as everyone tried to escape. In those days, it was illegal to dress as the opposite sex, except on Halloween, and this was not a Halloween party.

Crimes against nature were treated harshly in that less enlightened time. Lives were ruined when names and professions were printed in the newspaper after raids of gay bars. We were vilified for our otherness, treated as a lower caste, and the religious right took the anti-gay message in Leviticus, 17:22 very seriously as it does today. *Abomination* was a strong word freely thrown around. We were thought of as *twilight people* and the Mafia-run gay bars were smoky, dirty and had no windows.

And then, in the early sixties, we started going downtown on Sunday afternoons to see Jose Saria performing comic drag operas at the Black Cat Saloon. His shows always ended with a tentative call for equality when the audience sang a rousing chorus of *God save us nelly queens!* to the tune of *God Save the Queen.* Jose had unsuccessfully run for city supervisor in 1961 (a precursor to Harvey Milk), but his efforts were a beginning for gay political visibility in San Francisco. We weren't yet a significant voting bloc, but we would become a strong one in the future.

San Francisco, with its large gay population, had an upfront view of the gradual march to gay liberation. In 1968, gay culture was rocked by a ground-breaking play called *The Boys in the Band*. Its characters were mostly secretive, self-loathing queens, which seemed appropriate for that time, but the play provided a new visibility for gay life. The Stonewall riots in New York happened in June of 1969, and the message *we're queer and we're here!* rang out everywhere. Our rainbow flag was conceived by a gay man in San Francisco, and, almost universal now, it first appeared in the gay pride parade in 1978.

In 1977 and 1978, the San Francisco pride parades focused on two issues that galvanized the community. The first was pop-singer Anita Bryant's bigoted *Save our Children* campaign in Florida. Her efforts to prevent gays from adopting children ultimately failed.

The next year California State Senator John Briggs tried to get Proposition Six passed; that would have mandated the firing of all homosexual public-school teachers. I lived through the suspense of waiting to see if I would lose my job. But that election was the first time voters had rejected an anti-gay measure, and I was allowed to continue my career. After Stonewall and the defeat of the Briggs measure, some of my students asked to put up notices in my classroom for gay club meetings, even though I wasn't officially out to them. They must have figured me out by then – what would be better than the drama room and a teacher they trusted? I thought about it for a while, and then I discreetly let them do that as times were continuing to change. But I did my job well, never advocated a, proverbial, *homosexual agenda*, never touched anyone inappropriately, and generally stayed out of trouble.

*****

I took my first trip to Europe in the summer of 1967, Eurailing around the continent with a Damron gay guide in my luggage. One Sunday afternoon in London I met a young very British businessman named Andy Hawkins at the Star Tavern in Belgravia. I was drawn to Andy's exotic accent and *Britishness*, and his career as a businessman, something that always seemed intriguing from my point of view in my suburban classroom. He and I carried on a long-distance relationship (*geographically undesirable*) for a couple of years, with my spending two summers in England, until he was able to obtain a U.S. visa. I became a serious Anglophile and West End theater lover during those summers. When he was finally able to obtain a work visa, he joined me in California. He had passed himself off to Brooks Brothers as an expert on British fabrics. We bought a great house with wonderful views in the Oakland Hills for $33,000.

Andy was my third lover, and he now lives in Auckland, New Zealand with his partner Lindsay.

In 1970, after Andy and I split up, partly due to those cultural differences between us, I moved back to San Francisco where I knew most of the action was. I lived in a gentrifying neighborhood called the Castro. It was named for Castro Street, but we often called it *the gay ghetto* because gay immigrants from all over the country were displacing Irish and Italian families who then moved to the suburbs out of fear of that invasion. At that time, because of cheap rents, San Francisco was a city where anyone could come to reinvent himself. We flocked to the ghetto because we had the freedom to be ourselves in public there. It was a high-maintenance existence, however, with the sexual tension so palpable that I always felt I had to look my very best just to go grocery shopping. Everyone seemed to be thinking about sex all the time. We all felt like kids in a candy store. The thrill of the hunt always felt as if new prey might be just around a corner. *I wonder what his story is,* we would speculate, and *I wouldn't kick him out of bed,* was sometimes the verdict. But no one knew then that a terrible plague was incubating in the crevices of many of those encounters.

The neighborhood was dominated by the Castro Theater and its jumbo neon sign, which flashed and spelled out the word CASTRO one letter at a time. That attraction brought people to the neighborhood for films and helped establish the area for night life that included a number of gay bars. The Castro was mostly a repertory movie theater and showed old Bette Davis films and gay favorites like *The Wizard of Oz, Singing in the Rain, The Women* and *All About Eve.* It was always fun to be in a gay audience when everyone would shout out the well-known dialogue: *Fasten your seatbelts; it's going to be a bumpy night!* and *I don't think we're in Kansas anymore.*

Our ghetto was becoming an international gay destination. Bars, restaurants, discos, gyms and gay-owned shops were opened in repurposed Irish and Italian establishments. We danced to the music of The Village People, ABBA, Donna Summer and San Francisco's own Sylvester. I have always tried to keep fit by going to a gym, but I never pretended to be one of the muscle men who strutted around the neighborhood. I worked in a gay clothing store one summer where we sold all the latest trends in gay fashion, including t-shirts. My favorite one read "that's **Mister** Faggot to you, buddy."

Harvey Milk's political career began in his camera shop on Castro Street. I was teaching English on November 27th, 1978 when news of his assassination (along with that of Mayor Moscone) came to me. Harvey's legacy has dominated gay history ever since. I never considered myself an activist, but I twice carried a candle in evening marches with thousands of others from Castro Street to City Hall. Once was when Harvey was assassinated and another was when Dan White was essentially exonerated with an easy sentence. Harvey had been such an important leader of the gay community, both in San Francisco and across the country, that we all felt as if a rug had been pulled out from under us.

The gay revolution on the east and west coasts had heated to a boiling point in the seventies, and I hesitantly tried to keep up with the almost riotous hullaballoo. But I wasn't a cowboy or a leather man. I never wore colored handkerchiefs in my back pocket or had keys jangling off my belt to show what fetish or sexual proclivity I leaned toward. I *did* go to a sex therapist for a time and also to gay men's naked yoga classes. My body was pummeled at Rolfing sessions; I went to a regular gay support group; I learned to meditate and even toyed with signing up for EST (Erhard Seminars Training). I did get involved with the Advocate Experience, a personal growth seminar for gay men.

I could easily walk to Toad Hall, the most popular neighborhood gay bar in the early '70s. To get in the mood, I would dab on a little English Leather, smoke a joint and listen to Neil Diamond, John Denver and Bette Midler, the divine Miss M. There was the obligatory stroll around the block, and then a 50-cent beer, which I would drink sitting on a bench near the pool table. Before the beer loosened me up, I would sometimes hear suggestions that I smile, one of the worst pickup lines ever. In those days, cigarettes, which I never inhaled, were a benign character prop for me in my efforts to look as cool and self-assured as everyone else seemed to be.

I was never a hippie or a druggie, but marijuana helped put me in the present, as did a few party episodes with cocaine. I had one intense weekend on LSD carefully overseen by a more experienced guy at Stinson Beach. The seventies were in full swing, and we went to see Bette Midler before she became a superstar, celebrated with the Cockettes and even joined the now-famous human-be-in in Golden Gate Park. When I drove to a bar, I usually lit up a joint before getting out of my car. Sometimes, after the events of the evening, I would forget where I had parked and had to wander the streets until I found my ride home

The South of Market area, especially on Folsom Street, gradually became a center for leather and motorcycle men. In 1964, Life Magazine published a photo essay about gay bars there that excited a lot of people, and was an early instance of gay life appearing in the popular media. Most of those bars had names that suggested male sexuality: the Ramrod, the Tool Box, the Eagle, The Stud and the Boot Camp. I preferred the somewhat tamer places in the Castro like Toad Hall, The Midnight Sun and Badlands. But, even better, I enjoyed going to gay restaurants which were common then (in their eras there were Gordon's, Jackson's The Fickle Fox and Alta Plaza). The lighting was better, smoke didn't linger in the air, you didn't have to shout, and dinner gave everyone a common focus. Sometime in the early '70s a bar on Castro Street called The Twin Peaks introduced the concept of having windows to the street. Times were continuing to change, and now everyone could look in to get a glimpse of the gay party inside.

    I became one of thousands of *Castro clones* who roamed a neighborhood that radiated from the intersection of Castro and Eighteenth Streets. Our uniform was tight jeans, plaid flannel shirts suggestive of lumberjacks, and bushy mustaches. Until AIDS entered our lives, we would proudly display *hickeys* on our necks. Some gay men were accused of dressing too young, but part of that plan was to delay the passing of time. The spoils of the day belonged to the ever-young and beautiful. Some thought that a viable gay life was essentially over when you turned 35. Others believed that that was the entry point to gay *daddy-hood*.

    As with many of us, some of my energy was drawn to various investment schemes. First, was a plan with friends to turn an old synagogue on Geary Street into a very grand gay dance club. We were going to call it The House of Good. I would become a night-life entrepreneur. All went well at first until someone started letting too much coke go up his nose. Later, next door to our incipient club, was a building that became the headquarters for Jim Jones' People's Temple. I also put money into an early gay computer dating service which proved to be a scheme that arrived before its time. There weren't enough guys ready for that yet.

Investing in San Francisco real estate was not out of the question for a high school teacher in the '70s as it is now. A further attempt at fitting into the onrush of gay culture was my purchase of two Eastlake Victorian apartments in a nice area near Buena Vista Park. I had the mistaken impression that I needed to be part of what was referred to as the *A-gay crowd* of wealthy and influential gay men. So, I fluffed up my flat in order to entertain in style. I hired two inexpensive but ultimately unreliable hippies named Roscoe and Buffalo to help me sand the floors, put in a pantry and paint the apartment.

Lots of brunches, cocktail parties and dinners decorated with good-looking men were the glue holding that A-gay niche together. But having two rental units meant I had become a landlord too. Those flats and, later, my four apartments in Oakland were the extent of my real estate empire. My hands were full. I couldn't keep up with all the parties, and my investment in the A-gay crowd gradually simmered to the sidelines.

I did occasionally hold some parties at my Victorian flat on the southern end of Divisadero Street. On one Saturday night, I invited my sister Aileen and her husband to dinner. With candles on the table and surrounded by the fancy chinoiserie wallpaper and sconces I had installed in my diningroom, I offered a toast. I had planned this event as a grand coming-out announcement to them.

With enough alcohol and maybe a toke on a joint, I

stammered, "I have something I want to tell you."

There was a silence as we looked at each other through the candle light.

"We think we know what you want to say. We figured you out a long time ago. You haven't kept your secret from us, and we love you anyway." I was relieved, and we hugged and relaxed into an enjoyable evening.

Soon, my brother Harrison and his first wife Marcia knew, and I was supported by all of them. Marcia passed away in 1987, and Harrison's second wife Patti is extremely supportive of me as well.

*****

I was usually in a monogamous relationship, but when I wasn't, like everyone I knew, I had occasional one-or-two-night stands. Happiness, some have said, can depend on the quick glance of a stranger. I learned when to hold a gaze and when to look away and then turn back. Pretending to look in store windows was part of the mating dance as was touching knees at the movies. Sometimes a hot guy might be rejected after he opened his mouth to speak. Visuals can be deceiving at times. *Your place or mine?* If it wasn't mine, I always checked to see if the guy had books and what kinds. That was a deal-maker, or breaker, for me for the possibility of more than one night. If things didn't work out well, I could always announce that I had an early start the next day and needed to get some sleep. Most of us engaged in the perfunctory ceremony of exchanging phone numbers and casually promising to call. Anonymous sex was not my scene. I preferred a phone call or two and then a date. That was not how many in the gay community operated. Many felt they had fought for their sexual freedom, and they wanted to enjoy it – even in the pressing face of AIDS.

By the mid-seventies, gay life, once an almost forbidden subject, had become open for all to see as the topic appeared in the media almost daily. It was as if the straight world wanted in on the party that had only been whispered about for so long. About that time *The New Yorker* published a wonderful cartoon showing two little old ladies having a polite conversation: one says to the other, *"When you say "gay," dear, are you talking about being happy – or that other funny business?"* The *funny business* that everyone seemed to be talking about was everywhere. But that exclusive club I had joined years earlier was no longer secret. The furtive intrigue was gone and my compartmentalized subterranean life was open for most others to see.

My gay glossary lengthened with *fag-hag, camp and camping, flamer, bear, vanilla sex, miss thing, three-way, homophobic, homophile, switch-hitter, AC/DC, PFLAG, playing for the other team* and *Adam and Steve, not Adam and Eve*. The moniker *LGBT* now added a Q for *queer or questioning*. We had entered an era of specialties, and demanded the use of specific alphabetical listings. Earrings and tattoos began to appear on many, and I decided I needed to join that prevailing fashion. Never a tattoo, but I did get an ear pierced for a sparkling piece of jewelry. But after a few months, I decided it was too much trouble. Beards and mustaches came and went – and then came again. My baby face always seemed to fill out with at least some facial hair – usually a mustache but sometimes a beard too.

Outdoor sex in Buena Vista Park or at Land's End was never my scene. Many of us went to nude beaches on the San Mateo coast, excursions that ended in pick-ups for some people. The baths (many called them *the tubs*) and the gym were other options, but I was conservative enough that I only went to two or three bath houses out of curiosity – and only once to the sticky-floor backroom of a bar. The epidemic, originally referred to as gay cancer proved those to be fortuitous decisions.

In an attempt to stay safe, San Francisco gay men discovered alternate ways of meeting each other for relationships. At one time, there was a gay matchmaker in San Francisco, and the gay newspapers published want ads. Some of the ads were for sex, but mine and many others were in search of friends or lovers. After high technology entered our lives in the 1990s, cruising took a leap into the future. Internet want-ads and eventually *grinder* in 2009 provided almost immediate gratification. Your phone could alert you to any other willing gay men nearby. I did not participate in most of that, but it was all part of the gay culture I was living in.

The gay community blithely passed through those years of silent danger in the '70s when we didn't know that death was lurking all around us. But in the eighties everyone woke up and professed to having *safe sex* in the face of dying men everywhere. Safe sex was the mantra then just as masks, social distancing and vaccines are now professed, as I write this in the age of Covid-19. In the early days of the AIDS epidemic, people thought that the sexual stimulant amyl nitrate (We called them *poppers* because they popped when you snapped the glass vials.) could be responsible. That theory was disproven, but the universal need for condoms was not.

In the early '90s, I was an emotional support volunteer for a number of AIDS patients in Contra Costa County where I was living to be nearer to my suburban teaching job. The epidemic and a desire to cash in on the city's very high property values were beginning to decimate the Castro. People were either dying or moving to the suburbs. Today, Castro Street has new wide sidewalks, gay history plaques and trees, but the palpable excitement that could be felt on any evening or Sunday afternoon in the '70s is now gone. I see that magic decade as the good old days. The Castro as we knew it back then isn't going to come back. The city is too expensive now to support the heyday of what we remember. We young pilgrims had come to San Francisco at a time when the city was affordable and welcoming.

In the '70s and '80s, in addition to my sexual liaisons, I connected with a number of men in the gay community who became good friends. We cemented our relationships with activities like subscribing to the San Francisco Opera, water skiing at Lake Berryessa, river rafting in the Sierras, playing volleyball in a gay league, house boating on Lake Shasta and the Delta, planning city-wide scavenger hunts and organizing elaborate progressive dinner parties. We kept ourselves busy.

We now often gauge modern gay history as *before* and *after Stonewall* (1969), or *before and after AIDS* (1980). Those measurements were overlaid with the sexual revolution, which began in 1960 with the advent of the birth control pill, and pretty much ended with the appearance of AIDS around 1980. I lived in San Francisco in the 1970s while the virus was probably silently gestating, and in the '80s when the horror was in full bloom. A deadly combination of youth and beauty provided a formula for susceptibility. By all rights, I should have been a victim like so many others. I did deal with gonorrhea once, but that was hastily quashed with penicillin at the city clinic. But penicillin was not going to cure the new plague.

A personal AIDS scare came early on when I spotted dark spots in the back of my mouth. They turned out to be only shadows, but that was an example of how skittish we all were.

I did get tested, and a few days later I tensely went back for the results.

"How long have you known you were HIV positive?" was the first thing I remember the doctor saying.

The blood rushed out of my head and I slumped in my chair.

Then he confirmed my name and sheepishly admitted he had looked at the wrong file. I was reprieved. I think I survived because I was never very promiscuous; I preferred monogamy which was more predictable and comfortable and didn't require a constant search. Many on that hunt did not survive.

Frequent funerals, many weekly obituaries in the gay newspapers, the appearance of the AIDS memorial quilt and then the faltering promise of a medicine called AZT, reminded all of us that we were regularly losing our friends. My good friend Gary and I were both teachers, he in junior high and I in senior high. We were part of a close knit group that took cooking classes together. We traveled to China, Bali and Bangkok, where I feel he may have contracted the AIDS virus. When Gary was nearing death, he threw a small party in his apartment in order to bequeath belongings he would no longer need. He gave me a beautiful sweater and photos of our group from his albums. I still miss Gary and his wonderful sense of humor. And then, in no particular order, there were Mitch, Ned, Jerry, Michael, Frank, Jake, Tom and Derick – and more.

My relationship history makes it clear that monogamy –

or serial monogamy as it turned out to be – was my chosen lifestyle. As gay culture evolved, we called our partners by various names. My first was *boyfriend* (Duke) which sounded pretty high schoolish, but then, I was taught the term *lover*. There seemed to be a progression that usually went from one-night *trick* to *boyfriend* to *lover*. Often, in the tentative early stages of a relationship, there would come a time of decision for proceeding to the next stage of moving in together. I used the word *roommate* (Patrick) for as long as possible. But that wasn't believable after a certain age. If you looked young enough, you could get away with that, but *confirmed bachelor and his friend,* an old-fashioned term, was sometimes necessary. Later, the term *partner* entered our culture, to be finally followed by *husband* after 2015 with the Supreme Court's ruling. Scattered throughout were other terms such as *other half, better half, longtime companion* and *special friend.*

*****

One night at Toad Hall in 1974, I met my next partner Mark. As usual, I was sitting with my beer near the pool table which served as an innocent point of focus, when, in reality, my eyes, like everyone else's, were darting all over the bar.

"Hi, there. Things aren't as serious as all that. Give me a smile."

I immediately perked up and replied with that requested smile, "I'm just trying keep out of trouble."

Mark was tall, dark, sexy – and very outgoing. Our banter led me to think this was to be yet another one-night stand, but, months later, we were still seeing each other.

And it eventually led to a two-year relationship.

We never lived together, but in 1976 Mark and I decided to have an adventure and take a trip around the world. I received a year's leave-of-absence from my teaching, and we headed east. We crossed the country in his sports car and then flew to Europe. One morning, months after the hardships of travel had caught up with us, we found ourselves in the Tel Aviv airport. Mark headed west to Morocco, and I flew east to Teheran. Mark and I were finished as a couple, but I eventually completed my trip through Asia, arriving back in San Francisco in the fall. It was through Mark that I learned some of the newest gay lingo: *barebacking, Grinder, daddy, non-binary* and even *queer,* which a younger generation was using again as a point of pride.

The biggest mistake of that trip was selling my San Francisco apartments before I went away. I didn't anticipate that that year would see an unprecedented increase in property values, and I was out of the country, and out of the market, when that happened. That setback eventually righted itself, and I have gained back much of that lost value.

During my teaching career, I would go back to Honolulu for many Christmases and some summer trips. During all those years, Waikiki had become a high-rise jungle with thousands of hotel rooms, unlike the quieter Waikiki of my coming-out days. I liked spending time there revisiting the gay landscape where I first stumbled into gay life. That had been a time when I was excited every day about that new world opening up to me.

The Beachwalk bar where I had met Duke was long gone, but there were other watering holes in Waikiki. In the '70s and '80s the Stuffed Tomato and the Gay Nineties were near the corner of Kalakaua and McCully Streets. Guys would toggle back and forth between the two, hoping that Mr. Right was lurking in one of them. Hula's Bar and Lei Stand, under an old Banyan tree, was one of the more popular bars from 1974 to 1998, and I always felt very sophisticated at the Embers on Lewers Street, a New Yorkish lounge with smoky low lighting, which hosted the singer Ann McCormick and her jazz-style cabaret shows. In addition to my Hawaii trips, there were jaunts to the mountains for skiing, and obligatory trips to gay destinations where I could be part of the majority like Fire Island, Key West, Provincetown and the Russian River.

My relationships had moved from Duke to Patrick to Andy to Mark. But I have to admit, they didn't stop there. I had several brief affairs with local celebrities: one with Harry Britt, who had been appointed as a SF Supervisor after Harvey Milk was assassinated; another with the author of *Tales of the City*, Armistead Maupin, who had recently come to San Francisco; and Leonard Matlovich who in 1975 appeared on the cover of Time Magazine for challenging the military's ban on gay people.

And then I met Jim, a new-age Sufi who later died of AIDS after we had split up; Rick was a Deputy Attorney General for California, with whom I'm still friends. And William was a mover and shaker in Sacramento. Jim and I met at a fitness center; I met Rick through a social group called Other Ways, and William entered my life by way of an ad in The Bay Times. I was a member of a gay cooking class for a number of years where I was known as the Elizabeth Taylor of our group because of all my divorces. I wonder if I had just made poor choices in all those relationships. Or if I just struggled with the lonely vacuum of being single and settled for whomever came along next.

At least at the start, I had been seriously in love each time, but I know I learned about life from all of these guys, and I was enriched from the variety they provided in my life. Breaking up was never easy. My parents, the U.S. Army, long distance, AIDS, the strains of foreign travel and a lack of compatibility between two men's unique neuroses were some of the reasons for the breakups. A recent survey says that many think ninety days is the ultimate length of sexual love, then one comes to a realization that love isn't about one's appearance any more. I attracted attention in those days, perhaps because of my blue eyes, *de rigueur* mustache and very young looks, so there was always someone new on the horizon. Chance brought me to each of my relationships starting with my offhand decision to walk up Beachwalk on my way to the bus on the day I met Duke. *Happily-ever-after* had always eluded me in the past, but I've finally found a *keeper* in my husband Janek.

But first, there is a lead-up to that story: for two years, William and I had a commuter relationship – one weekend in Lafayette and the next in Sacramento. I enjoyed his lively sense of humor and we had a great adventure traveling in Greece and Turkey together. When our commuting routine finally became too cumbersome, we split up, and I spent the next twenty years as a single man. Along with various roommates and my faithful Westie Calvin (*Calvin and Hobbes*), I lived in my '50s ranch-style house in Lafayette where I had moved in 1989 from San Francisco. I assumed I would never hook up with anyone again.

But, in 2009 I decided to make one more stab at the mating game. I had a set of professional photos taken, and I signed on to a dating site called Match.com. Gay bars seemed like a dead-end at my age, and, besides, the word was that lots of guys were going online. My listing didn't say anything about *firesides* or *long walks on the beach*. But it did say:

Available Good Catch. Handsome, professional GWM (gay white man). Light brown hair, blue eyes, 5'11" with slim build (155 lbs.) and clean-cut good looks wants to meet an equally youthful but mature GWM to share the adventure of the rest of our lives.

The ad continued and included my age of 69. I counted on my flattering photos to compensate for a gentle white lie about my age, which was really 71.

I paid for my listing, and, with no great expectations, I let it sit on the site. I checked in on it every once in a while, but it did not become an obsession. One day, some months later, a response caught my eye. Janek Bubela had found me from Vancouver, B.C. That was definitely *geographically undesirable*, but we both took a chance. Janek was of the mind that a perfect match might be anywhere, when many local gay men wouldn't even cross the Bay Bridge for a date. After a few friendly emails, we gambled on a phone call. Amidst some initial small talk, I heard a broad smile in his voice as, I guess, he did in mine. Of course, he could have been an affable axe murderer, but his quick wit disarmed me, and I plowed ahead.

I learned he had been born in Poland in 1952 and had come to Canada with his parents when he was six years old. He grew up in a small town in Saskatchewan, and his career had been as a landscape designer and gardener. He had been married to a woman for 27 years and had four children who are now adults. He had also been married to a man for four years. None of our revelations were discouraging to either of us, including the fact that he had lived his life as a

Jehovah's Witness and had been aching to be free of that. Now he *is* free and is no longer religiously inclined. His age specification was 50-70, but I figured I could always come clean if the time presented itself.

And then, the time *did* come when I ventured a three-day visit to Vancouver – only three days in case things didn't go well. But *things did* go well, including that white lie about my age. If I hadn't lied about that, the computer would have eliminated me, and we would never have met. When we first saw each other at the airport, I liked his sparkling Slavic blue eyes and the fact that he kept himself in good physical condition. The serpentine dragon tattoo on his upper right shoulder wasn't a deal breaker either.

I could see that he wasn't a jerk or an axe murderer. He liked me and was a great host, showing me Vancouver from rented bikes that we rode around the city and the sea wall. We found out that we share a love of dogs, food, movies, theater, travel and adventure. The first of thousands of meals he has cooked for us in the last decade was a Polish dinner for me and a couple of his friends. I discovered that he is a great chef, expert gardener and all-around fixer – in other words, a handy guy to have around the house. He has taken excellent care of us for fifteen years. I love his gregariousness, something I am not blessed with. He can talk to anyone – and does – and makes good friends for both of us. He loves people, and we are constantly entertaining them. He's always threatening to *pull my gay card* when my more conservative way of being gay doesn't measure up to his style. I have always been shy about holding hands or showing affection in public. The Jehovah's Witnesses had forbidden him almost everything before he was finally *disfellowshipped* (excommunicated) and came out of the closet with bells and whistles.

Match.com had served us up to each other, and now it was our responsibility to take it from there. The courting included more phone calls, sessions on Skype, and visits to me in California. Eventually, our hands grazed each other almost by accident and led to a first tentative kiss. Down the line, we both figured out when to say *I love you*. As in an old-fashioned love story, he totally disarmed me by calling me his *prince* and writing me very romantic love poems:

Speak softly, my Love. Hold me warmly
Against your heart.
I feel your words, the tender trembling
Moments start.

He was the one to suggest we get married after the Supreme Court acted – something I never thought would happen to me – and I was happy to accept. I could see that his energy and relative youth would help keep me young. We are not jewelry people so we don't wear rings. Our unaffected wedding ceremony took place at the county court house in Martinez. Our good neighbor Marianne was our witness, and we followed up with a simple dinner at a small restaurant in Walnut Creek.

Life with Janek is never dull; his high energy keeps me on my toes. I feel liberated to not be on the hunt anymore. I even give myself permission to be happy staying home on Friday and Saturday nights.

The fact that we are married facilitated Janek's immigration status. First, on a normal tourist visa, next on a green card, and finally on an extended ten-year green card, Janek has gradually moved in with me – first into my house in Lafayette and then to our current home in a senior complex called Rossmoor in Walnut Creek, where we have made a number of gay friends including some lesbians. Many lesbians are to be commended for stepping up to care for sick and dying men during the AIDS epidemic. We travel back and forth to Vancouver, usually by car, to visit friends and his children. And I witnessed him being sworn in as a United States citizen on October 16, 2019 at the Paramount Theater in Oakland.

As I write this accumulating saga, I find myself regretting the trauma I put my long-suffering parents through because of who I am. My gay life happened to *me*, but it also happened to *them*, and I'm sorry that I put them through any worry or self-recrimination. I'm sure they wondered what they had done to cause it, and they may have blamed each other. I am also sorry that they are not here in this more enlightened and gay-friendly time for a fuller understanding of my story. I wish they could read this memoir for a better knowledge of who I really am. I'm ashamed that I may have taken them for granted when I had them with me.

When I first went away to Hawaii Episcopal Academy in seventh grade, Mom and Dad collected and numbered all of my letters. They lovingly continued to do that throughout my college time in Oregon and all the years I lived away from home on the mainland. My Dad outlived my mother, who passed away in 1973, and before Dad passed away in 1992, he presented me with a box of hundreds of letters that were essentially a time capsule of a good portion of my life. The letters were a loving gift that sparked memories contributing to my writing. I want to dedicate this memoir to them for helping me preserve my story and for loving me no matter what the drama was that separated us at one time. My letters to my parents did not report on the details of my gay saga – those would have to wait until now – but they gave me a time line for the structure I have used here. And I can read between the lines of those letters and dredge up the old secrets I was holding inside.

The most poignant letter I found was to my father and sums up my feelings after most of my secrets had already been spilled. The letter was written as an exercise for a gay seminar called the Advocate Experience. My mother would have been included in this, but she had already passed away. Even then, I was feeling guilt for what I had put them through. My wide-open closet door has now freed me from my internal homophobia and double life, but, because they are gone, I am powerless to free them any more than I already have. I'm grateful that Dad was alive to read this letter which probably dates from the late seventies:

Dear Dad, This past weekend I have taken a two-day personal-growth seminar designed for gay people called The Advocate Experience. Part of the process is to communicate some unfinished business with someone we love. My being gay has been a source of a lot of richness but also some sadness in my life as you and Mom knew for many years. We came to some understanding of sorts some years ago, but it was never talked about again. I know that it was always a source of pain for you, but I recognized and appreciated the fact that you continued to love and support me. Many gay people, I am finding, have not been as lucky as I am in this respect. I have heard some very sad stories in the last two days. I want to make sure that you understand I didn't choose to be gay, especially because of the pain it caused you is now very vivid in my mind. Every week when I receive your letter your great love is there behind it.

With lots of love, Carl

*****

I never did find out if Dr. Simpson was a homo – I suppose he could have been, but I suspect not. I *did* discover that I was one, however, not long after I found his name scratched on my desk in 1951. Puberty had circled and landed along with an asterisk by my name to indicate my special circumstances: at that age, going through puberty was bad enough – we were all doing that – what we weren't all doing was wrestling with being gay. The passing years have taken me from thinking I was the only one to a realization that there are millions of us. Here in the United States, almost everything about gay life has changed in my lifetime.

These days, because of all the coming out in the last few decades, almost everyone can say they know someone who is gay. I like to think that that exposure has diminished a fear of the unknown that used to make being gay so isolating. Coming out is easier for young gay people now because of that familiarity. I was of a generation that paved the way for current gay people, just as the generation before me had eased my way. One of our slogans in the AIDS era was *silence is death*, which encouraged many of us to speak up and come out. The closet now has an easier door to open, and has even been appropriated by the general public. You can be a *closet conservative* or a *closet liberal* or a *closet* almost anything else.

There was never a reason for me to think that I had made a choice in the matter, as I was always wired this way. I never chose to be attracted to my own sex. But, in a way, the religious-right is correct. I *did* choose to come out of the closet and lead a gay life in the gay culture. We flocked together as we had a primal quality in common. One chooses a lifestyle but not a sexual orientation. To live in the gay culture, I have discovered, is to put more chips on the table, and, even now, it is edgier and riskier to be gay than straight. Some of us have been asked hypothetically if we would take a pill if it would make us straight. I may have answered yes at one time when I was struggling with my identity, but, in retrospect, I'm glad I lived the rich and varied life that my homosexuality has allowed.

Being different from others was a great struggle for me at one time. Most children and teenagers want to be like their friends. But, as we mature, our individuality becomes more valuable. The difference that my being gay has bestowed on me is now an aspect of myself that I cherish. I have rid myself of my long-standing internal homophobia, a feeling that had been generated by a lot of personal shame.

As many gay men were doing in my era, I could have married a woman, and, perhaps made two people unhappy. But I gambled that a gay life was the correct choice for me. Was it a selfish choice? Single men, as a rule, have more disposable income than some, and there is a tendency to spend that money on experiences and comforts that many others are not able to afford. Without children to care for – except for the hundreds of teenagers I taught and befriended over the years – I was afforded a lot of freedom to live a life with a great deal of variety. I am a Sagittarius, *a searcher*, with a very long list (we didn't call it a *bucket list* back then) of places to see in the world. My lack of family responsibilities and generous summer vacations from teaching have allowed me to notch off 112 countries (including three trips around the world) and 50 states in the last 60 years. I have always liked to think that I am not just a superficial tourist, but a serious traveler. I'm glad I did all that traveling at a young age when I had enough energy. I could never do all that today.

*****

Today is February 8, 2020. A Time Magazine from May of 2019 sits on a pile in my study. Staring up at me is a cover picture of Democratic Presidential candidate Pete Buttigieg and his husband, Chasten, with the title *First Family* in large letters. Who would have predicted such a magazine cover in 1951 when I was first contending with my alternate identity and when gay life was thoroughly subterranean? I wish there had been a wise man like Mayor Pete to look up to when I was twelve years old.

I have lived through the long and continuing struggle for gay liberation that has seen the Supreme Court legalize same-sex marriage in 2015, and now marks the 50th anniversary of the Stonewall riots. We have now entered an age when gay people can live anywhere, not just in a gay ghetto. We don't even need all those gay bars anymore. We can meet each other on our computers.

After six decades of living a gay life, I am now adjusting to the reality of being an older gay man. Accepting my growing invisibility is a major aspect of that adjustment. People, young and old, look through me now, and there is no longer the electricity of chance encounters. My interest in cute guys has never gone away, but I no longer expect reciprocity. My husband, Janek, and I have been happily married for fourteen years (2023 now), and we live our lives for everyone to see. We don't hold hands in public, but I've finally become accustomed to calling him my *husband* ("*my husband and I . . .*"), a label I never imagined I'd ever live to use. Janek has four adult children so, in this age of two mommies and two daddies, I have become a father of sorts as well. After nearly a lifetime of gradually coming out to myself, friends, family and colleagues, writing and publishing this memoir is the ultimate opening of my closet door. If I were to find "Simpson is a homo" on a desk today, I would know exactly what it meant. The world has radically changed regarding gay people in the seventy years since 1953.

The Seventh and Eighth Grades at Hawaii Episcopal Academy – I am in the center at the bottom

Carl and Janek at the Punahou Reunion Luau

Carl and Janek at Waikiki Beach

Outside and Inside Red Hale

Red Hale
Prologue

For over fifty years, starting near the beginning of the twentieth century, a large beach house that family and neighbors called Red Hale (ha-lay, Hawaiian for house) was home to three generations of my family – the Davises, the Harrisons and the Spiegelbergs. With shifting characters, chronologies and locations, this story could be told from various points of view. I have decided to tell Red Hale's history by focusing, in turn, on each generation of my family that lived there or was associated with the house. As in the rest of this book, there are some overlapping events and years so there may be some repetitions.

The first member of my family to come to Hawaii was my maternal grandfather, Hoste McKean Harrison who arrived in 1900. In the following year, 1901, my great grandfather Edward Davis and his wife Margaret and daughter Susan (my grandmother) arrived. General Davis bought Red Hale in 1910 and put the property in his daughter Susan's name. She and her husband Hoste were the first generation of my family to live there. I have chosen to tell the General's story first, however, as it was he who originally purchased the property and later spent his retirement there. This will be followed by chapters on my grandparents, parents, and, finally, the Japanese family that helped run Red Hale as a family home. Chapter One is about an early personal encounter with the house, and Chapter Two is about the history of the real estate that Red Hale was associated with. I have tried to be accurate with this historical story based on the sources that were available to me.

The details of this history have been gathered from a number of sources: interviews, letters, diaries, obituaries, notes in the Davis family Bible, military archives, books on Hawaii, especially Waikiki, and memories from my childhood.

the Chippendale Chair

The Chippendale Chair

Shortly after World War Two – I think it was probably in 1947 when I was eight years old – I found myself in the grip of an ongoing childhood crush. The object of my affection was a well lived-in – but doomed – seaside home on the eastern end of Waikiki Beach. The inhabitants and their neighbors were affectionately calling the house *Red Hale,* (ha-lay, Hawaiian for *house*) and so I did too. They had recently heard that *"prosperity is imminent in our postwar world."* But, neither they nor I realized that *Grandma's house,* as my younger brother and I called the house, had only ten more years to *live.* Nor could most people interpret warnings already in the air – that, in about a decade, for example, passenger jet planes would have something important in store for Hawaii, Waikiki – and Red Hale.

My maternal grandmother's home had become a personal playground at the beach where my brother Harrison (our sister Aileen was a baby then) and I could go in our bathing suits to play and explore. We could ride our bikes, play hide-and-seek and tag with playmates in Manoa Valley where we lived, but *play* always seemed more interesting to me at Red Hale because of the large rustic red house with its ocean-side setting. The Waikiki Aquarium had shown me what lay under the sea, but the great expanse of water I could see from the seawall at Red Hale kept countries I'd heard of like China and Japan and, in another direction, a place called *the mainland,* at a distance. I didn't realize then that I lived in one of the Earth's most isolated places, so I sometimes vainly scanned the horizon for evidence of a greater world.

At the start of my *love affair* I was too young to know that my *childhood Red Hale* was already a fifty-year-old holdover from another era that would not exist in the next. I did know that my mother had been born and grew up there, but I didn't understand, for instance, that the house I knew was two structures, not one (Chapter Three), or that the post-war economic boom and its social fallout would take a significant toll on Red Hale and its neighborhood.

Now, over six decades later, with the aid of prodded memory, interviews, photos and letters, I have discovered the history of the house, but also the story of the American family that had lived there. I only directly knew my Hawaii grandmother as most of that family was gone by the time I was born. My extended family in Hawaii consisted only of Grandma and Mom's sister Aunt Peggy because uncles, aunts and a few cousins on my dad's side all lived on the mainland, a place I had not yet been to. The war and the Navy *did* briefly bring Dad's brother Uncle Herb to stay with us on his way to fight in the South Pacific. But it was my playground at Red Hale that provided evidence for me of a more complete family story.

During the first half of the Twentieth Century, the approximate lifespan of Red Hale, concrete high rises had not yet crowded out most of the coconut trees that fringed Waikiki Beach. For well over sixty years, an array of large wooden dwellings had made a notable show among those trees. That was the second generation of structures that had lined the beach. The first generation had been constructed of coconut fronds and *pili* grass that the first Hawaiians had brought with them from what we now call The Marquesas Islands. The third generation would be the wall of concrete and glass that diminished much of Waikiki's gentleness and public access to the ocean. Red Hale's land would host all three of these permutations – grass, timber and concrete. Early Hawaiians had built their grass huts near the shore, and the inevitability of concrete and glass would eventually sound a death knell and forge a conclusion for this story. But, it is the second generation – of large homes built of timber and plaster - that this memorial is about.

Many of these residences were grand, even grandiose, like palaces on the shore, while others, including Red Hale, were simply overblown beach houses that served as comfortable single-family homes. They all shared a commonality, however: the seaside land they were built on – then and today, some of the choicest residential real estate in Hawaii. All of those houses are gone now, but a few of their stories have been preserved beyond the finality of the wrecking ball.

Red Hale's tale, however, is one that has not yet been told. The house was an example of many fine wooden homes on the beach that made their unheralded exits in the 1950s and '60s. Red Hale's particular history took place just below Diamond Head's seaward summit. Waikiki Road, later named Kalakaua Avenue in 1905, came to its eastern end at Red Hale's driveway where one could turn the corner and connect to the road around Diamond Head.

2999 Kalakaua Avenue is a 17,000-square foot parcel of land that supported a spacious two-story, four-bedroom house. Its rusty red paint, weather-beaten by mountain rains and salt air, gave Red Hale its affectionate family nickname. That paint color helped disguise the iron-infused dust blown from Kapiolani Park directly across the street. For many years, the hooves of race horses and polo ponies, the wheels of horse drawn carriages, and marching soldiers had disturbed the dirt that trade winds blew out to sea. Except when the winds were occasionally from the south, Red Hale was directly in that path. The red dust had intensified the paint's color and given further credibility to Red Hale's name.

This biography – for the big red house certainly is the main character here – begins with the fortuitous rescue of a handsome antique Chippendale chair which now, far from its English origins, daily and mundanely serves as a depository for clean and sometimes dirty laundry in my California bedroom. Cabinet maker Thomas Chippendale had created graceful and ornate furniture that was fashionable in the second half of the eighteenth century. Today, Chippendale pieces can be either *by* or *in the style of* their designer. I am prepared to find out mine is *in the style of*, but it is beautiful and something I value because of its family story.

The symbolism of the chair's deliverance wasn't clear to me then, but the event serves as a convenient entry for this biographical account of Red Hale. It tells the story of my mother's ancestors and how they came to live in a neighborhood now thought rare. No one called that ground *the gold coast* then. Honolulu's real estate trade hadn't latched onto that phrase yet. But Red Hale's address would put it near the epicenter of that future marketing banner. We simply called it *Grandma's house*. Nevertheless, Hawaii's oligarchs of a certain era, and King Kalakaua's well-connected *haole* (Caucasian) friends, had, starting in 1876, finagled to claim what would eventually become *the gold coast* as their exclusive stomping ground.

*****

As usual, I wanted to go too. It would be another trip to Grandma's house, and I wanted to hitch a ride. I was an inquisitive and restless kid and was always ready for a trip that would take me anywhere, especially when playmates weren't available at home in Manoa Valley. Even then, I longed for travel, and a trip to Grandma's house invariably promised a diversion from the familiarity of our neighborhood and the dampness of our valley. Television, video games and texting weren't a part of childhood then. My visions of the greater world were fed by comedy and adventure on the radio, photos in Life and National Geographic magazines, Disney, Tarzan and Classic Illustrated comic books, the evening Star-Bulletin, The Hardy Boys and The Mighty Mouse Club at the Pawaa Theater on Saturday mornings.

Our dead-end block of Keahi St. near the back of Manoa Valley limited my outlook on the world, and errands with Mom were a means of widening it. Life was much richer to me in Waikiki, as there always seemed to be more happening there. This particular outing to Red Hale must have been in the summer as I wasn't in school, and I could tell it was a weekday because the tenants weren't there. The distance from our house to the beach was only about five miles. But the contrasting climates provided a measure of culture shock for an eight-year-old kid that arose, not only from the difference in climate and geography, but also from the fascinating antique house. Our three-bedroom, one-level home in Manoa, built in 1941, seemed small to me when compared to Red Hale. The large house served as a personal preserve where I could entertain myself with fantasies whetted by books, magazines, radio shows and movies.

*****

A car ride to Red Hale involved a gradual change in micro-climates. Rainbows and waterfalls gave way to coconut trees, surfers and a ten-degree rise in temperature. Our immediate rainforest and precipitous mountains gradually became brownish scrub and rounded hills as we drove out of the valley and could see that Diamond Head didn't have its overlay of winter greenery. The mountain's Hawaiian name, Leahi, means *brow of the tuna* in reference to its silhouette. That landmark was our destination, as Red Hale sat on a seawall where the head of that extinct volcano jutted out to sea.

I can do it all much faster if I go alone, my efficient mother would declare, but, always, my restless curiosity urged me to tag along if I could persuade her. Mom was constantly busy, and, with three kids she had to be practical with her time. Sometimes my brother Harrison would go with us. He was two years younger than I, and I think we were a handful when we were together. There could be teasing, poking and tickling, often, I must admit, at my big brother instigation.

I don't blame Mom when she sometimes announced, *you boys are going to drive me to Kaneohe. They'll take me to the pupule* (crazy) *house because of you two. We'll be good, we'll be good*, was often part of a spirited negotiation that sometimes allowed us to tag along.

During the day Dad was at work investigating pineapple diseases at The Pineapple Research Institute. Mom was a housewife and could help Grandma who was in her mid-seventies and lived with us in Manoa Valley at that time. Grandma had turned Red Hale into a fully furnished boarding house with a Japanese cook to feed the tenants and keep an eye on the house. Because of her age and the fact that she was a widow then, the house was rented to a succession of young Navy officers and defense workers who perpetuated the name Red Hale. There was never a painted sign announcing that name, but everyone in the neighborhood knew the house it referred to.

Mom would handle landlady duties for Grandma by collecting rents and keeping a weekly eye on the house and tenants. These visits must have been filled with nostalgia for her because she was returning to her childhood in a house that was now inhabited by strangers.

On the day of the Chippendale chair's rescue, a familiar bargaining session must have awarded me a place in the back seat of our car. Harrison wasn't with us that day. Mom may have been keeping us apart, and he was probably at home with our baby sister Aileen and Grandma. This certainly wasn't my first time at Red Hale, but it is the one that I have remembered most clearly because of what happened that day. Now I see that the near-loss of the chair was an early symptom of trouble – a proverbial canary in a coal mine – part of a bigger picture of socio-economic upheaval.

The chair was, after all, only a piece of musty furniture. It had come around Cape Horn from Washington D.C. with the rest of my great-grandparents' belongings when the U.S. Army posted Edward Davis and his wife Margaret, first to California, then to The Philippines during the Spanish-American War and finally to Hawaii in 1901. At any rate, I became acquainted with the chair that day, and now, with the perspective of an adult, I see its rescue as a warning of what eventually happened to Red Hale itself and a generation of timber homes on the shore. As my great grandfather had been in the habit of scouring second-hand and antique stores in Washington D.C., the chair's earliest history is unclear. But, as we shall see, it narrowly survived and now has connections to at least five custodians – originally in England, then Washington D.C., the Presidio in San Francisco, Waikiki, and now, once again, in California, in my bedroom.

*****

Our pre-war black Studebaker sedan would ease off the end of Kalakaua Avenue onto a sandy driveway where a bamboo thicket provided privacy from the street. My expectations would mount because Mom would always be preoccupied with the account books, Higuchi, the cook, and her inspection of the house. That routine gave me a window of freedom to entertain myself on the seawall, on the small beach next door and in the labyrinth of the big red house. We would first pass the separate washhouse where cook, resident custodian and widower Sadami Higuchi lived with his three children on the second floor.

More overgrown bamboo obscured the kitchen window, and Pathos vines clung to a substantial Ironwood stump which hid some of the upstairs bedroom windows. Two stone chimneys accented a pronounced double-gabled roof line, and star jasmine fringed over the rusty board-and-batten outer walls. As Mom was parking in the carport next to the kitchen, I would jump out of the slowly moving car, first onto the running board and then to the driveway. Because I was awed by the looming mountain next door, I would always take a quick glance up through the branches of the Ironwood trees to the summit of Diamond Head which rose over Red Hale. Mom's regular *be careful and don't go far* would partly register as I would scuffle in the sand to find bristly Ironwood cones before they could attack my bare feet. Another pathway led around the screened front porch to the ocean. There, startled mynah birds and doves would fly into the coconut trees that punctuated a lawn buttressed from the ocean by a public seawall. In Manoa our quiet dead-end street almost never offered interesting strangers. But in Waikiki I could always count on *real life* visitors on the seawall that offered public access to all. They seemed to be aimless pedestrians passing Grandma's front lawn, and I wondered where they were going on this sometimes wave-wet thoroughfare along the ocean.

To the east, the wall takes a sharp turn that cuts off vision in that direction, and keeps ships from the mainland from appearing until they pass that turn. During the war I had become fascinated by airplanes, but they didn't often appear above Manoa Valley. In Waikiki, however, they would regularly pass over as they made their climb toward California or descent to the Honolulu Airport. To the west I could see whitecaps on the reef and surfers using the natural break in the coral called the Kapua (*sea channel* in Hawaiian) Channel. Queen Kapiolani's beach house used to stand there, and the name *Queen's Surf* had been attached to that surfing area ever since.

Trade winds would carry the familiar scent of rainforest at home in the valley. But low tides at the beach permitted a fishy stink from the tide pools that hosted seaweed, *opihi* (edible sea snails), scuttling black crabs and the threatening possibility of moray eels among the rocks. High tides offered a briny mist rising from the regular assault of waves on the seawall. I wasn't allowed to go into the water there as sand didn't cover the slick rocks and sharp coral. But, immediately next door, to the east of Red Hale, there was a remnant of beach that the seawall and wave action had not yet eliminated. Early property owners had sometimes built their homes too close to the water, and the Army Corps of Engineers needed to build walls to protect them. The resulting altered wave movement had relocated the sand, and today all the small beaches are buried under seawalls and gardens. But, in the mid-1940s, at least one of those beaches still existed. There, I could play in shallow water and sit in the sand collecting shells and scouring for pieces of sea-washed colored glass.

*****

Smells of what would become Red Hale's dinner came from the kitchen that day, and I could hear Higuchi chopping and stirring to the muffled accompaniment of his Japanese radio station. Doors were seldom locked and the tenants weren't there on weekdays. The stage was set for me to summon plots from *Dick Tracy, The Green Hornet* and *The Whistler*. These stories could transform Red Hale into a castle, the interior of a cavern or even a large haunted house by the sea. There was no immense blue whale hanging overhead as one did at the Bishop Museum, but all the mahogany antiques and the musty smell of dust, beeswax, furniture polish and age reminded me of the Museum where the whale dominated the central hall. But at Red Hale there were no glass barriers or signs telling me not to touch.

My personal museum always seemed to have an overcrowded disorder that didn't suggest what I was used to at home. *Fashionable Victorian clutter* was not an explanation to me then, but there was **stuff** everywhere – an eclectic hubbub of mainland and island details. With each visit, the house offered up something new – an illustrated *Around the World in Eighty Days*, a book on Krakatoa and one about dinosaurs, a precariously placed ostrich egg, a tangle of Kukui nut *leis*, a precautionary box of gas masks and black-out curtains left over from the War, and even a stereopticon that showed me three dimensional images of exotic snow-capped mountains and European cities.

Gently creaking floors were covered with faded Persian carpets, and the walls hosted kilims and paintings hung frame to frame. Two exotic stone fireplaces generated fantasies of Santa Claus. I guess I was too old for Santa Claus, but why were two fireplaces necessary at the beach, I wondered. The mantles held crystal decanters and candlesticks, and an elegant grandfather clock set my imaginings to a rhythm as it chimed the time. More mahogany surfaces provided places for piles of books, framed photographs of dour overdressed ancestors, articles of Meissen and Imari porcelain, and hurricane and electric lamps. Some of them were always lit as outside light didn't fully penetrate from the beachside lanai to the center of the house. In Manoa, lots of windows filled our home with light, so the customary Victorian pall at Red Hale shed theatrical shadows on the stage sets in my mind.

This houseful of Victoriana mingled with an assortment of island accents: a hodgepodge of rattan, wicker and bamboo, a *koa* wood calabash, *tapa* wall hangings, a fishing net with Japanese glass floats that probably had been washed up on the seawall. There were fan-shaped peacock chairs and *lauhala* floor mats on the front lanai that had been woven by the wives of Hawaiian fishermen. A hammered-bronze and abalone shell decoration sat on top of the main staircase newel post. Today, it serves as an accent lamp in my California home.

Upstairs, furniture curiously called *highboys* and *lowboys* mixed with wrought-iron beds in the wallpapered bedrooms. Even there I was free to wander as I could often still hear voices discussing Red Hale's business. Usually, the upper windows were open, filling the bedrooms with hints of salt and jasmine, and the constant splashing at the seawall and the gentle roar from the reef. Mom's former bedroom had been on the ocean side of the house; living in Manoa, she missed the rhythm of the surf that would have always eased her to sleep at Red Hale.

A large dinner table with lion-clawed feet filled the dining room and was overhung by a green and white stained-glass chandelier; built-in cabinets with glass doors and a butler's pantry were full of formal silver serving pieces marked *D* for Davis, my great grandfather's name. Because of their living contents, an enclosed conservatory off the dining room and a walk-in canary cage on the *makai* lanai were particular curiosities to me. The conservatory held a jungle of ferns and orchids – and plots from my Tarzan comic books – and the aviary produced a chatter of canaries that blended with bickering mynahs and doves which had returned to the front lawn.

Even as an eight-year-old, I was a thoughtful book lover, so it was not surprising that the library/study was my favorite room. It sat in the center of the house with two living rooms and the dining room radiating from it. Amongst the ceiling-high shelves of book spines, were General Davis' epaulets in a *koa* frame and a ceremonial sword, probably from West Point or the Civil War. A family Bible with Davis signatures was a gift from the General's mother to his wife;

a large dictionary on a stand and a spinning globe would keep me company as I sat, knees to my chest, at Great-grandpa's desk thumbing through yellowing pages of musty smelling leather-bound books: a world atlas, an illustrated edition of Shakespeare's plays, works about Abraham Lincoln and others on military history, especially The Civil War. There was even a collection of Mom's childhood books including *The Wizard of Oz* and *The Tale of Peter Rabbit*. With third grade and possibly *show-and-tell* only weeks away, there were a number of possibilities in the library alone: the epaulets, the sword, a picture of the General or one of his books.

*****

Having eaten my tuna sandwich, I was climbing in the tangle of my favorite *jungle gym*, a gnarled *hau* tree which grew near the tenants' barbecue.

Mom's examination of the house had brought her to the seaside garden. *Oh, my God!*, I heard her scream as she picked up a well-crafted furniture leg from the grill's wood pile, and then another until there were about eight pieces of the Chippendale chair. Seemingly, a need for fire wood had driven someone to this "useless" antique. Moist salt air had probably taken a toll on its eighteenth-century glue, and the expediency of the wood pile must have been a practical solution for discarding junk. As survivors of World War Two, the tenants were probably looking ahead to a newer world. Pieces of an old chair with its venerable scars were reminders of the past, and they had been relegated to an immediate practical use before they were seen as something to be preserved and repaired.

Muttering that she was *mad as hell,* and calling out for Higuchi, Mom pulled me out of the *hau* tree to help carry the pieces of the chair, and we marched into the house. An antique chair meant very little to me at that age, but I was encouraged when I realized that I was not being blamed for that particular crisis. I see now that Mom might have felt the same violation one feels after a home burglary. Higuchi, of course, was innocent, so it was assumed one of the tenants was to blame. Today, there is no one to ask if Mom ever tracked down the culprit, but the crippled mahogany pieces were liberated in the nick of time and taken back to Manoa Valley for safekeeping.

*****

It was probably at this point that mom and Grandma began to rethink the strategy of leaving the furnished house in the care of its busy cook and tenants. The nexus of the disruption of the war and Grandma's advanced age had eclipsed the value of the house and its furnishings and put Red Hale on a course of inevitable decline – and eventual doom.

The Chippendale chair was the object of that specific rescue, but it was just the beginning of a process – moving many of Red Hale's furnishings from danger in a time that didn't seem to value them. Our house in Manoa began to resemble the inside of Grandma's house as it gradually filled with some of these period pieces: an assortment of Persian carpets, the grandfather clock, the *koa* desk, the formal dining set with lion claw feet, and several of the highboys from the bedrooms. There were also two sideboards, a Steinway upright piano, a large China cabinet containing formal dishes from James Monroe's white house and a gilt-framed portrait of Grandma as a young woman. And, of course, the Chippendale chair. Some of these rescued treasures now furnish my home and those of my siblings. Over the years, I have gradually claimed some of this Victoriana and imported them to California. They have outlasted the *antique-on-the-woodpile incident* and the tenants who had misunderstood and disrespected their heyday in the big red house.

The Chippendale chair had originally endured a voyage from England and then the hazards of Cape Horn only to be sidelined on a beachside barbeque in Waikiki. It would be cleaned and restored by an antique-collecting neighbor for another generation. Now, every time I use it as a holding place for laundry, it serves as a personal touchstone to Red Hale.

*****

Eventually, unlike the chair, the house itself could not be rescued. In the 1950s market pressures replaced it and many other houses with much larger buildings among the remaining coconut trees. As the world's cities continue to grow skyward, Red Hale's tale has become commonplace. Large homes in central or attractive areas are replaced and mostly forgotten when a generation of denser buildings and neighborhoods take their place.

My childhood affair with Red Hale has stayed with me as it and images of its departed family residents make appearances in my memory. Because she had left the house intact, Grandma had inadvertently created a time capsule of the late nineteenth and early twentieth centuries. I had encountered that time capsule in the midst of my formative years when I was filled with curiosity about the world. Without that immersion at my private museum, I wouldn't have been able to celebrate Red Hale's past - or soften its loss. Pieces of Red Hale's furnishings, mementos of an earlier time, have moved with me as I have changed homes. But I still sometimes vainly fantasize about a time machine that might afford me some more time to indulge my infatuation with the rambling house that my family called Red Hale.

Waikiki's Gold Coast under the rainbow where Red Hale stood

The mountains of Manoa Valley behind the Gold Coast

A Miracle Suburb on Yonder Beach

The history of Waikiki land is convoluted I discovered, including Red Hale's parcel. Please make the most of what I have written. Today, the seawall at 2999 Kalakaua Avenue protects twenty-seven apartments where Red Hale had housed a single family for over fifty years. In 1957, *Grandma's house* was replaced by nine floors of co-op units called The Tahitienne, becoming the first of the high rises that now crowd the base of Diamond Head. The land had gone from its initial feudal communal use by all Hawaiians to exclusivity for a few. We can imagine the possibility of Hawaiians living in *pili* grass huts by the shore in the early days of Waikiki that were replaced by large wooden homes just before the turn of the 20th century, and then in the 1950s by concrete towers. During the time of grass huts, Hawaiians had no concept of private property, hence no word for it in their language.[1] Had their land rights been easy prey in a twisting story of ambition, greed and public blunders that surfaced when I uncovered this history? Originally, I had merely set out to trace the chain of title for Red Hale's land, but, in the process, I dug up a story I had not expected to find. This chapter is a tale that dips into the sometimes sordid history of real estate in Waikiki. The information I have recounted here is backed up by my printed sources. Others may choose to interpret the story differently, but my perspective of it closely aligns with Red Hale's history.

---
[1] Julia Flynn Siler, Lost Kingdom, 2012, pg.19

On June 11, 1877, two years after his election to the throne, the 40-year-old King Kalakaua presented in fluent English the first of what would become his annual Kamehameha Day speeches. The mutton-chopped king, already stout but looking smart in his usual military uniform, stretched out his arms to indicate where *a miracle suburb* would be laid out *on yonder beach*.[2] Indeed, it was the beach and ocean overseen by an iconic cinder cone called Diamond Head that made this neighborhood so special. Here, during the holiday horse-racing festivities, he was setting aside a hundred and fifty acres of his land that bordered the sea for a public park named for his consort Queen Kapiolani. Through the Crown Land Commission, Kalakaua leased his acreage called Kaneloa to the park for one dollar a year. This would become the principal section of the park at its western or *ewa* end. The forty-eight acres of the Diamond Head end of today's park would, through leases and sales, be added separately. Red Hale would be built on the seawall directly across the street from that part of the park. Because Kalakaua was seen by a number of his critics of foreign businessmen to be sometimes unpredictable, self-indulgent and possibly corrupt, might there have been an ulterior motive in his generosity to the Hawaiian people? It should be noted that, to his credit, Kalakaua was known to be a scholar, a poet, a composer and a strong supporter of traditional Hawaiian culture. But how could a *suburb* be part of this public park?

Establishing Kapiolani Park and an association to govern it were parts of Kalakaua's vision for Waikiki, a district known for its white sands, gentle surf and *mauka* breezes that common people and *ali'i* alike had long used for rest

---

[2] Robert R. Weyeneth, Kapiolani Park: A History, 2002, pg.27

and recreation. The park would be both an aesthetic and a political focal point for Hawaii's expanding *sugar kingdom* which in 1876, had been bolstered by a reciprocity treaty for commerce and defense (Pearl Harbor) with the United States. Kalakaua was aware that a recently improved Waikiki Road was already bringing people to the tranquility of Waikiki four miles away from the noise and dust of Honolulu. Now he needed even loftier inducements for the *right people* to settle there.

Kalakaua had recently returned from a three-month tour (1874-'75) of the United States and Europe where he had been impressed with parks and recreation facilities for public use. But the elected king also had been harboring a belief in the divine rights of kings and an extravagant, almost comic-operatic, aspiration to become emperor of all Polynesia with Honolulu, and specifically Waikiki, as its capital.[3] His affinity for pomp and pageantry, outfitted with swords, military brass and braid and The Royal Hawaiian Band, provided a theatrical backdrop for his ambitions. Two years later (1879), the profligate king further impressed his citizens by building a royal residence called Iolani Palace to grandly house the Kalakaua dynasty. This over-budget project had indebted him to his missionary-descended advisors and the sugar barons including Claus Spreckels. It was suspected that Kalakaua had accepted a bribe from Spreckels to gain water rights for Spreckels' Maui sugar lands.[4] At any rate, Kalakaua had become a puppet monarch with American businessmen pulling the strings.

The king's park project was schizophrenic from the start. History has seen Kalakaua juggling his beloved people's

---

[3] Michael Dougherty, To Steal A Kingdom, 1992, pg. 156

[4] Siler, Lost Kingdom, pg.79

best interests with a need to satisfy the growing demands of *aliens* whom he needed for financial support. Kalakaua, it seems, wanted the status quo two ways: a government run by and for his own people but also the advice, cash and political backing of foreigners. Foreign sugar interests wanted the kingdom to be part of the United States. The *haoles* (came to mean Caucasian, literally meant *foreigner*) were already finding the quixotic king to be troublesome by keeping them out of administrative posts, and eventually the *Bayonet Constitution* of 1887 stripped him at gunpoint of personal power and gave it to the Legislature.

But, in the meantime, Kalakaua wanted something more splendid than a place for public amusement in Waikiki; the land-rich and cash-poor king's vision would attract the most influential foreign businessmen and local chiefs. A park *for the frequent and general resort of all of our citizens*[5] had more than a little self-interest embedded in it. The plan also included a scheme for a residential *suburb* that the rich could buy into. On the one hand, the park was for *all of our citizens* (the Hawaiian people), and on the other hand, for only *some* of the residents (rich foreigners) in this same vision. The notion of luxury mansions within the park was an offering to gain continued subsidy and political support from his rich *haole* friends. He owed them for their help in electing him over Queen Emma in 1874. Emma was the Dowager Queen of Alexander Lunalilo (Kamehameha IV), Hawaii's first elected monarch. After his untimely death from tuberculosis, an election was held between Emma and Kalakaua. David Kalakaua shared common descent with the Kamehameha ruling family from the 18th century. His park would be a gift to the Hawaiian people, but also, if he played his cards right,

---

[5] Weyeneth, pg.27

an appeasement to his debt holders and political backers.

There would be attractive amenities in his park: an improved first-class race track, carriage drives and ornamental ponds – but not for all. They would be for the wealthy who could afford a fifty-dollar share in the Kapiolani Park Association. Each share entitled its holder to a leasehold lot on the shore or on the slopes of Diamond Head. These fifty-dollar investments for home sites with striking views were seen as very secure, for Waikiki's healthy climate was already attracting members of the nouveau riche.[6] Honolulu's established society would surely follow and bring prestige to the king's vision. His notion of the public good for *all of our citizens*, especially rich foreigners, seemed to contradict itself and leave his detractors and future historians suspicious of his true intentions. "From the perspective of today, the origins of Kapiolani Park look like a lucrative real estate deal that benefited the king and his closest associates."[7]

*****

In retrospect, it was essentially the expanding sugar economy that first opened the door to land rights for foreigners. The original Hawaiians had brought sugar cane with them around 200 A.D. But in 1835, big agriculture had placed a foot in Hawaii's door with the establishment of the first sugar plantation on Kauai.[8] It was no coincidence that by the 1850s, Kamehameha IV's (Alexander Liholiho, 1854-1863) foreign advisors began to take an interest in sugar, and by extension, and more importantly, in Hawaiian land.

---

[6] Weyeneth, Kapiolani Park: A History pg.51

[7] Weyeneth, Ibid. pg.37

[8] Siler, Lost Kingdom, pg.33

Eventually, 1.8 million acres were seized from natives[9] – a kingdom stolen at the bidding of the sugar barons and missionary descendants.

In 1848, the *haole* inspired redistribution of the land called The *Great Mahele* (*division* of the land) opened the door to private ownership. This was the most important and influential document in Hawaii's history. Abruptly, the notion that the king controlled all the land for his people was swept away, and Hawaiian commoners were no longer permitted to settle where they wanted as they had in feudal times. The *Mahele* was achieved when a land commission inspired by foreigners in the court of Kamehameha III (Kauikeaouli, 1825-1854) began to settle long-standing property claims by Hawaiians for the land they had settled on under the old feudal system. Under this new policy, the land was divided into three parts: one third for the king, one third for the chiefs and one third for the commoners. In 1850, *aliens* were permitted to buy fee-simple land if they became Hawaiian citizens. Some *haoles* began renouncing U.S. citizenship to that end and settled in Waikiki.[10]

The *Mahele* had given commoners one third of the land, but it also charged a fee on one third of its value (values were based on what the land could produce) to farm or fish there. Most couldn't afford this fee to secure deeds so they sold their land instead, often to rich *haoles*. Their right to use the land now depended on legal ownership rather than Hawaiian feudal tradition. In this way, much of the common land ended up in the hands of influential foreigners. Less than one per-cent of the land ended up with Hawaiian commoners.[11]

---

[9] Siler, Lost Kingdom,.pg.xxx

[10] Dougherty,To Steal A Kingdom pg.108

[11] Siler, Lost Kingdom pg.20

The lot Red Hale sat on was one small piece of the land that the Great Mahele eventually siphoned off to foreigners.

*****

At this point, I must flash this narrative back to 1827 when the third company of Protestant missionaries arrived in Hawaii from Boston. Among them was the Reverend Gerritt Parmele Judd whose missionary zeal, knack for languages and extensive medical knowledge awarded him authoritative influence and a great deal of Hawaiian land including twenty-two prime acres in Waikiki near the area Red Hale would someday sit. Judd's name is not included in Red Hale's chain of title, but his tactics did award him land in the same area of Waikiki and reveals the manipulative measures some foreigners used to acquire Hawaiian land. The *Mahele* was Judd's idea so it was he who ultimately established the opportunity for foreign land ownership. The Boston mission headquarters had banned missionaries from mixing in private or political matters of the kingdom.[12] But the controversial Judd was determined to take advantage of the fact that he had arrived in Hawaii at a critical time when traditional customs were in conflict with new ones: old taboos were broken, and Christianity was adopted. Judd was not alone in exploiting the economic and political system in his own favor. There were other missionaries and their descendants who, as the saying goes, came to the islands to do *good* but had also done *very well*.

By 1847, *Judd's great land grab had begun in earnest. Certainly, no other event in the history of the kingdom had such shattering political, social and economic effect upon Hawaii's few*

---

[12] Dougherty, To Steal A Kingdom pg.103

surviving Polynesians. In one sense, it plunged Hawaii's commoners back into feudalism since the white man was soon to have control over their lands and their lives. There is no record of a missionary speaking out regarding the hypocrisy of preaching moral values to the Hawaiians on Sunday and then acquiring their land during the rest of the week.[13]

Within twenty years of Dr. Judd's arrival, a shortage of doctors and Judd's fluency in the Hawaiian language had bestowed on him a number of influential offices including Royal Physician, Minister of Foreign Affairs and official Court Interpreter. As interpreter, he was in a position to put his personal construction on all that was being said and done at court, and that would eventually be included as part of the public record in the Hawaii Archives.[14] He could edit history and perhaps cover up his opportunism in attaining Hawaiian land. Despite his official spin on Hawaiian history, the Judd-inspired *Mahele* could be seen as a land grab in the guise of land reform.

By 1824, literacy had been achieved for many Hawaiians including Kamehameha II (Liholiho, 1819-1824) who subsequently converted to Christianity. His *Kuhina-nui* (prime minister) Queen Kaahumanu, who had been the favorite wife of Kamehameha the Great, also converted, and later, as the regent of Kamehameha III (Kauikeaouli), she shared her beliefs with him. Because of her religious influence on the young king, and possibly a mercenary proposal by the opportunistic Dr. Judd, the division of the land allowed special real estate discounts to foreign missionaries for bringing the word of God and literacy to the islands.[15] It is no surprise

---

[13] Dougherty, To Steal A Kingdom pg.107

[14] Dougherty, To Steal A Kingdom pg.110

[15] Dougherty, To Steal A Kingdom, pg.115

that Judd himself would become one of those beneficiaries.

*****

Ultimately, my research uncovered what proved to be a complicated tangle of land maneuvering that suggested greed and deceit. I had to wonder if members of my family could have been implicated in any such finagling for Red Hale. Surely they were just innocent land buyers and not conniving oligarchs. Crooked land deals seemed a long way from the tranquil domesticity that I knew had taken place at Red Hale. But I wanted to *follow the money* to see if my great grandfather's purchase in 1910 could have been part of any of the tainted land acquired by others.

*****

Kalakaua's Park would be created predominantly from two large tracts of land: Kaneloa and Kapua were both part of the much larger Waikiki *ahupuaa* (traditional triangular shaped Hawaiian land divisions that stretched from the mountain tops to the sea). Before the creation of the park in 1877, the king had owned both parcels as part of his one-third share of the land. At the time of the park's creation, however, he owned only Kaneloa at the western or *ewa* end of the park. According to hearsay and some written sources, he possibly lost part of Kapua (the eastern tract where Red Hale would later stand) in a poker game to a Swedish immigrant named Allan Herbert.[16] This probably took place at Kalakaua's boathouse at Honolulu Harbor which was the setting for much of the *Merrie Monarch's* pleasure: card

---

[16] Weyeneth, Kapiolani Park: A History pg.36

games, drinking, lavish luaus and enjoying the hula that the missionaries had tried to outlaw. Poker was known to be Kalakaua's favorite pastime. *The king's poker games were infamous as it was well known he regularly lost assets that rightfully belonged to the people. His chief asset was Hawaiian land.* His sister Liliuokalani was known to chastise him for gambling and frittering away the royal treasury. This is according to a friend Fred C. McCorriston whose great grandfather regularly played poker with the king. So, it is possible that the poker game with Herbert was a reality as it was entirely in Kalakaua's character. In 1884, as the new owner of a section of Kapua, Herbert opened his seaside residence as one of Waikiki's earliest hotels: Sans Souci (*without a care*) became a favorite resort of Robert Louis Stevenson, and the name survives today on a condo building overlooking San Souci Beach.

Before Kapua was possibly lost to a foreigner, and well before it belonged to Kalakaua, it had been administered by Queen Kaahumanu. Here, she fished, swam and surfed in the winter months while summering on the cool *ali'i* side of upper Manoa Valley. Interestingly, my family lived near both of these sites – two blocks from where her Manoa retreat was eventually discovered in a neighbor's backyard, and at Red Hale in the Kapua section of Waikiki.

*****

On a recent trip to the islands, I spent some time maneuvering a number of large dusty ledgers at the bustling public records office in Honolulu. My search paid off when one of these weighty books supplied me with the Hawaiian name Pehu in the chain of title to Red Hale's property. Pehu seemed to be the first non-royal who was associated with that land. In 1823, Kamehameha ll (Liholiho, 1819-1824) had presented Kapua as part of a tribute to a member of his court, Chief Iona Pehu, who had managed a successful fishing operation in the area. The land must have been agreeable and productive, for Pehu and his wife lived there for many years, and their descendants continued ownership until a remaining section of Kapua was sold to Allan Herbert by the fourth husband of Pehu's widow in 1877.

Kapua, meaning *sea channel*, has a critical break in the reef, and has a history of its own: that natural formation gave Oahu its first, if smaller, protected harbor in addition to the later and much larger deep water port at Honolulu. It also produces angled wave action for superior surfing conditions which came to be known as Queen's Surf. In 1853 Kapua Channel was used as access to a quarantine station for arriving visitors during a smallpox epidemic. And, in 1902, the channel was an obvious site for the Commercial Pacific Cable Company to lay a telegraph line through the reef from Sans Souci to San Francisco's Ocean Beach. The first transmission was a New Year greeting relayed to Theodore Roosevelt in Washington D.C.[17]

*****

As it became clear to me that Mom's grandfather had no association with finagling oligarchs, it also became evident that, in addition to Reverend Judd and Allen Herbert, one William G. Irwin (English, 1843 – 1914), probably had. Unlike Judd's and Herbert's trajectory to Hawaiian land, Irwin

---

[17] Andrea Feeser, Waikiki, A History of Forgetting and Remembering, 2006, pg. 119

(a partner of Claus Spreckels) was already one of Hawaii's wealthiest sugar and banking magnates and had the means to purchase land he wanted.

By the early 1880s, Irwin and Spreckels had attained great political clout through a virtual monopoly of Hawaiian sugar. As one of the principal investors in the Kapiolani Park Association, Irwin owned 41 shares and held proxy rights to another 31 – all due to his wealth and great influence in the Park Association. In 1878, two years after Kalakaua established the Park, the Park Association began distributing leasehold residential lots by auction. One could bid on as many parcels as one had shares, so the wealthiest shareholders could outbid others for the best oceanfront lots.[18] In 1893 Irwin purchased a section of Kapua from Allan Herbert and in 1895 another section from Adolf Spreckels.

By 1896, bidding wars and purchases from Herbert and Spreckels had awarded Irwin a good portion of Kapua as well as some of Kaneloa. On July first, he orchestrated a series of convoluted deals that led to the Republic of Hawaii converting thirty-seven of his leasehold lots to fee-simple status. Nineteen of those lots were on the ocean where the Waikiki Natatorium and Aquarium are today, just outside of Kapua's boundary. One of Irwin's maneuvers was a *benevolent* land gift to the park of part of his land – but only a part of it, as he saw that Kalakaua's vision was becoming a reality: the area was developing as a fashionable neighborhood for large homes.[19] History kindly credits him with this bequest to the public park, but it seemed to be a business decision that drove him to retain the balance, the nineteen waterfront lots at the eastern end of Kapua – a maneuvering

---

[18] Weyeneth, Kapiolani Park: A History pg.51

[19] Weyeneth, Kapiolani Park: A History pg.48

that won him control of some very coveted property.

*****

In 1893, American business leaders and merchants, the power elite of their day, overthrew the Hawaiian monarchy with the aid of the United States' Army. They established a republic which was, in reality, an oligarchy under Hawaii's first governor Sanford B. Dole and his rich cohorts. In 1895, Hawaiian nationalists initiated a failed attempt to restore the monarchy; a military encounter took place on Diamond Head not far from Red Hale's future site. In 1898, the United States annexed Hawaii as a territory, disappointing the many supporters of Queen Liliuokalani, Kalakaua's younger sister. At this point, Hawaii became part of the Manifest Destiny movement which was marching westward.

In any event, the door had been opened to foreign land ownership, and General Davis, my great grandfather, was at liberty to purchase his property. Nevertheless, political ambition, personal greed, government blunders – and perhaps the luck of the draw in a royal poker game – had all contributed to a windfall for foreigners and a devastating loss for natives. Red Hale's section of Kapua had become off limits for Hawaiian commoners to live in *pili* grass huts, but my great grandfather *The General,* as he was known in the family at the time of his purchase, was able to buy lot number seven of William Irwin's beachfront tract in 1910. By 1893, *haoles* controlled four-fifths of the island's arable land. King Kalakaua never became emperor of all Polynesia, but his *miracle suburb*, including Red Hale, did take its place on the *shore* as he had predicted.

The twisting tale of Red Hale's land concluded in 1985

when The Hawaiian Trust Company sold my grandmother's property to the residents of The Tahitienne, the nine-story condo building which had replaced Red Hale in 1957. Known records show the chain essentially starting in 1793 when Kamehameha the Great landed his army in war canoes in Waikiki to conquer Oahu. Under the old tradition, the land belonged to him, and he could dictate how it was used. He saw this as a sacred area, for two *heiaus* (pre-Christian places of worship and sacrifice) were established there, one on either side of Red Hale's future site. Kupalaha Heiau was near Queen's Surf just west of Red Hale, and the greater Papaenaena Heiau was situated nearby on the slopes of Diamond Head where the old Dillingham home La Pietra (now a girl's school) sits.

In 1819 Kamehameha II inherited control of the land, and he bestowed Kapua on Chief Iona Pehu in 1823. This was confirmed by The Great *Mahele* in 1848. The chain continued with Allen Herbert in 1877, William Irwin in 1893 and my grandmother Susan Harrison in 1910. Her father, The General, purchased the property with a house on it and put it in Susan's name where it remained until 1957. The Hawaiian Trust Company then convinced her to lease the land to Tahitienne Incorporated for a nine-story high rise. The only part of the puzzle Hawaii's ledger books has not revealed is who built the original house. I assume it was Irwin as he deeded the property with a house on it to the General.

*****

Long after his original vision, a collection of concrete towers has replaced King Kalakaua's graceful *suburb on the beach* that Red Hale was a part of. At any event, then and today, Diamond Head looms over all, and the ocean that has always made this area so remarkable endlessly doubles over on itself and breaks up its white froth on the seawall which still protects the land.

Bibliography

Dougherty, Michael, To Steal a Kingdom, Island Style Press 1992

Freeser, Andrea, Waikiki, A History of Forgetting and Remembering, University of Hawaii
Press, 2006

Henry, J. Patrick, Pehu and the Kapua Section of Kapiolani Park, unpublished manuscript

McCorriston, Fred C., private conversation

Siler, Julia Flynn, Lost Kingdom, Grove Press, 2012

Weyeneth, Robert R., Kapiolani Park: A History, Kapiolani Park Preservation Society, 2002

The Tahitienne Today

The General

The General, his wife Mardi, My Grandmother and My Great Uncle

The General and Camp McKinley

"I guess you must have been one of those proverbial Army brats."

I occasionally hear that quick rejoinder whenever I inform people that I am originally from Hawaii. I am not an Army brat in the usual sense as my parents were not in the military, but, in the long run, I am a Hawaiian and an Army brat because of my great grandfather Brigadier General Edward Davis. I suppose I should give ultimate credit for my provenance to a detonation in Havana Harbor, Cuba on February 15, 1898. The sinking of the Battleship Maine set in motion a chain of events which established me, three generations later, as a Hawaiian *Army brat*. As such, I occasionally *remember the Maine* and the Spanish-American War for ultimately bringing my great grandfather, the General, and my family to Hawaii.

In his retirement at Red Hale, he was most often identified as *the General* – not Grandpa or Great Grandpa, but, by the time I knew of him, *the General*. I knew his name was Edward Davis, but his final military rank and his physical bearing in photographs were most often referenced when I was getting to know of him as a child. I never actually met the General because he passed away twenty-two years before I was born. But there is family lore that has told me a lot about him.

"The General would take his walk each morning on the seawall or across the street in Kapiolani Park."

"The General would come back to Waikiki from the

Tantalus house each autumn after the summer heat."

"The General always requested that there be no visitors in the afternoon when he was napping on the *pune'e* (Hawaiian daybed) on the oceanside lanai."

"The General always wanted his dinner served on time."

"The General wanted quiet when he was reading or working in his library."

This formidable man seems to have enjoyed being *"the general"* as he played the part in every way. While he was a retired resident there, daily life at Red Hale was managed for him. The discipline of a very long military career had led him to expect respect, and, indeed, that is what he always received.

At first, I didn't know what the word *general* meant, but a usual tone of deference made it sound important. Military photos, including the one used for his Honolulu Star-Bulletin obituary in 1918 revealed a lot as well. The headline read "Gallant Soldier Long Resident of Honolulu Answers Final Roll Call." He appears in uniform with brass, ribbons, epaulets and a stern countenance. His smart beard and the features of his Scots-Irish face seem to be saying that he was in charge of any situation. I now know that most people in the General's time set their faces still and hard for photos, partly because it was the fashion and partly because of the exposure time needed to record the image. Today, I would be happy to see his severe image brought to life so I could witness other film frames of his demeanor. Maybe he had been smiling just before or after the shutter clicked. Perhaps I would not have allowed his photos to be so intimidating if I could have seen behind the curtain of that military façade.

Reports from the Japanese family who helped at Red Hale reveal that he was respected for running a *tight ship,* paying his bills on time and displaying a strong sense of patriotism. He always vowed America could never lose in any war. He was admired for his fairness and love of family, and, yes, apparently even a good sense of humor, but, as a child, his photos cowed me and I never felt that he was someone whose lap I could have crawled up on.

When I first knew Red Hale as a child, its weighty 19th century atmosphere seemed to reflect the formality of the General's photographs. An extensive collection of Victoriana, brought to Hawaii to accompany his next-to-last tour of duty, ornamented the house: the rescued Chippendale chair was part of a collection that also included heavy claw-footed furniture, a library full of military and history books, his West Point sword, epaulets from his Spanish American War uniform, and family photographs of ancestors encased in heavy clothing. I always wondered how they endured the Hawaiian climate in so many layers. No one wore shorts in those days. In one photo the General is surrounded by his wife Margaret, my great-uncle Alexander and my grandmother Susan. All of them stare into the camera with the stiff unsmiling presence fashionable at the time.

*****

In 1901, Major Davis (he wasn't the General yet), his wife and their daughter Susan sailed to Honolulu from a posting in the Philippine Islands where he had been serving with John Pershing in response to a Muslim uprising just after the Spanish-American War. The 1898 war with Spain was over, but there was still a fight against Filipino rebels who resisted American rule. I hope my readers will indulge me for some turn-of-the-century history as I set the stage for the

General's presence in Hawaii. His story is full of history.

At that time, Edward was 56 years old, his wife Margaret was 60, and their daughter Susan was 29. Hawaii was to be his penultimate assignment and it corresponded with the first United States presence there. He was in charge of the new Camp McKinley, originally a tent city in Kapiolani Park and a stopover for the Army to adjust to the tropics on its way to the Philippines.

It is now believed that the sinking of the Battleship Maine was caused by a tragic accident, but the incident was used by President McKinley as a pretext for going to war because Randolph Hearst's yellow journalism was calling McKinley weak for not standing up to Spain. The explosion killed 267 sailors and set in motion a chain of events that led to the 112-day conflict, the Spanish-American War.

Because the hostilities extended across the Pacific to the Philippines, Hawaii was seen as a strategic key to that ocean and an imperialistic opportunity for the United States. European powers had already colonized most of the world leaving few openings for U.S. expansion. The Hawaiian Islands, ruled by David Kalakaua, an elected monarch, were perceived as possibly *available*. This realization ultimately led to U.S. annexation in 1898 – *the stealing of a kingdom*. The establishment of Camp McKinley followed, as did the arrival in Hawaii of Major (soon-to-be Brigadier General) Edward Davis.

By the early 19th century, Spain had lost most of its colonies through wars of independence. Spain considered Cuba to be part of its national territory, as opposed to a colony, so it was in Cuba to protect these interests. The Monroe Doctrine (1823) declared the western hemisphere to be protected from outside interference, so the United States sent the Battleship Maine to guard our interests there. After its sinking, the U.S. issued an ultimatum to the Spanish government to end its presence in Cuba. Spain refused this, and on April 25, 1898 President McKinley asked Congress for a declaration of war.

Because the Philippines were a part of Spain after over 300 years of rule, the war reached the far side of the Pacific. In those days, battleships couldn't cross the ocean without refueling or supplying, so Hawaii (and Pearl Harbor) became an important stopover and an added reason for its annexation. Admiral Dewey's victory at Manila Bay destroyed the Spanish fleet on May 1st and led to Spain's eventual surrender on August 12, 1898. Peace was declared, and The Treaty of Paris was signed on December 10th. These events awarded the U.S. temporary control of Cuba (including a perpetual lease of Guantanamo Bay) and ownership of Puerto Rico, Guam and the Philippines.

Camp McKinley, the first United States military presence in Hawaii, was established four days after annexation in 1898. A temporary tent city was set up among the surrounding *kiawe* trees near King Kalakaua's race track in Kapiolani Park. The camp housed 1300 soldiers of the New York Volunteer Infantry Regiment which sojourned there while making its way to the Philippines. They were hurried there to relieve Admiral Dewey and to seize Manila. But first they needed this Hawaiian stopover to bridge the Pacific.

King Kalakaua's permission for the camp was originally meant for only a few days, but then grew to months, and then years. By November of 1898, a permanent camp was built on the current site of the Waikiki fire station on Kapahulu Avenue. Its name became Camp McKinley in honor of the President and remained there until 1907 when Fort Shafter was established.

Major Davis had recently come, first from duty on Angel Island in San Francisco Bay (it served as the Ellis Island of the west coast, admitting Chinese immigrants), then The Presidio in San Francisco, and finally the Philippines. His command at Camp McKinley lasted from July 22, 1901 to January 9, 1903.

*****

A man named John Davises (sic.) of Cambridgeshire, England has the honor of providing the first printed record of the Davis (son of David) name sometime in the year 1327. Three hundred years later, as part of a Puritan movement to the new world, the HMS Speedwell brought the Davis name (common in England and Wales) to Boston in 1638, eighteen years after the Mayflower arrived in 1620. It took another two hundred years for the Davis name to disseminate and make its way, first to Virginia, and then to Kentucky where, still a long way from Hawaii, my great grandfather Edward Davis was born on July 7, 1845 in Louisville. According to Ancestry.com, my DNA can be traced to Kentucky and the Ohio River Valley. Edward's parents, Benjamin Outram Davis and Susan Frey Speed had married in 1836. A long family connection to Abraham Lincoln began as Susan was the sister of the Honorable James Speed who became Lincoln's second Attorney General. His brother Joshua was Lincoln's best friend – some have speculated *intimate friend* – from early childhood.

Edward's path to Hawaii and Red Hale began when, as a young man of 17, he volunteered with the 5th Kentucky Cavalry in 1862. The Civil War had started the year before, and young Edward spent fifteen months fighting as a Second Lieutenant in the Union Army. Military records show that he entered the Army as a first level officer. Kentucky was a border state just north of the Mason-Dixon Line, and Edward was decidedly a Yankee.

Edward's 1918 obituary reports "gallant and meritorious conduct" and an award for valor at the infamous Battle of Chickamauga in northwestern Georgia. This was a decisive Confederate victory with great Union losses. Family history does not report if he ever killed anybody. I wonder if his "gallantry" extended to a rescue of fellow soldiers. Images in my mind emanate from Ken Burns' documentary on the Civil War and the sometimes-grisly war photography of Matthew B. Brady.

With hostilities ongoing, Edward's Civil War service ended in 1863 when President Lincoln appointed him to West Point. Family evidence vouches that this was based on merit (*gallantry and valor*) and not because of any connections to the Speed family. Ulysses S. Grant presented Edward with a West Point diploma in1867, and, in that same year, because the War had ended in 1865, he was free to marry Margaret (Mardie) Davis (no blood relation) in Washington D.C.

During forty years of service at posts throughout the country, Edward rose through the ranks to eventually become the General: Second Lieutenant, 1867; First Lieutenant, 1873; Captain, 1896; Major, 18898 and Brigadier General in 1905. He was a Captain when he was sent with his wife and daughter Susan to Zamboanga in the Philippines. (His son Alexander was already serving in the Army elsewhere.) The 1898 war with Spain was over, but there was still a fight against Muslim Filipino rebels who resisted American rule. America's current struggle with Islamic forces, it seems, is not just a contemporary phenomenon.

While in the Philippines, Captain Davis served with and became close to John Pershing who later rose to be Commander in Chief of the American forces in France during World War One. As a close friend, Davis consoled Pershing after his wife and three daughters died in a tragic fire at the Presidio in San Francisco. This happened while Pershing was chasing Poncho Villa along the Mexican border. In Zamboanga Edward founded an Episcopal mission that later became an established church, and he was also instrumental in getting Captain Pershing promoted to Brigadier General.

*****

Red Hale did not yet stand on the seawall at Waikiki when the Davises arrived in Honolulu in 1901. Hawaii had become a territory of the United States only three years earlier. Queen Victoria had died in January and most Americans welcomed the dawn of the twentieth century as an era of peace, prosperity and progress. But it was still a man's world in which women did not vote, the average life expectancy was only forty-six years, and a typical weekly wage was $12.75. By 1900, however, the process of technological and scientific progress had started to accelerate.

Honolulu was growing up and anticipating greater contacts with the rest of the world. Electricity had started lighting the city in the 1890s. Telephones were in use, and a trans-Pacific cable to San Francisco was being planned. Honolulu had four newspapers, and its citizens were reading about current trouble spots in the world: the Boer War in South Africa, the Boxer rebellion in China, the Spanish-American War in two hemispheres and the ominous rise of

Germany. They also read with fascination about the experiments of a man names Guglielmo Marconi and two brothers named Wright. Marconi would imminently link Hawaii wirelessly to the rest of the world, and Orville and Wilber would make history at Kitty Hawk in 1903, heralding far-ranging implications for Hawaii, the most isolated populated islands on Earth.

The United States had become a continent-wide nation of forty-five states that was looking westward, even across an ocean. The country still relied on a predominantly agricultural economy, but "skyscrapers" had appeared and population was starting to fill the empty spaces to the west coast. A new western frontier would now stand across 2500 miles of water. In that respect, Honolulu was about to build a first-class hotel on the beach at Waikiki that would be an exclamation point to the collection of large beach houses that soon would include Red Hale.

*****

As their ship moved into Honolulu's deep-water port in 1901, masts, stacks and funnels framed the sight of a small city that recent census reported to have 45,000 people. In heavy military uniform and full skirts, the Davises welcomed the usual trade winds pushing the clouds around on the tops of the Koolau Mountains. These served as a backdrop in their view of downtown Honolulu's salient landmarks: King Kalakaua's Iolani Palace, the rooftop and spire of Kawaiahao Church, and the extinct cinder cone called Punchbowl.

The old Russian fort was long gone from the port, but they would have seen its namesake, the recently paved Fort

Street which was home to Honolulu's banks and chief shopping emporiums. Camp McKinley was near Diamond Head, so they were escorted on a dusty ride to the east in either a horse car or one of Honolulu's new electric trollies. Among the horses and buggies, they might have glimpsed one of the two horseless carriages that had arrived two years before.

Coconut and *Kiawe* trees, and picket fences lined the sometimes untidy streets of the city. As they approached Diamond Head, Waikiki Road (to become Kalakaua Avenue in 1905), took them on a trestle over rice and taro paddies, and around banana fields and duck ponds, which were fed by the spouting fresh water (*Waikiki* in Hawaiian) of natural springs and the runoff of mountain streams.

Near the royal coconut groves at Helemoa (today's site of the Royal Hawaiian Hotel), they would have passed the brand new five-story Moana Hotel, Hawaii's tallest structure then and a punctuation mark in what was still a largely rural Waikiki. It would become known as *The First Lady of Waikiki* and was a sign that the beach near Diamond Head was starting to become a tourist destination.

Turning left onto Kapahulu Avenue, the Davises would have immediately seen the barracks of Camp McKinley. It had been commissioned in1898, three years before Edward took command, and after the original camp near Diamond Head had been abandoned. Today, the Waikiki Fire Station stands where the new camp had been, and the eastern end of the Ala Wai Canal is located across the street. But in 1901 the Davises were delivered to a guard house and then a camp road leading to four large barracks buildings with separate bath houses for each. A headquarters building and the base hospital completed the site. If they had looked further east, through the *kiawe* and ironwood trees, and past King Kalakaua's racetrack to the base of Diamond Head, they might have seen the location where the General – he would have become the General by then – would spend most of his retirement years. The site of Red Hale was less than a mile away, but Edward did not yet know it would be home to a significant chapter of his future.

Only a year into his Camp McKinley command, on September 22, 1902, the Davises took possession of a large home at 1516 Hasting St. (now Nehoa St.) in Makiki. That investment made clear the Major knew the end of his career was forthcoming, and he had chosen Hawaii for his retirement. He and his family would live in that house for ten years making additions and alterations. Their 30-year-old daughter Susan (my grandmother) lived with them, at first single and then with her husband and a young daughter. The Hastings Street house sat just below Round Top near an access road to a second Davis home on Tantalus, a cool retreat favored by the well-to-do in the summer months.

After his Camp McKinley command, Edward and his wife returned to Washington D.C. for his final two years of service. As an Adjutant General (his job description, not a military rank) in an administrative job, he assisted commanders in keeping their soldiers combat ready. The Davises then returned to Honolulu to retire, and Edward stepped down on April 11, 1905. But on the day before, on April 10th, his good friend and colleague General John Pershing had him promoted from Major to a one-star Brigadier General, skipping the ranks of Lieutenant Colonel and full Colonel. At length, he had become the General, the man whose spirit hung over Red Hale when I was a child.

Hastings Street had been home to the Davises from 1902

to 1912 when the General's wife Margaret passed away from a cerebral hemorrhage when she was 71 years old. In 1910, anticipating his retirement, Edward had purchased a beach house at the Diamond Head end of Waikiki and put it in his daughter's name. That is the house that would become known as Red Hale. Because he was now alone at the Hastings Street house, the General was moved to Waikiki and Red Hale by his daughter and son-in-law.

In addition to walks in Kapiolani Park, naps serenaded by a cage of prized canaries and trips to the cooler climate on Mount Tantalus, Edward's 1918 obituary (he died of Arterio-sclerosis at age 73) reveals ample pursuits to fill his retirement. An interest in civic affairs led to his memberships on the Territorial Board of Prisons and the Board of Reclaimed Marshlands on Oahu. Edward was an ardent Episcopalian having paid for a new building for Saint Mary's chapel on King Street, originally meant to serve the poor. Like the church he had founded in the Philippines, St. Mary's was a mission that then became a church. He dedicated St. Mary's to his wife Margaret in 1917.

Red Hale itself was filled with evidence of an active and interesting man. His library where I spent time as a child, was proof of his intellect and held books on world affairs and history, particularly The Civil War in which he had served. Abraham Lincoln was the subject of many of those books, and that collection attracted the attention of the community at large. He enjoyed a house full of antiques, including a set of China from the White House of President Monroe that had been bought in a second-hand store in Washington D.C.

*****

I now have in front of me obituaries from The Honolulu Star-Bulletin and The Pacific Commercial Advertiser, reports of a man who belied the impression I had had of Edward when I was a child. The surviving children of Red Hale's Japanese help remember him being stern but fair and generous; he was diligent, patient and full of good stories, probably about his colorful career. Perhaps the stiff old-fashioned photographs had given me the wrong impression. His obituaries present a distinct picture of a man who was obviously esteemed by his community: *he leaves a host of friends in both military and civilian circles who have the most admiring things to recall and deeply regret his passing. He had a wide circle of friends here to whom his affable and kindly nature were a source of pleasure and inspiration.*

The obituary goes on to speak of his love of family and friends. His friendships would have included fellow parishioners at St. Andrews Cathedral, members of The Oahu Country Club, many civilian and military companions and neighbors in Makiki and Waikiki.

As I studied the glowing reviews of this man, I began to discount my childhood impressions. Everyone looked grave in those old photographs, but happier secrets could be embedded there too. And obituaries don't lie, do they? It gives me comfort to think that he was called *affable, kindly* and *loving* and perhaps would have warmly welcomed me on his lap after all. And, oh, the war stories he could have told this thrice-removed *Army brat* who grew up in Hawaii because of him. Mardie and the General, along with their son Alexander, now rest in Arlington National Cemetery. In 1958, as part of an extensive road trip, our family visited their headstones – a long way from Red Hale but a well-deserved resting place of honor.

Susan as a Young Woman

Hoste as a Young Man

Susan and Hoste at Washington Place

Susan and Hoste were my maternal grandparents. Susan war born in Detroit, Michigan in 1870, and Hoste was born in Belfast, Northern Ireland in 1871. They met each other when they were party guests at Queen Liliuokalani's royal residence Washington Place in Honolulu, Hawaii in 1901.

HOSTE

You'll never see that boy again. There were good reasons for the doctor's foreboding words. They lingered in his family's ears as Hoste's ship pulled away from the Liverpool dock and steamed for Cape Horn and the western world. His precarious respiratory condition (probably a form of tuberculosis) was reason enough for that prediction, but California was on the other side of an ocean and a continent,, and long sea voyages could not necessarily be counted on for success in 1891.

The doctor's advice had been for nineteen-year-old Hoste to seek out a warmer and dryer climate than the one that had contributed to his condition in Northern Ireland. Belfast was often damp and cold, and its air could likely kill him. A successful voyage to southern California was not a certainty either. So, the Harrisons reluctantly said goodbye to their son and brother, realizing that the doctor just may have been speaking the truth.

But they would all be proven wrong. Hoste's health

would be restored by baking out his illness in the dry warmth of Riverside, California, then a resort that people from all over the world sought to regain their health. It would be another fifty or sixty years before Los Angeles smog and population inundated the air and orange groves of Riverside, and the Mission Inn, built in 1876, was the premier destination for those fitness seekers. It's not clear if Hoste stayed at that Inn, but as his lungs cleared and grew stronger, he lay out in the sun, worked hard in the orange groves and invested in real estate. After nearly ten years, in 1900, another destination pulled him farther west to an even more healthful climate when he sailed to Honolulu.

SUSAN

The single word *"polo"* constitutes my grandmother Susan's first entry (New Year's Day) in her *Dainty Diary* for 1902. She doesn't reveal with whom, but perhaps she attended a match in Kapiolani Park, near her father's post at Camp McKinley. She would not have realized then that, in eight years, her future home Red Hale would be nearby on Kalakaua Avenue. On January third, her diary continues with: *my first dip in the Pacific, bathing* and later, *lunch party at Governor Dole's in Makiki*. She doesn't reveal where her first Pacific swim took place, but it was on the same day as a luncheon with Hawaii's governor. It's not clear how she came to be socializing with the upper crust, although it probably was through her father who commanded the U.S. military at Camp McKinley. Perhaps she attended the *lunch party* with her parents whom the governor was reaching out to. Indeed, her father's military connection was also probably the circumstance that led to her first meeting with Hoste as well.

Family lore has it that she first met Hoste at a royal party at Queen Liliuokalani's Greek Revival home Washington Place which was built by wealthy trader and sea captain John Dominis in 1847. After he was lost at sea, John's son inherited Washington Place and he married the Hawaiian princess who would become Queen Liliuokalani. In the course of Hawaii's annexation by the United States, the Queen was arrested in 1895 but was allowed to live out her life at Washington Place where she gave gala parties like the one at which Susan and Hoste first met. For years, our family has passed on the story that they met at a *royal ball*, but Liliuokalani was no longer the queen when they met. The party was probably one of her *galas* even if *royal* was not at that time an appropriate indication. For many years Washington Place served as Hawaii's governor's mansion until a new house was built elsewhere on the property in 2008.

The social connection for Susan's invitation is not clear. It could have been through her father, or perhaps because the Queen was the next-door neighbor of St. Andrew's Episcopal Cathedral where Susan and her parents worshiped every week. Official guest lists show that other Cathedral members and clergy had been the Queen's guests, so it is likely Susan had been as well. The source of Hoste's invitation is also a mystery, but it may have been because he was an Episcopalian too.

There were no witnesses to document their meeting so my imagination defaults to lyrics in the song *Some Enchanted Evening* from the musical play *South Pacific*. *You may see a stranger across a crowded room* as the song goes. If the party had been in the afternoon, as I imagine, Hoste was probably wearing a white linen suit and Susan a white floor-length party dress. They were both good looking young people, but his blue eyes and Irish accent may have been the clinchers for her. A large family portrait shows Susan to be beautiful at that age. I had only known her as an older woman, but she was always very stately and had a striking facial bone structure. Photos of Hoste reveal a very handsome man as well.

Reading my grandmother's handwriting was always known for its difficulty, and her *Dainty Diary* (January first through August eighth, 1902) is no exception. It only provides a seven-month glimpse of her life and is fairly cryptic. Perhaps she wrote it because it covers a romantic and ultimately pivotal time for her. Her diary continues on January 11th – a Saturday, when Mr. Harrison's name appears for the first time. The entry is brief and casual. This could have been their first meeting, but I feel she might have made more of him if it was. Their Washington Place meeting was probably near the end of 1901.

On February 22nd, she merely says *Mr. Harrison – ping-pong,* and again on March 7th, *ping-pong* along with a copy of her personal card on which she has written his name *Hoste McKean Harrison*. Susan doesn't let us know where these ping-pong games were held or indeed where most of the diary events took place, but it should be remembered that she still lived on Hastings Street with her parents and would not move into Red Hale until 1910 after she had become Mrs. Harrison. But it is clear that, in early 1902, ping-pong was considered a chaste and acceptable activity for two single people of the opposite sex.

As the diary progresses, other men's names are mentioned in social situations (a Mr. Lansdale, a Mr. Newton and a Mr. Robinson), but eventually Mr. Harrison's name prevails, and the others disappear. The diary continues with various card parties, luncheons, receptions, teas, tennis matches, dances, carriage rides and her birthday on March 19th. None of these events mentions Mr. Harrison, but again on April 3rd, we read again *ping-pong with Mr. Harrison*. The diary traces a courtship that moves from the innocence of ping-pong to dancing with Mr. Harrison on April 18th, a picnic with him on the 19th, and a dinner on the 28th. In her May 20th entry, there is a decidedly tender *Moonlight around Diamond Head with Mr. Harrison*. He is still formally referenced as *Mister*, but the single word *moonlight* seems to advance the possibility for an affair of the heart. It was clearly a night of encouragement for new lovers.

On June 11th: *took a moonlight cruise with Mr. Harrison*. More moonlight! And on June 16th: *drove to the Pali with Mr. Harrison*. June 21st she *stayed all night at Mr. Harrison's*. The formal *Mr.* seems to contradict *stayed all night*. It's not clear where he lived at that time or what these circumstances were, but within the context of 1902, and knowing my grandmother, we must see only innocent implications in *stayed all night*. On June 24th, Susan had an unspecified surgical operation, and on the 25th, flowers were sent from several people including Princess Kawananankoa and Mr. Harrison. The Princess was related by marriage to the house of Kalakaua. I wonder why Susan was receiving get-well flowers from a presumptive royal heiress? Hoste followed up his gift by sending carnations on the 28th. His consistent attentions clearly indicate that a courtship was under way. There are almost no dates in July when Mr. Harrison's name is not mentioned (*called, spent evening, dined, lunched*), and finally for July 16th I can just make out her handwriting to read *Hoste here and after supper . . . moonlight under the . . .* (not readable), and on July 20th, *Hoste to supper*. She had taken her time to finally use his first name, but references to *moonlight* and *carnations* suggest lyrics in a love song or at the least an intrigue of flirtation.

Tucked into the pages of the diary is what seems to be a formal dance card with no date attached. Among the seven names on the card is Hoste M. Harrison. For a few entries, Susan reverts to *Mr. Harrison* – perhaps as a devout churchgoer, she couldn't help herself – but her very last entry on August 8th says *Mr. Harrison stayed over …Hoste went with Dad to …* I can't read where they went, but a portentous meeting between a father and a future son-in-law is suggested. In this last entry, she moves from *Mr. Harrison* to *Hoste*, and then the diary ends. Perhaps a proposal had been made, and the courtship in the diary had fulfilled itself. At any rate, by the end of the diary, Hoste seems to have stolen Susan's heart. They did not marry until December 29, 1903, so a long engagement, perhaps a custom of the time, filled most of the following year. I'd like to be able to report on that year, but no information is provided. *Hoste* is almost the last word of her diary so we can venture that they were *Hoste and Susan* from then on.

HOSTE

His first name was officially William as evidenced by his naturalization certificate in 1922 – William Hoste McKean Harrison – but in my memory, he was always called Hoste. The name was French and came to Britain in the wake of the Norman Conquest in 1066. In English, the name meant *host* and was most likely originally used by innkeepers. By the 13th century, the family had come to Ireland from Scotland, probably for the purpose of subjugation of the Irish by the

British. And on February 6, 1871, Hoste was born, the fourth child (out of seven) to Robert and Charlotte Harrison in Dromore (a small market town near Belfast), County Down, Ireland. During the course of the seventeenth century, colonists from Scotland and England were allowed to set up plantations on land taken from Gaelic chiefs. The purpose was to subjugate, anglicize and civilize Ulster, a northern province of Ireland that had been most resistant to English control. These immigrants were required to be English-speaking, protestant and loyal to King James l.

*****

When Hoste arrived in Honolulu from Riverside, California at the turn of the twentieth century, he was twenty-nine years old. At once he became part of the office staff at the British importing and trading firm Theo H. Davies & Co., then the largest retail company in Hawaii. By the time of his retirement, he had become *Chief Cashier*, a British term for Treasurer or Chief Financial Officer. When I was a child, we periodically visited the Clive Davies (son of Theo) family in Nuuanu. Theo was instrumental in the founding of St. Andrews Cathedral, and he and Clive, pillars of the church, were very close to the Davises and the Harrisons. Susan's Dainty Diary is scattered with references to the Davies family.

SUSAN AND HOSTE

Major and Mrs. Edward Davis request your presence at the marriage of their daughter Susan Speed to Mr. Hoste McKean Harrison. It is clear by the wedding invitation that his name in the family was to be Hoste as his first name William is not used. The year-long engagement is circumspect and perhaps was necessary to overcome reservations held by his father-in-law that an Irishman was not a suitable match for his Anglo-Saxon daughter. But love was love, Hoste was gainfully employed, and besides, Susan was already thirtyish. The marriage took place at St. Clement's Church in Makiki, and the couple moved in with Hoste's in-laws on Hastings St. and lived there for seven years before moving to Red Hale in November of 1910. Their first child Margaret (my Aunt Peggy) was born in 1906, the year after Susan's father had been promoted and became *The General* while they still lived on Hastings St.

Perhaps because he was familiar with Waikiki where he had commanded Camp McKinley and was looking for a change of locale for his retirement, the General bought a large rambling beach house on the seawall near Diamond Head in 1910. Landowners had built their mansions on the shore and buttressed them with seawalls with the cooperation and help of the Army Corps of Engineers. The Hawaii Supreme Court had ruled that the seawalls were public property as access to the beach. Having overcome his reservations about Hoste and deciding the couple needed a home of their own, the General put the Waikiki house in Susan's name. She and Hoste would call the house *Red Hale*, a name that persisted until the end of its life – and after.

Maybe it was propitious for the Harrisons that planet Earth passed through the tail of Halley's Comet on May 19, 1910. At any rate, that celestial event occurred a few months before the drays came to move the young family from Makiki to their new home in Waikiki. Susan was at the end of a pregnancy at the time of the move, and their second and last child, my mother Charlotte Stuart Harrison, was born on November 15, 1910, a few days after her parents had settled into their new home. Her older sister Peggy had wanted a kitten and was disappointed to receive a sister instead.

SUSAN

Susan was twenty-nine years old when she first came to Hawaii with her parents in 1901. Her entire adult life began and eventually ended (in 1956) in Honolulu. She had been born in Detroit, Michigan, one of her father's military assignments, and she continued to move with him wherever he was needed by the Army. Hawaii was to be Susan's *last assignment* with her father when Major Davis assumed command of Camp McKinley. After his final promotion, Susan always thought of herself as The *General's daughter*, but she was also a devoted wife and the mother of two daughters.

Red Hale was never a house full of servants, but, in light of a major move and the birth of a new granddaughter, the General wanted to hire a personal maid and nanny to help Susan. Tsuta Ogai (the story of the Ogais will appear soon.), who had come from Japan at age 15 in 1906, was engaged to help in the house and care for the children. Her husband (Takachi Naka) took his wife's name Ogai which was a sometimes-followed Japanese custom of the time if the man was not the eldest son. He would become the Harrison Family cook. Tsuta, who later had four children of her own, considered my mother Charlotte to be her first daughter as she had been hired to take care of her from birth in 1910.

The family, including the Ogais, easily settled into life at Waikiki: Letters simply addressed to *The Harrisons, Diamond Head, Honolulu* were successfully delivered, the children were well cared for, and their parents became devoted communicants and committee members at St. Andrew's Cathedral. Hoste became part of the governing board and Susan was on the Altar Guild. At first, Hoste's work at Theo H. Davies & Co. (one of Hawaii's *Big Five* companies) was as an accountant and auditor. The Waikiki line for the streetcar ended in front of Red Hale where Mr. Matsu-ojisan sold candy, cracked seed, *li hing mui* and *see mui* (Chinese preserved fruits) from his cart. Hoste would take the open-sided streetcar to town every day in his customary coat, tie and hat. The large Theo H. Davies building stood on Bishop Street, Honolulu's chief business thoroughfare. Sometimes his work as auditor took him to neighbor islands, especially the Big Island where his company had sugar interests, to examine the books at the plantations.

Folded into Susan's Dainty Diary I found a cache of letters from Hoste in excellent handwriting that spanned the dates from 1910 to 1921. The first of these seems to indicate that he had to be at Kukaiau Plantation on the Big Island at the time of the Waikiki move. *I hope that the moving day was not too much for you.* And later, *Did the dray come from the construction companies?* suggests that the addition to the house to make room for the General was already underway at the time of the move. *With my dearest love to you my wifey and also to my baby* (Peggy) *and give her a big hug from her daddy. Your loving husband.* On New Year's Day 1913, he seems to be spending time at the Oahu Country Club: *golf – beat the Governor,* who at the time was Walter Frear. In October of 1913 he is at the Hilo Hotel – *will go to Laupahoehoe by rail on Sat. tummy trouble- took Dr. Keller's quack medicine.*

Geo-politics seems to be on his mind when on August 5, 1916 he writes in reference to World War One (The Great

War): *The news today is not so good, as you will see by the paper today.* And a year later, he writes: *I hear Dr. Schuman left a photo of the Kaiser in the Tantalus house with my pertinent remarks written on same. Please be careful of this photo as it can be used to put the gentleman (Schuman) behind bars.* Later: *war news is better for us – I can tell you there are a number of blue looking Germans around town.*

*****

In September of 1921 Susan and her daughter Peggy were on their way to Washington D.C. to put Peggy in school for her junior year at the National Cathedral School for Girls. Charlotte was eleven and stayed at home with her father who wrote: 'The Buckeye State leaves for San Francisco tonight so I must let you know how we are getting along'. In those days, letter writers in Hawaii had to gauge writing their letters by the schedule of departing ships. Later in September, he notes: 'The Sherman leaves here on the 11th and I won't have time tomorrow to write so will now. And then 'The Niagara will be in from Vancouver this afternoon', which was included in another letter. Today, there are few letters written anymore, so where will future writers get their family information?

I'll be very glad when the next eight weeks is over. Waikiki is anything but attractive without you. If Cha (Charlotte) *were not here I wouldn't go near it.* In those days, it was a two-month trip from Honolulu to Washington D.C. and return, and Hoste would be alone for the duration. Later, in the same letter: *annual meeting of the Country Club so stayed on after golf. There is an effort to change the bylaws in order to permit Counsel General Yata becoming a member. There is strong sentiment against admitting any Japanese. This proposed amendment caused quite a stir.* The amendment did not pass. Hawaii, it seems, wasn't always the comfortable melting pot that it is today.

One letter without a date, probably in the summer, suggests that Susan was up at their cooler Tantalus house with the children, and Hoste was writing from Waikiki. *I'll sleep on the veranda at night instead of in the room. I'll come up on Saturday. After dinner, we went for a motor drive around Diamond Head, and we saw light on the hill bright and clear. Kisses to the weeuns.* Almost all of his letters to Susan begin with *Dearest Wifey* or *My dear Suse* and end with *Ever your very loving husband, Hoste.*

*****

Two years after their move to Red Hale, Susan's mother Mardi's (Margaret) health began to diminish at the Hastings St. home. Mardi passed away suddenly from a stroke on April 1, 1912. The General was now alone, so his Makiki house was sold and he was moved to Red Hale in Waikiki. We can imagine that this move may have been part of his long-range plan for his retirement when he bought the Waikiki house for his daughter.

It was not a small house, but plans had been made to enlarge it to comfortably contain three adults, two growing children and the Ogais. 5,543 square feet was purchased from the *ewa* or western neighbors for $1,000. George *Dad* Center was a well-known swimming coach who trained Olympians such as Buster Crabbe and Duke Kahanamoku and helped found the Outrigger Canoe Club. I assume Dad Center was renting his home as the deed of sale came from a Mr. Waterhouse. Red Hale was transformed by adding a second living room and enclosed lanai on the first floor, and a master bedroom and screened lanai on the second floor. At the same time, a wash house with second-floor quarters for the Ogais was built nearer the street. Family photos show the construction in progress.

*****

The streetcar went everywhere in those days, and Susan, too, could get rides – to St. Andrews Cathedral downtown and to St. Mary's in Moilili, which the General had donated to the Episcopal Diocese in 1912 to honor his deceased wife. Susan would play the organ there at evening services for the church's orphan boys. Her days were spent in church activities including periodic visits by ladies for afternoon tea and sandwiches. She loved to bake, and her pies and celebrated chocolate cake were a special part of the entertaining. Snapshots show that these were sometimes dressy affairs in ankle-length dresses and hats on the lawn near the sea wall. Japanese women (Tsuta?) are seen in kimonos serving the ladies.

The money for this lifestyle came from the General as Hoste was not a rich man. Hoste was a well-liked gentleman and the Ogai children remember his playful nature, calling him *a boo boo* which is what he said when he came around corners to scare them in fun. They all loved him and Susan and felt lucky to work for the Harrisons who treated them as part of the family and not as servants as other households in the area were known to do. Hoste was seen as an old style Christian gentleman, and both Susan and Hoste became godparents to the Ogai children.

Until 1927, life at Red Hale changed gracefully as the

house and its inhabitants gradually grew older. In the years between the wars, Waikiki was not yet the bustling tourist mecca it would be in the future. The Moana Hotel, built in 1901, could be counted on for a very good dinner for about two dollars, and was the home of radio's *Hawaii Calls* in the 1930s. And the new Royal Hawaiian Hotel (1927) hosted rich travelers and added great glamour to Waikiki. But people didn't lock their doors at night, delivery services brought ice, bread, milk and eggs, and flowers came from Manoa Valley. Christmas was celebrated each year with a spruce tree next to the grandfather clock and was decorated with clip on candles, bird ornaments and strands of popcorn. Easter saw an egg hunt in the dining room for Peggy and Charlotte and the Ogai children. On Fourth of July the lanai was always festooned with flags and palm fronds.

Toward the ocean, Red Hale looked out at surfers who used the nearby excellent surf conditions in the Kapua Channel; fishermen who unfurled their nets, sometimes using flaming torches at night; human traffic passing along the public sea wall, and the comings and goings of all the ships on their way to and from California. One could organize the day by the arrivals and departures of the ships which brought movie stars and other wealthy people and could be counted on for new mail and fresh fruit and vegetables from the mainland. The ships took five or six days to get to the coast, and air flights took about seventeen hours then. Other regularities at Red Hale were sunsets over the Waianae Mountains and the Southern Cross constellation rising just above the horizon in the winter.

The General occupied himself with his books in the library, feeding the canaries and tending the ferns and butterfly orchids in the glassed-in conservatory off the dining room. Susan always presided over the dinner table which was set with silver serving dishes monogramed with *D* for Davis. The best dining service was used at Waikiki while the plated silver was relegated to the Tantalus house on the mountain. Sometimes the family took the streetcar downtown to see movies at the Hawaii and Liberty theatres. Peggy and Charlotte went off each day on the streetcar to Punahou School. Not yet called *the gold coast,* the neighborhood gradually became a high-class area with neighbors such as the Walter Dillinghams (developer and head of the Oahu Blue polo team) at their La Pietra estate on the slopes of Diamond Head, and the James B. Castles (Castle and Cook, one of the *Big Five* companies) who built a gigantic four-story mansion a few houses west on the seawall. The Harrisons got to know these people as neighbors, at St. Andrews Cathedral and at Punahou School.

*****

In 1909, a year before the move to Red Hale, and before Susan was pregnant with my mother Charlotte, the Harrisons and their daughter Peggy made a trip that took them to Belfast, Northern Ireland, discrediting the prediction that the family would *never see that boy again.* But Hoste did reunite with his brothers and sisters who remembered the doctor's dire warning of 1891. They were proud that he had been successful on the far side of the world. They remembered his rascally school days when he would regularly be sent home from school, but were pleased to know that in his adult years he was always known as a true British gentleman.

Hoste was naturalized in 1922, and his health which had never been robust, began to be more precarious in the 1920s.

He took early retirement in 1923, and he passed away of a heart attack in 1927. He was only fifty-six years old. Susan had cared for him for several years with the help of the Ogais who had postponed moving to a house of their own. That year, 1927, was the year Hawaii read of Charles Lindberg flying to Paris which notified the islands that they would soon be more readily joined to the rest of the world. The General had already passed away in 1918 after the end of The Great War. Life at Red Hale altered dramatically after Hoste passed away.

Susan was now in charge, and she made adjustments to her lifestyle after the two men in her life were gone. She was less secure financially, and she had two modest duplexes built on the street side of Red Hale to house rental units. She hired a new family, the Higuchis, to replace the Ogais who had moved to their own home in Palolo Valley. Higuchi became the cook and chauffeur and fed the boarders whose welfare was now the main business of Red Hale. We can well imagine that the ambiance of the home changed significantly. The family was replaced by paying guests who came and went according to their own agendas.

Among these lodgers were the Warwicks, a Navy officer's wife and her young son Billy who lived there as a haven away from Pearl Harbor during the war; Mrs. Clemens whose husband had killed himself; a public school teacher named Edith Fitch; and a woman whose father had owned "half of Los Angeles" at one time and who ended up on a chicken ranch on the mainland after living at Red Hale. At times, there were defense workers and Navy personnel as well. After her marriage to Pete Pringle in 1929, Susan's daughter Peggy lived there too. Pete was a newspaper and radio reporter at the Star-Bulletin who read the comics

(*Tarzan, Mutt and Jeff* and others) on the radio every Saturday morning. He loved kids and was known as *Pete-san* by the Ogai kids who would periodically go with him in his red convertible to Kau Kau Corner for ice cream.

After the attack on Pearl Harbor in 1941, Susan left the management of Red Hale to the Higuchis and she went to live at the Pleasanton Hotel near Punahou School for a time and then into our house in Manoa Valley. For a time, after the war in the 1940s, Susan lived with her older daughter Peggy and her second husband John Lutz in Washington state and California. Back in Hawaii in the 1950s, Susan ironically spent the last few years of her life in another well-run boarding house on Lanihuli Drive in lower Manoa Valley.

But for years she had been preoccupied with a simmering enterprise she could not get out of her mind. In the wintertime when the northern hemisphere tips south, one can see just above the horizon a constellation known as *the Southern Cross*. This is the most well-known constellation in the southern hemisphere and is visible from only a few places north of the equator, including Hawaii. Perhaps because of its Christian symbolism Susan was drawn to this phenomenon which she could view every year from the front porch and seawall at Red Hale.

By the mid-1950s, as Red Hale's land became more valuable, and especially after Hoste had passed away, Susan was advised by the Hawaiian Trust Company, where she had been a client since 1920, to consider projects to make the best use of her ocean-side property on Kalakaua Avenue. She had already built some apartments and taken in boarders, but her advisors felt the land could be used for further benefit. Two pathways were suggested: the property could be sold in order to purchase a diversified collection of securities, or the house could be razed to build an apartment building. These plans were to produce income for her, her two daughters and her grandchildren. Susan favored the construction of an apartment building. The name of the building had already been chosen: *The Southern Cross*.

Susan always said she would do this or that *when my ship comes in,* so the Ogai children would search the Waikiki horizon for her ship. The Southern Cross apartment project was surely her most important *this or that*. A loan would have to be taken out for construction, but, because she was eighty years old, this might be difficult. It was assumed that the securities she owned would be enough to pay for estate and inheritance taxes. An effort was made to determine the extent of demand for rentals in this part of Honolulu. Condominiums were still a concept of the future and co-ops were not considered at first. Family friend and architect Edwin Bauer designed a nine-story building, and a news story with an artist's rendering appeared in the Honolulu Star Bulletin. Twenty-six prospective renters responded for 1956 rents of $150. - $200 a month.

In the mid-1950s Henry J. Kaiser, variously called a genius or a dictator, was known for saying that he had *missed the boat* in the Florida land rush, but he would not do so in Hawaii. The convergence of two projects – Susan's Southern Cross Apartments and Kaiser's Hawaiian Village Hotel at the opposite end of Waikiki – created a financial impasse because of post-war competition for still-scarce construction materials. This sent the cost of Susan's Southern Cross skyward making it more expensive than the loan amount of $210,000 (secured by the value of the future building) that had been offered by The Prudential Insurance Company. The Hawaiian Trust directors stated that their approval was conditioned on receiving construction bids no greater than the loan that could be obtained. This ominous ruling was the start of what our family has always considered *being sold down the river* by the Hawaiian Trust Company. But, in reality, it was Henry Kaiser who should be seen as the villain in this case. His deep pockets were responsible for The Hawaiian Village to take precedence in the marketplace and, eventually, to cover the Kalia end of Waikiki with concrete towers.

There were deposits and signed five-year leases for The Southern Cross from six prospective tenants. But at this critical time, Susan was admitted to Queen's Hospital with acute leukemia, so The Hawaiian Trust Co. began looking for a developer to lease the land and construct its own building. They found Tahitienne Inc. a Hawaiian corporation, and a lease was signed on August 1, 1957, thus dooming Red Hale and helping to bring about the end of the era of wooden mansions on the beach. The Tahitienne opened in July of 1958 initiating the concrete and glass era on the property and becoming the first high rise co-op building to begin a wall of concrete surrounding Diamond Head. Advertisements began extoling exclusive luxury residences for island residents: *Stunning picture postcard views of turquoise blue waters and dramatic sunsets*. There would be 22 units for families with children and retirees. Each unit was to have *mauka (mountain) and makai (ocean) views, a covered garage, elevator service, a garden terrace, a shared pool and a lanai*. Long term leases were available and *a distinguished list of tenants* had already signed on.

Susan's Southern Cross apartment house was never to be. The Tahitienne would be built in its place, but would be controlled by others. It would be built in advance of additional *gold coast* properties such as Castle Surf, Tropic Seas, Coral Strand and Sans Souci. Susan and her daughters received monthly payments for the use of the land, but the amount was never thought to be just compensation for the value of this unique property. The fifty-five-year lease was renegotiated after twenty- five years, and then, finally, The Hawaiian Trust sold the property to the Tahitienne corporation for $1,200,000 in November, 1985. The proceeds were put into securities, and Susan's grandchildren now enjoy a supplemental income based on those investments. Susan passed away a few months before the Tahitienne was completed, so she didn't have long to lament the passing of her home. At least Red Hale never went into disrepair, the fate of some other large houses on the beach. I had graduated from Punahou School in 1957 and was a freshman at The University of Oregon when Red Hale was razed. I was relieved I didn't have to see the destruction of the object of my early affection. And it's a blessing that Susan didn't have to witness it either. She passed away in October of 1956, a year before the lease was signed with Tahitienne Inc.

In the early sixties, there were plans by the Honolulu City Council and The City Planning Commission to increase the land parameters for further Diamond Head development. News articles inflamed the public, especially conservationists and the *haole* (Caucasian) elite (including the Dillinghams at La Pietra) who would lose their ocean views if those who would profit had their way. In 1960 a movement called *Save Diamond Head* was organized to stop the Chinese developer Chin Ho's plan to build a solid line of high rises east around Diamond Head from The Tahitienne to the Kahala Hilton. By the mid-sixties, after a number of lawsuits, the city put a stop to the high rises in the area that had become known as *the gold coast* of Waikiki. Today, the concrete and glass towers that were built at the foot of Diamond Head cannot be rebuilt if anything were to happen to them. But the inadvisability of glass towers was not heeded in the central tourist area of Waikiki, and development there has been rampant.

*****

I am a lady, and Episcopalian and a Republican, in that order, was Susan's quick response when informed they were going to give her a Wasserman test for syphilis during her final illness. Why a Wasserman test for a sweet, dignified old lady is not now clear. But her response was very much in character and sums up the way I remember her. Her first twenty-nine years, corresponding with the end of the Victorian Era, were spent learning a strict social code of conduct from her parents. This emphasized family, motherhood, and respectability. Sexual restraint was a Victorian ideal that suggested that a lady should know nothing of sex until her wedding night. It's not clear if that was true with Susan, but her formative years had certainly taught her dignity and conformity to socially respectable behavior.

We all – my brother and sister and I – remember her as an old lady as we didn't get to witness her and Hoste meeting *across a crowded room* at Washington Place and courting with physical activities like tennis, swimming, picnics – and ping-pong. She was the only grandparent we ever knew as our father's parents and Hoste had passed away before we were born. We always associated her with St. Andrews Cathedral – she was a classic *church lady* – in that she regularly attended service at eleven o'clock on Sundays and was a member of the Altar Guild taking care of the silver and vestments. She had donated a chalice with a gold cross on its face in loving memory of Hoste. The chalice is still used today. We were brought up at that church – baptism, Sunday school, confirmation, acolyte duties, young people's social activities – and saw her each Sunday, with dignified posture, decorous dress that included a hat and white gloves and loads of white hair pulled up on her head that was held in place by tortoise shell combs.

Susan invariably had what we thought of as a clean *old lady smell*, perhaps because of the soap and powder she used. Or, maybe it was the smelling salts that she always kept at the ready, or the glass of sherry she ritually drank before bedtime. Except for the sherry and communion at St. Andrews, she imbibed in moderation, but was known to express herself when she had had too much: *It stimulated me so I couldn't close my eyes.* To her, women did not sweat, but *glowed*, and gentle people should never talk about sex. At the table one should respond, *I am replete*, as *I am full* was coarse and not ladylike.

We also remember Grandma as being very generous with her money and her time. She paid for me to go to an Episcopal boarding school on the Big Island in seventh and eighth grades, and she helped pay the tuition for all three of us to attend Punahou School. As her father had done for her (paying for a cook, maid and nanny), she paid for a young Japanese woman named Sadako Shimabukuro to help with our mother's cooking and housework. She played the organ for the orphan boys at St. Mary's and taught English to the sons of a Chinese taro farmer whom she had taken under her wing. The two Choi brothers grew up to be doctors, one a dentist and the other an ophthalmologist, and they never forgot her or her generosity. Money for some of this benevolence came from her investments in the Honolulu Iron Works, The California and Hawaii Development Company, and Theo H. Davies & Company.

Because Dako, as we called her, was live-in help, there was no comfortable room for Grandma in our house. She had returned from staying on the mainland with our Aunty Peggy and preferred living at a boarding house for retirees not far from us in Manoa Valley. Hillcrest served meals in a formal dining room where everyone had an assigned table. The food was tasty and the atmosphere was friendly. I remember visiting her there in her sunny corner room which was perfumed with *the old lady smell* we associated with her.

Grandma's final residence, a far cry from Red Hale, was a private room at Queen's Hospital where she passed away from leukemia on October 7, 1956 at age 86. When she was on her deathbed, the nurses tried to take out what they assumed were false teeth. Not able to communicate clearly, she had to struggle to indicate that the teeth were her own and had been all her life. St. Andrews was packed on the day of her funeral service, and she was buried in our family plot in Oahu Cemetery in Nuuanu Valley where Hoste was already resting. The family requested that flowers be omitted and contributions be made to the Altar Guild at St. Andrews Cathedral – a gesture that would have pleased her greatly. Even after all these years, we miss her loving spirit.

Susan and Hoste and family

Charlotte and Spieg

Charlotte and Spieg
In Waikiki and Manoa

Charlotte and Spieg (short for Spiegelberg and everyone called him that.) were my parents. Charlotte was an island girl, a *kamaaina*, born in Waikiki in 1910. Spieg was a newcomer, a *malihini*, born in St. Louis, Missouri in 1898. His family moved to eastern Washington and bought a farm there when he was 14 years old. He came to Hawaii in 1930 for a scientific job working for the pineapple industry. They met at the dinner table at Red Hale and got married on October 31st, Halloween, in 1936. They raised three children and lived the rest of their lives together in Manoa Valley.

SPIEG

To use a familiar expression, one might say that Spieg was *fresh off the boat,* or more precisely, fresh off the American President Line's S.S. President Madison from San Francisco. At any rate, he was a new guy in town in January of 1930 when he was 31 years old and starting to get used to living in the middle of the Pacific Ocean. He was learning that Honolulu's Rapid Transit trolleys were essential to navigating his new city. Trolly lines crisscrossed Honolulu to far-flung districts and could take him downtown and to such neighborhoods as Kalihi, Manoa, Kaimuki and Waikiki. Every weekend Spieg would hop on one of those cars to explore his sprawling new town.

No matter what route he chose, he always rode to the end

of the line where the cars turned around. He would get off and stretch his legs and then reboard and return to where he began. In time, he rode on all of the lines and got to know Honolulu well. But he favored the Waikiki route as it ran near the ocean and ended at Diamond Head. The Waikiki cars reached their turn-around point in about thirty minutes from downtown's Fort Street.

At the end of the line was an inviting rusty-red house that promised ocean views from the seawall and had an aura of domesticity that teased him with memories of home in Washington State. The house sat just opposite the final Waikiki trolley stop so his attention was always focused there. He wondered who lived in the house and why the scene was so attractive to him. Was there a family there like the one he grew up with in Kennewick, Washington? On his first trip there he had no idea that he would later get to know that family, the Harrisons, intimately, but for the present they were just people living in one of the large houses along the shore.

Spieg spent his first night in Hawaii at the Pleasanton Hotel close to Punahou School, and then, for a short time, he lived at the nearby McDonald Hotel where he paid $60 a month for room and board. Soon, he moved closer to the ocean where he settled into a cottage at the Niumalu Hotel next to a seawall where Henry Kaiser would build his Hawaiian Village Hotel in the 1950s. There was no actual beach there in those days, but the hotel had a cozy family-friendly atmosphere that helped stave off his homesickness.

To get to the trolley on Kalakaua Avenue, he would cross the grounds of Ft. DeRussy. There, he would step up on a running board and then into an open-sided car that contained parallel rows of wooden benches. The cars looked like overgrown versions of San Francisco's cable cars and had inexplicably large cow-catchers that protruded from their fronts. These were either an affectation mirroring classic railroads or testimony to the still rural quality of some of Honolulu's neighborhoods.

Spieg's ride toward Diamond Head took him east along Kalakaua Avenue. First, the Army's Fort DeRussy was on his right and then there was the wooden fence that surrounded the gardens of the brand new Royal Hawaiian Hotel. Small businesses and cottages dotted the way, but the Moana Hotel, where he would sometimes eat his dinner, punctuated Waikiki with four stories of late Victorian elegance. The car would run along Kuhio Beach and then pass the intersection with Kapahulu Avenue where Kapiolani Park began. Australian ironwood trees overlooked the rest of the route to Diamond Head. He would pass by the Honolulu Aquarium which had been built by the city to lure trolley passengers to Waikiki, and then the new War (The Great War) Memorial Natatorium and Sans Souci Beach. Other large mansions including the five-story Castle estate marked the route and, finally, Red Hale, that inviting house on the seawall, sat at the end of the line.

There is no way to know if those in the house ever noticed Spieg at their trolley stop or if he ever glimpsed Charlotte there, but it is clear that, had Charlotte been at home, they could have been in each other's company a few years before they actually met. He had no idea that his imminent future included marriage to a beautiful girl who lived in that house. It may be a stretch, but we might imagine Charlotte as a princess in a tower and Spieg as a suitor looking up to where she lived. Rapunzel she was not, as Charlotte sported a stylish short bob that was popular at the time. Later hindsight would remind Spieg that he had been in the presence of his future bride, even as he merely stretched his legs in front of the big red house she lived in.

He was born (and christened soon after in the Lutheran Church) Carl Henry Spiegelberg on August 26th 1898 in St. Louis. But I always heard him called *honey* or *Spieg*. *Spiegelberg* is a mouthful so it's not surprising that everyone (friends, colleagues and his spouse) called him *Spieg*. I can understand that need for a shortcut as I inherited his first and last name, and all my high school English and Drama students called me *Spieg* for thirty-seven years. It was a nickname I always bore with pride.

Spieg was raised by working-class immigrant parents. His father Frederick was a house painter and wallpaper hanger who had come to St. Louis, Missouri from lower Saxony in western Germany in 1881. In about 1884 he met his Danish wife Augusta in the immigrant community there, and, together, they raised a large family of seven boys and three girls. Spieg was the third youngest child of these ten. In 1913, when he was fifteen years old, his family moved to Kennewick in central Washington State where they bought a small farm that grew apples. Spieg learned to speak some German from his father, but that demonstrated itself mostly in swear words (*dummkopf* and *scheisse meier* were favorites of his) that I learned from him when I was growing up.

Spieg's route to Hawaii and the trolley stop in front of Red Hale followed a meandering path that took him from working in his parents' apple orchard, to graduation from Kennewick High School in 1919, to a bachelor's degree and then a master's degree from Washington State College. Always interested in botany, his esoteric thesis was about fungi and canker disease in blackberries. His master's degree in agriculture was awarded in 1925. There was a short stint in the cranberry bogs of western Washington, a time at the University of Maryland for further classes and research, probably in plant pathology, and a brief teaching assignment in Puerto Rico. In June of 1927 there was correspondence with Thomas Edison about a possible position as an expert on latex bearing plants; Edison was looking into producing rubber in the U.S., but Spieg did not take that job. Then, there was a brief and unlikely sidetrack to Sweeny's Automobile School in Kansas City for an eight- week course that didn't seem to impart much auto expertise. At least he never passed on any mechanical know-how to my brother, sister and me. Eventually, a job offer from the Pineapple Research Institute brought him to Honolulu. PRI was an entity that supported the entire pineapple industry with research on canning, spoilage and diseases.

CHARLOTTE

Charlotte Stuart Harrison, named after her father Hoste's mother and sister in Belfast, Northern Ireland was born at home at Red Hale on November 15, 1910. Her aunt in Ireland was nicknamed *Cha* so, at times, Charlotte was called that as well. Her Japanese nanny Tsuta Ogai called her Cholly or *Miss Cholly*.

Charlotte was the younger of two sisters. From the start, there was a sharp dissimilarity between the two girls. They were only four years apart, but it was as if they were born and raised in different eras. As the first child, Peggy had inherited the Victorian values of her parents and grand-parents, but Charlotte was born well inside the Edwardian era, between the Victorian age and the jazz age that came to be characterized by *the new woman*. Peggy was the proper one who always wore shoes and toed her parents' line. Peggy eventually spent most of her adult life living on the mainland. Charlotte, on the other hand, spent most of her life in Honolulu and was a thoroughly modern tomboy, a flapper, a rebel and a flirt. She wandered barefoot whenever she could and probably rolled her stockings below the knee.

Charlotte's formative years were influenced by the attitude that girls could be emancipated and independent. She grew up seeing women working outside the home, gaining voting rights with the nineteenth amendment when she was nine years old, and, thanks to Henry Ford's revolutionary assembly line, driving automobiles. Young women of that era were told that smoking cigarettes would curb their appetites and keep them slim. Charlotte always remained svelte but at the cost of a smoking habit for the rest of her life. Family snap shots almost always showed a cigarette in her hand. I wonder if the rest of the family ever suffered from second-hand smoke. Her unfiltered Lucky Strikes ultimately led to her untimely death in 1973. The movies, or *flickers* as they were casually known as then, reflected this new era on the screen. Her childhood was spent without much global conflict as The Great War came and went on the other side of the world before she was ten years old.

As a child, Charlotte was treated to riding lessons at the nearby Waikiki Stables. There, she could feed the horses with sweet beans from the *kiawe* trees in Kapiolani Park. She would visit the Waikiki Aquarium and the new zoo where she could feed the chief attraction, Daisy the elephant. Charlotte could be a rascal, and she teased Mrs. Clemens (an early boarder at Red Hale) and her dog Wrinkles. She was fascinated by the white ocean liners that passed Red Hale and always searched for *leis* that might wash up on the seawall when departing passengers threw them overboard in hopes of returning to Hawaii. She loved taking Oahu Railway trains to Haleiwa on the north shore where a special treat was riding on the glass-bottomed boats. For one of those trips, her dad had given her a camera and film which she used to take pictures of everything. There were concerts at the bandstand in Kapiolani Park across the street, and hide and seek with her playmates, the Castle children, in the cavernous house they lived in just west of Red Hale on the seawall. It is ironic that I played hide and seek in that same house many years later when it had become the Elks Club. The Elk's *Exalted Ruler* was our next-door neighbor in Manoa.

Charlotte's teen years were marked by a society searching for normalcy after the Great War. According to Hollywood, it was an era of vamps, flappers and flaming youth. Talking movies appeared in 1927 when Charlotte was seventeen, and in 1929 when she graduated from Punahou School, she saw Joan Crawford in a picture called *Our Modern Maidens*, a portrait of Charlotte's generation. Skirts came up, knees were powdered and hair was shorn. Barbaric music like jazz and the Charleston annoyed her parents in an era of prohibition, bootleggers, flag pole sitting, dance marathons and flight.

The Harrisons' next-door neighbor was a man named George *Dad* Center who was a renowned swimming coach. He had co-founded the Outrigger Canoe Club in 1908 and helped develop beach volleyball as a sport. He and his swimmers captured 16 of 30 medals in the 1920 Olympic games in Belgium. Among his swimmers whom he trained at the Waikiki Natatorium were Duke Kahanamoku and

Buster Crabbe who went on to star in a movie serial called *Buck Rogers*. Some of Dad's swimmers lived at his house next to Red Hale, as did, for a time, R. Alex Anderson who wrote *Lovely Hula Hands*, *Mele Kalikimaka* and over two hundred other songs.

Dad was a great pal of Charlotte's. She helped him make home brew during prohibition, and she loved flirting with *Dad's* swimmers and was popular with all of them. Apparently, they all looked like *Greek gods*, but she had a favorite named Ginger (in reference to his hair color, I assume) whom she dated, as she did Buster Crabbe whom she also knew at Punahou School.

In 1928, Charlotte left Punahou for her junior year to go to the Episcopalian National Cathedral School for Girls in Washington D.C. Perhaps this was considered a finishing school for her, and she returned to Punahou where she was a member of the 1929 graduating class. Her Punahou annual, The Oahuan, says this about her next to her senior picture: *frank, Irish blue eyes – a sunburned, windblown bob, a coat of tan envied by every other blonde in school, and a genuine smile with an accompanying giggle ready for everyone – that's Charlotte. Those who think her shy and reserved have missed too much by not knowing her out of school and during zero period. When she forgets her dignity, she is anything but in expressing her subtle sense of humor. She has managed to pull through in whatever she has undertaken from Miss Barnhard and Miss Porter.*

I have little evidence of Charlotte's other social interactions at Punahou. I know she had a couple of best friends named Sis Larsen and Lily Watson, and I assume she did some dating. Buster Crabbe is the only one she ever spoke of, and I assume it was because he became a film star. Her reported flirtations with *Dad's boys* will have to serve as documentation of her teenage social life. The yearbook description of her sounds like she was popular, but there are no autographed letters or mash notes there; perhaps it was not the custom to do that then. We will have to wait for the journal of her post-high school trip to Europe to discover more.

SPIEG

Spieg's first impression of Honolulu, despite the extensive trolley system, was that it was a *one horse town.* There were no traffic lights when he arrived. "They were tried, but no one paid attention." At the Niumalu Hotel he met and then shared a cottage with Cyril Murphy who would be a life-long friend. Later, he and *Murph* shared a house on Black Point Road for a year that, at the time, was cheap enough for two young bachelors. Today it is a picturesque and very expensive neighborhood. Spieg's social life began to expand when he and Murph threw parties for friends including Naval officers and their wives and girlfriends. The parties always involved a bootlegger and plenty of Hawaiian liquor called *okolehao,* which was distilled, sometimes in bathtubs, from the root of the *ti* plant.

A major leap in time and some insightful excerpts from his much later eulogy provide a glimpse into Spieg's character that we, his children, remember from our lives with him. He passed away at age 94 close to midnight on New Year's Eve in 1992. All three of his children were at his bedside. This eulogy (a collaboration by my brother, sister and me) was delivered on January 6, 1993 at Our Redeemer Lutheran Church, and he is buried in our family plot at Oahu Cemetery in Nuuanu Valley.

A place to begin would be to mention his strong character. He never left a doubt as to what kind of person he was. There was always a right way to do things and he could be a perfectionist which is very German. And indeed, he was very German and proud of it. We suffered from this at times because he was exacting in how we should do things, but it taught us discipline and hopefully enriched our characters as well. He was a scientist through and through and always used the scientific method, never taking anything for granted, always wanting proof. He would say "show me" which is appropriate because he was born in Missouri, the show-me state. He was the ultimate list maker, which, again, drove us crazy at times, but because of it, we grew up with ordered lives.

Through a great deal of perseverance and hard work, he was the only one of his large family to go to college and, despite setbacks such as having to repeat the seventh grade three times due to illness, he wasn't satisfied until he achieved a PhD in Plant Pathology and Soil Bacteriology.

His strong work ethic was certainly evidence that he believed in work before play, but he also said 'everything in moderation' and this allowed him a single beer or high ball at exactly 5:30 every day. Another piece of philosophy that used to puzzle us, but which now gives us a further metaphor to live by is 'anything is a weed if it grows where you don't want it.'

He was one of the most honest and straight forward people we have ever known. He hated pretension in any form and was always intolerant of gilding the lily.

'Anyone can get a PhD' he used to say, 'you just have to work hard and be stubborn.' He loved his home and being comfortable, but he lived simply and never threw *anything out until it had completely served its purpose. He was basically a shy and reserved person, but he had a good sense of humor, could tell and appreciate a good story, and he loved to sing and laugh. Despite his eccentricities and stubborn German nature, we always felt a strong sense of unconditional love which we miss very much.*

CHARLOTTE AND SPIEG

We must now go back in time to nudge Spieg and Charlotte together for the first time. A few of his colleagues at the PRI were rooming at a large pink house on the beach three doors west of Red Hale. It was owned and run by a Miss Ermine Cross who managed the kindergarten at Punahou School. Perhaps transportation was difficult from Black Point without a car so Spieg and Murph separated for the time being, and he moved back to the convenience of the trolley line. Fatefully, Miss Cross did not serve meals so Spieg discovered he could have his dinners at the nearby home called Red Hale. And that is what he did, returning to the rambling red house he had admired so much from the Waikiki trolley line. Charlotte was living there then after a post-high school European trip so there is no doubt they met at the dining table which was always properly presided over by her mother.

CHARLOTTE

In 1930, three years after her father Hoste passed away, Charlotte, who was nineteen years old, made an extensive trip, probably her version of the grand tour, to the east coast and Europe with her mother Susan. Her sister Peggy was married by then and living at Red Hale with her husband Pete. Charlotte's trip coincided with Spieg's first year in Hawaii, but they were not aware of each other then. Charlotte's travel journal, (*My Trip Abroad*, embossed in gold lettering on black leather) is filled with intermittent entries, beginning on May 25th1930 as she was leaving New York for Belfast on a ship called the R.M.S. Adriatic (the White Star Line). I was fortunate to find this travel journal amongst her things after she passed away.

Eavesdropping on part of a parent's life that took place ten years before I knew her can be very illuminating – and surprising. But it also feels slightly subversive and perhaps a little intrusive. Today, Charlotte's journal is almost shocking to me as it reveals a woman who was far different from the one I knew when I was growing up. My mother was a mature, practical and busy woman who liked to have fun but took care of her family's needs first. She was not the flirtatious flapper seen in her journal which seems to be catching her in the last throes of adolescence. I wonder if I was ever meant to read these revelations? Probably not. Today, she would be well over one hundred and twenty years old so maybe a kind of statute of limitations absolves me of this intrusion.

Charlotte's social life on the crossing was packed with activity that involved men who were attracted to her blue eyes, blonde bob, Hawaiian tan and very presentable gams. Perhaps it would not be out of order to refer to her as *the bee's knees* or the *cat's meow*. Immediately, a major theme of her journal presents itself. It is clear that Charlotte had not lost the flirtatiousness she had indulged with her neighbor Dad Center's swimmers and was clearly still boy-crazy. The first words of her journal say, *Freddie on the way over - Had a grand time.* Whist, patience, bridge, rummy and hearts were the card games of the time, and, apparently, she spent time playing all of them, perhaps with Freddie. Other men appear – Bob, Skipper, Pat, Murdock and Rudolf – but Freddie's name is paramount in her diary during that crossing.

There were other shipboard amusements like concerts, shuffleboard, horseshoes, horse races, tea dances and formal dances for which, not surprisingly, Charlotte always had a full dance card. Toward the end of the crossing, after a number of intimate talks, she confronted Freddie, and he revealed that for two and a half years he had been married to a woman named Elizabeth. Then, suddenly, we read: *it was the last I saw of him.* And, indeed, we hear no more of him as the Adriatic tendered some of the passengers into Glasgow and then took the rest of them to Belfast.

Her father Hoste's family occupied a great deal of her time in Belfast. There were Aunty Cha, Uncle Maitland, Aunty May, Uncle Herbert, Cousin Betty and Cousin Helen. Some of her entries showed a preoccupation with shopping – for gloves, garter belts, hats, dresses and evening gowns. She also mentions a letter she received that came on the first mail delivery service of the Graf Zeppelin. She saw an appropriate movie called *College Coquette* and then, on July 4th, she speaks of a certain Bunny Masters (*looks like Freddie*) for the first time.

Bunny had come for tennis, and she lets us in on her first impression of him: *I fell in love with Bunny at first sight, absolutely darling.* I wonder if *Bunny* was a nickname, and, if so, for what? But she also mentions a Harold and a Tony and a Dick and a Reginald in the same entry so we can see that Charlotte's head was being turned from all sides. They would *ring* her up, and she would spend time with them in the *tank* (swimming pool), at jigsaw puzzles, tennis and croquet. There was no mention of ping-pong that had occupied her mother when she was being courted by Hoste.

On July 28th something special between Charlotte and Bunny seems to be heating up. She writes: *Bunny is a perfect darling and I fear I'm falling in love again. I mean I **know** I'm in love.* Apparently, he was teasing her about her long finger nails and the way she talked. Today, I wonder just how she talked then. Impulsively, she goes on to say, *told Mom about Bunny and want to stay over for the winter, but Mom said no. So, I asked if I could stay if I was in school, and she said maybe.* I think that was Susan's version of *we'll see* which I know is just a delaying tactic that I heard a lot of when I was growing up. She continued: *wrote to Sis and Peg* (her best friend and her sister, both in Hawaii) *and told all about Bunny. Bunny is precious.* In this same entry, she finishes with *Fell off the roof.* Google tells me that that was then a delicate euphemism for menstruation.

June and July were primarily spent socializing with all those aunts, uncles and cousins. And then she and Susan took a trip to Scotland, down through England and to Paris. Most of her comments were about sightseeing, (*Follies Bergere, wasn't so shocked as I thought I'd be.*) but she did find moments to refer to Bunny. On July 7th, she mentions that *Bunny is a darling and has Japanese eyes. Still love Bunny.* Japanese eyes?! She mentions meeting Bunny's mother and teaching her how to do the *hula*. Was this meeting an indication of something serious?

In September, Charlotte seems to be back in Belfast, and we read *Bunny is as darling as ever.* Also: *Bunny sat next to me at tea!* Several times she mentions playing the *Vic* together;

I assume they were sharing some of the latest music on the Victrola. *The Sheik of Araby*; *Runin' Wild*; *Yes, Sir! That's My Baby* and *Ain't We Got Fun?*

At one of these sessions Charlotte mentions that she could bend her fingers all the way back, and Bunny said, '*You know what that means?' I said it wasn't true about being a flirt, but he insisted and said it was a psychological fact.* For some reason, he chose this conversation to announce that he was going to go into the ministry. Charlotte draws tears on the page and Bunny's name doesn't appear again after that. I assume this was a sad goodbye after a torrid but, I assume, chaste holiday romance. The entire *Bunny affair* brings me up short, as here in her journal was a portrait of a woman I had never known. And Bunny certainly was not the name of my father.

On Sept. 18th: *We sail for home a month from today.* And then there is another *fell off the roof* and then another *Saw an adorable man* and yet another *darling man playing tennis*. It seems that bending her fingers all the way back may, indeed, suggest her propensity for being a flirt.

Soon after, she mentions a dance at which she had a partner for every dance, including someone named Tony. She asked Tony if he liked to *molly coddle* (Google tells me it meant treating someone very indulgently or protectively as in a courtship) and then Tony asked her for the last dance. Sept. 29th: *Met Molly Coddle and saw the film 'Rio Rita' – my seat broke and I went into fits.*

Another entry: *Aunty May's for dinner. My partner was a Mr. Johnson, a young barrister.* There are no adjectives to describe Mr. Johnson so, perhaps, he wasn't a *darling* like the others had been. On Oct. 7th: *Trevor asked me to go to a club dance with him. Fooled around.* Was that a gentle version of our 1950s term *made out*? And who was Trevor?

On October 16th we hear more about Tony who seemed to be her focus of attention for the rest of the trip. *Tony is absolutely adorable and is a darling dancer. He was asked 'who is the striking-looking girl' he was going around with? I was thrilled. We played the Vic and fooled around. Mom called for me to come home but I stayed in Tony's arms for a while. I curled his hair and eyebrows until finally he couldn't stand it any longer and took off his glasses which I wanted him to do. Then he kissed me, I couldn't help it. He's so darling.*

Her next encounter with Tony seems to be at the dock where she and Susan are about to board the tender to the Adriatic which would take them back to New York. *He gave me a necklace and I thanked him with a kiss. The goodbye was awful. I shocked everyone by kissing Tony goodbye, but I had to. I did it twice and he said 'goodbye, dear' and then the tender left. I may never see him again.* Through none of the *Tony* entries do we hear another word about Bunny. Was my mother a fickle flirt or were her hormones just getting the best of her?

There is one more flirtatious episode in her diary that brings Charlotte back to New York. This one involves a Freddie, or maybe it was the same Freddie from the eastbound crossing. Could this have been a major coincidence? Or was this a new Freddie? Or did Freddie work on the Adriatic? Anyway, if it had been the same Freddie, her earlier declaration that *it was the last I saw of him* was not correct.

On October 24th: *Freddie and I had a heart-to-heart talk on love and the like and he asked me if I had any spare time in New York.* It seems possible that this was a new Freddie because she had pulled away from the earlier one when she learned he was married. On the last night of the voyage: *We had our last confidential talk. I had a beer at dinner and felt quite frisky and went running up to Freddie after dinner to the lounge and he laughed at me for being so peppy. Then Mom came to drag me away to pack, but I couldn't go and Freddie made me. After packing I met Mr. Kaltner (who was he?) and we went up to the first-class lounge to change money, but the man wasn't there, so we waited listening to the orchestra. Finally, we left and crashed two parties and went to the bar for cocktails, and Freddie came up there after the concert.* We should remember that prohibition was the law in the United States but not in Britain or on the high seas.

On the morning of the Adriatic's arrival in New York: *Had breakfast and found Freddie for a minute, missed the Statue of Liberty and talked by the rail, and I got low about saying goodbye to him, nearly cried when I said goodbye for the last time, but I didn't know it then because we were expecting to see each other Friday for lunch at the Metropolitan Museum. He's a darling fellow.* And those are the last words of her journal. I'll never know if that planned meeting at the Museum ever took place. Neither Bunny nor Tony are mentioned again. I know it doesn't work that way, but I wonder if, under other circumstances, one of them could have become my father.

Then there would have been a train journey to San Francisco and a sailing on the Matsonia to Honolulu. Vacation romance seemed to be the major theme of Charlotte's journal – first Freddie, then Bunny, then Tony and then, possibly, Freddie again. Remembering my mother, I am certain that, despite some occasional *fooling around,* all of the intrigue of her journal was virtuous. After all, she was under the watchful eye of her mother who, as a staunch Episcopalian, served as an attentive chaperone. Charlotte would be nearly 120 years old today (2024), but it is a lovely treat to glimpse the high-spirited flapper swooning and throwing her dignity to the wind in 1930. I'm glad she took that trip and I'm glad I had the opportunity, through her journal, to witness her having so much fun just before she settled into the more serious business of a long and successful marriage.

CHARLOTTE AND SPIEG

Charlotte and Spieg met in Waikiki – at Red Hale – and then spent the rest of their lives together raising a family in Manoa Valley. It is conceivable they met in Red Hale's dining room over dinner. Spieg was taking his evening meals there, and Charlotte was back living at home after returning from her swirling trip abroad. I have no idea what their first words were, but Charlotte was likely attracted to Spieg's serious intellectual nature, a far cry from the playboys she consorted with in Europe. She probably decided it was time to settle down, and here was a substantial gentleman. Spieg was twelve years older than Charlotte, and she may have seen him as a steadying influence. To use his words, he was *footloose and fancy free* for a few years. Then he recognized that time was moving on, he had come to be happy living in Hawaii, and he had met a very attractive and eligible young lady.

The proposal is a mystery, but I think it happened during the period when Spieg and Murph were palling around and all of them were socializing with young naval officers and their wives and girlfriends. An artifact among Charlotte's old papers is a radiogram from Manila in November of 1934 that says, *Will you sign with me for long-term contract and if so when? Answer via Navy radio, Mark.* Here was yet another proposal, but who was Mark? And I wonder how many other proposals Charlotte received before she fell for Spieg.

I can't report on their courtship as it happened, of course, before I knew them, but it was periodically interrupted by Spieg having to be in residence in Madison, Wisconsin for his PhD.

It is known that Charlotte promised to marry Spieg if he completed the PhD he was working on at the University of Wisconsin in Madison. That was the leading center for study of a certain bacteria that was spoiling pineapples in Hawaii, so to advance his career at the Pineapple Research Institute, he agreed to study there. There were several trips to Wisconsin in order to fulfill his residency requirements. He was there when he wrote to Susan asking permission to marry her daughter.

The engagement was announced in the Honolulu Star-Bulletin on July 8, 1935, providing a decorous year-long engagement. Spieg was still in Wisconsin when the final marriage plans were settled, and he returned to Honolulu in September of 1936, a month before their wedding on October 31st. They did not plan to marry on Halloween, but it happened to be a Saturday, and they could arrange for their ceremony, officiated by Dean William Ault, at St. Andrews Cathedral. The newspaper society pages (they still had those in the 1930s) had announcements of a number of parties, dinners and showers some of which Spieg was able to attend. As clippings from the social pages indicated, there was a *kitchen shower* for fifty guests and a *glass shower* and tea at Waioli Tea Room. Spieg's best man was Cyril *Murph* Murphy from his Niumalu Hotel and Black Point days. Charlotte's only attendant at their relatively small wedding was Lily Watson, a close friend and classmate from Punahou School.

Charlotte wore her mother's wedding dress and carried

a bouquet of white ginger and Night-blooming Cereus from the wall that surrounded Punahou School. The wedding was at four P.M., so it's not clear how the blooms were encouraged to open at that hour – perhaps by putting them in a closet until the time of the ceremony. Grandpa 'Gai (Ogai), Red Hale's original cook, had driven the honeymoon car to the church to prevent tin cans and signs being attached. The buffet reception was catered by the then current Japanese cook Higuchi and was held on the lawn near the seawall at Red Hale. The honeymoon took place at the home of Sis Larsen (another great school friend of Charlotte's) at Ka-a-awa (sic.) on the windward side of Oahu. Later, the home became a popular restaurant called The Crouching Lion Inn named for a rock formation on the hill above it.

The happy couple moved back to Red Hale after the honeymoon until Spieg had to, once again, go back to Madison for residency work in 1937. Again, it feels like prying when I read a playful letter from Charlotte that says: *Hello, cute little babykins! You thot I'd send an empty envelope, but I fooled you. Youse is an awful sweet baby and I love you. Cholly.* It is obvious that they loved each other as even across many miles there was a close connection.

*****

Except for an occasional trolley ride, Spieg didn't know much about Manoa Valley, a place where he would spend the rest of his life. Charlotte had heard from a realtor friend that the Bishop Estate was selling lots in their Manoa Uplands development at a good price. They went to look, and Spieg thought, with his knowledge of plants, he could build a three-bedroom house and create a beautiful garden there.

There were two last contiguous lots available, but another guy was interested. So, they rushed downtown to present a check and the other guy was right behind them. They paid $1,580. for two lots of soggy property that had a spectacular mountain view. The land, the house and architect fees came to about $10,000 in 1940 dollars.

A final summer session in 1940 finished Spieg's residency, and he received his PhD in Plant Pathology. He returned to Honolulu to oversee the building of their house. Moving day was in August of 1941, a few months before the bombing of Pearl Harbor. Up in the valley they did not hear the bombs; when they tried to use the telephone that day, they heard someone shouting, *Get off the line! Get off the line! Don't you know there is a war on?!* They didn't.

The neighborhood was in a dither when rumors went around that the Japanese had landed near us in upper Manoa Valley. This proved to be false, but everyone was on edge, and many families (including close friends) left the islands and returned to the mainland for safety. Charlotte was a *kamaaina* (born in the islands) so our family did not leave. It wasn't until the Battle of Midway and a decisive American victory in June of 1942 that nerves began to calm and people started to feel safe. But martial law had been declared, and everyone adjusted to new routines: gas masks, blackout curtains, rationing for food and gasoline, hoarding, victory gardens, blue headlights on cars and early evening meals to avoid using house lights.

*****

Charlotte and Spieg bought their two lots in 1940 – partly because they were contiguous and partly because they were on a slope which offered a spectacular view of mountains, rainbows and waterfalls at the head of the valley - besides, they were the last lots available in the Manoa Uplands tract. In early times the neighborhood had been the stomping grounds of Hawaiian royalty because it was cooler than the other side of the valley. It was protected from afternoon sun by very steep and looming mountains. Spieg, with his background in botany, saw the possibility of creating a remarkable garden. And so, they built their house on one of the lots leaving the other for the garden he wanted to create.

The vicinity, because of its 100 inches of annual rain (30 inches in Waikiki), was soggy but very green. This entire part of the valley was littered with volcanic rocks that had come from an ancient eruption of a volcanic vent near Mount Tantalus. Spieg's first challenge was to deal with those rocks, so he created paths, rock walls and terraces which became the hardscape of his remarkable garden. He meticulously sifted the earth for planting through a large strainer he had created to prepare the soil.

He planted a small forest of trees – plumeria, lemon, lime, grapefruit, macadamia, lychee, papaya, avocado and guava – which provided produce for us and presents for neighbors in the years to come. Every year at Christmas he would harvest the grapefruit and Charlotte would decorate them with foil and ribbons for the neighbors. Other plants were bird of paradise, hibiscus, croton and mock orange. As a true scientist, he loved to experiment to see what would thrive.

Every afternoon when he came home from a day of solving pineapple problems, he would change into his *yard clothes*, have a cup of coffee and a sweet roll. Then he would go outdoors to improve and maintain his garden. He worked hard which served as exercise and probably contributed to his living to be ninety-four years old. This was his hobby, and he lovingly tended to it. Sometimes we would help him with the weeding and mowing, but it was his know-how that created this project, and he loved to show it off. Another aspect of his garden was the caring for a rain gauge, and every morning he would measure the rain for the Hawaii Department of Agriculture. We would sometimes help measure, but he, being a true scientist, always kept the careful records.

*****

Charlotte had come from an upper-class family that could pay for live-in help, so you might say that she *married for love* when she decided to spend her life with a scientist on an academic salary. Charlotte had worked for two years in the Occupational Therapy Department at Queens Hospital. Then she became a busy middle-class housewife with no outside career which was very common in those days. She devoted herself to her family including her mother Susan who lived with us for a time after the war. She was always aware of the budget we had to live on and spent time saving money where she could. There were the expenses of raising three children including private school tuition. One area of her saving were the clothes she made for us, at first on the treadle sewing machine that she had inherited from her mother. We always had new clothes to go back to school in each year. And she painted the inside of our house twice to save the money.

Probably because she had grown up with a family cook, Charlotte hated to plan, shop and cook our family meals, but she dutifully did it for many years anyway. We ate well, with roasts on Saturday night and simpler meals for Sunday night, like her special spaghetti casserole which we all loved. Charlotte did like making guava jelly, mango chutney and papaya sherbet. She would send us up the valley to forage for guavas and mangos, but the papayas always came from our own back yard. For four years Grandma Susan paid for a live-in Japanese girl named Sadako who did the evening cooking, but, being our mother, Charlotte was never idle and kept things humming in our home.

There was always a division of taste at our dinner table. Spieg's German upbringing leaned him toward meat, potatoes, and sauerkraut. Charlotte and we kids preferred more exotic island fare like Asian and Hawaiian food. We would laugh when Dad ate his rice with milk and sugar. And he hated onions of any kind, so often there had to be a separate preparation without the onions.

Periodically, Charlotte and Spieg would put on dinner parties for friends and neighbors. There was always a Japanese lady named Mrs. Nishioka in the kitchen who prepared dinner – sometimes the Japanese dish called *hekka* (a peasant version of the more refined sukiyaki) or shrimp or chicken curry with all the condiments. At times, Mrs. Nishioka cleaned the house and did the ironing as well.

In my lifetime, Mom always did the driving which she didn't mind as she was nervous when others drove. But the real reason was that Spieg had had an accident as a teenager when other boys threw some nails that put out his left eye. Later he was fitted for a glass eye and suffered from glaucoma and cataracts in the other eye. In the summer of 1976, he and I went on a tour to Alaska. It was partly on a cruise ship and also on a bus and train. I served him as his eyes for that trip. My siblings and I also served as his eyes when going into places with low lighting like restaurants. Late in life he had surgery on his one eye which gave him a new lease on life. But he never drove again, and Charlotte became the family chauffer running all of us to work, school, appointments and fun.

Both Charlotte and Spieg were life-long Republicans in an era when Republicans still had a good name. Hawaii was then what we would now call a *red state* (or territory), probably because of the influence of the Big Five companies that controlled Hawaiian business. A reflection of this was the fact that we had a couple of parakeets named Ike and Mamie. Charlotte had a like-minded best friend named Dorothy. For relaxation, they would share Lucky Strike cigarettes and Lucky Lager beer and gossip about local and national politics. The *red scare* was often part of the discussion. Sometimes they would call in to the local radio shows and broadcast their ideas to the rest of the city. Spieg shared many of these views, but he was too busy tending his garden, so he kept them to himself.

Charlotte was a staunch Episcopalian (sometimes referred to as *Catholic lite*), probably because of the influence of her father Hoste who was from Northern Ireland. Once, upon coming home from seventh grade on the big island, I told her about a film I had seen that fascinated me. She was horrified and thought I might be edging toward Popism. The film was *The Miracle of Our Lady of Fatima*. That was too close for comfort, and I was lectured about the dangers of Roman influence.

Both my parents loved to share what they called a *high ball* (sometimes a beer) every evening. When we were teenagers, we were allowed to have small versions of this (the theory was that if we were allowed, we wouldn't sneak it and would stay out of trouble). They would buy bourbon by the case when it was on sale at Long's Drugstore. When we would go out, their favorite drinks were Old Fashioneds and Manhattans, and I have inherited that taste. I always enjoyed it when they relaxed with their evening cocktails because they would become playful with each other and that made me feel happy and secure. Whether at home or at a friend's house, the echoing tinkle of Charlotte's ice cubes always indicated when she needed a refill. But it wasn't always peaches and cream in their relationship. They did share the same conservative political views, but there were tensions over the fact that they went to different churches (Episcopalian and Lutheran), and tempers could be flared because they didn't share the same dispositions. Charlotte was very outgoing and Spieg tended to be quiet and introverted. I tell you this because I want this memoir to be an honest view of their lives. Another incident I must report on was when Charlotte fell down our very long outdoor back staircase. Unfortunately, she was pregnant with twins at the time My brother Harrison survived this but his twin sister Carol Marie died shortly after she was born. She rests in our family plot at Oahu Cemetery in Nuuanu Valley.

    The dinner dishes were not a chore to them. It was a time to share the events of the day. We wanted to give them a dishwasher for their 25th wedding anniversary in 1961, but they didn't want to lose their *together time,* so we got off cheaply with a garbage disposal instead. Every Sunday afternoon they would work on a letter intended for the three of us. At first, we were at various colleges on the mainland and my brother in the Navy, but later my sister and I continued to live in California. The letter was a mutual effort on their part summarizing the week's events and ideas and was produced with three copies using carbon paper. We each got a lovingly written letter every week, and we all learned the importance of family connections which, because of them, my brother and sister and I have continued to this day.

In 1954, when television first came to Hawaii, we three kids pushed for having a set. But Dad thought it was a waste of time, and, besides, it would cost too much. My bother Harrison decided to buy one himself with money he had saved from his paper route. Our first set was a small Crosley, and, low and behold, Dad loved it and was glued to it every evening. Because of his poor eyesight then, he sat very close and had the sound turned up as his hearing began to fail. We eventually got used to his cursing at the set when the advertisements came on. Long before the use of remotes, he would lean forward to turn off the sound at the least hint of a commercial.

In 1948 and 1958 Spieg was eligible for sabbatical leaves from the Pineapple Research Institute, so the whole family went to the mainland for those two years. Spieg would be doing research for his job, we three kids were in school and Charlotte managed her usual job of being an efficient housewife. On the first trip we lived in Riverside, California, and, on the second, we were in Corvallis, Oregon. Summer-long road trips around the country followed each of those school years. Before they had kids, Charlotte and Spieg went on other mainland trips, partly to fulfill Spieg's PhD residency requirements, and partly to visit his family.

*****

The trolleys that originally brought Spieg to Red Hale -

and to Charlotte - are long gone, and Red Hale itself is never going to come back. But they found each other there, and, of course, I am grateful. Over the years, they joined each other to become exemplary parents who forged the people my brother and sister and I became. They set examples of good citizenship, diligence, a strong work ethic and close family ties. Spieg was never happier than when the whole family was all together. And there was always an adjustment period for him, especially after Charlotte died, after any of us visited home and then would leave to return to the mainland.

From 1947 to 1955 there was a series of movie comedies featuring the characters Ma and Pa Kettle. Our whole family loved those films, and, in honor of them, we three kids began to call Charlotte and Spieg *Ma* and *Pa* in an ironic way. Eventually, those nicknames stuck and they have been Ma and Pa to us ever since. Ma passed away in 1973 when she was 63 years old of stomach cancer. At Christmas time of that year, we felt her great love when we realized that she had bought and wrapped presents for all of us even as she was dying.

Pa outlived Ma until 1992 when he died of liver cancer at age 94. Harrison was the sibling who had remained in Hawaii, and living next door to Pa, he took very good care of him, cooking, running errands and taking him to his doctor appointments. Both Ma and Pa lived at our home in Manoa Valley when they died, Pa dying in his own bed. All three of us were at his bedside holding his hand when he died. I wish I could show them what I have written about them. In a way, they both helped write this memoir as Ma was full of stories, and, before he died, Pa, ever the scientist, dictated a meticulous memoir of his life to me which I have on audio tape. Ma and Pa are both gone now, but I wish they could have read what I have said about them. I wish they could have experienced the love I feel in writing this memoir.

Charlotte

Charlotte

Charlotte and her mother Susan

Charlotte and Spieg

Charlotte and Spieg

Charlotte and Carl Before He Knew He Lived on an Island

Grandma and Gramma 'Gai Celebrating Their Birthday Together

My Japanese Grandparents

It never seemed out of the ordinary to me, especially as a child, that I would be blessed with Japanese grandparents. You see, I am not Asian. I am entirely of northern European descent – Irish, English, Scots, German and Danish. So, where did the Japanese come from? Even the racial melting pot of Hawaii didn't explain that situation to me. I called my mother's mother *Grandma,* but I also called an older Japanese couple *Gramma and Grampa 'Gai.* Their last name was actually Ogai, but my brother and sister and I first heard their name as *'Gai* without the other syllable. Even when we became adults and came to know better, we never stopped calling them *Gramma and Grampa 'Gai.*

For more than twenty years, the Ogais served as nanny, housekeeper and cook at Red Hale. When the Harrisons first moved there in 1910, Susan's father, *the General,* felt it was necessary for her to have some live-in help to care for a new baby (my mother Charlotte) and to manage the larger house that had recently been expanded. Red Hale would never have functioned as well as it did without the devoted assistance of the Ogais. A special association developed between our two families that still exists today over a hundred years later. The Ogais had four children who spent their childhoods at Red Hale, and the youngest of those has only recently passed away at age 94. This chapter tells the story of one Japanese family's assimilation into the multi-ethnic population of Hawaii.

At a little over five feet tall, both Gramma and Grampa 'Gai were slight in stature as those of Japanese ancestry often were in those days. They were lean from hard work and a healthy diet. I always remember Gramma 'Gai wearing wire-rimmed glasses that gave her a thoughtful responsible look. Both exuded a humility and a gentle kindness that matched their soft-spoken manner. They were attentive parents and grandparents to their family – and to mine.

A part of the island culture I grew up with was influenced by the Japanese and the Ogai family. I remember wearing a kimono and *tabis* (Japanese socks that fit like mittens on our feet) when I was very little. I was proud to be able to count in Japanese *(ichi, ni, san, shi)*, and I learned to play a traditional Japanese card game called *hanafuda* in which you matched stylized pictures and symbols. My brother Harrison was urged back to health when he was eight years old by Japanese physical therapy when he broke his collar bone. And we lavishly exchanged gifts with the Ogais at Christmas time.

And oh, the food. We often visited the Ogais at their Palolo Valley home where we enjoyed their Japanese graciousness and hospitality and learned to love their food like chicken *hekka* and a cucumber salad called *namasu*. There was never a visit in which we were not showered with enthusiasm and refreshments when we were barely in the front door. Their house was modest, but it always felt full of love and generosity. Despite her Japanese reticence, we always hugged each other when we left their home.

By the time I realized they were not *real* relatives, I was old enough to value the unique relationship we shared. All of my aunts, uncles and cousins lived on the mainland so, because of their proximity, the Ogais loomed as the only extended family, Japanese or not, that I grew up with. This kind of cross-cultural connection would probably be rare today, and I value it as an important part of my island upbringing.

*****

Tsuta Ogai's story began when she was born in 1891 in a farming village called Otani on the shore of Japan's Inland Sea. Ehime Prefecture is on the island of Shikoku in southwest Japan. Her father who was principal of a small school and then became mayor, had heard about Hawaii and came out of interest about a new land. His village was crowded and he knew opportunities would be greater there. He paid his own way so was never part of the plantation system as were most of the 15,000 workers who came to work in the cane fields from that part of Japan. For many of these immigrants, this was to be temporary. They could accumulate 3000 yen and be able to return to their villages. More than half of them did return, but many stayed in Hawaii, and after 1896, the Japanese became the largest ethnic group in the islands.

When Tsuta's father, Kumao Ogai, came to Hawaii, he temporarily left his wife and four children to whom he expected to return. Kumao had the means to open a plantation store in Waialua which did well enough for him to send for some of his family. Tsuta was the oldest, so she followed him to Hawaii in 1906 when she was 15 years old. She traveled with a friend, Takeyo Watanabe, who was older and was going to Hawaii as a *picture bride* for the Japanese cook who worked for John Waterhouse of Alexander and Baldwin. From her arrival, Tsuta taught herself to speak English and easily integrated into the fabric of the Honolulu community.

At first, she followed the Buddhist beliefs she had been

born into, but, because Honolulu was smaller and was a closer-knit community at that time, she was connected to a Reverend Philip Fukao and his wife and went to live with them. They were part of the Japanese congregation at the Episcopalian Holy Trinity Church. That was downtown on Queen Emma Square near St. Andrews Cathedral where Susan, Hoste and the General worshipped.

Grampa 'Gai, who was known as Takachi Naka at the time, was born in 1888 and grew up in the village of Otani as Tsuta had. Originally, there was nothing romantic between them in Japan, but they knew each other and would be reacquainted in Hawaii. Takachi, like his future father-in-law, independently traveled to Hawaii searching for new opportunities. When Tsuta and Takachi were both in the islands, her father nudged them together and arranged a marriage. He knew Takachi was a good man and wanted to see his daughter wed. They were joined by Reverend Fukao in the Episcopal Church when Gramma 'Gai was 18 years old. After he had seen his daughter successfully married, Tsuta's father returned to the rest of his family in Japan.

As was the Japanese custom at that time, Takachi took Tsuta's surname because he was the middle son, not the eldest. They became Takachi and Tsuta Ogai and both became Episcopalians because of Reverend Fukao's influence. Or, according to her daughter Seiko, maybe she didn't like being a Buddhist because a Buddhist fortune teller had once told her she had stolen and eaten a neighbor's chicken thus permanently impairing her eyesight in one eye. This had actually been caused by a childhood illness. At any rate, they were a perfect match as domestics for the Harrisons who were devout Episcopalians. They were referred to the General, Hoste and Susan by Deaconess Potter who worked with Reverend Fukao, and in 1910 they went to live and work at Red Hale for over twenty years.

*****

In the beginning, there was the sugar cane (the first plantation opened in 1835 at Koloa, Kauai) and then the necessity to grow, harvest and refine it. Hawaiians filled that need at first, but, as demand for sugar and the industry grew, there was a need for a greater labor force. Chinese laborers began coming in 1851, but soon they too, were insufficient to fill the labor need. In 1868, 142 men and 6 women came from Japan. This was the first year of the Japanese Meiji era, a period in which Japan moved out of isolated feudalism to engage with the rest of the world. Hawaii was part of that outside world and was a handy destination for Japanese people looking outward for greater opportunities. Other waves of immigrant laborers, Portuguese, Puerto Rican and Filipino, were yet to come.

Three major waves of Japanese immigration to Hawaii eventually totaled 180,000 workers. The first and greatest wave, from 1886 to 1897, was mostly men going to work in the cane fields. The second, from 1898 to 1907, included women, some of whom were picture brides – this was the era when Takachi, Tsuta and her father came. The third wave, 1908 to 1924, included many women and children being sent for by workers who had decided to stay. They came to a xenophobic society that didn't offer a strong welcome. But because Hawaii was dependent on this outside labor, feelings against foreigners were kept quieter as opposed to the more virulent racism against the Chinese in California.

But Hawaii's media of the time spoke of the *Japanese menace* and the *Japanese problem.* On the plantations, the Japanese generally did not integrate but stuck to their own culture and ideas. In 1921, my grandfather Hoste spoke about the problem of admitting Japanese people into the Oahu Country Club. It was even controversial when there was an effort to admit the Japanese Counsel General. On the other hand, the Chinese laborers did integrate and intermarry, often with Hawaiian women. They started businesses and became more urban, living away from the plantations. Chinese/ Hawaiian is a very common ethnic mixture in Hawaii today.

The first generation of Japanese immigrants to Hawaii was known as *Issei.* Their descendants the *Nisei* (second generation) and *Sansei* (third generation) were warily viewed by the Caucasian establishment. They feared a time when all the Japanese would go to the polls (which they eventually did) changing Hawaii from a Republican territory to one led by Democrats in the early 1950s.

Throughout the 1920s, the Japanese were kept out of federal and territorial jobs; their Japanese newspapers were regulated and some Japanese language schools were closed. And, of course, there was discrimination during World War Two. It was assumed they could not be Americanized, and some blamed local Japanese for the attack on Pearl Harbor. Everyone wondered who you could trust, perhaps not even your Japanese yard boy. The Japanese were warned not to speak their language, wear kimonos or even eat their food lest they raise suspicions. Buddhist and Shinto shrines were closed and some Japanese (priests, school teachers and others who might have influence in their community) were interned in local camps, and later others were sent to camps on the mainland. But the federal government was told that

Hawaii's economy would collapse if all the Japanese were to disappear; besides, there were too many to lock up everyone. None of the Ogais was ever interned.

Ultimately, there were no acts of sabotage, and gradually there was a softening of the idea that Asians, especially the Japanese, were inferior. It was seen that they had a great penchant for education and a respect for strong family values. Many began to move off the plantations into other occupations such as shop keeping, running tea houses and public baths, and settling in Honolulu's valleys, especially Manoa, as flower and vegetable farmers. Grampa 'Gai's *Issei* journey to integration began when he went to night school to learn to cook which prepared him when he went to work at Red Hale. He was also employed at the Diamond Bakery on McCully Street where he eventually became chief baker and treasurer. When one of the original founders decided to return to Japan, Takachi was able to buy into the business.

*****

When they lived at Red Hale, the Ogais were the only Japanese family in a *haole* (Caucasian) neighborhood. The Castles and some others had Chinese servants, but the gossip was that they were not as well cared for as the Ogais were by the General and the Harrisons at Red Hale. Other neighborhood servants were envious of the Ogais who essentially became an extended part of the Harrison family. This was the domestic situation I grew up with as a child. It was as if they were protected from any prejudice or racism that was part of the culture in the rest of the city.

Protected as they were, the Ogais went about their business of contributing to a second generation (*Nisei*) of

Hawaii's Japanese. Gramma 'Gai began caring for her own children in addition to my mother and aunt, Charlotte and Peggy. From the beginning, Tsuta called Charlotte *Miss Cholly*, and the name stuck. I always wondered if, despite obvious differences, Gramma 'Gai's job as nanny or nurse maid could be compared to the custom in the American south of having blacks caring for white children. The Ogais moved into the second-floor apartment of an out-building built near the street to contain a laundry and to relieve crowding in an over-extended main house.

The Ogai offspring started arriving in 1916 when Yuki Ogai was born, seven years after her parents were married. This happened at Tripler Army Hospital as she was considered part of General Davis's household. Yuki started a career as an elementary school teacher, but this was cut short because of racial bias after the bombing of Pearl Harbor because of her Japanese ancestry. She worked for many years as a clerk in the radiology department at Tripler Hospital. She married Yasu Takenouchi and had a *Sansei* (third generation) daughter named Sharon.

The Ogai's second child Seiko happened to be born in Japan in 1920 when the Ogais took Yuki to visit her grandparents. Another reason for the trip was that Tsuta's brother was dying of tuberculosis. Tsuta's pregnancy made it too dangerous to travel back to Hawaii so Seiko was essentially an *Issei* (first generation) because she was born in the old country. Seiko graduated from the University of Hawaii in English, History and French, but, again, because of her Japanese citizenship, she had trouble getting a teaching job in Hawaii and worked for the Methodist Church in Chicago for many years. She married Shigeo Oshita and had no children. I want to express my gratitude to Seiko for providing much of my information about her family, in addition to a great deal about Red Hale in general. She had an exceptional memory even at the age of 96 when she passed away in 2016.

Tomotaru (Tomo) was the first Asian born in the new Kapiolani Hospital in 1923. He went to Columbia University on the G.I. Bill and had a top management career at the state tax department of Hawaii. He married Mildred Naito and had two sons, John and James and a daughter Amy. Tomo was a member of the famed 442nd Regimental Combat Team during World War Two.

Atsuko was delivered by a mid-wife at Red Hale in 1925. She attended the University of Hawaii and became a microbiologist working for the Hawaii Department of Agriculture. She married Bob Kato and had no children. Atsuko was the youngest of the Ogai children, and passed away in 2019. After Seiko died, Atsuko, also with an excellent memory, provided answers to more of my questions about her family and Red Hale.

When I was growing up, I often heard the Ogais call my grandmother Susan *Godmother*. For, indeed, Susan and Hoste became the godparents of all four Ogai children when they were baptized and confirmed at St. Mary's Episcopal Church. They were like *haole* (Caucasian) grandparents to the Ogai children just as their parents had been like Japanese grandparents to my brother and sister and me. All six of the Ogais, the whole family, lived with and worked for the Harrisons and were fundamentally *adopted* by them. Gramma 'Gai always thought of my mother as her *first daughter* as she came to Red Hale to care for her from birth. Coincidentally, my two grandmothers, the *haole* one and the Japanese one, shared a birthday, March 19th – St. Joseph's Day when the swallows come back to Capistrano. They always celebrated together – their birthdays and their long friendship.

*****

When they moved off the plantations, many Japanese settled in a neighborhood of Honolulu called Moiliili near the entrance to Manoa Valley. This was especially true in the 1920s when Buddhist temples and Shinto shrines were established there along with Japanese businesses such as florists and nurseries. In 1923, the Ogai family began looking for property so they could build a home of their own. They were Christian so they did not need a proximity to the Japanese religious establishments in Moiliili. Palolo Valley in Kaimuki was not far away, and, before the end of 1923, they bought a 50 by 200 -foot lot on 9th Avenue for $1000. The property ran all the way down to Palolo Stream and allowed lots of room for a colossal greenhouse which would always be filled with orchids, ferns and anthuriums. I always loved wandering through Grandpa 'Gai's collection when we visited. Their plan was to build a house, but my grandfather Hoste became ill with kidney and circulatory problems, and Susan was needed to care for him. Out of loyalty and gratitude to the Harrisons, the Ogais postponed their move until 1929 after Hoste had passed away. They had built their house in 1925, but it sat empty until they thought they could move there.

The Ogai children spent their early childhoods at Red Hale before their family moved away. When they moved, Yuki was 13, Seiko was 9, Tomo was 6 and Atsuko was 4. They were all younger than Charlotte and Peggy so their playmates tended to be other servant children in the neighborhood. They didn't play in Kapiolani Park as that was mainly used for polo and horse racing at the time. They did become friends with the prisoners who came to clean the park. They also became friendly with Mr. Masako who was the stable hand at the Dillingham family's stables. He would pay them ten cents a bunch for the sweet *kiawe* beans that the horses loved. As I did years later, they would climb in the jungle-gym of the *hau* tree near Red Hale's bar-b-que; they loved collecting dates from the trees at the Castle estate, and they played hide-and-seek in the ironwood thicket near the house. String, bent pins and bamboo became fishing poles, and they swam at high tide when the water was deep enough near the seawall. At times, they ventured as far as San Souci Beach for picnics. Many of Susan's friends called her Susie, and Seiko remembers thinking they had named San **Souci** Beach after her godmother. Susan occasionally took the Ogai children on outings downtown to the Princess Theatre to see religious movies such as *King of Kings* and *The Sign of the Cross*.

*****

After their move to Palolo Valley, Charlotte would pick up Tsuta once a week so she could come back to Red Hale to help clean for the tenants who lived there after Hoste was gone. In 1932, the Ogais recommended friends, another Japanese family, to Susan, and the Sadami Higuchis came to Red Hale and stayed until 1950. Mr. Higuchi was a widower with four young children, and they lived in the second-floor apartment of the wash house where the Ogais had lived. Because Susan and Charlotte were then living alone in the main house, they were happy to have Higuchi and his children use the big house as well.

Both Mr. and Mrs. Higuchi had been born in Japan, had come to Hawaii in their teens and were married there. Chie Higuchi had died in childbirth along with their last child in early 1932 in the Palama neighborhood, and Mr. Higuchi wanted to move his children to a better area so they would not become *hoodlums*. Red Hale in Waikiki was a perfect fit for them, and Sadami would become the cook, gardener and chauffeur. The Higuchis did not become surrogate family as the Ogais had, but they are a significant part of Red Hale's story.

Asa Higuchi, the second to oldest (he was eight years old when he first came to Red Hale) remembers a pleasant childhood there that was similar to what the Ogai children experienced. Their friends envied them living at the beach where they could swim, surf, fish, sometimes with torches at night, and play touch football in the park. Asa is the Higuchi who has supplied me with most of my material about his family.

As with the Ogais, Susan got all of them to St. Mary's where they were baptized and confirmed. Hoste was gone by then so she, as a godparent to them, served as a mother figure. Asa recounts: *the outstanding memory that I have is the great love, compassion and kindness that your grandmother bestowed on me and my family during our entire residence in Waikiki. For that, I am forever grateful.* They, too, moved to Kaimuki when they left Red Hale in 1950, and Sadami died there in 1977 when he was 73 years old.

Today, Asa has become a friend, and he continues to tell me tales of Red Hale. (Asa has now passed away in 2022.) On April 1, 1946, his sister Sakiko woke him early. *Asami, wake up, tidal wave!' But this was not an April Fool's joke. I ran* *to the back yard which was right next to the beach. I could see miles out to sea with coral reefs showing way above the sea level. It was really eerie and gave me 'chicken skin' (*slang for goose bumps*). Then the waves came crashing back to shore covering most of the backyard. April Fool, indeed!*

Asa also remembers their neighbors who lived where Dad Center's swimmers had tantalized Charlotte when she was a teenager. The composer R. Alex Anderson lived there with his family then. He had written over 200 songs including *Beyond the Reef, Lovely Hula Hands* and *Mele Kalikimaka*. He famously had introduced Hawaiian music at the Panama-Pacific Exposition in San Francisco in 1915. The Anderson children became playmates of the Higuchi kids.

On the morning of December 7, 1941, when Asa was a senior at McKinley High School, he was practicing his backstroke for a 100-meter race at the Waikiki Natatorium. *I saw a Japanese plane with red dots on the wing pass over me. That was my first exposure to World War Two.* But it was not his last. *I had just started my second semester at the University of Hawaii in 1942. It was announced by the government that it would accept Japanese-Americans for the Army. They asked for about 1,500 volunteers, but I learned later that over 10,000 came forward. On March 23, 1943, I was inducted into the Army. First, we went to Schofield Barracks for initial training. In April, we boarded the S.S. Lurline which had been converted to a troop ship and sailed to San Francisco. From there we went to Camp Shelby, Mississippi where we were told that our outfit would be designated the 442nd Regimental Combat Team.* All of its members were second generation Japanese (Neisi), about two-thirds of them from Hawaii. It wasn't clear then that great fame and honors would be bestowed on that unit.

In 1951, when I was twelve years old, I went to see a

movie at the Waikiki Theater called *Go For Broke*. I didn't know at the time that that strange sounding title was pidgin English for *give it everything you've got*. The film tells a story of the 442nd in which a Caucasian platoon leader gradually comes to terms with his prejudice against his Neisi men. Asa's unit was first sent to Oran in North Africa and then to Naples where their job was to patrol and report enemy activity. While they were advancing up the Italian peninsula, word came to Asa that he would become part of a 442nd swim team that, for morale purposes, would compete with others in the 34th Division. They were sent to Rome for two weeks, away from the front lines and harm's way, for training and the competition. Asa always had mixed feelings about that swim meet as it may have saved his life, but it also left him with guilt as his buddies continued to face hardship and danger.

    Asa's unit was sent to France in September of 1944 where they became involved in the rescue of the *Lost Battalion* of the 36th Division. Members of the 1st Battalion of the 141st Texas Regiment found themselves cut off and surrounded behind enemy lines in the Vosges Mountains with little food and water. The 442nd was ordered to rescue them, and, after six days of combat, did so with over 800 casualties of their own. This led to the question of whether the Nisei soldiers were used as *cannon fodder* or whether they were given this difficult assignment because of their record of outstanding performance. Asa was part of this effort as support staff although he wasn't involved in the actual shooting. The 442nd was collectively awarded a Congressional Gold Medal for this effort. *Go For Broke* became their motto, and the 442nd was the most decorated unit in World War Two. Asa says, *the most coveted award among us front-line GIs was the combat infantry badge awarded to all infantry soldiers in combat.*

After the French campaign, the 442nd was sent back to Italy just north of the Arno River. There, in April 1945, they broke through the German defenses which had been holding off the Allies for months. Then, in May 1945, the Germans surrendered, and World War Two ended in Europe.

During a mop-up period after the shooting stopped, the Army allowed men to take college courses. Asa did so at the University of Milan where, by chance, he met and had his picture taken with Tomo Ogai – both were members of the 442nd and both had lived at Red Hale as children. They had been in separate battalions so they never fought together, but both Tomo and Asa were awarded Bronze Stars for their efforts in the Italian campaign.

Asa remembers: *In November 1945 while still guarding German prisoners in Northern Italy, I was one of several 'old timers' ordered to be returned home to Hawaii to be discharged. The homecoming for us was relatively subdued – no bands, no ceremonies as we had been coming home in scattered groups a few at a time. The big parade and hoopla in Washington D.C. for the 442nd was later when the entire group (consisting mostly of replacements) came home. We original members of the 442nd came home quietly and without fanfare.*

And Asa did come home to Red Hale where a reminder of the war sat under the beach-side *hau* tree. A five-foot deep bomb shelter had been dug in the sandy soil but had never been used. Asa continued to live at Red Hale while he finished his education at the University of Hawaii. He went on to become a social worker and officer at the University's School of Public Health. He married Yoshiko Imahiro at St. Mary's in 1951, and they had a son Clyde and a daughter Lynne. Tomo Ogai returned to his family in their new home in Palolo Valley before continuing his education at Columbia University.

*****

Gramma and Grampa 'Gai were founding members of the Good Samaritan Episcopal Church near their home in Palolo Valley. They continued to live on 9th Avenue, and that is where I remember feeling their hospitality and extreme gratitude for grandma Susan's kindness to them whenever we visited. In the Japanese culture, there is a sense of obligation and a need to give back that my family always felt from the Ogais. Takachi passed away in November of 1962 when he was 74 years old, and Tsuta died in November of 1978 when she was 87.

Gramma 'Gai cared for my mother Charlotte from cradle to grave, from 1910 to 1973. Our family will be forever grateful for their love and devotion. In the early 1950s Susan gave a bronze communion set to the Ogais' Good Samaritan Church. On it was inscribed, *A thanks offering to almighty God for the years of loving service and companionship of Tsuta Oga*i. Gramma and Grampa 'Gai, my Japanese grandparents, are buried under three shade trees at Diamond Head Memorial Park, not far from their two homes in Hawaii, in Palolo Valley and at Red Hale.

Gramma 'Gai Caring for My Mother and Aunt Peggy

Tomo and Asa of the 442nd at a Reunion in Italy

Epilogue

No story has a definitive ending. The finish always comes when one chooses to leave off telling the tale. Red Hale, the family house at the end of Kalakaua Avenue is no longer there – that tale is finished. But the land that supported that history continues to carry the stories of a new generation which now lives vertically in a nine-story concrete tower called The Tahtienne. Pili grass huts and large beach houses have disappeared, and today there are twenty-six apartments (some of the original spaces have been joined to create larger units) where a single family had lived for many years. Some of these apartments are second homes, and most of the inhabitants are professionals who can afford to live on Waikiki's "Gold Coast."

The endangered Chippendale chair is now safe in my California bedroom, but the object of my childhood crush, the house called Red Hale, is only a memory. King Kalakaua would not recognize the "miracle suburb on the beach" he touted in 1876. And the Davises, Harrisons, Spiegelbergs and Ogais can only remember an era and a way of life that, one might say, has gone with the trade winds. The mauka breezes, the trade winds, still transport a hint of rain forest; a few of the old coconut trees still stand; Diamond Head still looms above the neighborhood; Kapiolani Park is still across the street, and the seawall still holds back the ocean. But, as the Earth's climate warms, might this story have a finish that can't be predicted? As those who remember continue to disappear – someday my memories will be gone as well – perhaps this uncommon biography of Red Hale will, one day, be the only evidence of a rich and colorful time gone by.

The Southern Cross

The Southern Cross is a one-act play based on characters and situations that are recounted in the six chapters about Red Hale. Some changes have been made in order to fit the dramatic structure of the play. Charlotte Stuart is based on my mother who in reality was married with children; Lily Cameron is based on my Aunt Peggy, Charlotte's sister; Higuchi is based on Sadami Higuchi who actually worked at Red Hale; Ben Tarpley is a composite invention based on tenants at Red Hale; Gordon Lum was an actual employee at the Hawaiian Trust Co. and Susan Stuart is based on my grandmother Susan Harrison.

A One-Act Play
By Carl Spiegelberg

Cast of Characters

Charlotte Stuart
Lily Cameron, her sister
Higuchi, a Japanese manservant
Lt. Cmdr. Ben Tarpley
Mr. Gordon Lum
Mrs. Susan Stuart

The Southern Cross is a play about a specific time and place and a few of the people who experienced the onrush of change that happened there. While the characters of the play are extremely important, it should be clear that another principal protagonist here is the house called Red Hale and Hawaii itself.

The setting is the eastern end of Waikiki Beach in July of 1959, on the brink of the age of commercial jet travel. It is an historical fact that the first passenger jet liner arrived in Honolulu at that time, and the citizens of Hawaii voted for statehood in June of that year. It is very important that the costumes and general atmosphere of the play be tied to that summer.

> The scene is the backyard and lanai of a large beach house near the foot of Diamond Head in Waikiki. The front edge of the stage apron represents the seawall and it becomes clear that the audience is viewing the set from a point just offshore looking in at the land. This is the back of the house, and the driveway to the street is around the side of the house to the right. The house is rambling and comfortable, and its natural wood and stone give it a warm feeling. At stage left there is a daybed that could be used for napping in hot weather. There is a table with several chairs and an oriental sideboard at stage right. Wind chimes hang at one edge of the lanai and a tapa cloth hanging is on one wall. Fish nets hang about and some bedraggled party decorations including a sign reading "One More to Go" are taped here and there. Steps lead down to the yard where there is a bench down right near the seawall, and an outdoor bar-b-q with firewood sloppily piled next to it in a wood box. The suggestion of

a coconut tree or two rise at the edge of the
stage. There is a feeling of transition about the
home - household articles are stacked about in
the process of being inventoried and stored. It
should be clear, even though there is a sense of
disrepair and disorderliness about the house,
the total effect of the scene should be old,
relaxed, comfortable and, most of all,
Hawaiian.

As the lights come up, there is a stillness and
oppression that comes from two or three
days of southerly Kona heat. The wind chimes
are silent. The time is five o'clock in the
evening. As the play progresses, the lights
gradually dim, and the play ends in darkness
except for the glow of artificial light from the lanai.

A car horn is heard from the driveway; we
hear a woman's voice call out: "Who left this
lawn chair in the drive?" Interior footsteps
are heard and a male voice answers: "I
come." We hear the sound of the chair being
moved and the car coming to a stop with
its door opening and closing.

We see CHARLOTTE enter the yard from the
driveway at stage right. She is an attractive
woman of about 50. There is a sense of
purpose about her, accompanied by a certain
amount of nervous energy, but even though
she is in a hurry and annoyed at the

> moment, she is pleasant and should be
> played in a sympathetic manner. She calls
> back over her shoulder:

CHARLOTTE

Thanks, Higuchi. I want to pack some more of mother's things and take them with me tonight. I'll need the car as close to the house as possible.

> She surveys the disarray of the yard and
> party decorations on the lanai and shakes
> her head as if in response to the job ahead
> of her. She proceeds to the bar-b-q and is
> looking over the pile of firewood next to it.
> Something catches her attention and she stops.

CHARLOTTE

Oh, for crying out loud! What's this doing here? (turns toward the house) Higuchi!

HIGUCHI

(Enters from drive with lawn chair which he leans against the house.) Yes, Cholly.

> HIGUCHI is an elderly Japanese man of
> perhaps 70. He came from Japan years
> ago to work in the cane fields but was
> able to move from that and has been a
> domestic in this home for many years.
> He is familiar with everything here
> including the family members who treat
> him with respect. He speaks with a typical

pigeon English island accent. We hear his
Japanese radio station coming from the kitchen.

CHARLOTTE
(Picking up a piece of wood from the woodpile) Darn those tenants. How long have these been out here?

HIGUCHI
(Not understanding) Don't know. I nevah see.

CHARLOTTE
This is part of the old Koa dining set. What is it doing in the bar-b-q wood box?

HIGUCHI
That firewood for hamburger. Party last night. Men make house all a mess, all kapakahi.

CHARLOTTE
(Outraged, not at him but at the fact)
This is not firewood. It was one of the General's favorite chairs as part of his koa dining set. (She continues to pull pieces of the chair out of the box and arranges them on the lawn.) He bought that dining set at auction when he first came here.

HIGUCHI
Boarding men put it there, I think. I ask Mrs. Stuart.

CHARLOTTE
What could those men be thinking of? – No, don't say a word to mother. We're getting her moved none too soon.

HIGUCHI
Oh, you take Mrs. Stuart away now?

CHARLOTTE
(sighing) Yes, Higuchi, I think tonight. She must move now. I'll take her to my house in Manoa this evening, and then, we'll see. This will be difficult – for all of us, but we only have until the end of the month. How have things been for her today?

HIGUCHI
I think she no sleep last night. Plenty noise.

CHARLOTTE
Well, I hope she'll be ready for our appointment this evening. I'm never quite sure what she remembers.

HIGUCHI
Oh, yes, I help. (pause) And I no think she see chair.

CHARLOTTE
No, she probably hasn't noticed this kind of thing for some time.

HIGUCHI
I try to keep up with tenants, but –

CHARLOTTE
You've been a great help, Higuchi. Let's not tell Mother about the chair – and let me deal with her about the move. You could go up and get an overnight bag packed for her while we're eating out here. She can come down when the

dinner is ready. (Going up onto the lanai) I want to get some more of these things listed for the appraiser and the auctioneer, and I can do it faster alone.

HIGUCHI
Yes, Cholly.

CHARLOTTE
(Starting to work – she lists and packs household items into boxes) I don't suppose my sister is here yet. Has she called? I really don't want to wrangle with Lily tonight. I think her flight got in this morning. She's staying at the Moana Hotel.

HIGUCHI
No, she not here yet. When you want dinner?

CHARLOTTE
Before too long. I don't want mother to tire out.

HIGUCHI
I do shopping this afternoon. We have chicken hekka and rice - used to be your favorite.

CHARLOTTE
You know, I still miss your cooking after all these years.

HIGUCHI
Not change since long time.

CHARLOTTE
These boarders do live well. Are you still going to that old store in Kapahulu?

HIGUCHI

Oh, yes.

CHARLOTTE

I can remember begging to go with you on the trolly.

HIGUCHI

That trolly gone long time now.

CHARLOTTE

Along with lots of other things. (Dusting off an old Chinese vase) I haven't seen this for years. It's survived a lot around here. (Continues the packing. Higuchi helps her.) Heavens, it's hot out here at the beach. We feel the Kona weather up in the valley, but not like you do out here. The wind chimes are perfectly still.

HIGUCHI

Men sleep on outside lanai for two nights.

CHARLOTTE

I guess that explains some of this mess. (pause) I tried to get away earlier, but I had students after school, and I wanted to pick up some things for my apartment from Liberty House before the weekend. Things to make mother comfortable. This has been quite a week.

HIGUCHI

Today boat day, Cholly.

CHARLOTTE

Oh, did I miss the Lurline? (Coming down toward the sea

wall) You remember I used to love watching the ships sail around Diamond Head. I'd imagine the flowers being thrown overboard.

HIGUCHI
Not so many now.

CHARLOTTE
When I first went up to boarding school, I threw a lei and I imagined it had come ashore right here on the seawall.

> We hear a voice from inside call out. "Charlotte, are you out there?" LILY, Charlotte's sister, appears opening the screen door from inside. She has come from the mainland to help with closing down the house. She is a plump woman who is extravagantly dressed with more make up and jewelry than is necessary and wears her idea of fashionable beach wear – sunsuit, large picture hat, high heels and carries a large bag of beach accessories. She speaks with a slight nasal tone which becomes exaggerated when she becomes self consciously "cute." She is not a practical woman. She and CHARLOTTE have never seen eye to eye. She has just removed a large pair of sunglasses

which she holds while fanning
herself and trying to move some air
into the house.

LILY

Oh, here you are, Charlotte. It's dark in here – and not a breath of air.

CHARLOTTE

Hello, Lily. (They kiss formally) I'm glad you're on time. Supper won't be late. Mother is upstairs napping. How was your flight?

LILY

Oh, the usual. I haven't seen that airport in ages. I took a taxi from the Moana a little early – Oh, hello, Higuchi – I thought I might be able to help. (She is wandering away from the work out toward the sea wall) And, of course, I want to see mother. I haven't called her since I landed. God, it's hot. (fanning) I notice you still have the Red Hale sign on the house out front.

CHARLOTTE

You must remember that Daddy put that sign up when the neighbors started calling the house Red Hale. The house is painted red, of course, but also, he always thought, because of the red dust blowing from the park. Now everyone calls this place Red Hale. I guess I left the sign in Daddy's honor.

LILY

I guess we're a neighborhood landmark now. We should get some more of these reminders cleared away before mother sees them. The simpler we make this the better.

CHARLOTTE
Let's hide this Hawaiian calabash, part of the General's collection.

LILY
I thought he was going to give some of this stuff to the Bishop Museum.

CHARLOTTE
I still want to do that.

LILY
It was going to be all of the Hawaiian stuff -the feather leis and the tapa hangings. A lot of junk from the old days – useless stuff.

CHARLOTTE
It is not useless. These are things we grew up with. Our childhoods. I don't want an argument with you right off the bat.

LILY
OK, I'll try to behave myself.

HIGUCHI
Long time since you were here, Lily.

LILY
The last time was when Daddy died, and, I guess before that – just before the war. Oh, yes, and when we added on to the

house to make room for the General.

CHARLOTTE

It was when granddaddy retired. It's lucky for us Mom was able to buy part of Dad Center's lot for the expansion.

LILY

It seems just as gloomy in here as it ever did.

CHARLOTTE

It's an old house – and please don't talk that way when mother comes down. I want to have a pleasant evening. I don't want to wrangle with you.

LILY

Such a shambles. It's just a big old beach house, nothing remarkable. What has she been allowing to happen here? Nothing like the Castle mansion down the seawall.

CHARLOTTE

You know very well mother doesn't really see what's going on here anymore.

LILY

I don't think it's so much her eyes as it is her sense of reality.

CHARLOTTE

Don't be flippant about your mother, Lily.

LILY

The gothic quality of a senile old woman in the attic is a bit out of character in our family, don't you think?

CHARLOTTE
Stop being dramatic, Lily. And don't exaggerate.

LILY
That's what I've imagined from your letters.

CHARLOTTE
I never mentioned the word senile. She's old and. . . .

LILY
You've got to face facts, Charlotte – we're moving her because she doesn't- how shall I say it?- have a handle on the here and now any more.

HIGUCHI
(Moving toward kitchen) I fix dinner now.

CHARLOTTE
Oh, yes, Higuchi. Thank you. Tell mother I'm here, will you? I'll be up soon.

HIGUCHI
Yes, Cholly. (He goes up stairs)

LILY
And those boarders take advantage of her – living like kings in this place – right on the beach and with a servant and all their meals cooked for them, well, they might as well be living at the Royal Hawaiian Hotel. Just so she could stay on here in the house.

CHARLOTTE
You knew we had to take in boarders after Daddy died.

LILY
Yes, but I don't see why they have to have the run of the place.

CHARLOTTE
The property taxes have to be paid. And an old house needs constant upkeep. (pause) I guess I wrote she's been getting worse in the last year.

LILY
Heavens above! I don't understand you allowing her to stay here with those men.

CHARLOTTE
We had to have them. The taxes were ruining her. I wrote you that Daddy's stocks are practically gone. Honolulu Iron Works and Castle and Cook. Mr. Austin got those men in here to help out until the demolition. And besides, we've always had upright Navy men. Officers.

LILY
The Kamaaina Trust was so damn quick to make an outside deal. They've wanted us out of their hair for years.

CHARLOTTE
You know how much mother relied on Mr. Austin after father was gone.

LILY

I think they're just out to make a buck – whatever is best for the Kamaaina Trust Company. And with no thought to mother's plan for the Southern Cross. That apartment building would have set us up just fine.

CHARLOTTE

Yes, well, I think it's final now. We just need mother's signature on a few more papers. I think Mr. Lum will be here for that.

LILY

Thank God, you've come to your senses about getting her out of here anyway.

CHARLOTTE

Do you think it's easy after so many years? She has stubborn ideas about this place, and I felt with Higuchi here to take care of things – but he's getting old too. She loves this place. (It is clear that Charlotte does too)

LILY

That's no reason under the circumstances –

CHARLOTTE

I think that when her mind is clear she feels she wants to die here – where father died.

LILY

Don't be morbid. But, of course, I seem to remember there was one other reason that's kept her here. I wonder if she still remembers that you never found a man. She wanted you to move in here with a husband.

CHARLOTTE

I've stopped worrying about that. And, besides, it's none of your business.

LILY

She didn't want to leave here 'til everyone was neatly tucked in.

CHARLOTTE

Edward was a war casualty in the south Pacific – Saipan – and there has been no one else. And you don't have to be vulgar about it.

LILY

Well, if it's still one of the obstacles here, it's your responsibility, not mine. (pause) The view was always the best thing about this place, but we were so far away from things out here. It took an hour to get downtown to Fort St. on the trolly. I always felt like we were living in the country here.

CHARLOTTE

But if the trust company has its way, there will be a nine-story building here. It won't feel like it's out in the country any more.

LILY

That's a lot of concrete. If there is any more of that they will build a wall around Diamond Head. The neighborhood is going to change, and that little Red Hale sign is going to be lost in the dust.

CHARLOTTE
But, as you said, it was always the view. (Pointing toward the ocean) The view, yes. In the winter, whenever we see the Southern Cross on the horizon –

LILY
Is she still talking about that Southern Cross nonsense? I thought she had forgotten about that constelation. I never understood a church lady like mother being so taken up with all that astrology hocus-pocus.

CHARLOTTE
It wasn't that at all. The cross has just always been a symbol, a reminder of the church for her.

LILY
(Fanning herself) My God, it's hot.

CHARLOTTE
For a while, after her plans to put up her apartment house fell through, she wanted to pass the property to St. Andrews for a church retreat and name it after the cross – to keep it in local hands.

LILY
I didn't realize she was still hanging on to that idea.

CHARLOTTE
But Mr. Lum says the estate can't afford it now. Henry Kaiser is building his Hawaiian Village Hotel at the other end of Waikiki, and that has put pressure on the cost of building materials. It's all gone sky high. (pause) I think

about her apartment building too when I see that constellation the way we did in winter. At least her apartment house idea was a way of honoring what mother loved.

LILY

Yes, well, don't bring that up and get her off on it. That – and the church. Let's get her moved to your place in Manoa Valley without any sermons or fantasies.

CHARLOTTE

She does talk sometimes as if the church was already here. She forgets.

LILY

Forgets! She doesn't know the difference. I had no idea she had gotten that bad.

CHARLOTTE

It will help to get her away from here and living with me in Manoa. The view of the Southern Cross is always a reminder of the old days for her. I'll let her settle in with me in Manoa, and then we'll find a nice retirement home for her. A place that can take care of her and where she can get her meals.

LILY

I assume she doesn't know about her imminent departure.

CHARLOTTE

I've tried to talk to her about it, and I think she realizes it's inevitable.

LILY

But does she know she's going to be spirited out of here tonight?

CHARLOTTE

No, I just thought we'd have an early dinner here on the lanai and then go for an after-dinner ride to Manoa.

LILY

A bit sneaky, but maybe for the best.

CHARLOTTE

(She has returned to the chair pieces on the lawn) I can't understand how Higuchi could have allowed this chair to end up on the bar-b-q.

LILY

(She has taken the lawn chair and set it up down right) Don't you suppose he has enough to do without policing after our paying guests. What good is it in that condition? It might as well be firewood.

CHARLOTTE

They don't make furniture like this anymore – and all the parts seem to be here.

LILY

For crying out loud, put them in a box and take them with you. The house is full of old useless things. I hope you don't think I'm going to take any of this stuff back to the coast with me.

CHARLOTTE
That isn't the point.

LILY
The only point I see is that we have an old lady to move to a rest home, and I don't want to worry about furniture too.

CHARLOTTE
Lily, I'm tired of your criticism, and it would be nice if you supported what I'm trying to do here. Please stop talking like that.

LILY
(Bored and restless, fanning herself) This southerly weather in the summer has always been unbearable – and unhealthy too, I have no doubt. I hope the trades come back soon.

CHARLOTTE
We know she won't want to leave here, but they've waited as long as they could. The demolition can't take place with people still living here. I've notified the Trust Co. when you would be here. I asked Mr. Lum to come out here with the final papers this evening when we would all be here.

LILY
Oh, really, Charlotte. Do we have to do all these unpleasant things in one night?

CHARLOTTE
There are some things that you and I have to sign too, and I think Mr. Lum may have some things to say to her that may help.

LILY
(Taking off her shoes and arranging herself on the chair) I wish you luck.

CHARLOTTE
If someone from outside, like Mr. Lum, can talk to her –

LILY
Of course, at this point and in her condition, I see no reason why you shouldn't tell her what she wants to hear too.

CHARLOTTE
I will not invent some man just so mother can think –

LILY
I'm not suggesting you invent. I thought Red Hale was crawling with eligible men.

CHARLOTTE
There are only two of them living here now.

LILY
Nice Navy men? That would strike a familiar – and believable cord.

CHARLOTTE
They are officers, but, really, not like the men we ran around with before the war.

LILY
As for the men here, a little white lie wouldn't hurt anyone. (She steps on some Ironwood cones on the lawn) Damn

these Ironwood cones.

CHARLOTTE
(sarcastically) Your feet have gotten tender, Lily. Don't forget that you grew up running around here barefoot.

LILY
We're a bit more civilized than that in California, thank you.

CHARLOTTE
(Pause as she returns to her work on the lanai) It breaks my heart to have to leave here, especially since we're now dealing with a mainland builder. I feel so helpless.

LILY
Personally, I don't care who builds as long as we don't have the headache of taking care of all this anymore – and worrying about those men and mother.

CHARLOTTE
If the architects had acted more quickly –

LILY
You know it was that damn Henry Kaiser and all his projects that prevented them from giving more time to this.

CHARLOTTE
Meanwhile construction costs have been going up.

LILY
And another thing – it's those slant eyes who have taken over everywhere.

CHARLOTTE

Really, Lily.

LILY

Charlotte, you know you never used to see Orientals in public office. It's really getting to be a liability to be a haole any more.

CHARLOTTE

I wish you wouldn't talk that way.

LILY

You have to have a relative in those agencies or have the right color skin to get anything done. But I can't be bothered with it all. I could have stayed cool in the hotel. (Putting suntan lotion on) I'm going to get some color to take back if it kills me.

CHARLOTTE

You're not going to get any at this time of day.

LILY

I could use a drink. (wistfully) I suppose it's cooler up in Manoa. You know, I was asked more than once at work how long it took for my eyes to get less slanted when I came to the mainland. What idiots.

CHARLOTTE

(Trying to assemble pieces of the chair) Yes, idiots. Of course, it's cooler in the valley. I hope it won't be too big a change at her age. It took some time for me to sleep easily when I left here. I had gotten used to the sound of the waves on the seawall. I suppose it's like rain on the roof for some people.

LILY

I wonder if Higuchi has time to bring us a drink.

CHARLOTTE

At least mother is used to the mountain air from her trips to Tantalus in the old days. Going to the Tantalus house was always a break from the Waikiki heat. When daddy was alive we'd all go up there. (pause) I hope I can save this chair. There's a crack in it. I'll put all the pieces in a box to take to Manoa.

LILY

(Calls loudly) Higuchi!

CHARLOTTE

Lily, the neighbors.

LILY

They're probably used to all the carrying on over here. (calls) Higuchi! I half expected to run into some kind of shore leave orgy. Where is the fleet, anyway?

CHARLOTTE

They know we're having this last evening here. I asked them to have dinner in town.

HIGUCHI enters

Yes, Lily.

LILY

Higuchi, be a dear and bring me a glass of - sherry. That's what mother still keeps out here, I imagine. No vodka, I suppose.

HIGUCHI

Oh, no. Plenty sherry. Good for sleep. Cholly?

CHARLOTTE

Maybe some iced tea, Higuchi. (She has the chair pieces in a box and places it on the lanai)

HIGUCHI

Yes, (he goes)

LILY

(Noticing decorations from the night before) It looks as if the boys and their guests had a final fling. And what will become of dear Higuchi when this place shuts down?

CHARLOTTE

You know his son and daughter-in-law have a house in Palolo Valley. I'm sure they'll take him in. I think he's planning on going there.

LILY

I hope so. I used to love his cooking and the way he takes care of things here.

CHARLOTTE

We should get rid of those decorations too.

LILY
(Getting up) Do they know they have to be out by the end of the month?

CHARLOTTE
I had Mr. Lum send them letters.

LILY
(She begins pulling down the decorations) I'll be glad to see them go. We've put up with just about –

CHARLOTTE
Just a minute, Lily – you take all this burden on yourself but you haven't set foot in this house for years.

LILY
Don't blame me for that. Lots of others left the islands at that time. The Japs bombed Pearl Harbor and it was safer to be on the west coast. And besides, the Red Cross gave me time to come over here, and I'm using my vacation time to help you. Someone will pick up the slack and deal with my clients.

CHARLOTTE
I thank you for that. (pause) You know mother always hoped one of us would take over the house.

LILY
I was bored stiff out here – besides, I met Walt and – You made your choice. You and mother could have gone too. We never knew when the Japs might…

CHARLOTTE
Lower your voice. Do you want Higuchi to hear you?

LILY
He knows I don't include him. He's family. He's different. If it wasn't for Pearl Harbor –

CHARLOTTE
Yes, I did make the decision to stay. Mother needed me.

LILY
(Sarcastically) It suddenly didn't seem like "paradise" – to lots of people. But I came back for the grand finale, didn't I?

CHARLOTTE
Here, you might as well help with this. I don't want to be at it all evening. (Hands her a pad and pencil) You can list some of these things for the auctioneer.

LILY
Just remember, I did take time to come over here. Walt will fend for himself while I'm gone. (Looking over items on lanai) What in the world is this old thing?

CHARLOTTE
It's some sort of Philippine lamp shade. I think the General brought it back after his last tour of duty. He told me he wanted something to remind him of that – the Spanish-American War in the Philippines.

HIGUCHI
(Enters with drinks on a tray) Here on table. OK?

LILY

(Noting on her pad) Grandfather's Philippine lamp. Is that all right?

CHARLOTTE

Yes, fine. (To Higuchi, indicating bench on the lawn) Down there might be better, Higuchi.

LILY

(Higuchi is serving her) And where will you go when the house is closed, Higuchi? I hear you have children in Palolo Valley.

HIGUCHI

I go live with my son and daughter-in-law. They have room for me. I do the cooking.

CHARLOTTE

I hope you didn't think we'd close up here without a place for Higuchi. He's been one of the family for years.

LILY

Since Daddy died and all through the war.

CHARLOTTE

Higuchi, I know mother would want you to have something from the house. Is there anything here ... ?

HIGUCHI

Oh, no, Cholly, I could not.

LILY

Of course, you should, Higuchi. These things will just end up gathering dust somewhere else.

CHARLOTTE

Maybe your daughter-in-law could use some of the Japanese Imari dishes.

HIGUCHI

Very nice, but I don't know.

CHARLOTTE

You've always liked them, and mother and I did discuss this back in her better days.

LILY

Well, you think about it.

HIGUCHI

(Begins to straighten table and lanai for dinner) Yes, Lily.

> At this moment a healthy man of about 40 runs in along the sea wall from the left. This is Lt. Cmdr. Ben Tarpley, one of the tenants in the house. He has bare feet, wears swim trunks and a t-shirt and carries a towel and drink cooler. He is intelligent if a bit unrefined and is a man who will make his mark in business when given a chance after his military hitch. He speaks with a mid-western accent

that is clearly not of Hawaii, but he is tanned and seems very much at home in the beach milieu. He is not drunk, but it is clear he has been drinking.

BEN

Oh, the advance guard of the eviction service. Beer's getting warm. Join me for one? (Sets down cooler and opens a beer for himself) As promised, I'll be away for dinner. I just want to get changed.

CHARLOTTE

Lily, this is Mr. Tarpley who…

BEN

Call me Ben.

CHARLOTTE

… who has been living in the mauka bedroom. My sister from California, Lily Cameron.

LILY

Oh, the Navy on liberty? (flirting) Did you have a nice day at the beach?

BEN

(Brushing off sand) I walked along the wall to just below the Diamond Head lighthouse.

CHARLOTTE

I think Higuchi told you we want to use the lanai for dinner with mother this evening.

BEN
The last supper, eh?

CHARLOTTE
(indicating the party decorations) There seems to have been some goings on here last night too.

BEN
A few friends around the bar-b-q. Beer?

LILY
Well, yes, I don't mind if I do. (She looks to Charlotte to remind her about their earlier discussion about men.) Charlotte? (But Charlotte purposely ignores this)

CHARLOTTE
(Referring to the chair) I see you were in need of firewood.

BEN
Oh, yes, ah…

CHARLOTTE
That is not your property, Mr. Tarpley.

BEN
We were helping Higuchi keep things ship shape. That chair has been in pieces under the lanai ever since I came here.

CHARLOTTE
Do you know what that is?

BEN
A fire hazard, we thought. – your mother never mentioned it.

CHARLOTTE
And please don't clutter up the driveway; we need to have access to the yard.

BEN
If you rent a place furnished, you must expect some use to be made – And, besides, that broken chair just may be a forewarning of what is going to happen to this house in the end . . . . and other old houses here on the seawall. (Sees decorations are being removed) Were those a problem?

CHARLOTTE
We're going to move mother this evening, and I don't want her to see all this.

BEN
Yes. Higuchi, I guess I'll be away for dinner.

HIGUCHI
Yes, Mr. Tarpley. (Starts to go with tray and bottles)

LILY
Just leave that, Higuchi. I'll bring it in.

HIGUCHI
Yes, Lily. (He goes)

LILY
(Pouring another drink) Frankly, Mr. Tarpley – Ben – my sister

and I disagree on the value of a lot of this junk. A chair is not very useful in pieces like that, is it? Of course, she's lived with it longer. (She has gone back to listing items) Here's a wooden bowl that's cracked down the side. Surely, you don't want –

CHARLOTTE

That's an old Hawaiian calabash I've urged mother to give to the Bishop Museum. I'll have it fixed first, of course.

BEN

It was a salad bowl last night.

CHARLOTTE

Just list everything, please.

> From this point to the end of the play, the stage becomes progressively dark. A sunset takes place during this time which the audience sees as an amber glow that washes over the entire scene. Charlotte goes about her business but shows some annoyance at the flirting that LILY is doing with BEN.

BEN

(Looking out front toward the setting sun) The sun's getting ready to disappear behind Barber's Point. I'm going to miss that, and we always looked for the Southern Cross in winter – just above the horizon. Your mother has pointed that out to us a number of times.

LILY
I grew up with that sunset and always took it for granted.

BEN
We used to see great sunsets from the peaks of Hong Kong – but, somehow coconut trees are a better compliment for a sunset than all those tall buildings.

LILY
Were you stationed in the far east?

BEN
I've been all over the Pacific on five tours. (Refers to party sign "One More to Go") One more before I can retire.

LILY
You certainly are the traveler.

BEN
"Join the Navy and see the world "to coin a phrase. I first came here as an ensign in 1945.

LILY
And your next stop?

BEN
A staff position in Washington – good for my career if I was staying in. Jesus, three more eastern winters. But, hell, the full retirement will give me something to invest in the future. (pause) I hate to leave here. Red Hale has been a wonderful home. The end of a hitch and – being dispossed too.

LILY
I guess that explains last night. (Indicating party decorations)

BEN
Yes, ma'am. (Lifts bottle toward the house) A toast – and farewell – (He turns out toward the ocean) and to the Southern Cross. There's going to be a hell of a sunset.

LILY
(She drinks and comes closer to Ben; Charlotte is working but keeping an eye on Lily's maneuvers) And what will a young retired Navy officer do with himself?

BEN
I could go back to Ohio and work in the family business – concrete.

LILY
Won't that mean more winter?

BEN
Or I could come back to Hawaii and watch what happened to Hong Kong happen here – bring in the family product. A lot of money is going to be paid to watch that sunset. You're going to see a major viewing stand built along this beach. Just watch what happens to Waikiki.

CHARLOTTE
That's a rather far-fetched picture, isn't it?

BEN
I've been in and out of here a lot of times since the war, and I've learned at least one thing – the value of what I see around here. (Gesturing toward Waikiki) Know what an Ohio winter is like?

CHARLOTTE
I have some idea.

BEN
The sad thing is that it's not always going to be so unique when the world rushes in.

LILY
When I first went up to the coast, people thought I grew up in a grass shack and wondered why my eyes weren't slanted.

BEN
All that mystery is nearly gone. It can't be stopped.

CHARLOTTE
I can't believe...

BEN
Culturally, you're going to become an extension of California, and you know what's happening there. They had a gold rush once upon a time too.

LILY
I live in Los Angeles.

BEN

Hawaii will become its own state soon, perhaps later this summer – the 50th. I have a feeling I've been plunked down in the proverbial "right place at the right time."

CHARLOTTE

This is a woman's home, not a commercial commodity.

BEN

It's a pity so many of you islanders don't have any real idea of what you have here. And I wonder what the Hawaiians will think of what is going to happen. It was originally their land. They probably lived on this property in grass huts – before the era of these big wooden beach houses, to speak nothing of the concrete and glass that's going to replace them.

LILY

I don't know about the Hawaiians, but he's right, you know, Charlotte. Deep down, I thought the world was all just like Honolulu until I finally got away.

BEN

A case of home-grown island fever?

LILY

I couldn't wait to get off this rock when I was a teenager.

CHARLOTTE

And eventually you found a reason to do it.

LILY
Yes. (To Ben) Honolulu can be a very inbred small town.

CHARLOTTE
(To Ben) You men have had a good deal here for a few years, but it couldn't go on forever.

BEN
That's right. You've had to lease this land in order to survive, but others will do it to cash in on a good thing. These other big houses on the seawall won't last. (pause) What will replace this one?

CHARLOTTE
A co-op apartment building – the first one in this area.

LILY
In our own backyard. (She is still working with the items on the lanai) Here's another relic of the past. (She holds up an Oriental ceramic piece)

BEN
On Okinawa those are meant to protect houses from evil spirits.

LILY
Well, it didn't work here in the end.

BEN
"Crossroads of the Pacific" – they're not kidding. This kind of cultural hodge-podge is just going to speed up with those jet planes that will be coming in here. BOAC is going to start

twice weekly flights here next month, a stopover between the east coast and the Orient. (He is settling into the lawn chair with another beer)

CHARLOTTE
Planes have been coming here for years – there used to be the China clippers.

BEN
This is different. Five hours to California, and that's going to change your neighborhood, ladies. It's an end to the charm of long distance.

LILY
I wonder if I can get on one of those jets when I go home.

CHARLOTTE
I just hope mother won't have to see what you're talking about.

BEN
Have you ever looked closely at a map of the Pacific? Thousands of miles of ocean and suddenly where there are no other islands –

CHARLOTTE
There are plenty of other islands out there.

BEN
Not where these are. You know you can go half way between here and California and you're further from land than you can be anywhere on Earth.

CHARLOTTE

(She is preparing to go upstairs) But this is the backyard where I grew up. (pause) Lily, I'll go up and see that mother is ready and ask Higuchi to start setting dinner. Maybe you could finish up here and get a few of the boxes around to the car. Excuse me, Mr. Tarpley. (She goes)

BEN

Good night.

LILY

(After a pause) There has never been any love lost between my sister and me. But she **has** stayed here and taken care of mother.

BEN

Your mother is very devoted to this place and the memory of your father.

LILY

She won't want to leave. But Charlotte has written me that her mind has been slipping recently, so maybe it won't be as great a shock.

BEN

I sometimes talk with her in the evening. She often refers to me as if I'm one of the family.

LILY

Oh, really?

BEN
It's just old age – and the mind protecting itself from change. (pause) I think I'll content myself with just one more (opens another beer) – and then- I don't want to be in the way.

LILY
Would you mind helping me with a few of these boxes?

BEN
Sure.

> There is a silence while they gather up some of the boxes and head for the driveway. The following dialogue is heard while they are moving things.

LILY
I guess it's too bad to have to move all this stuff now. But when my sister never married, there was no family to fill up this place.

BEN
Did you ever consider coming back?

LILY
Some people are meant to live on islands and some people aren't. (pause) It's strange to think about finally becoming a state after years of talk.

BEN
It had to come. Alaska just recently.

LILY
For a long time, Hawaii thought it would be the 49th state.

BEN
Don't you think there's a distinction to being 50th?

LILY
You seem to take great delight in these changes around here.

BEN
It's just very interesting, that's all – to watch the inevitable from my vantage point – just ahead of a new wave of conquerors. You know Henry Kaiser has said he missed out on the gold rush in Miami Beach, but he didn't want to miss out here. And there will be others. You can't put a lid on Pandora's box or put the genie back in the bottle.

LILY
Yes, I think I see what you mean.

BEN
(Looking around at the house) Sometimes old things outlive their purpose and a new use can be found.

> The doorbell rings and Lily looks up; we
> hear Higuchi going to answer it.

MR. LUM
(offstage) Good evening, I'm Gordon Lum from the Kamaina Trust Co. I've come to see Mrs. Stuart – or perhaps her daughter.

HIGUCHI

Oh, yes, Mr. Lum.

LILY

(Putting on an after-beach outfit over her swimsuit) I think it's the voice of those conquerors.

BEN

Time for me to disappear.

HIGUCHI

(Bringing Mr. Lum onto the lanai) Mr. Lum from the trust company, Lily.

> During the following scene
> Higuchi goes to the side of the
> house to pick some ginger which
> he carefully arranges in a bowl
> on the table.

LILY

How do you do? I'm Lily Cameron, Charlotte's sister from California.

MR. LUM

> (He is a young Chinese
> businessman of about 35. He is
> eastern educated, very intelligent
> and speaks standard English. He is
> sensitive to the job he has come
> here to do but also knows that it
> must be done.)

Oh, yes, there are two daughters. How do you do?

LILY

We were expecting you. This is Mr. Tarpley, one of mother's tenants.

BEN

The second guard of the eviction service. A pleasure, but I have a date at the Waikiki Grill. (He starts to exit)

LILY

Goodnight, Ben. Thanks for the help.

BEN

Think nothing of it. It just might be fitting that I have a hand in this move. I think maybe it's the cement contractors – my bailiwick – who are going to find a new use for the land under this old place and all the other old houses along the beach. (He takes one more box and disappears to the driveway laughing).

LILY

(Pause as she looks after Ben. Then turns to Mr. Lum) My sister has told me you took over the estate after Mr. Austin died.

MR. LUM

Yes. I've attempted to fill his shoes. I've brought the release papers as your sister requested. Is she here?

LILY

She'll be right down. Charlotte has told me that all this was inevitable, but it seems to me –

MR. LUM
We feel this is the best course to take for the good of the estate. The property can be used to best advantage if we don't wait much longer. Costs are still going up, and these co-ops are the coming thing.

LILY
My mother will be very unhappy to leave her home, Mr. Lum.

MR. LUM
Yes. I believe she has spoken of leaving her property to the church – in lieu of building her apartment house. The Southern Cross. But we've had an offer from a San Francisco company that is interested in leasing this land. And I feel we should consider that.

LILY
This all seems a bit hasty.

MR. LUM
Fee simple land right on the seawall with this view is very desirable. I'm sure you realize that $10,000 a year is no small sum.

LILY
It seems to me there was some rush in putting through this deal. But personally, I'll be happy to be rid of the worry.

MR. LUM
(Looking around the yard to the view out front) I've been out here just once before, but your mother has had us managing

the income from your rentals for some time.

                    LILY

Mother and Mr. Austin were great friends, but she's old now and – has become – eccentric. I'm not sure what we should expect of her this evening.

                    MR. LUM

Yes, I understand. We'll want to do this as gently as possible. I guess this has been her home for many years.

                    LILY

They paid $1,000 to a part Hawaiian family for the land just after the turn of the century.

                    MR. LUM

This was countryside then – out past the Waikiki swamp and duck ponds.

> Lily and Mr. Lum are moving
> about the yard looking up at
> the house. HIGUCHI is putting
> the last-minute touches to the table.

                    LILY

(Referring to what HIGUCHI is doing) I think it's a bit sentimental, but Charlotte insisted we have a last dinner here on the lanai to please mother.

                    MR. LUM

I understand.

LILY

I just hope the sentiment doesn't make things touchier.

MR. LUM

I hope I won't be in the way, but your sister said this would be a good time to come.

LILY

The distractions of dinner might make this as good a time as any. Higuchi, why don't you ask Charlotte to bring mother down.

HIGUCHI

Yes, Lily. (He goes upstairs)

MR. LUM

You know, your mother should feel fortunate that these mainland investors came along when they did.

LILY

An nine-story building here on the beach is going to change the looks of things around here.

MR. LUM

You'll be pioneers. This will be the first of these co-ops out here, but they've proved to be very successful back east.

LILY

As long as we have a guaranteed rental on the land. We'll let the developer risk selling off the apartments. I'm glad we won't have that to worry about.

MR. LUM

This is the best way.

LILY

I can't help remembering how people fled from here in 1941. You couldn't give things away.

MR. LUM

Fifteen years is a long time. Instead of barbed wire on the beach, you have catamarans, outriggers and tourists now – and you know we'll be celebrating statehood before this summer is over.

LILY

Yes, I've been hearing.

MR. LUM

Hawaii has been trying for that for over fifty years.

> Lily and Mr. Lum are now down right near the bench. At this moment, Charlotte leads in her mother Mrs. Stuart who is a very stately woman of about 85. She moves slowly as her sight is poor. She is a proud, strong woman who was probably very beautiful at one time. Her movements and voice show signs of age, but, despite the fact that her mind moves from the present to the past, she shows vestiges of an alertness and intelligence that were hers

at one time. Her long hair is piled upon her head and she wears an elegant kimono.

CHARLOTTE
Out here, mother. We'll eat out here on the lanai.

MRS. STUART
How lovely.

LILY
Hello, mother. I didn't come right here as I wanted to get settled in the hotel first.

MRS. STUART
Give me a kiss, Lily.

LILY
Of course, Mother. (they kiss)

MRS. STUART
What is that fragrance, Cha? Something lovely is in bloom.

CHARLOTTE
It's the ginger from the *ewa* side of the house. Higuchi has put some of it on the table for us.

MR. LUM
Good evening, Mrs. Stuart.

CHARLOTTE
Hello, Mr. Lum. I thought mother would enjoy the air. This

stillness can be very oppressive.

MR. LUM
I'm sure we'll be eating outdoors at our house as well.

CHARLOTTE
You're welcome to join us. We planned for you.

MR. LUM
Thanks very much but I'm expected at home.

CHARLOTTE
Mother, this is Mr. Lum who has come to talk with you about the property – the Southern Cross.

MRS. STUART
Is it time for the stars to be out, Cha? The Southern Cross?

CHARLOTTE
Soon, mother.

MR. LUM
Good evening, Mrs. Stuart. You look well tonight.

MRS. STUART
I can feel a glow on my face. It's so warm here at Diamond Head. Higuchi, are you there?

HIGUCHI
Yes, Mrs. Stuart.

MRS. STUART
I think we'll pack the dray and go to Tantalus. Diamond Head has been brown for weeks, and it's so green up on the mountain.

CHARLOTTE
Mother, the trades will be back soon and it's a long way to go. You know how much you love it here when the breezes return. (a thought occurs to her) But, perhaps we can take a ride to the mountain after supper.

MRS. STUART
The eucalyptus up there always smells so lovely in the summer – father will insist that we go as usual.

CHARLOTTE
Mother, the trust company has come to see us.

> HIGUCHI brings in the dinner on a tray and is setting the plates around the table.

MRS. STUART
Oh, yes. Is Mr. Austin here?

LILY
No, it's Mr. Lum who is handling the estate now. He says he has some papers for you to look at.

> CHARLOTTE gives LILY a look

(Charlotte gives Lily a sign not to pursue this yet.) Not now, Lily.

HIGUCHI

Dinner ready now.

CHARLOTTE

Thank you, Higuchi

> CHARLOTTE leads her mother
> and they all move to the table.
> HIGUCHI sets a chair next to
> the table for MR. LUM.

LILY

I assume I may bring my drink to the table.

MRS. STUART

Lily, you mustn't have much of that. You want to act like a lady as I've always taught you.

LILY

Yes, of course, Mother.

MRS. STUART

Not to act like a proper lady is far worse than robbery my mother always said.

LILY

(With a laugh) You know you take some yourself on occasion.

MRS. STUART

Only in moderation, dear. I learned my lesson the night I met your father at Queen Liliuokalani's house party. That darn stuff stimulated me so much I didn't dare lie down because the room went around in circles.

LILY
I hope they didn't have to carry you from Washington Place.

CHARLOTTE
(a warning) Lily.

MRS. STUART
Don't be cheeky with your mother, darling. But a little before bedtime is always permissible for my daughters. A little sherry.

CHARLOTTE
Wouldn't you like some sherry, mother? You know how much better it makes you sleep on hot nights.

MRS. STUART
Is it my bedtime?

CHARLOTTE
No, mother, but we're also celebrating some news that Mr. Lum has for us.

MRS. STUART
Yes, some sherry would be nice.

CHARLOTTE
(Offers sherry) Mr. Lum?

MR. LUM
Yes, thank you.

> They are all seated and HIGUCHI is pouring the wine. CHARLOTTE begins eating and they proceed with dinner until the exit at the end of the scene. After Mr. LUM is served the wine, he looks out toward the setting sun.

MR. LUM
You have some wonderful sunsets out here. The clouds are just right over the Waianae Mountains tonight.

MRS. STUART
When my father, the General, came to live with us, we would often eat our meals out here on a lovely Koa dining set. (LILY and Charlotte exchange glances) This lanai was a favorite spot of my husband's too. And we used to have such lovely garden parties out here on the lawn.

MR. LUM
> During the following scene it is clear that he is sensitive to the delicacy of the situation.

It's wonderful that, after all these years, this land will remain with your family, Mrs. Stuart. (pause) I think there was an idea for you to build an apartment house here.

LILY
Until there was trouble qualifying for a loan.

MR. LUM
Yes, the building materials got too expensive. There was no way we could outbid Henry Kaiser. But at one time it was Mrs. Stuart's idea to give the home as a church retreat by the sea, I believe.

CHARLOTTE
My father was a pillar of the St. Andrew's parish. But it was mother's idea to call her apartments the Southern Cross.

MRS. STUART
We would often sit out here with the Southern Cross on the horizon in the winter time. I realized the Lord meant this place for his work.

MR. LUM
That shows a great deal of faith, Mrs. Stuart.

MRS. STUART
These islands saved his life. They said, "You'll never see that boy again" when he sailed from Belfast.

CHARLOTTE
He was tubercular and was sent around the horn as a young man for his health.

> The stage is almost dark now and the sunset is in its final stages. HIGUCHI has lit the

lights on the lanai which cast a
warm glow over the scene.

MRS. STUART

The linen mills would have been your father's death. But the Lord saw fit to send him here and he lived.

LILY

He did die of a stroke in 1948.

MRS. STUART

But his lungs were strong when he died, Lily, and I believe it was the Cross that looks over here that gave him that strength.

LILY

Surely the climate had something to do with it.

MRS. STUART

The Lord works in many ways. And I know He wants me to die here at Waikiki.

LILY

Please, mother, let's not talk of dying.

MRS. STUART

My time is coming and I want to be here at home by the sea.

LILY

(Trying to change the subject) This is particularly good hekka.

CHARLOTTE
We were very fortunate to have you come here, Higuchi.

HIGUCHI
For me too. More betta than working in da cane fields.

CHARLOTTE
Mother, don't you remember we thought it would be nice for Higuchi to have something from the house?

MRS. STUART
Yes, dear.

CHARLOTTE
This dinner set is another thing we can save by putting it into good hands.

MRS. STUART
(she looks closely at a piece) They were a wedding present from our friends the Dowsetts. All of these old things should have a place to be, Higuchi. (CHARLOTTE nods to him)

HIGUCHI
Thank you, Mrs. Stuart.

CHARLOTTE
(Reaches for his hand) Thank you for everything, Higuchi. (pause) Mother, I think Mr. Lum wanted to discuss a plan for the use of your property. (pause)

MR. LUM
It seems to us at the trust company, Mrs. Stuart, that your

home could be much more valuable to you and your heirs – and much simpler for your estate to manage – if we let another company build here and let you collect the rental from the lease.

MRS. STUART

Is that what Hoste and I planned with Mr. Austin?

MR. LUM

No, not exactly, Mrs. Stuart, but –

LILY

It's the best way, mother, under the present circumstances.

CHARLOTTE

The house is old now, and you know the expense we've had maintaining It. And you living here with those officers has been a worry to us.

MRS. STUART

That nice Mr. Tarpley sometimes visits me. You girls have such nice friends. You must always feel free to bring your young men to the house.

CHARLOTTE

(After a pause and a meaningful look at Lily) Mother –

MRS. STUART

You girls always know how to behave properly with your young men. I raised my daughters to be Republicans, Episcopalians and, above all, perfect ladies.

MR. LUM
(There is another pause and then Mr. LUM decides he can proceed) I've asked for one provision in this agreement that, I'm sure, will make it more acceptable. I'd like to see one of the apartments in the building reserved for your use.

CHARLOTTE
That way, mother, we could all come here to visit at any time.

MR. LUM
You wouldn't have to feel that it was no longer your home.

MRS. STUART
I would want it for you girls. This is your home too. I want you both to be taken care of.

LILY
I think Charlotte and I feel well taken care of, mother.

MRS. STUART
I want to be where my husband passed away when my time comes.

CHARLOTTE
Of course, mother.

MR. LUM
Another building can't change this wonderful setting by the sea.

MRS. STUART
I've been smelling the sea all day; perhaps it's the moisture in the air. Hoste and I would often sit out here in the evenings – when the stars began to come out.

MR. LUM
You can begin to see that now, Mrs. Stuart.

MRS. STUART
Do you also see the torch fishermen on the reef this evening, Cha?

CHARLOTTE
There are lights but I think it must be a fishing boat. There haven't been torches out here for years.

MR. LUM
I remember seeing them near Queen's Surf when I was a boy. But I'm afraid that's a thing of the past – like the boys who dove for coins at the harbor.

LILY
They were still doing that when I left at the start of the war.

MR. LUM
But this land is something that won't disappear – and the increased value will be renegotiated from time to time. Meaning more income for you as time goes by.

LILY
I hope I won't have to be wheeled in to see that.

Soft Hawaiian music begins playing
at a distance coming from the
house next door to the right.

CHARLOTTE

The Thurstons must be entertaining again.

LILY

Good heavens, do they still live there?

MRS. STUART

Who is it, Cha?

CHARLOTTE

The neighbors. They have music playing.

MRS. STUART

How lovely. We often have music and gaiety here in the house, Mr. Lum. Especially when the girls bring their young men.

CHARLOTTE

(She is trying to change the subject) I wonder what the neighbors think about all these building plans.

MR. LUM

Since the zoning was changed for this area, it was only a matter of time. It could be very profitable for them all if more buildings could be put up here.

CHARLOTTE

(Indicating the papers) Mr. Lum.

MR. LUM

These are the agreements that we must look at, Mrs. Stuart.

MRS. STUART

My, I do wish that we could get a breath of air.

CHARLOTTE

If we let Mr. Lum go, we can be on our way to Tantalus. (There is a pause; Mr. Lum has taken the papers out of his briefcase) Lily and I will sign these first, mother.

> There is a pause as LILY and CHARLOTTE sign the papers where Mr. LUM indicates. The papers are passed to MRS. STUART. There is another lengthy pause in which we see MRS. STUART look over the papers and then she bows to the inevitable.

MRS. STUART

You know, Charlotte, I have always trusted the Kamaaina Trust Company with our best interests. Mr. Austin never led me astray, so we must trust Mr. Lum as well. (trying to read the papers, she picks up the pen) Help me with these, will you, dear? I don't see them as clearly as you do. What am I signing here?

MR. LUM

These are agreements that allow us to negotiate with a firm in San Francisco. They are going to pay you for the use of your land.

MRS. STUART
We've had this land for many years. If I remember correctly, we have the last property on Kalakaua Avenue.

MR. LUM
Yes, that's correct. And the building will be a punctuation point just before the Avenue ends. Please let me show you where to sign. (he does so)
(There is silence while the papers are being signed)

> HIGUCHI has come in with an overnight bag which he has packed for MRS. STUART. He nods to CHARLOTTE who sees him but indicates to wait a moment.

MRS. STUART
(Reaching for the flowers on the table) Oh, my, the fragrance of this ginger – mixed with the smell of the sea. (pause) Hand me the bouquet, Charlotte.

CHARLOTTE
Yes, mother.

> CHARLOTTE takes the flowers from the vase and hands them to her mother. MRS. STUART smells them as she is standing.

MRS. STUART
Now help me to the seawall, dear.

> CHARLOTTE helps her mother to
> downstage center. LILY moves
> down also but stays to the side.
> MR. LUM comes with them when
> he realizes he is being addressed.

You know, Mr. Lum, it is not uncommon to find leis washed against our wall from some passing liner – the Niagra, or the Manoa, or the Lurline – we often watch them go around Diamond Head on their way to the mainland. I suppose it's a silly superstition that those visitors would return if their flowers washed ashore – but tonight, I, too, feel that if this ginger were to go into the sea…

> MRS. STUART drops the bouquet
> over the edge of the seawall. There
> is a long silence that is finally broken.

CHARLOTTE
Come, Mother. Higuchi has our bags packed.

MRS. STUART
(She turns and allows CHARLOTTE to begin leading her off toward the drive) We'll see the lights of the mountain house from the Waikiki Road. Father always goes ahead to air out the place for us. His fortnight leave from Camp McKinley has come none too soon with this Kona weather.

CHARLOTTE
(There is a struggle within her but she finally comes out with a humoring statement aimed at her mother) We don't want to keep the General and grandmother waiting.

> CHARLOTTE gestures for LILY to come help MRS. STUART to the driveway. LILY does this and exits with her mother while the following lines are spoken.

LILY

Come, mother.

CHARLOTTE

(She moves over to MR. LUM) Thank you for helping with a very sensitive situation, Mr. Lum.

MR. LUM

Certainly. If I can be of any further assistance, please contact me downtown or at my home.

CHARLOTTE

(They shake hands) Yes, we will. Higuchi, would you see Mr. Lum out – and then get a few more of these boxes around to the car?

HIGUCHI

Yes, Cholly.

MR. LUM

Good night.

> HIGUCHI leads MR. LUM out the front screen door.
> CHARLOTTE surveys the scene, picks up one more box and

> then quickly moves around to
> the driveway.
>
> Momentarily, HIGUCHI returns,
> picks up another box, blows
> out the candles and follows
> where CHARLOTTE has gone.
> We hear the car doors shut
> and then the car backing out
> of the driveway.
> There is a silence and then BEN appears
> dimly through the screen door. He is
> sharply dressed in a silk Aloha shirt. He is
> on his way out to dinner, but seeing the
> lanai is now empty, he lights a cigarette
> and comes out on the lawn toward the
> seawall. HIGUCHI appears for one last
> check of the dining area. BEN sees him and…

BEN

You know, Higuchi, one day, not too far in the future, this area will be called Honolulu's Gold Coast. And I plan to be a part of it. I'll be sure to cash in on what is coming – it's inevitable.

> As BEN smokes his cigarette looking out
> toward the sea, the wind chimes start a
> faint sound and, then, gradually, the
> breeze gets stronger and the chimes get louder. The
> lights fade out on him as he is staring into the
> southern sky.

CURTAIN

ABOOKS

ALIVE Book Publishing and ALIVE Publishing Group
are imprints of Advanced Publishing LLC,
3200 A Danville Blvd., Suite 204, Alamo, California 94507

Telephone: 925.837.7303
alivebookpublishing.com

www.ingramcontent.com/pod-product-compliance
Lightning Source LLC
Chambersburg PA
CBHW040745020526
44114CB00049B/2914